D0761113

LANGUAGES, COMPILERS
AND
RUN-TIME SYSTEMS FOR
SCALABLE COMPUTERS

LANGUAGES, COMPILERS AND RUN-TIME SYSTEMS FOR SCALABLE COMPUTERS

EDITED BY

Boleslaw K. SZYMANSKI
Rensselaer Polytechnic Institute
Troy, NY, USA

■

Balaram SINHAROY
IBM Corporation
Poughkeepsie, NY, USA

KLUWER ACADEMIC PUBLISHERS
Boston/London/Dordrecht

Distributors for North America:
Kluwer Academic Publishers
101 Philip Drive
Assinippi Park
Norwell, Massachusetts 02061 USA

Distributors for all other countries:
Kluwer Academic Publishers Group
Distribution Centre
Post Office Box 322
3300 AH Dordrecht, THE NETHERLANDS

Library of Congress Cataloging-in-Publication Data

Languages, compilers and run-time systems for scalable computers /
  edited by Boleslaw Szymanski, Balaram Sinharoy.
      p.   cm.
    Includes bibliographical reference and index.
    ISBN 0-7923-9635-9
    1. Parallel processing (Electronic computers)--Congresses.
  2. Software engineering--Congresses. 3. Computer architecture-
  -Congresses. I. Szymanski, Boleslaw. II. Sinharoy, Balaram, 1961-

  QA76.58.L37 1996
  005.4'2--dc20
                                                              95-37540
                                                                  CIP

Printed on acid-free paper.

Printed in the United States of America

CONTENTS

Contents

Contents   xi

CONTRIBUTORS

G. Agrawal, G. Edjlali, J. Humphries, W. Pugh, J. Saltz, A. Susman, D. Wonnacott, J. Wein
Dept. of Computer Science
University of Maryland

D.P. Agrawal, S. Kumar
Dept. of Electrical & Computer Engineering
North Carolina State University

F. André, F. Bodin, O. Chéron, J. Erhel, M. Hahad, J. Pazat, T. Priol
IRISA/INRIA, Rennes

H. E. Bal, R. Bhoedjang, K. Langendoen
Dept. of Mathematics and Computer Science
Vrije Universiteit, Netherlands

I. Banicescu, S. Flynn Hummel, C.-T. Wang, J. Wein
Dept. of Computer Science
Polytechnic University

G. Becker, N. V. Murray, R. E. Stearns
Dept. of Computer Science
University at Albany

G.D. Benson, R.A. Olsson
Dept. of Computer Science
University of California, Davis

C.L. Bottasso, M.S. Shephard
Scientific Research Computation Center
Rensselaer Polytechnic Institute

P. Brezany, B.M. Chapman, K. Sanjari, H.P. Zima
Institute for Software Technology and Parallel Systems
University of Vienna, Austria

T. Bubeck, W. Küchlin and W. Rosenstiel
Wilhelm-Schickard-Institut für Informatik
Universität Tübingen, Germany

S. Chakrabarti, D. Culler, E. Deprit, J.A. Feldman, S. Goldstein, A. Krishnamurthy, C.-P. Wen, K. Yelick
Computer Science Division
University of California, Berkeley

S.W. Chappelow, P.J. Hatcher, J.R. Mason
Dept. of Computer Science
University of New Hampshire

M. Chen
Dept. of Computer Science
Boston University

Y. Choo, B. Sinharoy
IBM Corporation

G. Craig
Dept. of Computer Science
Syracuse University

F. Deelman, J.E. Flaherty, E. Kaltofen, W. Kaplow, C. Ozturan, M. Samadani, B.K. Szymanski, J. Teresco, P. Tannenbaum, L. Ziantz
Dept. of Computer Science
Rensselaer Polytechnic Institute

W. Denissen
Institute of Applied Physics
Netherlands Org. for Applied Scientific Research
Delft, Netherlands

T. Derby, R. Schnabel, B. Zorn
Dept. of Computer Science
University of Colorado at Boulder

P. Dinda, D.R. O'Hallaron
School of Computer Science
Carnegie Mellon University

I.T. Foster, D. Kohr, Jr., R. Olson, S. Tuecke, M.Q. Xu
Mathematics and Computer Science Division
Argonne National Laboratory

K. Ghose, N. Mehdiratta
Dept. of Computer Science
State University of New York, Binghamton

L. Hendren
Dept. of Computer Science
McGill University, Canada

J. Hummel, A. Nicolau
Dept. of Computer Science
University of California, Irvine,

S.P. Iyer
Dept. of Computer Science
North Carolina State University

K. Kennedy, N. Nedeljković, A. Sethi
Dept. of Computer Science
Rice University

D. Kulkarni, M. Stumm
Dept. of Computer Science and Dept. Electrical and Computer Engineering
University of Toronto, Canada

S. Kumaran, M. J. Quinn
Dept. of Computer Science
Oregon State University

D. Lea
Dept. of Computer Science
State University of New York at Oswego

C.-C. Lim
International Computer Science Institute
Berkeley

A. Müller, R. Rühl
Centro Svizzero di Calcolo Scientifico
Manno, Switzerland

M. O'Boyle
Dept. of Computer Science
University of Manchester, U.K.

S. Pai
Dept. of Computer Science
Yale University

J. Ramanujam, A. Thirumalai, A. Venkatachar
Dept. of Electrical and Computer Engineering
Louisiana State University

M. Rosing
Pacific Northwest Laboratory

K.E. Schauser
Dept. of Computer Science
University of California at Santa Barbara

C.K. Shank
Dept. of Computer Engineering
Rochester Institute of Technology

M. Ujaldon, E.L. Zapata
Computer Architecture Department
University of Malaga, Spain

PREFACE

This book contains the papers presented at the Third Workshop on Languages, Compilers and Run-Time Systems for Scalable Computers. This international meeting of leading researchers in parallel software engineering provides an overview of current state-of-the-art in this area and charts the directions of future developments. The book contains 20 articles based on the Workshop presentations and 13 extended abstracts from the poster session.

The chapters of the book cover the most relevant areas of research today. The book starts with new developments in classical problems of parallel compiler design, such as dependence analysis (the first chapter describes nonlinear array dependence analysis and the second chapter is about dependence testing in the presence of dynamic, pointer-based data structures), and an exploration of loop parallelism (there are chapters on computation decomposition and alignment through transformation of an iteration space, on optimization of the stencil computation, and on load balancing and data locality via fractiling). Two chapters address the issues of compiler strategy for specific architectures: the first one describes a compiler for shared virtual memories, whereas the second one concentrates on runtime support for irregular computation executed on a network of workstations. Several chapters focus on programming environments. One chapter discusses parallel programming using the divide-and-conquer paradigm while another focuses on the use of object-oriented templates in this paradigm. There is a chapter on the Multipol runtime layer, which provides an efficient and portable abstraction underlying the data structures, and another one on a preprocessor developed for supporting distributed arrays on parallel machines.

Several chapters investigate support for multi-threading and communication optimization. There is a chapter on using multi-threading for masking cache misses and another one on integrating data and task parallelism via multi-threading. Chapters on communication optimization discuss communication generation for cyclic(k) distributions and point-to-point communication using migrating ports. Issues on the boundary of language and operating system support are addressed in a chapter devoted to the design of micro-kernel support for the SR concurrent programming language, in another chapter on primitives for compiling parallel languages, and also in a chapter on impact of address relation caching on message passing performance. The load balance issues are discussed in two chapters, first in the context of sparse matrix computation, and then in iteratively balanced adaptive solvers for partial differential equations. Some additional topics are also discussed in the extended abstracts from the poster session at the end of the book.

xviii

The chapters are ordered in the sequence in which they were presented at the workshop, with the poster presentations following the regular papers. Each chapter provides a bibliography of relevant papers by the authors and other researchers. Hence, this volume can be used as a reference book of the current research in parallel software engineering. The book constitutes the timely coverage of the most important topics in parallel software engineering.

The workshops on Languages, Compilers and Run-Time Systems for Scalable Computers are held every two and a half years. The first one was held at ICASE, NASA in Hampton, Virginia in May 1990; the second was at the University of Colorado, Boulder in October 1992; the third was held at Rensselaer Polytechnic Institute in Troy, New York in May 1995 and gathered about 70 participants from many countries. The papers presented at the workshop were selected from over 60 submissions. The selection was made by the Program Committee consisting of: Joseph E. Flaherty (Rensselaer Polytechnic Institute), Ken Kennedy (Rice University), Chuck Koelbel (Rice University), Piyush Mehrotra (ICASE), Joel Saltz (University of Maryland), Bobby Schnabel (Colorado University), Balaram Sinharoy (IBM Corporation), Boleslaw Szymanski, Chair (Rensselaer Polytechnic Institute) and Hans Zima (Vienna University). In addition to the Program Committee members the submitted papers were reviewed by the following referees: E. Mehofer, Thomas Fahringer, Bernd Wender, Stefan Andel, S. Benkner, Viera Sipkova, Mario Pantano, Kamran Sanjari, Beniamino DiMartino from Vienna University; Ray Loy, Can Ozturan, Wesley Turner and Louis Ziantz from Rensselaer Polytechnic Institute; Tom Derby, Rich Neves and Chung-Shang Shao from Colorado University; Ira Pramanick and Chungti Liang from IBM Corporation; Matthew Haines from ICASE, NASA; J. Ramanujam from Louisiana State University. On behalf of the Program Committee, the editors express thanks to all referees for their involvement in the workshop.

The Workshop was run by the Organizing Committee from Rensselaer Polytechnic Institute led by Ewa Deelman and assisted by Charles D. Norton and Peter Tannenbaum. The committee was supported by a group of volunteers including Wesley Kaplow, Austin Lobo, William Maniatty, Mohan Nibhanupudi, Wesley Turner and Louis Ziantz. In addition to the members of the Program Committee, the sessions were chaired by Dharma P. Agrawal (North Carolina State University), Susan Flynn Hummel (Polytechnic University) and J. Ramanujam (Louisiana State University). The discussion was vivid and in many cases it influenced the final versions of the chapters in this book. The Workshop received financial support from Rensselaer Polytechnic Institute and IBM Corporation. Finally, the authors wish to thank the editor at Kluwer, Alex Green, whose encouragement and advice enabled us to prepare and publish this book shortly after the workshop.

Boleslaw K. Szymanski   Balaram Sinharoy
Rensselaer Polytechnic Institute, Troy, NY   IBM Corp., Poughkeepsie, NY
July, 1995

1

NON-LINEAR ARRAY DEPENDENCE ANALYSIS †

William Pugh, David Wonnacott

Department of Computer Science,
University of Maryland, College Park, MD 20742

ABSTRACT

Standard array data dependence techniques can only reason about linear constraints. There has also been work on analyzing some dependences involving polynomial constraints. Analyzing array data dependences in real-world programs requires handling many "unanalyzable" terms: subscript arrays, run-time tests, function calls.

The standard approach to analyzing such programs has been to omit and ignore any constraints that cannot be reasoned about. This is unsound when reasoning about value-based dependences and whether privatization is legal. Also, this prevents us from determining the conditions that must be true to disprove the dependence. These conditions could be checked by a run-time test or verified by a programmer or aggressive, demand-driven interprocedural analysis.

We describe a solution to these problems. Our solution makes our system sound and more accurate for analyzing value-based dependences and derives conditions that can be used to disprove dependences. We also give some preliminary results applying our techniques to programs from the Perfect benchmark suite.

1 INTRODUCTION

Standard algorithms for determining if two array references are aliased (i.e., might refer to the same memory location) are posed in terms of checking to see if a set of linear constraints has an integer solution. This problem is NP-Complete [7]. Both approximate and exact algorithms have been proposed for solving this problem.

Unfortunately, many array dependence problems cannot be exactly translated into linear constraints, such as Example 1. The lhs and rhs of the assignment statement

---

†This work is supported by an NSF PYI grant CCR-9157384 and by a Packard Fellowship.

```
                               for i := 1 to n do
                                 for j := 1 to p do
                                   A[i,j] := A[i-x,j]+C[j]
```

```
if p > 2 then
   for a := 1 to n do                      Example 2
     for b := 1 to n do
       for c := 1 to n do       for i := 1 to 100 do
         a[a^p+b^p] = a[c^p]       A[P[i]] := C[i]
```

Example 1   Example 3

might be aliased if and only if

$$\exists a, b, c, p, n \text{ s.t. } 1 \le a, b, c \le n \land p > 2 \land a^p + b^p = c^p$$

Allowing arbitrary constraints makes checking for solutions undecidable (not to mention difficult). Disproving the above conditions is the same as proving Fermat's last theorem.

The standard approach in cases such as this is to simply omit any non-linear constraints when building the set of constraints to be tested. For the above example, we would simply check the constraints:

$$\exists a, b, c, p, n \text{ s.t. } 1 \le a, b, c \le n \land p > 2$$

Omitting the non-linear constraints gives us an upper bound on the conditions under which the array references are aliased. Checking this upper bound for solutions will give us a conservative solution, which is what we need if we are to prove the safety of a program transformation that requires independence.

However, there are a number of situations in which this approach is unsatisfactory. It is inadequate when we want to know the conditions under which a solution exists, rather than just testing for the potential existence of a dependence, or when we wish to produce dependence information that corresponds to the flow of values in the program (rather than memory aliasing).

1.1 Symbolic dependence analysis

We represent data dependences as relations between tuples of integer variables. The input tuple represents the values of the loop index variables at the source of the dependence, and the output tuple the values of the loop index variables at the sink. Consider Example 2: we can describe the flow dependence carried by the outer loop as a relation from source iteration i, j to destination iteration i', j':

$$\{[i, j'] \to [i', j'] \mid 1 \le i < i' \le n \land 1 \le j, j' \le p \land i = i' - x \land j = j'\}$$

Since all the terms are affine, we can use techniques described in [13] to compute the conditions on symbolic constants (x, n and p) that must be true in order for a flow dependence to exist: $1 \le x < n \land 1 \le p$.

Once we compute these conditions, we might use more powerful analysis techniques to see if they can be disproved, allow the user to assert that they are false, and/or check at run-time to see if they are false. As described in [13], we can eliminate the test $1 \leq p$ as uninteresting.

If a program contains non-linear expressions and we simply omit the corresponding non-linear constraints from the dependence problem, we will be unable to accurately compute necessary and sufficient conditions for the dependence to exist. For example, if we omit the non-linear terms in

$$\{[i] \to [i'] \mid 1 \leq i < i' \leq 100 \wedge P[i] = P[i']\}$$

(the relation describing the output dependence in Example 3), we would conclude that a dependence is inevitable. However, if we include the non-linear constraints, we can determine that there is a dependence iff $P[1:100]$ contains repeated elements.

1.2 Computing value-based dependences

Standard array data dependence tests only determine if two array references touch the same memory location; they are oblivious to intervening writes. For a number of program optimizations and transformations, it is desirable to also compute "value-based" dependences [6, 13, 14, 16, 9], in which there are no intervening writes. In our approach [14], we start with a set of constraints describing the iterations that touch the same memory location and then subtract out the pairs clobbered by an intervening write. Our techniques for handling negation are described in [14]. Note that our techniques are intended for use in analyzing array references; other techniques can analyze value-based scalar dependences more efficiently [19].

For example, the memory-based flow dependence in Example 4 is

$$\{[i,j] \to [i',j'] \mid 1 \leq i \leq i' \leq n \wedge 1 \leq j = j' \leq m\}.$$

When we subtract out the pairs clobbered by an intervening write:

$$\{[i,j] \to [i',j'] \mid 1 \leq i < i' \leq n \wedge 1 \leq j = j' \leq m\}$$

We find that values are only communicated within iterations of the i loop:

$$\{[i,j] \to [i',j'] \mid 1 \leq i = i' \leq n \wedge 1 \leq j = j' \leq m\}$$

This approach cannot be applied with conservative approximations of the dependences: subtracting an upper bound from an upper bound gives something that is neither an upper bound nor a lower bound. So we can't just blindly omit non-linear constraints if we wish to compute value-based dependences, even if we are willing to settle for a conservative approximation. If we tried to do so in Example 5, we would conclude that there cannot be a loop-carried flow dependence, even though there can. In Section 5.1, we will see that our techniques produce a correct, though approximate, result for this example. In some cases, we can produce exact value-based dependence information despite the presence of non-linear terms (Section 5's Example 11 shows one such case).

```
for i := 1 to n do              for i := 1 to n do
  for j := 1 to m do              for j := 1 to L[i] do
    work[j] := ...                  work[j] := ...
  for j := 1 to m do              for j := 1 to m do
    ... := work[j]                  ... := work[j]
```

Example 4   Example 5

1.3   Representing control-flow information

There have been two approaches to the calculation of array data-flow information. Some methods, like ours, are based on extensions of array data dependence techniques. Others are based on extensions of scalar data-flow equations to deal with array sections. In general, the former are better at dealing with complicated subscripts, and the latter handle more complicated control flow. As we will see in Section 3, a sufficiently rich constraint language will let us handle control flow constructs other than **for** loops and structured **if**'s.

When we want to analyze value-based dependences or find the conditions under which a dependence exists, we must have some way to avoid making approximations whenever we are faced with a non-linear term.

This paper describes our use of constraints containing *uninterpreted function symbols* to represent non-linear expressions from the program, and thus avoid the problems described above.   In Section 2, we describe the class of constraints that we can manipulate.   In Section 3, we show how to use uninterpreted function symbols for program analysis. Sections 4 and 5 show that these more powerful constraints let us perform accurate symbolic and value-based dependence analysis in the presence of non-linear terms. We present our conclusions in Section 7.

2   PRESBURGER FORMULAS WITH UNINTERPRETED FUNCTION SYMBOLS

Presburger formulas [8] are those formulas that can be constructed by combining affine constraints on integer variables with the logical operations $\wedge$, $\vee$, and $\neg$, and the quantifiers $\forall$ and $\exists$. For example, the formulas we constructed for the analysis of Examples 2 and 4 in Section 1 are Presburger formulas. There are a number of algorithms for testing the satisfiability of arbitrary Presburger formulas [8, 4, 14]. This problem appears to have worst-case complexity of $2^{2^{2^{O(n)}}}$ [11].

We formulate value-based array data dependence in terms of (simple) Presburger formulas, with only two nested alternating quantifiers. Memory-based array data dependence can be formulated in terms of even simpler Presburger formulas, with only a single quantifier. Fortunately, the formulas we generate for array dependence analysis of real programs can be solved quite efficiently [14].

Presburger arithmetic can be extended to allow *uninterpreted function symbols*: terms representing the application of a function to a list of argument terms. The functions are called "uninterpreted" because the only thing we know about them is that they are functions: two applications of a function to the same arguments will produce the same value. The formula we used in the analysis of Example 3 is in this class (since the array P is not modified, it is equivalent to a function). Downey [5] proved that full Presburger arithmetic with uninterpreted function symbols is undecidable. We will therefore need to restrict our attention to a subclass of the general problem, and produce approximations whenever a formula is outside of the subclass.

We are currently restricting our attention to formulas in which all function symbols are free, and functions are only applied to elements of the input or output tuple of the relation containing the formula, possibly with a constant offset. For example, in a relation from $[i, j]$ to $[i', j', k']$, a binary function f could be applied $f(i, j)$, $f(k', i')$, or $f(j + 2, i - 5)$. In many cases (and in our current implementation), we only need consider applying a function to a prefix of the input or output tuple (e.g., $f(i, j)$ or $f(i', j')$). Note that the formula we used for Example 3 is in this class.

2.1   Manipulating Presburger Formulas with Uninterpreted Function Symbols

Our techniques for manipulating Presburger formulas with uninterpreted function symbols are based on our previous work with regular Presburger formulas. Our approach is based on conversion to disjunctive normal form and testing each conjunct via Fourier's method of elimination, adapted for integer variables [12]. We have developed a number of techniques to ensure that the number and sizes of conjuncts produced do not get out of hand for the formulas that we encounter in practice [14].

Shostak [18] developed a procedure for testing the satisfiability of quantifier-free Presburger formulas with uninterpreted function symbols, based on the following observation: Consider a formula F that contains references $f(i)$ and $f(j)$, where i and j are free in F. Let F_0 be F with f_i and f_j substituted for $f(i)$ and $f(j)$. F is satisfiable iff $F' = (((i = j) \Rightarrow (f_i = f_j)) \wedge F_0)$ is satisfiable. Shostak provides several ways of improving over the naive replacement of F with F'.

Our techniques also rely on this fact. We convert each formula into a specialized disjunctive normal form, in which every conjunct that contains multiple uses of a function also contains either an equality constraint between the function arguments or some constraint that contradicts this equality. In other words, a conjunct containing both $f(i_1, i_2, i_3)$ and $f(j_1, j_2, j_3)$ could contain either $i_1 = j_1 \wedge i_2 = j_2 \wedge i_3 = j_3$ or $i_2 > j_2$ (or some similar inequality). Thus, in any one conjunct, we can either unify a pair of functions applications or treat them as unrelated.

Some of the relational operators supported by the Omega Library , such as "compose" or "domain", replace the variables of the input or output tuple with existentially quantified variables. For these operation, we approximate any constraint that contains

```
                                   for i := 1 to n do
                                     for j := 1 to n do
                                       for k := 1 to n do
                                         if p[i,j,k] < 0 then
for i := 1 to n do                         goto L1 // 2 level break
  A[m*i] := ...                            A[i] := ...
  ... := A[i]                            endfor
endfor                                 endfor
                                   L1:
        Example 6                  endfor
```

```
                                            Example 7
for i := 1 to n do
  for j := 1 to n*i do
    a[j] := ...
  endfor                           for i := 1 to n do
  for j := n*i+1 to m do             for j := 1 to m do
    a[j] := ...                        for k := 1 to p[i] do
  endfor                                 a[q*i+k] := ...
  for k := 1 to m do                   endfor
    ... := a[k]                        ...
  endfor                             endfor
endfor                             endfor
```

```
        Example 8                        Example 9
```

a function application that cannot be written as a function of the input or output tuple in the result. When we approximate, we may wish to produce either an upper or a lower bound on the relation. We can relax any conjunction of constraints containing $f(x)$, where x is existentially quantified, by replacing $f(x)$ with a new existentially quantified scalar. We can tighten such a conjunction by replacing it with **False**.

For a more detailed description of these techniques, see [15].

3   USING FUNCTION SYMBOLS IN DEPENDENCE ANALYSIS

Consider a program that contains a non-linear term, such as Example 6. For each non-linear expression e that is nested within n loops, we use an n-ary function $f(\mathcal{I})$ to represent the value of e in iteration $\mathcal{I}$. For example, the flow dependence in this example is

$$\{[i] \to [i'] \mid 1 \leq i \leq i' \leq n \land f_{m*i}(i) = i'\}$$

Of course, we do not know the value of f_{m*i} at compile time, but we can use it in the constraints that describe a dependence (after all, we're using n, and we don't know what it is).

This basic technique works for non-linear expressions in subscript expressions, loop bounds and the guards of conditional branches that do not jump out of loops. This technique doesn't work well for breaks (i.e., jumps out of a loop). The problem is that to describe the conditions under which iteration i of a loop executes, we must express the fact that the break was not taken in any previous iteration. We therefore use a slightly different approach for breaks: we create a function symbol whose value is the iteration in which the break is performed. In Example 7, there may be different breaks for each iteration of i. So we create function symbols $b_j(i)$ and $b_k(i)$ to describe when the break occurs. The constraints describing the iterations of the assignment statement that are executed are:

$$\{[i,j,k] : 1 \leq i,j,k \leq n \land (j < b_j(i) \lor j = b_j(i) \land k < b_k(i))\}$$

We treat **while** loops as **for** loops with infinite upper bounds (i.e., no upper bound) and a **break** statement.

3.1 More Sophisticated Selection of Functions

The previous representation is somewhat crude: the only thing it captures is that a value computed at some iteration of a statement has some fixed but unknown value. We can do substantially better by recognizing when values computed at different points must be the same. For example, if we use the same function to represent the two occurrences of n*i in Example 8, we can show that there are no upwards exposed reads. Also, an expression may be partially loop invariant. In Example 9, the expression q * i is independent of the j loop, and would be represented as a function of i. If p is constant, p[i] is also independent of j.

4 SYMBOLIC DEPENDENCE ANALYSIS

In previous work [13], we discussed a general method for finding conditions that prove independence in programs without non-linear terms, and described some ad-hoc methods for applying our techniques in the presence of such terms. Our use of uninterpreted function symbols gives us a general framework for performing this analysis in the presence of non-linear terms.

4.1 Symbolic dependence analysis without non-linear terms

We begin with a review of our previous work. If a relation contains no function symbols, we first replace the variables representing the iteration space with existentially quantified variables, giving the conditions on the symbolic constants under which a dependence exists somewhere in the iteration space. For example, recall the flow dependence in Example 2:

$$\{[i,j'] \rightarrow [i',j'] \mid 1 \leq i < i' \leq n \land 1 \leq j,j' \leq p \land i = i' - x \land j = j'\}$$

This dependence exists iff $1 \leq x < n \land 1 \leq p$.

These conditions often contain conditions that are false only in situations in which we don't care if the loop is parallel (in this case, $1 \leq p$). We wish to avoid asking the user about such constraints or generating run-time tests for them. We avoid this problem by collecting another set of constraints that give the conditions that must be true for the dependence to be interesting: each surrounding loop executes at least one iteration, the loop that carries the dependence executes more than once, plus any facts about the program provided by user assertions or other analysis.

We then consider only the *gist* of the dependence conditions given these uninteresting conditions [17]. Informally, gist p given q is the conditions that are interesting in p given that q holds. More formally, it is a minimal set of constraints such that (gist p given q) $\land$ q = p $\land$ q.

If we find that there are interesting conditions under which the dependence will not exist, we might choose to compile a run-time test or query the user about whether the conditions can actually occur (for example, the programmer might have knowledge about x in Example 2 that is not available to the compiler).

4.2   Symbolic dependence analysis in the presence of non-linear terms

When a Presburger formula contains no function symbols, we can eliminate any arbitrary set of variables. This ability derives from the fact that our methods are based on a variation of Fourier's method of variable elimination, which relies on classifying individual constraints as either upper or lower bounds on the variable to be eliminated. However, a constraint like $p(i) > 0$ constrains both p and i, but it is neither an upper nor a lower bound on i. Therefore, we cannot eliminate i exactly if $p(i)$ remains in the formula.

This fact limits our ability to eliminate arbitrary variables from a formula. For example, we cannot simply eliminate i and i$'$ from the relation describing the output dependence in Example 3:

$$\{[i] \to [i'] \mid 1 \le i < i' \le 100 \land p(i) = p(i')\}$$

We therefore leave in the relation any iteration space variables that are used as function arguments. In this example, we cannot eliminate any variables, and the relation is not changed in the first step of our symbolic analysis. Fortunately, the uninteresting conditions on these variables are eliminated in the second step: the gist of the above relation given $1 \le i \le i' \le 100$ is

$$\{[i] \to [i'] \mid p(i) = p(i')\}$$

Note that we may wish to include the "uninteresting" conditions in any run-time tests we compile (to check for repeated elements only in p[1:100]) or dialogue with the programmer ("Is it the case that p[i] != p[i'] whenever $1 \le i < i' \le 100$").

5 VALUE-BASED DEPENDENCE ANALYSIS

Our use of function symbols to represent non-linear expressions increases the accuracy of our value-based dependence analysis. We can compute value-based dependence information from access A to C by subtracting, from the relation describing the pairs where memory aliasing occurs, all the pairs in which the memory location is over-written by some write B. One way to compute this is to subtract is the union of all compositions of a dependence A to B with one from B to C (more efficient techniques that produce the same answer are described in [14]). This composition operation may produce results that are outside the class of relations we can handle, and therefore produce approximate results.

For example, we cannot produce exact information about the loop-carried flow of values in Example 10. To do so, we would have to calculate the composition of the loop-carried flow dependence with the loop-carried output dependence, which produces the relation:

$$\{ [i,j] \rightarrow [i'] \mid \exists [i'',j''] \text{ s.t. } 1 \leq i < i'' < i' \leq n \land p(i) > 0 \land p(i'') > 0$$
$$\land 1 \leq j'' = j' \leq n \land j = j'' = i' \}$$

Since this relation contains $p(i'')$, an application of a function to a quantified variable, it is outside the class of formulas we can handle. It is possible to apply the techniques described in [18] to the formula in this relation, but these techniques simply test for satisfiability; we need to subtract this relation from the relation giving memory-based dependences. Since we cannot handle this exactly, we handle it approximately as follows. We convert $p(i'')$ to a quantified variable, $\alpha_{p(i'')}$. This produces a looser set of constraints (i.e., an upper bound):

$$\{ [i,j] \rightarrow [i'] \mid \exists i'',j'',\alpha_{p(i'')} \text{ s.t. } 1 \leq i < i'' < i' \leq n \land p(i) > 0 \land \alpha_{p(i'')} > 0$$
$$\land 1 \leq j'' = j' \leq n \land j = j'' = i' \}$$

We can, however, exactly compose the loop-independent flow dependence with the loop-carried output dependence. Since $i'' = i'$, we can replace $p(i'')$ with $p(i')$. When we subtract this from the relation that describes the memory-based dependence, we eliminate any loop-carried flow dependences to iterations in which $p(i) > 0$.

Normally, when we can not compute dependences exactly, we wish to compute an upper bound on the true dependences. When computing $R_1 - R_2$ where R_2 is an upper bound, we can use R_1 as upper bound on the result. Of course, if $R_1 \cap R_2$ is infeasible, then R_1 is an exact answer.

We can produce exact value-based dependences for Example 11. There are two compositions of output dependences and flow dependences that describe potential kills. We can represent each of these exactly, and when we subtract them both from the loop-carried memory-based dependence, nothing is left.

```
                                    for i := 1 to n do
                                      if p[i] > 0 then
                                        for j := 1 to n do
                                          a[j] := ...
                                        endfor
 for i := 1 to n do                   else
   if p(i) > 0 then                     for j := 1 to n do
     for j := 1 to n do                   a[j] := ...
       a[j] := ...                      endfor
     endfor                           endif
   endif
                                      ... := a[i]
   ... := a[i]                      endfor
 endfor
```

Example 10   Example 11

5.1   Symbolic array data-flow analysis

We can apply the techniques of Section 4 to value-based dependence relations, even if they are inexact. For example, we cannot produce an exact description of the data flow in Example 5. If we choose to be conservative, we can show that the value-based loop-carried flow dependences are a subset of

$$\{ [i,j] \rightarrow [i',j'] \mid 1 \leq i < i' \leq n \wedge 1, l(i') + 1 \leq j = j' \leq m, l(i) \}$$

We eliminate j and j', producing

$$\{ [i] \rightarrow [i'] \mid 1 \leq i < i' \leq n \wedge 1, l(i') + 1 \leq m, l(i) \}$$

When we take the gist of this relation given our usual set of uninteresting conditions, we get:

$$\{[i] \rightarrow [i'] \mid l(i') < l(i), \mathtt{m}\}$$

Thus, we can disprove a dependence by asserting that L is nondecreasing, or that all elements of L are greater than m (in which case the read is covered). Therefore, we could privatize the `work` array and run this loop in parallel under either of these conditions. Similarly, we could conclude that Example 10 could be run in parallel if p is always greater than 0. However, the inexactness of our result keeps us from showing that this example can also be parallelized if p is nondecreasing.

5.2   Related Work

Paul Feautrier and Jean-Francois Collard [3] have extended their array data-flow analysis technique to handle non-linear terms in loop bounds and **if**'s. They also give a precise description of the set of programs for which they can provide exact dependence information. However, their system cannot be applied to programs with non-linear array subscripts, and according to Section 5.1 of their work, extending it to handle this case is "very difficult". Furthermore, there is no discussion of any way of introducing information about the values of non-linear expressions, as we describe in Section 3.1. We have not been able to come up with a precise mathematical comparison of our methods, but have so far not found an example in which one method cannot disprove a dependence that is disproved by the other, without resorting to non-linear subscripts or the techniques in Section 3.1.

We believe that the most significant distinction between our work and [3] is our ability to relate the non-linear terms in our dependence relations to expressions in the program, and thus discuss the program with some external agent (such as the programmer), as described in Section 4. The techniques described in [3] produce information about the possible sources of a value that is read from an array, but do not provide information about which expressions in the program control which source actually produces the value. In other words, they provide no mechanism for deriving the fact that Example 5 can be parallelized (after array expansion) if L is nondecreasing.

Vadim Maslov's work on lazy dependence analysis [9] can handle some non-linear constraints. The value-based dependences his system can disprove are a strict subset of the ones we can disprove, but the dependences his system fails to disprove do not appear to be common. However, his system cannot determine the conditions that would disprove a dependence or utilize the optimizations described in Section 3.1.

6 RESULTS

We have implemented techniques to manipulate relations in which functions are applied to a prefix of the input or output tuple of the relation (this is sufficient to handle everything described in this paper except example 9 from Section 3.1).

We have tested the effectiveness of our techniques on the five Perfect Club Benchmarks studied in [10]. This study compared the loop-carried flow dependences found by memory-based analysis to the number of cases of inter-iteration data-flow that occurred during a test run. This comparison indicates the degree to which dependence analysis can be used to estimate loop parallelism (which is fundamentally limited by inter-iteration data-flow). Memory-based dependence analysis was found to over-estimate data-flow by more than a factor of 5.

Figure 1 shows the number of loop-carried value-based flow dependences found for these same programs, using the techniques described in Sections 4 and 5 and three different approaches to non-linear terms:

U.F.S. Non-linear terms are represented with uninterpreted function symbols, as described in Section 3. For those cases that are beyond the scope of our current implementation, we applied our techniques by hand.

Affine bound We compute an affine upper bound for any memory-based dependence that involves a non-linear term. During value-based analysis, we use R_1 as an upper bound on any subtraction $R_1 - R_2$ in which R_2 is an upper bound and $R_1 \cap R_2$ is satisfiable.

Analysis	Non-linear	Dependences			Total
		Proved	Conditional	Inexact	
Memory aliasing	Affine bound	543	40	567	1150
	U.F.S.	972	176	0	1148
Value flow	Assume dependence	160	11	619	790
	Affine bound	160	5	200	365
	U.F.S.	161	69	0	230

Figure 1   Dependences found by various tests

Assume dependence   When a non-linear term appears during value-based analysis, we assume there is a dependence (this reflects the results of a test that is not applicable in the presence of non-linear terms).

Before performing our analysis, we manually performed inter-procedural constant propagation, and inlined one subroutine call. To compare the dependences found by our techniques and those reported in [10], we removed the following dependences from the set found by our analysis:

- conditional dependences with infeasible conditions (these could be removed via programmer assertions),
- conditional dependences that did not occur during the test run,
- and all dependences in procedures that were not called during the test run.

The remaining set of dependences matched the inter-iteration data-flow found during the test run in [10] exactly. Thus, we believe that our techniques provide an accurate static estimate of the run-time data flow of programs that are similar to these benchmarks.

Figure 2 shows the amount of time required on a Sparcstation 10/51 for our implementation to perform memory and value-based dependence analysis on the array variables of several routines from the Perfect Club Benchmark Suite [1]. The routines shown in this table all contain many non-linear terms.

While these times may be to great to allow the use of our techniques during regular compilation, they are not excessive for a system that interactively assists programmers in the detection and elimination of dependences that prevent parallelism.

7   CONCLUSIONS

Standard array dependence analysis techniques produce conservative approximations by ignoring any constraints arising from non-linear terms in the program. This approach is not adequate for tests that perform value-based dependence analysis or provide information about the conditions under which a dependence exists.

Procedure	time for our analysis	time for £77 -fast
BTRIX	2.3s	3.8s
CFFT2D1	9.0s	1.0s
INTERF	10.2s	2.2s
NLFILT	4.6s	1.4s
OLDA	4.2s	2.1s

Figure 2   Analysis times for array data dependences in several procedures

We use uninterpreted function symbols to represent non-linear terms in our constraint system. This approach lets us calculate conditions that are sufficient and necessary for a memory-based dependence to exist. Furthermore, it seems to be at least as powerful as other methods for computing approximate value-based array dependences in the presence of non-linear terms. We can determine the conditions under which a value-based dependence exists, although in some cases these conditions will be conservative. This approximation occurs when we cannot rewrite the function symbols occurrences in the kill terms to be functions of the write or read iteration, and we just ignore the kill term. Alternatively, we can make the function symbol occurrence in the kill term just a existentially quantified variable. In this case, the result of the subtraction will be a lower bound on the actual dependence.

Our techniques provide information that is useful in determining that some code from the Perfect Club Benchmark programs can be run in parallel. This information is not provided by standard analysis techniques. Some of this information might be derived by advanced interprocedural analysis techniques [2], but it may be more efficient to derive such information in a demand-driven way, rather than trying to derive all interprocedural information that can be proven.

A partial implementation of our approach is distributed with version 0.95 of the Omega library and the Petit dependence analyzer.

REFERENCES

[1] M. Berry et al.   The PERFECT Club benchmarks: Effective performance evaluation of supercomputers. *International Journal of Supercomputing Applications*, 3(3):5–40, March 1989.

[2] William Blume and Rudolf Eigenmann. Symbolic analysis techniques needed for effective parallelization of the Perfect benchmarks. Tech. Report 1332, Univ. of Illinois at Urbana-Champaign, Center for Supercomputing Res. & Dev., 1994.

[3] Jean-François Collard and Paul Feautrier. Fuzzy array dataflow analysis. Tech. Report N° 94-21, Laboratoire de l'Informatique du Parallélisme, Ecolo Normal Supérieure de Lyon, Instiut IMAG, July 1994.

[4] D. C. Cooper. Theorem proving in arithmetic with multiplication. In B. Meltzer and D. Michie, editors, *Machine Intelligence 7*, pp. 91–9. American Elsevier, New York, 1972.

[5] P. Downey. Undeciability of presburger arithmetic with a single monadic predicate letter. Tech. Report 18-72, Center for Research in Computing Technology, Havard Univ., 1972.

[6] Paul Feautrier. Array expansion. In *ACM Int. Conf. on Supercomputing, St Malo*, pages 429–441, 1988.

[7] Michael R. Garey and David S. Johnson. *Computers and Intractability: A Guide to the Theory of NP-Completeness*. W.H. Freemand and Company, 1979.

[8] G. Kreisel and J. L. Krevine. *Elements of Mathematical Logic*. North-Holland Pub. Co., 1967.

[9] Vadim Maslov. Lazy array data-flow dependence analysis. In *ACM '94 Conf. on Principles of Programming Languages*, January 1994.

[10] Dror Eliezer Maydan. *Accurate Analysis of Array References*. PhD thesis, Computer Systems Laboratory, Stanford U., September 1992.

[11] D. Oppen. A $2^{2^{2^{pn}}}$ upper bound on the complexity of presburger arithmetic. *Journal of Computer and System Sciences*, 16(3):323–332, July 1978.

[12] William Pugh. The Omega test: a fast and practical integer programming algorithm for dependence analysis. *Communications of the ACM*, 8:102–114, August 1992.

[13] William Pugh and David Wonnacott. Eliminating false data dependences using the Omega test. In *SIGPLAN Conference on Programming Language Design and Implementation*, pages 140–151, San Francisco, California, June 1992.

[14] William Pugh and David Wonnacott. An exact method for analysis of value-based array data dependences. In *Lecture Notes in Computer Science 768: Sixth Annual Workshop on Programming Languages and Compilers for Parallel Computing*, Portland, OR, August 1993. Springer-Verlag.

[15] William Pugh and David Wonnacott. Nonlinear array dependence analysis. Technical Report CS-TR-3372, Dept. of Computer Science, University of Maryland, College Park, November 1994.

[16] William Pugh and David Wonnacott. Static analysis of upper and lower bounds on dependences and parallelism. *ACM Transactions on Programming Languages and Systems*, 14(3):1248–1278, July 1994.

[17] William Pugh and David Wonnacott. Going beyond integer programming with the Omega test to eliminate false data dependences. *IEEE Transactions on Parallel and Distributed Systems*, 1995. To appear.

[18] Robert E. Shostak. A practical decision procedure for arithmetic with function symbols. *Journal of the ACM*, 26(2):351–360, April 1979.

[19] Eric Stoltz and Michael Wolfe. Detecting value-based scalar dependence. In *Proc. of the Seventh Annual Workshop on Languages and Compilers for Parallel Computing*. Cornell University, August 1994.

PATH COLLECTION AND DEPENDENCE TESTING IN THE PRESENCE OF DYNAMIC, POINTER-BASED DATA STRUCTURES†

Joe Hummel, Laurie Hendren* and Alex Nicolau

UC-Irvine, Irvine, California USA

* McGill University, Montreal, Quebec Canada

ABSTRACT

Memory references to dynamic, pointer-based data structures are best summarized by paths through the structure. Accurate collection of such paths is critical to data dependence testing, and plays an important role in guiding data distribution. In this paper we present a new approach to path collection that enables general dependence testing, and then demonstrate its importance in parallelizing a real application.

1   INTRODUCTION AND MOTIVATION

The problem of data dependence testing in the presence of pointers is beginning to receive a good deal of attention. The reason for this is two-fold. Firstly, there is an increasing use of languages by the community which support pointers, in particular C, C++, FORTRAN90 and HPF. Secondly, there is a growing recognition that dynamic pointer-based data structures, like arrays, are important tools for achieving efficient solutions. For example, the *Quadtree / Octree* data structures are used in a number of application areas, including computational geometry [24], N-body simulations [1], and computer-aided design [7]. Likewise, *Sparse matrices* are an important tool in circuit simulations [18], *Bipartite graphs* are useful in electromagnetic simulations [2], and *Patricia trees* have found important applications in computational biology [8].

---

†This work supported in part by the NSF, ONR, FCAR, NSERC, and McGill Faculty of Graduate Studies and Research.

Having accurate dependence information enables the compiler to perform a wide-range of optimizing transformations, e.g. loop parallelization. In the particular case of compilers for scalable parallel architectures, memory issues become a more dominant problem, and thus the target of a good deal of the compiler's optimization effort. Accurate dependence information plays an important role in this effort as well. For example, knowing that different processors access disjoint segments of a data structure can enable each processor to prefetch an exclusive copy of its segment [21, 15]. Also, the selection of an appropriate, application-specific memory consistency model [9] or cache coherence protocol [23] can be aided by dependence information. Finally, dependence information is certainly necessary for any compiler optimizing C programs for a scalable multiprocessor [3].

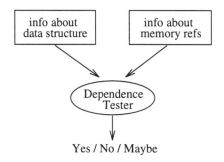

Yes / No / Maybe

Figure 1   Components for an accurate solution.

The goal of our work is the same as that of traditional array-based analysis and optimization efforts: accurate dependence testing. The difference is that we are focusing solely on dynamic, pointer-based data structures. As shown in Figure 1, three components are needed to perform accurate data dependence testing in the presence of pointer-based data structures. The compiler needs information about the data structure, information about the memory locations being referenced, and the actual dependence test itself. Given the difficulty of automatic recognition of dynamic data structures [12], we have proposed both high and lower-level languages for obtaining data structure information from the user [12, 13]. We have also developed the first general dependence test for use with dynamic data structures [14]. Unlike existing approaches, our test is not limited to a particular class of structures — its accuracy is limited only by the accuracy of the information provided.

What remains is an accurate approach for summarizing memory references, which is the subject of this paper. Not only is this information critical to dependence testing, it is important in its own right; e.g. to guide data distribution decisions [3]. In the next section we present related work, followed by a discussion of our approach in Section 3. Then in Section 4 we demonstrate the importance of our approach in parallelizing a real application. Finally, in the last section we present our conclusions.

2 RELATED WORK

We are concerned with summarizing memory references to dynamic, pointer-based data structures. Existing approaches fall into one of two categories: *store-based* and *storeless* [5].

Store-based approaches, first proposed by [17] and typified by [20], are much too conservative in their approximation. This is due to the use of a naming scheme which labels the nodes of a potentially unbounded data structure with a small, finite set of names. Improvements to this core approach are limited to particular types of data structures [4, 22].

Storeless approaches are potentially much more accurate, since they can provide an essentially infinite namespace. The idea is to label a given node based on its relationship with other nodes, in particular some notion of the *paths* between these memory locations. Existing storeless approaches however are either limited to a particular set of structures [10], limited in accuracy due to the use of more restrictive paths [16, 6], or limited by the kinds of paths collected [19]. Furthermore, none of these approaches enable general data dependence testing.

We propose a storeless, path-based approach which is both generally applicable and captures multiple paths for more accurate dependence testing in the presence of loops. Similar to [19], we use regular expressions to summarize memory references. Regular expressions exhibit important theoretical properties such as decidability, and support the accurate analysis and mapping of standard program constructs into paths—statement sequence via concatenation, selection by alternation, and iteration by kleene star. Unlike existing approaches, the paths we collect enable general dependence testing, including that of memory references within complicated loop nests.

3 PATH COLLECTION ANALYSIS

In this section we first outline our overall approach to data dependence testing, then we will outline and define our approach to path collection.

3.1 Overall Approach to Data Dependence Testing

Figure 2 summarizes our general approach to the problem of dependence testing in the presence of dynamic, pointer-based data structures. Information about the data structure is currently provided by the user, in either a high-level or lower-level form. Ultimately, higher-level information is automatically translated into the lower-level form, which is viewed as a series of *axioms* about the data structure. Information about memory references is then collected in the form of *access paths*, which denote paths rooted at a particular node in the data structure. Dependence testing is performed in a manner similar to theorem proving—the axioms are applied to the access paths in an attempt to prove dependence or no dependence. Since axioms and access paths are based on regular expressions, the dependence tester is both general and decidable.

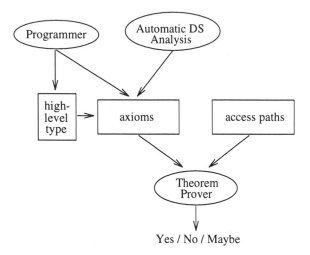

Figure 2 Components in our approach to accurate data dependence testing.

3.2   Definitions

A *path* is defined as a regular expression of pointer fields connecting two nodes in the data structure. The regular expression ϵ denotes the empty path, i.e. for any node n, traversing the path ϵ from n yields n. A *handle* denotes a particular node in the data structure; unlike program pointer variables, once a handle is defined it always refers to its associated node. Paths are collected relative to handles, and thus an *access path* is a tuple $H.P$, where H denotes a handle and P a path.

The motivation for collecting paths in this manner is that it facilitates dependence testing. Existing approaches collect information relating the program's pointer variables to *each other*. The result is program-point specific information that is valid for the given statement, but becomes invalid once the analysis crosses a pointer-updating statement. Hence information from different statements cannot be compared, preventing general dependence testing. Access paths, however, which are based on handles and thus *independent* of the program's pointer variables, can be compared even if they originate from different program statements.

During analysis, the compiler collects access paths in *access path matrices*. An entry in an access path matrix (APM) represents the statically-traversed path, or some conservative approximation of this path, from a handle to a set of nodes. Access path matrices exhibit two important properties. Firstly, an APM does not summarize at compile-time all the possible paths that may exist at run-time. Instead, an APM captures only those paths that are explicitly traversed by the statements in the program. This greatly reduces the amount of information that must be collected, yet retains what we consider the crucial information—the paths actually being used by the program.

An important side-effect of reducing the amount of information collected is that it enables the use of more accurate collection strategies. The reader should note another implication of this approach: if an APM entry is empty, this does not imply the absence of a path between nodes, only that no definite path has yet been explicitly traversed by the program.

Secondly, each entry in an APM is a *must*-path, i.e. at least one string in the regular expression is guaranteed to lead from the given handle to the destination node(s). Note that this restriction does not prevent the accurate analysis of control flow branching (e.g. conditionals), since must-paths can be constructed using the alternation and kleene star regular expression operators. It merely reduces the amount of needless information stored in the APMs, since dependence testing cannot be performed with *may*-information.

3.3 Collecting Paths: Building APMs

Initially, the analysis process starts with an empty access path matrix. After analyzing a program statement S which updates some program pointer, a new APM is produced and associated with S. Hence APMs are program-point specific, even though the access paths contained within are not.

During the analysis of S, a handle is added to the APM based on the source node referenced by the RHS. A path is then constructed from this handle to the destination node (denoted by the LHS) based on the pointer fields traversed by S. For example, consider the following C statement:

$$S: \quad p = q\text{->next};$$

Assuming an empty APM before reaching S, the following APM is produced after the analysis of S:

APM_S	q	p
$\$h_S$	ϵ	next

In short, the handle $\$h_S$ is added and defined as equivalent to q, the column for q is then copied to p, and the field next is appended to every path in p.

Pointer-updating statements can be simplified into one of five types [11]. Though our examples are based on C, this classification is valid for any imperative language with pointers and dynamic memory allocation:

```
1. p = NULL;
2. p = malloc(...);
3. p = q;
4. p = q->F;
5. p->F = q;
```

In the case of (1), the analysis does not add a handle, and sets all entries in p's column to • (signifying that p points nowhere). For (2), a handle $\$h_S$ is added with a path of ϵ to p, while the remaining entries in p's column are set to •. In (3), a handle $\$h_S$ is added with a path of ϵ to q, and then q's column is copied to p. In the case of (4), the analysis proceeds as discussed in the previous paragraph (add handle, copy column, append F to every path). Note that handles are deleted from an APM when they no longer *anchor* any path, which can occur anytime a pointer variable is assigned a new value.

What remains is the analysis for statement type (5). The effect of this statement is quite different from that of (1) through (4), since it updates the *structure* of the data structure (vs. updating a program pointer variable). This may invalidate one or more access paths computed before the statement, as well as invalidate one or more axioms about the data structure. At present our analysis simply produces an empty APM after such a statement, resulting in overly conservative but correct behavior.

3.4   Merging Access Path Matrices

APMs need to be merged in two cases: conditionals and loops*. In the case of conditionals, the branches are analyzed separately and the resulting APMs merged to summarize the effect of taking either branch. An accurate summary is achieved by using the alternation regular expression operator. Loops are handled by repeatedly summarizing the body of the loop until the APM at the loop header reaches a fixed-point, i.e. each entry in the APM converges. The kleene star regular expression operator plays a critical role in this case. We will refer to these as *conditional-merge* and *loop-merge*, respectively.

Conditional-merge

Given two APMs A and B, the first step is to eliminate *may*-information, i.e. information not common to both APMs. If a program pointer variable p does not appear in both APMs, then all entries in p's column are ignored during the merge. Likewise, if a handle $\$h_i$ does not appear in both APMs, and it cannot be proven that $\$h_i$ is equivalent to some other handle $\$h_j$, then all entries in $\$h_i$'s row are ignored.

The second and final step is to merge the remaining, common information to produce a single APM R. For each corresponding entry $a \in A$ and $b \in B$ (i.e. for each pair of entries with the same row and column header), the resulting merged entry is computed as follows:

---

*The ideas presented here can be extended to handle other cases that will occur, e.g. case statements and recursive subroutines.

```
if both are paths then
    if path_a ⊆ path_b then entry is path_b
    else if path_b ⊆ path_a then entry is path_a
    else entry is path_a|path_b
else if both are • then entry is •
else entry is empty
```

Loop-merge

Iteration over dynamic data structures is most often structured as a `while` loop, iterating an unknown and unpredictable number of times (0 or more)[†]. To analyze the effect of an entire loop, the idea is to repeatedly analyze the loop body until the *per iteration path change* for each APM entry in the loop header converges. Once each $\Delta path$ is known, the effect of the entire loop is easily and accurately summarized by applying the kleene star regular expression operator (if necessary) to these Δ values.

The advantage of calculating per iteration path changes, versus simply collecting longer and longer access paths and then summarizing, is to facilitate loop-based dependence testing. For example, the compiler may want to unroll the loop by one iteration; knowing how the access paths change from one iteration to the next enables dependence testing without the need for further analysis. Likewise, loop-carried dependences are easily tested by comparing the access path for a given iteration to that of an access path one or more iterations away, i.e. $(\Delta path)^+$.

Given a while loop L, the APM reaching L becomes the initial loop header APM, denoted APM_{L0}. The body of the loop is then analyzed as normal, eventually producing APM_{L0n} which summarizes the first iteration of the loop. This APM is then merged with APM_{L0} as follows, producing APM_{L1}:

1. *may*-information is discarded

2. for each corresponding entry $a \in APM_{L0}$ and $b \in APM_{L0n}$, compute the per iteration path change as follows:
   if both are paths then the $\Delta path$ is b *minus-prefix* a
   else $\Delta path$ is empty

3. for each corresponding entry $a \in APM_{L0}$ and $b \in APM_{L0n}$
   if both are paths then entry is b
   else if both are • then entry is •
   else entry is empty

In short, APM_{L1} is produced by propagating around the loop the values from the previous iteration APM_{L0n}, while per iteration path changes are computed based on the change in path from one iteration to the next.

[†]Since other loop structures are easily converted in `while` loops, our approach focuses solely on this loop type.

APM_{L1} becomes the new loop header APM, and then the body of the loop is analyzed once again. This analysis eventually results in APM_{L1n}, which must be merged with APM_{L1} to produce the next loop header APM, APM_{L2}. The only difference now concerns step (2), since the new $\Delta path$ must be merged with the previous value. The merging process is done as follows:

> if both $\Delta path$ values are paths then
> > if $\Delta path_{new} \subseteq \Delta path_{L1}$ then $\Delta path_{L2}$ is $\Delta path_{L1}$
> > else if $\Delta path_{L1} \subseteq \Delta path_{new}$ then $\Delta path_{L2}$ is $\Delta path_{new}$
> > else $\Delta path_{L2}$ is $\Delta path_{L1} \mid \Delta path_{new}$
> else $\Delta path_{L2}$ is empty

The loop analysis repeats until a loop header APM is produced in which all $\Delta path$ values are equal to their previous value; we denote this APM as APM_{LN}. At this point the loop analysis has converged, and a summary APM, denoted APM_L, can now be accurately generated by merging APM_{L0} and APM_{LN}. For each corresponding entry $a \in APM_{L0}$ and $b \in APM_{LN}$, where Δp denotes the associated $\Delta path$ value from APM_{LN}, the resulting merged entry is computed as follows:

> if both are paths then
> > if $b \subseteq \Delta p$ then entry is $a(\Delta p)$?
> > else entry is $a(\Delta p)^*$
> else if both are • then entry is •
> else entry is empty

In other words, the kleene star operator is used—if appropriate—to summarize the effect of the while loop, namely traversing $\Delta path$ 0 or more times. Given a loop body consisting of n statements, convergence in the worst case requires n analysis iterations.

3.5   Putting It All Together

As an example, consider a two-way linked-list as shown in Figure 3. The forward pointers are labeled with F, and the backward pointers are labeled with B.

Figure 3   A two-way linked-list.

We will analyze the code fragment shown in Figure 4, and assume an empty APM before starting the path collection analysis. The first step is to analyze statement S1, a statement of type (4). This results in the addition of a new handle $\$h_{S1}$, the addition of

```
S1:    p = hd->F;
W:     p->d = ...;
S2:    if (...)
S3:       q = p->F;
       else {
S4:       q = p->B;
S5:       r = p->F;
S6:       p = hd;
       }
R:     ... = q->d;
```

APM_{S1}	hd	p
$\$h_{S1}$	ϵ	F

APM_{S3}	hd	p	q
$\$h_{S1}$	ϵ	F	FF
$\$h_{S3}$		ϵ	F

APM_{S6}	hd	p	q	r
$\$h_{S1}$	ϵ	ϵ	FB	FF
$\$h_{S4}$			B	F

Figure 4   Example code fragment; APMs after analysis of S1, S3, and S6.

two program pointer variables hd and p, and the definition of two access paths $\$h_{S1}.\epsilon$ to hd and $\$h_{S1}$.F to p.

Since S2 denotes a branch in the control flow, analysis first proceeds separately along the different paths with APM_{S1} serving as the starting APM in each case. Analysis of the *then-branch* produces APM_{S3}, while analysis of the *else-branch* produces APM_{S6}. These APMs are then merged to complete the analysis of statement S2. The resulting APM is shown below:

APM_{S2}	hd	p		q	
$\$h_{S1}$	ϵ	ϵ	F	FF	FB
$\$h_{S3}$				F	B

Note that the handles $\$h_{S3}$ and $\$h_{S4}$ were merged (and not deleted) since it could be proven that these both refer to the same node ($\$h_{S1}$.F).

How is this information used for dependence testing? Consider the statements W and R shown in Figure 4, which denote a write and read, respectively. To prove there is no data dependence from W to R, it suffices to prove that p in W and q in R refer to different memory locations. Thus, the corresponding APMs—APM_{S1} for W and APM_{S2} for R—are searched for common handles with non-empty entries for p and q, and the resulting access paths are then fed to the dependence tester. In this case, the access paths $\$h_{S1}$.F and $\$h_{S1}$.FF | FB are selected, which are easily proven to lead to distinct memory locations if the dependence tester knows that the data structure is a two-way linked-list.

4   A REAL EXAMPLE

Figure 5 shows a Bipartite graph, a dynamic, pointer-based data structure used in the EM3D electromagnetic simulation application [2].

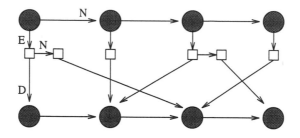

Figure 5   A (partial) Bipartite graph.

The core computational loop nest in this application is given in Figure 6. In short, for each node n on one side of the Bipartite graph, n is updated due to its neighboring nodes on the other side of the graph. This core loop nest is applied to both sides of the graph, and this is repeated for the number of time steps in the simulation.

An obvious and highly-effective transformation is to parallelize the outer loop. However, existing approaches cannot enable such a transformation, since they cannot break the numerous, false loop-carried dependences involving statement RW. This is due to both the inability to collect appropriate paths for loop-based testing (weak path collection), and the DAG-like nature of the data structure (weak dependence tester).

```
S1:  p = hd;
OL:  while (p!=NULL) {
S2:     e = p->E;
IL:     while (e!=NULL) {
S3:        d = e->D;
RW:        p->v += p-
>c*d->v;
S4:        e = e->N;
        }
S5:     p = p->N;
    }
```

APM_{OL}	hd	p
$\$h_{S1}$	$\epsilon\,[\epsilon]$	$N^*\,[N]$

APM_{IL}	hd	p	e
$\$h_{S1}$	$\epsilon\,[\epsilon]$	$N^*\,[\epsilon]$	$N^*EN^*\,[N]$
$\$h_{S2}$		$\epsilon\,[\epsilon]$	$EN^*\,[N]$

APM_{S3}	hd	p	e	d
$\$h_{S1}$	ϵ	N^*	N^*EN^*	N^*EN^*D
$\$h_{S2}$		ϵ	EN^*	EN^*D
$\$h_{S3}$			ϵ	D

Figure 6   EM3D's core computational loop; key APMs after path collection.

Our approach to path collection, coupled with our dependence tester, is able to break all false dependences and thus allow the outer loop to be parallelized. The important APMs are shown in Figure 6; $\Delta path$ values are depicted within [ ]. The APMs are used as follows in order to break the false LCDs. Firstly, consider the possible output-dependence from RW to itself due to the write of p->v. Given that p's $\Delta path$ is N, we can break this dependence if we can prove that $\forall p$, $p.\epsilon <> p.N^+$. This is easily done since in a Bipartite graph, the appropriate N field is acyclic. Next, consider the possible flow-dependence from RW to itself, due to the write of p->v and the read of d->v. Given p's $\Delta path$ and the fact that a path exists from p to d (see row $\$h_{S2}$ of APM_{S3}), this dependence can be broken if we can prove that $\forall p$, $p.\epsilon <> p.N^+ EN^* D$. Given that the top and bottom sets of nodes in a Bipartite graph are disjoint, this is easily proven. Finally, there exists a possible anti-dependence from RW to itself, which is similarly broken.

5 CONCLUSIONS

Dependence testing in the presence of dynamic, ponter-based data structures is an important problem. Accurate path collection is a crucial component for accurate dependence testing. This paper presented a new approach to path collection that enables general dependence testing, and we demonstrated the importance of this approach in parallelizing a real application.

REFERENCES

[1] Josh Barnes and Piet Hut. A hierarchical O(NlogN) force-calculation algorithm. *Nature*, 324:446–449, 4 December 1986. The code can be obtained from Prof. Barnes at the University of Hawaii, or from jhummel@ics.uci.edu.

[2] D. Culler, A. Dusseau, S. Goldstein, A. Krishnamurthy, S. Lumetta, T. von Eicken, and K. Yelick. Parallel programming in Split-C. In *Proceedings of Supercomputing 1993*, pages 262–273, November 1993.

[3] M. Carlisle, A. Rogers, J. Reppy, and L. Hendren. Early experiences with Olden. In U. Banerjee, D. Gelernter, A. Nicolau, and D. Padua, editors, *Proceedings of the 6th International Workshop on Languages and Compilers for Parallel Computing*, pages 1–20, August 1993. Available as Springer-Verlag LNCS 768.

[4] D.R. Chase, M. Wegman, and F.K. Zadek. Analysis of pointers and structures. In *Proceedings of the SIGPLAN '90 Conference on Programming Language Design and Implementation*, pages 296–310, 1990.

[5] A. Deutsch. A storeless model of aliasing and its abstractions using finite representations of right-regular equivalence relations. In *Proceedings of the IEEE 1992 International Conference on Computer Languages*, pages 2–13, April 1992.

[6] A. Deutsch. Interprocedural may-alias analysis for pointers: Beyond k-limiting. In *Proceedings of the ACM SIGPLAN Conference on Programming Language Design and Implementation*, pages 230–241, June 1994.

[7] R. Dutton. 3D information models and parallel libraries for integrated TCAD. In *Proceedings of the High Performance Computing Software PI Meeting*, pages 18.1–18.14. ARPA Computing Systems Technology Office, September 1993. TCAD is an ongoing project at Stanford University.

[8] G. Gonnet, M. Cohen, and S. Benner. Exhaustive matching of the entire protein sequence database. *Science*, 256:1443–1445, 1991.

[9] K. Gharachorloo, D. Lenoski, J. Laudon, P. Gibbons, A. Gupta, and J. Hennessy. Memory consistency and event ordering in scalable shared-memory multiprocessors. In *Proceedings of the 17th Annual International Symposium on Computer Architecture*, pages 15–26, May 1990.

[10] Vincent A. Guarna Jr. A technique for analyzing pointer and structure references in parallel restructuring compilers. In *Proceedings of the International Conference on Parallel Processing*, volume 2, pages 212–220, 1988.

[11] L. Hendren, C. Donawa, M. Emami, G. Gao, Justiani, and B. Sridharan. Designing the McCAT compiler based on a family of structured intermediate representations. In U. Banerjee, D. Gelernter, A. Nicolau, and D. Padua, editors, *Fifth International Workshop on Languages and Compilers for Parallel Computing*, volume 757 of *Lecture Notes in Computer Science*, pages 406–420. Springer-Verlag, 1993.

[12] L. Hendren, J. Hummel, and A. Nicolau. Abstractions for recursive pointer data structures: Improving the analysis and transformation of imperative programs. In *Proceedings of the SIGPLAN '92 Conference on Programming Language Design and Implementation*, pages 249–260, June 1992.

[13] J. Hummel, L. Hendren, and A. Nicolau. A language for conveying the aliasing properties of dynamic, pointer-based data structures. In *Proceedings of the 8th International Parallel Processing Symposium*, pages 208–216, April 1994.

[14] J. Hummel, L. Hendren, and A. Nicolau. A general data dependence test for dynamic, pointer-based data structures. In *Proceedings of the ACM SIGPLAN Conference on Programming Language Design and Implementation*, pages 218–229, June 1994.

[15] M. Hill, J. Larus, S. Reinhardt, and D. Wood. Cooperative shared memory: Software and hardware for scalable multiprocessors. In *Proceedings of the 5th International Conference on Architectural Support for Programming Languages and Operating Systems*, pages 262–273, September 1992.

[16] Laurie J. Hendren and Alexandru Nicolau. Parallelizing programs with recursive data structures. *IEEE Trans. on Parallel and Distributed Computing*, 1(1):35–47, January 1990.

[17] N. D. Jones and S. Muchnick. A flexible approach to interprocedural data flow analysis and programs with recursive data structures. In *9th ACM Symposium on Principles of Programming Languages*, pages 66–74, 1982.

[18] K. Kundert. Sparse matrix techniques. In A. Ruehli, editor, *Circuit Analysis, Simulation and Design*, pages 281–324. Elsevier Science Publishers B.V. (North-Holland), 186.

[19] James R. Larus and Paul N. Hilfinger. Detecting conflicts between structure accesses. In *Proceedings of the SIGPLAN '88 Conference on Programming Language Design and Implementation*, pages 21–34, June 1988.

[20] W. Landi and B. Ryder. A safe approximation algorithm for interprocedural pointer aliasing. In *Proceedings of the SIGPLAN '92 Conference on Programming Language Design and Implementation*, pages 235–248, June 1992.

[21] T. Mowry and A. Gupta. Tolerating latency through software-controlled prefetching in scalable shared-memory multiprocessors. *Journal of Parallel and Distributed Computing*, 2(4):87–106, 1991.

[22] J. Plevyak, V. Karamcheti, and A. Chien. Analysis of dynamic structures for efficient parallel execution. In D. Gelernter, A. Nicolau, and D. Padua, editors, *Proceedings of the 6th Annual Workshop on Languages and Compilers for Parallel Computing*, pages c1–c20, August 1993.

[23] S. Reinhardt, J. Larus, and D. Wood. Tempest and typhoon: User-level shared memory. In *Proceedings of the 21st Annual International Symposium on Computer Architecture*, pages 325–336, April 1994.

[24] Hanan Samet. *Applications of Spatial Data Structures: Computer Graphics, Image Processing, and GIS*. Addison-Wesley, 1990.

3

CDA LOOP TRANSFORMATIONS

Dattatraya Kulkarni and Michael Stumm

Department of Computer Science and

Department of Electrical and Computer Engineering

University of Toronto, Toronto, Canada, M5S 1A4

ABSTRACT

In this paper we present a new loop transformation technique called *Computation Decomposition and Alignment* (CDA). *Computation Decomposition* first decomposes the iteration space into finer computation spaces. *Computation Alignment* subsequently, linearly transforms each computation space independently. CDA is a general framework in that linear transformations and its recent extensions are just special cases of CDA. CDA's fine grained loop restructuring can incur considerable computational effort, but can exploit optimization opportunities that earlier frameworks cannot. We present four optimization contexts in which CDA can be useful. Our initial experiments demonstrate that CDA adds a new dimension to performance optimization.

1 INTRODUCTION

The introduction of linear transformations in 1990 as an algebraic framework for loop optimization [5, 22] was a major contribution for three reasons: First, the framework provides a unified approach to loop restructuring since most existing loop transformations [19, 23] and arbitrary sequences of these transformations can be represented by a single transformation matrix. Second, the framework allowed the development of a set of generic techniques to transform loops in a systematic way, independent of the nature of transformations in the compound transformation. Finally, it made possible semi-quantitative evaluation of candidate transformations [4, 13, 15, 22].

A linear transformation changes the structure of a loop so as to change the execution order of the iterations. But it does not change the constitution of the iterations themselves: a given iteration in the new iteration space performs the same computations as the corresponding iteration in the original iteration space, only at a different time.

29

In the last three years Computational Alignment (CA) frameworks have been proposed that extend linear transformations [9, 11, 21]. CA applies a separate linear transformation to each statement in the loop body. Since the new execution order of a statement can be different from that of another statement, CA transformations can alter the constitution of the iterations. A statement is, however, always mapped in its entirety. The origins of the basic idea in CA can be traced to loop alignment [2, 18] which is a special case of CA. The statement level transformation retains the advantages of linear transformations while enabling additional code optimizations. For example, a CA can be used to align the lhs references in statements so that all lhs data elements accessed in an iteration are located on the same processor. This eliminates ownership tests and thus improves the efficiency of SPMD code.

CDA is a generalization of CA and goes a step further in that it can move computations of granularity smaller than a statement. Instead of transforming the statements as written by the programmer, CDA first partitions the original statements into finer statements. This creates additional opportunities for optimization. Thus, a CDA transformation has two components. First, *Computation Decomposition* divides the statements in the loop body into smaller statements. Then, *Computation Alignment* linearly transforms each of these statements, possibly using a different transformation for each.

We intend to show in this paper that there are benefits in transforming a loop at subexpression granularity. Because CDA is a generalization of linear loop transformations and CA, it has all their advantages and can achieve everything they can and more. CDA can potentially exploit much of the flexibility available in loop structures to extend existing local optimizations, or to minimize constraints that are otherwise treated global. CDA does, however, also have drawbacks. The derivation of a suitable CDA requires considerable computational effort. The search space for CDA's is so much larger than that for linear transformations that good heuristics are even more important. Other drawbacks are that CDA may increase memory requirements, may introduce additional dependences, and may produce complex transformed code. However, we believe there are many situations where the benefits of CDA outweigh its drawbacks.

We present an overview of Computation Decomposition and Computation Alignment in Sections 2 and 3, respectively. A simple example of how CDA is applied is given in Section 4. The fine grain manipulation of the loop computation and memory access structures enables the application of CDA to several optimization contexts; four of them are listed in Section 5. We present the results of some representative experiments that demonstrate the promise of CDA as a loop restructuring technique in Section 7.

2 COMPUTATION DECOMPOSITION

Computation Decomposition first decomposes the loop body into its individual statements and then may additionally decompose individual statements into statements of finer granularity. Because of this, CDA has more alignment opportunities than does CA alone. The choice of subexpressions that are elevated to the status of statements is a key decision in CDA optimization. As we see later in Section 5, the optimization objective influences this decision.

A statement is decomposed by rewriting it as a sequence of smaller statements that accumulate the intermediate results and produce the same final result. Consider a statement S_j in a loop body :

$$S_j : w_j \leftarrow f_{j.1}(R_{j.1}) \; op \; f_{j.2}(R_{j.2})$$

where w_j denotes the lhs array reference. $R_{j.1}$ and $R_{j.2}$ are the sets of references in subexpressions $f_{j.1}(R_{j.1})$ and $f_{j.2}(R_{j.2})$ respectively. The above statement can be decomposed into the following two statements to produce the same result :

$$S_{j.1} : t_j \leftarrow f_{j.1}(R_{j.1})$$
$$S_{j.2} : w_j \leftarrow t_j \; op \; f_{j.2}(R_{j.2})$$

where t_j is a temporary variable introduced to accumulate the intermediate result. We can repeatedly decompose a statement into possibly many statements, with the result of each new statement held in a different temporary variable. The decomposition does affect the loop bounds. The temporary variables are typically chosen as arrays in order to reduce the number of dependences introduced by the decomposition, allowing for more freedom in the subsequent search for alignments.

The decomposition of statements adds two main complications. First, the temporary arrays may reduce the degree of cache locality achievable, may increase the number of references to memory, and may add to space requirements. However, there are also several optimizations that can reduce some of these overheads. In the best case, a temporary can be eliminated altogether, for example if the lhs array or a dead variable can be used in place of the temporary. Otherwise it may be possible to reduce its dimension and size.* Also, sometimes temporary arrays can be reused in loops that follow.

Second, the loop independent flow dependence on a temporary array can later become a loop carried dependence because of alignments that follow. In practice, this often does not introduce additional constraints, for example if it is identical to an already existing dependence.

3 COMPUTATION ALIGNMENT

A sequence of decompositions produces a new loop body that can have more statements than the original. We can now employ CA to transform each statement of the new loop body [9, 11, 21]. Analogous to the iteration space, the computation space of a statement S, $CS(S)$, is an integer space representing all execution instances of S in

---

*Note that for some optimizations it is desirable to use the temporary array, for example to reduce data alignment constraints (see Section 5).

the loop. A separate linear transformation is applied to each computation space. That is, if the decomposition produces a loop body with statements $S_1, \ldots, S_K$, which have computation spaces $CS(S_1), \ldots, CS(S_K)$, then we can separately transform these computation spaces by linear transforms $T_1, \ldots, T_K$, respectively. The transformed computation spaces together define the new iteration space as follows. Suppose $(i_1, \ldots, i_n; S_j)$ denotes the execution instance of statement S_j in iteration $(i_1, \ldots, i_n)$. An iteration $(i_1, \ldots, i_n)$ in the original iteration space then consisted of computations:

$$(i_1, \ldots, i_n) \equiv \{(i_1, \ldots, i_n; S_1), \ldots, (i_1, \ldots, i_n; S_K)\}$$

The corresponding iteration in the new iteration space consists of computations:

$$(i_1, \ldots, i_n) \equiv \{(T_1^{-1} \cdot (i_1, \ldots, i_n); S_1), \ldots, (T_K^{-1} \cdot (i_1, \ldots, i_n); S_K)\}$$

Intuitively, the mapping results in a relative movement of the individual computations across iterations. As a result, a new iteration may consist of computations that originally belonged to different iterations. This computation movement is explicitly reflected in the text of the new loop structure. It is for this reason that CDA (and CA) is fundamentally different from traditional linear loop transformations.

If computation space $CS(S)$ is transformed by T, and r is a reference in S with reference matrix R, then r has a new reference matrix, $R \cdot T^{-1}$, after the transformation. The dependence relations change as well. Consider statements S_w and S_r in the original code, where S_r is flow dependent on S_w. Let w be the write reference in S_w and r be the corresponding read reference:

$$w[d_{wr} \cdot \mathtt{I}] \rightarrow r[\mathtt{I}]$$

If T_w is applied to $CS(S_w)$ and T_r is applied to $CS(S_r)$, then the dependence is transformed to:

$$w[d_{wr} \cdot T_w \cdot \mathtt{I}] \rightarrow r[T_r \cdot \mathtt{I}]$$

which can be rewritten as:

$$w[d'_{wr} \cdot \mathtt{I}] \rightarrow r[\mathtt{I}]$$

with $d'_{wr} = T_w \cdot T_r^{-1}$. The transformation is legal if the new dependence relations are positive. This can be easily verified if the dependences are uniform and the transformations are simple offsets: we just have to verify that the last column in d'_{wr} is lexicographically negative (i.e. the write is earlier). If the dependences are non-uniform, then more sophisticated techniques are necessary, such as those that reason with symbolic affine constraints [6, 20]. There are cases, when the only violated dependences are (0) flow dependences between statements, and textual interchange will then suffice to make these positive again.

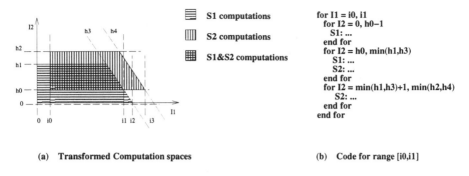

(a)   Transformed Computation spaces   (b)   Code for range [i0,i1]

Figure 1   Segmenting the union.

The new loop bounds have to account for each of the transformed computation spaces. The basic idea is to project all computation spaces onto an integer space that becomes the iteration space of the transformed loop. Because transformations $T_1, \ldots, T_K$ can be different, the resulting iteration space can be non-convex. There are two basic strategies that can be pursued to generate code. First, it is possible to take the convex hull of the new iteration space and then generate a *perfect* nest that traverses this hull, but this requires the insertion of *guards* that disable the execution of statements where necessary.

A second, alternative strategy is to generate an *imperfect* nest that has no guards. Guard-free code is usually desirable for better performance, but a perfect loop may be desirable in some cases, for instance to avoid non-vector communications or to avoid loop overheads. An algorithm to generate a guard-free loop for T when all statements require the same loop stride is described in Kelly et al [9]. They also developed an algorithm to generate code for general linear transformations but with conditionals [10]. These algorithms reduce to the algorithm developed by Torres et al. when the transformations are simple offsets corresponding to loop alignments [21].

For completeness, we illustrate a typical way to generate guard free code in Figure 1. The full details can be found in the literature [9, 10, 11, 21]. Assume a loop with two statements S_1 and S_2. The basic idea of the algorithm is to partition the new iteration space into segments that contain iterations with S_1 computation only, or those that contain S_2 computations only, or those with both computations. First split the I_1 axis into ranges that demarcate these segments. For the I_1 range $[0, i_0 - 1]$, the lower bound of the segment is given by 0, and the upper bound by h_1; this segment has only S_1 computations. For the range $[i_0, i_1]$, three segments must be defined. The first is delineated by 0 and h_0 and has only S_1 computations. The second is delineated by h_0 and $min(h_1, h_3)$ and has both S_1 and S_2 computations. The third segment is delineated by $min(h_1, h_3) + 1$ and $min(h_2, h_4)$ and has only S_2 computations. Further segments are defined for the ranges $[i_1 + 1, i_2]$ and $[i_2 + 1, i_3]$.

Given these segments, we can construct a program with a sequence of four loops, one for each defined I_1 range. Each of these loops consists of a sequence of inner

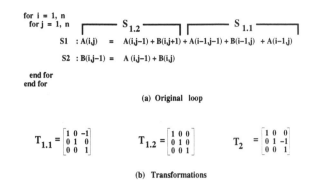

(a) Original loop

(b) Transformations

Figure 2   An example loop and a CDA transformation.

I_2 loops, one for each segment defined in that particular I_1 range. The individual bound expressions are chosen so as to delineate the segment. Figure 1b shows the code generated for the three segments defined in the range $[i_0, i_1]$.

4   ILLUSTRATION OF A SIMPLE CDA TRANSFORMATION

We will use the loop of Figure 2a to illustrate the application of a simple CDA transformation (Figure 2b) and its effect on the computation and memory access structures. We assume that there are no pre-existing data alignments. Our goal here is to minimize the data alignment constraints and eliminate the ownership tests.

The loop body of Figure 2a has two statements, $L = (S_1; S_2)$, each with its own computation space: $CS(S_1)$ and $CS(S_2)$. We partition S_1 into two smaller statements $S_{1.1}$ and $S_{1.2}$, using a temporary array t to pass the result of $S_{1.1}$ on to $S_{1.2}$. This effectively partitions $CS(S_1)$ into $CS(S_{1.1})$ and $CS(S_{1.2})$ for a total of three computation spaces as shown in Figure 3b. We chose this particular decomposition for S_1, because all references in $S_{1.1}$ now have the same data alignment constraint with respect to A(i, j) along the i-dimension; that is, the first index in the references are all $i - 1$. The remaining references in S_1 and S_2 align to A(i, j) along the i-dimension as they are. This partitioning allows us to align $CS(S_{1.1})$ to $CS(S_{1.2})$ to eliminate the data alignment constraints along the i-dimension for all three references in $S_{1.1}$, without affecting the references in $S_{1.2}$ and S_2.

After this decomposition, iteration (i, j) has the following computations :

$$(i, j; L) \equiv (i, j; S_{1.1}) < (i, j; S_{1.2}) < (i, j; S_2)$$

We can now transform the three computation spaces separately by applying transformations $T_{1.1}$, $T_{1.2}$ and T_2 of Figure 2b to $CS(S_{1.1})$, $CS(S_{1.2})$ and $CS(S_2)$, respectively. The transformations required in this case turn out to be simple offsets. Computation spaces $CS(S_{1.1})$ and $CS(S_2)$ move relative to $CS(S_{1.2})$, which is applied an identity transformation. $CS(S_{1.1})$ moves one stride in direction i in order to change the

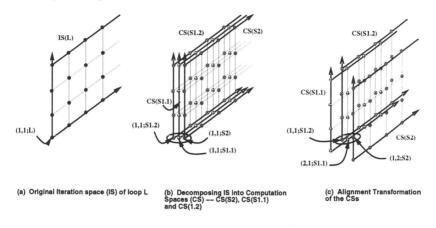

(a) Original Iteration space (IS) of loop L   (b) Decomposing IS into Computation Spaces (CS) -- CS(S2), CS(S1.1) and CS(1.2)   (c) Alignment Transformation of the CSs

Figure 3   Illustration of a simple CDA transform on the example loop.

$(i-1, *)$ references $(i, *)$, and $CS(S_2)$ moves one stride in direction j in order to align $B(i, j-1)$ to $A(i, j)$ to remove the need for ownership tests. Figure 3c shows the transformed computation spaces and highlights three computations that are now executed in one iteration.

The new iteration space is defined by the projection of the transformed computation spaces onto a plane which becomes the new iteration space (Figure 4a). Iteration (i, j) in the new iteration space now has the following computations:

$$(i, j; L') \equiv (i, j; S_{1.2}) < (i, j+1; S_2) < (i+1, j; S_{1.1})$$

Notice that it was necessary to change the order of the statements in the loop so that $S_{1.1}$ is executed after the other two statements. Before the transformation, $S_{1.1}$ had a loop carried flow dependence from both $S_{1.2}$ and S_2. These dependences become loop independent after the alignment, thereby necessitating the reordering.

Figure 4a shows which iterations need to execute which computations. The new iteration space is non-convex. We choose loop bounds to correspond to the convex hull and hence require guards to step around computations that should not be executed. The resulting code is listed in Figure 4b. Code without guards could have been produced as described in Section 3.

The above CDA, although simple, can be very effective, whether targeting a parallel system or a uniprocessor. The transformation has achieved our two main objectives:

(i) The CDA reduced the number of data alignment constraints, thus reducing the amount of communication required. Assuming both $B(i, j)$ and $t(i+1, j)$ are aligned to $A(i, j)$, and assuming the use of the owner computes rule, then the original loop accesses elements $A(i-1, j-1), A(i-1, j)$ and $A(i, j-1)$ in iteration (i, j), while it only accesses $A(i, j-1)$ and $t(i, j)$ in the new loop. Similarly, the original loop accesses, elements $B(i, j), B(i-1, j)$ and $B(i, j+1)$, but only accesses $B(i, j+1)$

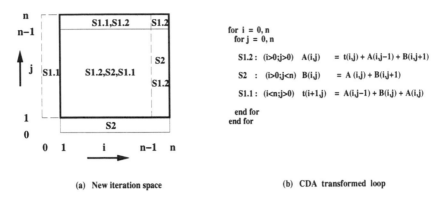

(a) New iteration space

for i = 0, n
   for j = 0, n

S1.2 : (i>0;j>0)   A(i,j)   = t(i,j) + A(i,j−1) + B(i,j+1)

S2 :   (i>0;j<n)   B(i,j)   = A (i,j) + B(i,j+1)

S1.1 : (i<n;j>0)   t(i+1,j) = A(i,j−1) + B(i,j) + A(i,j)

   end for
end for

(b) CDA transformed loop

Figure 4   The CDA transformed loop.

in the new loop. In comparison, a CA transformed loop would still need to access a total of 6 elements.

(ii) The original loop needed ownership tests, unless A(i, j) was aligned to B(i, j − 1). The CDA transformation eliminated the need for these tests, without requiring a data alignment of B to A. Moreover, the execution of statement S_1 is now spread over two processors, effectively implementing a modified computation rule.

This transformation has a number of other side effects on the loop that were not specifically part of our goals, but that cause improvements in performance nevertheless.

(iii) The new loop accesses A and B in a fundamentally different way, with the dependences changed from:

$$flow : \{(1,1),(0,1),(1,-1),(1,0)\}, anti : \{(0,1),(0,2)\}\}$$

to:

$$flow : \{(0,1),(1,0)\}, anti : \{(0,1)\}, output : \{(1,0)\}\}$$

In comparison, a CA (without first decomposing S) would change the dependences to:

$$flow : \{(1,1),(0,1),(1,0)\}, anti : \{(0,1)\}\}$$

The (1,1) dependence results in non-vectorizable communication with some distributions. CDA could eliminate the (1,-1) dependence (so could a CA). Thus the loop is blockable as is, with indexing and loop bounds simpler than if the loop had first been skewed.

(iv) If the the array sizes and the cache geometry are such that A(i − 1, j) and B(i, j) conflict in iteration (i, j) of the original loop, then the transformation eliminates these conflicts without any changes to the data layout.

(v) The CDA transformation reduces the cache context of B from 2n to n elements. This is as a result of bringing the two accesses to each element of B in i and $i + 1$ outer loop iterations to the same iteration (i). A similar effect on array A is negated by the cache context required for the temporary.

(*vi*) The transformation modifies the overall number of loads and stores per iteration from 8 distinct array element accesses to 6 (5 if t is replaced by A). This can have an impact on register pressure.

5 APPLICATIONS OF CDA

In this section, we list a number of optimization objectives and describe how they can be targeted by CDA. However, it should be noted that CDA is often used to augment existing techniques and is not necessarily intended to replace them.

Removing data alignment constraints
Data alignment transformations are a popular way of removing data alignment constraints. For example, a data alignment transformation T_{da} maps array B onto A so that references r_B to B and r_A to A go to the same (hopefully local) processor if

$$T_{da}r_B = r_A$$

Such a data alignment is a global change, since every reference r to B in the program is changed to $T_{da}r$.

In some cases, a CDA transformation can have exactly the same effect without having to (data) align array B. First, the CDA would have to decompose the loop body so that references to A and references to B occur in different statements.[†] Second, the linear transformation T_{cda} that satisfies

$$r_B T_{cda}^{-1} = r_A$$

would have to be applied *legally* to each statement with a reference to B.[‡] (The identity transformation is implicitly applied to all other statements, particularly those with references to A.)

However, the power of CDA allows more localized optimization. Instead of applying T_{cda} to each statement with a reference to B, it is applied to only those statements with references r_B, leaving the other references to B in other statements undisturbed.[§] This is illustrated with the example of Figure 2, assuming that B(i, j) is aligned to A(i, j). The CDA transformation $T_{1.1}$ changes the reference B(i − 1, j) to B(i, j). The same transformation also illustrates what we call *self-alignment*, where reference A(i − 1, j) is aligned to A(i, j) without affecting accesses to A in other statements.

Data alignment and CDA each have their own advantages and drawbacks. Data alignment does not affect dependences and satisfies a constraint between a pair of arrays without affecting other arrays. But, it only satisfies a single constraint, and it modifies the references to the array globally, possibly undoing alignments in some other

---

[†] This is not always beneficial in practice, as in the following statement: $r_A = r_B + c$.

[‡] T_{cda} will change *all* references in the statement s being transformed.

[§] It is sufficient to decompose the loop body so as to separate only those references to A and B with indexing as in r_A and r_B into different statements.

loop.¶ CDA transformations on the other hand are local to the loop, can potentially remove several data alignment constraints, and do not require data layout changes. However, CDA changes dependences (so legality checking is necessary) and changes all references in a statement. An integrated algorithm might attempt to exploit the advantages of both data alignment and CDA.

Optimizing SPMD code
The elimination of ownership tests results in better performing SPMD code, because a processor does not have to execute every iteration just to check whether it has work to do or not. One way to eliminate ownership tests is to ensure that all statement instances in an iteration are to be executed by the same processor. This can be achieved by transforming statements so as to *collocate* all the lhs references of the loop body if this can be legally done [21]. To achieve this in the CDA transformed loop, we first choose a lhs reference, say $A(i,j)$ that serves as a basis. Each temporary array is data aligned so that its lhs reference is collocated with $A(i,j)$. Then, each statement with a lhs reference r is applied a linear transformation, T, such that rT^{-1} and $A(i,j)$ are collocated. We eliminated the need for ownership tests in the example of Figure 2 by data aligning $t(i+1,j)$ to $A(i,j)$ and (computationally) aligning S_2 to $S_{1,2}$ so that all three lhs accesses in an iteration become collocated, allowing the entire iteration to be executed by the same processor.

The example of Figure 2 also shows that in general CDA can be viewed to be implementing a class of flexible computation [7] rules with the aid of a fixed computation rule such as owner-computes. The original statement S_1 is executed in parts by two processors instead of the owner of $A(i,j)$ alone.

Reducing cache conflicts
Array padding is a simple and popular technique that changes the data layout in memory to eliminate cache conflicts. However, array padding is a global change and requires that the size of the arrays be known a priori. More seriously, array padding can be illegal without proper inter-procedural analysis.

CDA can also be used to eliminate cache conflicts. The loop is decomposed into statements such that all (most) references in a statement do not conflict so that conflicts are (mostly) between references in different statements. Computation alignment then moves each statement with respect to the other statements until there are no conflicts. This spreads the conflicting data accesses in an iteration across different iterations. CDA is an attractive alternative to array padding since it does not change data layouts and is therefore always legal. Even when the array sizes are unknown, a simple conditional on the size and the cache geometry can dynamically select between the original code or a CDA transformed code at run-time. However, CDA is constrained by dependences and therefore may not be able to eliminate all conflicts. Moreover, CDA may introduce extra loop overhead compared to array padding.

Reducing communication for a reference stencil
A communication optimal distribution of an array depends on its reference *stencil*

¶ Realignment of data at run-time is usually expensive.

in the loop [1, 3, 8]. A CDA can modify the reference stencil, thus providing an additional dimension of optimization in the choice of distribution. Conversely, if an array distribution is given, then it is possible to change the reference stencil to suit the given distribution better.

6 EXPERIMENTAL RESULTS

We summarize the results of five experiments run on the SUN Sparc 20 and the KSR1 platforms to demonstrate the flexibility loops have at fine granularity and how this flexibility can be exploited both on parallel and uniprocessor systems. It should be noted that the KSR1 has a COMA architecture, where the data automatically moves to the processor accessing it.

We chose *mg*, *rtmg*, *slia*, *swm256*, and *wanal*, so as to show improvements over existing transformation frameworks. The loops do not benefit from any linear transformation as such. Three loops, namely, mg, rtmg, and slia have a single statement in their loop body, so CA cannot be applied directly, but only transformations that can be applied at subexpression granularity. Listings of the original and transformed loops, details of the applied CDA, and all of the measurement data can be found in [12].

SLIA
Objective: Removal of data alignment constraints.
SLIA is a synthetic two dimensional loop with $i \pm c$ references to three arrays A, B, and C [12]. The original loop needs data alignment of both $(*, j - 1)$ and $(*, j)$ references of arrays to $A(i, j)$. Clearly, a data alignment can satisfy only of those. We applied CDA to remove the $(*, j - 1)$ data alignment constraints. We decomposed the statement in the loop body to have one statement with all $(*, j - 1)$ references and the other statement with oall ther references. We then aligned the first statement to obtain $(*, j)$ references. The execution time on the KSR1 improved by 30%-38% when using up to 16 processors.

Swm256
Objective: Elimination of ownership tests without data alignment.
The calc1 subroutine of the SPEC benchmark, SWM256, has 4 statements, with lhs references to $CU(i + 1, j)$, $CV(i, j + 1)$, $Z(i + 1, j + 1)$ and $H(i, j)$. The loop requires ownership tests unless $CU(i + 1, j)$, $CV(i, j + 1)$ and $Z(i + 1, j + 1)$ are aligned to $H(i, j)$. Hence, we aligned the statements so that their lhs references are all of the form (i, j). The transformed version does not require ownership tests and does not require any data alignments. Because of the shared address space and relatively low cost of remote accesses on the KSR1, the execution time of the transformed code improved by only 17%.

Wanal
Objective: Improving cache locality.
Wanal is a wave equation solver that is part of the Riceps benchmark suite [14]. The three dimensional loop has two statements in the body. A linear transformation cannot

improve cache locality here, because only one statement requires a loop interchange, while the other does not. A CDA, which is equivalent to a CA in this case, can be applied to the one statement to achieve locality. On the KSR1, the parallel execution time improved by 45-50%.

Rtmg
Objective: Elimination of cache conflicts on a SUN Sparc 20.
The rtmg loop from the Arco Seismic benchmarks suite is a two a dimensional loop with a single statement in the loop body which accesses two dimensional arrays p1 and p2 [16]. There are cache conflicts between the lhs reference p1(i, k) and the rhs reference p2(i, k) on a Sparc 20 (with a 1MB, direct-mapped cache). We decomposed the statement into a statement S_2 with references p1(i, k) and p2(i − 1, k) and statement S_1 containing all other references . We then aligned S_1 to S_2 such that the p2(i, k) reference became p2(i + 1, k), leaving the S_2 references unchanged. The indexing of the temporary was chosen so as to not conflict with p_1 and p_2. The data accesses in an iteration now map to different cache lines and therefore do not conflict, improving the execution time by about 50-55%.

Mg
Objective: Elimination of cache conflicts on the KSR1.
NAS mg is a multigrid solver in the NAS benchmarks suite [17]. We CDA transformed the psinv subroutine. The loop has iterators i, j, and k, and accesses three dimensional arrays U and R with $(i \pm c_1, j \pm c_2, k \pm c_3)$ reference patterns, where the c's are either 0,1, or -1. For a given i iteration, the loop accesses elements in the ith plane of U, and elements in the $(i − 1)$, i and $(i + 1)^{th}$ planes of R. The references with similar j indexing conflict in cache. We decomposed the only statement in the loop into a statement with references to the $(i − 1)^{th}$ plane of R (i.e. all R(i − 1, ∗, ∗) references) and another statement with the other references. We then aligned the two statements so that the R(i − 1, ∗, ∗) references become R(i, ∗, ∗) references, effectively eliminating the references to the $(i − 1)^{th}$ plane of R.∥ The transformed loop, therefore, has fewer planes with similar j indexing, and hence, fewer conflicts, and results in a speedup by a factor of 2 over the original b the original code when using up to 32 processors. However, the dependence introduced by CDA did reduce the available degree of parallelism, but this is not noticeable with only 32 processors.

7   CONCLUDING REMARKS

With respect to optimization, loop structures have considerable flexibility at the subexpression level. Computational Decomposition and Alignment (CDA), which we introduced in this paper, provides a framework to linearly transform loops at this relatively fine granularity. It can be applied to target a number of different optimization objectives. However, heuristics are a key to applying CDAs successfully, since the derivation of a suitable CDA is more complex than say the derivation of a linear transformation.

∥ In this case, we can eliminate the need for the temporary by using the lhs array, U, to hold the intermediate results.

Nevertheless, we are hopeful that it will be possible to find good heuristic algorithms that find near optimal CDAs, similar to the way linear transformations are found today.

We believe that CDA will be particularly effective in the context of global optimization, because it can help reduce constraints that are otherwise treated global. It is also interesting to observe that CDA can be applied both to extend current control optimization techniques, as well as to optimizations that are traditionally handled by data layout changes.

In our current work, we are focusing on deriving CDAs that improve cache performance on both uniprocessors and multiprocessors. For example, we are comparing CDA and array padding in reducing the number of cache conflicts on numerous benchmark codes, and intend to develop algorithms capable of automatically deriving suitable CDA transformations for this purpose.

Acknowledgments

We thank Ron Unrau at IBM, Toronto Laboratory and Wei Li at the University of Rochester for their contribution to certain aspects of the CDA framework. This work was supported in part by the Natural Sciences and Engineering Research Council of Canada and the Information Technology Research Center of Ontario.

REFERENCES

[1] Abraham, S.G., and Hudak, D.E. Compile-time partitioning of iterative parallel loops to reduce cache coherency traffic, *IEEE Transactions on Parallel and Distributed Systems*, 2(3):318–328, July 91.

[2] Allen, R., Callahan, D., and Kennedy, K. Automatic decomposition of scientific programs for parallel execution, In *Conference Record of the 14th Annual ACM Symposium on Principles of Programming Languages*, pages 63–76, Munich, West Germany, January 1987.

[3] Ancourt, C. and Irigoin, F. Scanning polyhedra with DO loops, In *Proceedings of the 3rd ACM SIGPLAN Symposium on Principles and Practice of Parallel Programming*, volume 26, pages 39–50, Williamsburg, VA, April 1991.

[4] Anderson, J. and Lam, M. Global optimizations for parallelism and locality on scalable parallel machines, In *Proceedings of the ACM SIGPLAN '93 Conference on Programming Language Design and Implementation*, volume 28, June 1993.

[5] Banerjee, U. Unimodular transformations of double loops, In *Proceedings of Third Workshop on Programming Languages and Compilers for Parallel Computing*, Irvine, CA, August 1990.

[6] Feautrier, P. Dataflow analysis of array and scalar references. *International Journal of Parallel Programming*, 20, 1991.

[7] Gilbert, J. and Schreiber, R. Optimal expression evaluation for data parallel architectures, *Journal of Parallel and Distributed Computing*, 13:58–64, 1991.

[8] Irigoin, F. and Triolet, R.   Supernode partitioning,   In *Conference Record of the 15th Annual ACM Symposium on Principles of Programming Languages*, pages 319–329, San Diego, CA, 1988.

[9] Kelly, W. and Pugh, W.   A framework for unifying reordering transformations, Technical Report UMIACS-TR-92-126, University of Maryland, 1992.

[10] Kelly, W., Pugh, W., and Rosser, E.   Code generation for multiple mappings, Technical Report UMIACS-TR-94-87, University of Maryland, 1994.

[11] Kulkarni, D. and Stumm, M.   Computational alignment: A new, unified program transformation for local and global optimization,   Technical Report CSRI-292, Computer Systems Research Institute, University of Toronto, January 1994. *http://www.eecg.toronto.edu/EECG/RESEARCH/ParallelSys.*

[12] Kulkarni, D., Stumm, M., Unrau, R., and Li, W.   A generalized theory of linear loop transformations,   Technical Report CSRI-317, Computer Systems Research Institute, University of Toronto, December 1994. *http://www.eecg.toronto.edu/EECG/RESEARCH/ParallelSys.*

[13] Kumar, K.G., Kulkarni, D., and Basu, A.   Deriving good transformations for mapping nested loops on hierarchical parallel machines in polynomial time, In *Proceedings of the 1992 ACM International Conference on Supercomputing*, Washington, July 1992.

[14] Li, C.H. Program wanall. ftp://ftp.cs.rice.edu, Rice University, 1992.

[15] Li, W. and Pingali, K.   A singular loop transformation framework based on non-singular matrices, In *Proceedings of the Fifth Workshop on Programming Languages and Compilers for Parallel Computing*, August 1992.

[16] Mosher, C. Arco Seismic Benchmarks, ARCO E&PT.

[17] NASA, Ames Research Center. NAS Parallel Benchmarks

[18] Padua, D. Multiprocessors: Discussion of some theoretical and practical problems, Phd thesis, University of Illinois, Urbana-Champaign, 1979.

[19] Padua, D. and Wolfe, M.   Advanced compiler optimizations for supercomputers, *Communications of the ACM*, 29(12):1184–1201, December 1986.

[20] Pugh, W. and Wonnacott, D.   An exact method for analysis of value-based array data dependences, Technical Report CS-TR-3196, University of Maryland, 1993.

[21] Torres, J., Ayguade, E., Labarta, J., and Valero, M.   Align and distribute-based linear loop transformations, In *Proceedings of Sixth Workshop on Programming Languages and Compilers for Parallel Computing*, 1993.

[22] Wolf, M. and Lam, M.   An algorithmic approach to compound loop transformation, In *Proceedings of Third Workshop on Programming Languages and Compilers for Parallel Computing*, Irvine, CA, August 1990.

[23] Wolfe, M. *Optimizing supercompilers for supercomputers.* The MIT Press, 1990.

4

OPTIMIZING DATA-PARALLEL STENCIL COMPUTATIONS IN A PORTABLE FRAMEWORK

Stephen W. Chappelow
Philip J. Hatcher
James R. Mason

Department of Computer Science
Kingsbury Hall
University of New Hampshire
Durham, NH 03824 U.S.A.
{swc,pjh,jrm}@cs.unh.edu

ABSTRACT

We have developed a communication optimizer that concentrates on stencil communication patterns. This optimizer has been done in the context of the UNH C* compiler that targets distributed-memory MIMD computers. Our work has two distinguishing features:

■ The compiler/optimizer is designed to be highly portable. We achieve this goal by providing efficient support for the optimizations in the run-time library.

■ As well as performing aggregation for messages that share the same source and destination, we employ a specialized store-and-forward protocol that reduces the total number of messages initiated.

1   INTRODUCTION

At the University of New Hampshire we have developed a series of compilers for data-parallel dialects of C. Our most recent compiler is for the C* programming language designed by Thinking Machines Corporation for their Connection Machine series [7]. We have developed C* compiler back ends and run-time systems for both shared-memory and distributed-memory MIMD computers*.

Our C* compiler exploits the technology we developed in earlier projects for the translation of data-parallel programs [9]. Our strategy is to produce an equivalent SPMD program for loosely-synchronous execution on MIMD hardware. C* compilation is aided by the language's explicit construct for declaring (potentially) distributed data

---

*Our compilers are available via anonymous ftp to ftp.cs.unh.edu, directory pub/cstar.

43

machine	initiate (μsec)	per byte (μsec)	break-even (bytes)
Intel Delta	120	.150	800
Meiko CS-2	20	.025	800
nCUBE-2	154	.572	269
IBM SP-2	46	.035	1314
Linux cluster	1141	1.324	862

Figure 1 Communication costs for five distributed-memory MIMD computers. The *break-even* column is the message length for which the initiate cost equals the per-byte transmission cost. The *Linux cluster* is a collection of 66MHz PCs running Linux augmented with UNH Net* [6] and the UNH SBP protocol [11].

and by its explicit operator for sharing the data. This obviates the need for array index analysis that is required in languages, such as High Performance Fortran (HPF), that are based upon the distribution of arrays and implicit communication. This index analysis is necessary to identify operands that will need to be communicated in a distributed-memory target machine.

Once communication operations are identified, however, C* compilers share with HPF compilers the difficult problem of optimizing to reduce communication costs
This paper reports on a portable communication optimizer we have developed for stencil computations. This optimizer targets distributed-memory machines that have high message-initiation costs (i.e. latency) relative to the per-byte transmission costs. Figure 1 lists the communication characteristics of the machines we are initially targeting. This paper contains performance data for the Intel Delta and the Meiko CS-2.

2 THE C* PROGRAMMING LANGUAGE

This section describes the C* programming language and is organized around the example program in Figure 2. This program implements the Jacobi algorithm to find the steady-state temperature distribution on an insulated two-dimensional plate, given constant boundary conditions.

C* introduces a new data type, the shape type, that describes array-like objects that are operated on in parallel. A shape specifies the rank, dimensions, and layout of explicitly parallel data. Shapes can be used in the declaration of arithmetic, structure and union types. When a declaration includes both a base type and a shape type, then a parallel object is declared consisting of an object of the base type at each position of the shape. Line 5 of Figure 2 declares a shape and lines 6–9 declare a set of parallel variables[†].

Parallel objects can be operated on in parallel via the overloading of standard C operators. The operator is applied as if simultaneously at each position of the shape.

[†] C* also includes a Boolean data type, used in line 6 of Figure 2.

```
1.   #include <math.h>
2.   #define SIZE     128        /* Resolution of grid */
3.   #define TEMP     50.0       /* Arbitrary cut-off  */
4.   #define EPSILON 0.1

5.   shape [SIZE][SIZE]cell;
6.   bool:cell  active;     /* 0 if cell boundary; 1 otherwise */
7.   float:cell change;     /* Change in temperature */
8.   float:cell new;        /* Newly calculated temperature */
9.   float:cell old;        /* Previous temperature */

10.  main () {
11.     float maxerr;       /* Largest change in temp. over grid */
12.     int   cool_cells; /* Number of cells with temp. < TEMP */
13.     with (cell) {              /* Initialize grid */
14.        where (((!pcoord(0)) || (!pcoord(1)) || (pcoord(1) ==
15.                   (SIZE-1))) {
16.           active = 0;
17.           old = new = 0.0;
18.        } else where (pcoord(0) == (SIZE-1)) {
19.           active = 0;
20.           old = new = 100.0;
21.        } else {
22.           active = 1;
23.           new = 50.0;
24.        }
25.        do {    /* Compute steady-state temperatures */
26.           where (active) {
27.              old = new;
28.              new = ([.-1][.]old + [.+1][.]old +
29.                     [.][.+1]old + [.][.-1]old) / 4.0;
30.              change = fabs(old-new);
31.              maxerr = >?= change;
32.           }
33.        } while (maxerr > EPSILON);
34.        cool_cells = (+= (new < TEMP));
35.     }
36.     printf ("There are %d cells cooler than %5.2f deg\n",
37.        cool_cells, TEMP);
38.  }
```

Figure 2   Example C* program for the Jacobi algorithm.

To specify a parallel operation, a current shape must first be established by a `with` statement. A `where` statement is provided for masking off positions of the current shape. Lines 13–24 of Figure 2 use the overloaded assignment operator to initialize parallel variables. The `pcoord` intrinsic function creates a parallel value of the current shape with each position containing its coordinate along the specified axis.

C* also overloads most of the assignment operators to perform reductions of parallel values to a single scalar value. Line 34 of Figure 2 uses a unary `+=` operator to perform a sum reduction computing the number of positions whose new temperature is less than the cut-off temperature, `TEMP`.[‡]

C* allows parallel variables to be indexed. However, indexing a parallel variable may be expensive on machines where the parallel variable is spread across the distributed memories of a set of processors. To emphasize this potential inefficiency, the index operator is moved to the left of the indexed variable. When indexing a parallel variable by scalar indices, the left index operator produces a scalar value. When indexing a parallel variable by parallel indices, the left index operator produces a parallel value.

This dichotomy—parallel variables with left indexing and arrays with right indexing—improves the *transparency* of programs. That is, the concepts of parallel variables and left indexing improve programmers' ability to predict the performance of their programs. A programmer knows that in C*, as in C, an array index is always very efficient. In C*, however, the programmer knows that a left index of a parallel variable is potentially very expensive. This transparency also, of course, simplifies the compiler's task of locating potential communication points as they are indicated by specific syntax.

The dot is used as a shorthand notation within a left index expression. The dot stands for a `pcoord` call on the axis being indexed. This allows for the convenient referencing of neighboring values in a shape. Lines 28–29 demonstrate the reference of the four neighboring values in a two-dimensional shape. Such references are known as *grid* communications.

3 A PORTABLE COMPILATION FRAMEWORK

Our compiler translates C* code to C code. The C code is then linked with our run-time library. We enhance portability by making in the run-time library any decision concerning the number of processors or the topology of the processors. Two prime examples of such decisions are the distribution of data across the processors and the generation of communication schedules.

Despite the delayed decision making, the compiler still has considerable work to do. The C* programming model includes a synchronous grid of virtual processors. The compiler is responsible for generating loosely-synchronous SPMD code that correctly

---

[‡]C* has added two new binary operators for min, `<?`, and max, `>?`, which also have reduction forms, `<?=` and `>?=`. The max reduction operator, `>?=` is used on line 31 of Figure 2 to control the enclosing loop.

```
/* grid ops clustered here
 *    CS__GridRead parameters: defer flag, destination
 *    variable, source variable, type, rank and list
 *    of relative indices.
 */
CS__GridRead(CS__DEFER, CS__temp_5, old, CS__FLOAT, 2, -1, 0);
CS__GridRead(CS__DEFER, CS__temp_6, old, CS__FLOAT, 2, 1, 0);
CS__GridRead(CS__DEFER, CS__temp_7, old, CS__FLOAT, 2, 0, 1);
CS__GridRead(0, CS__temp_8, old, CS__FLOAT, 2, 0, -1);

/* virtual processor emulation loop
 *    CS__current points to the current shape, which contains
 *    info about data distribution (e.g. number of data values
 *    storedlocally) and about the set of currently active
 *    virtual processors (the context).
 */
for (CS__limit = CS__current->CS__num_local,
     CS__context_ptr = CS__current->CS__context,
     CS__vpi = -1;
     ++CS__vpi < CS__limit;
     /* Nothing */)
{
    if (*CS__context_ptr++)
    {
        new[CS__vpi] = (CS__temp_5[CS__vpi]+CS__temp_6[CS__vpi]
            + CS__temp_7[CS__vpi] + CS__temp_8[CS__vpi]) / 4.0;
    }
}
```

Figure 3 Illustration (i.e. many details suppressed) of the C code generated by the UNH C* compiler for lines 28-29 of the Jacobi program of Figure 2.

and efficiently implements the source program. The compiler is also responsible for performing program analysis and program restructuring to support communication optimization.

The compiler clusters communication operations within basic blocks. Communication operations are moved as far toward the front of the basic block as safely possible. For example, a read communication of an operand cannot be moved before a statement that potentially changes that operand. In this manner clusters of communications are identified that can be performed in any order or all at once.

The compiler places a call to the run-time library in the output code for each communication operation. A cluster is identified by passing a "defer" flag to the library. All operations in the cluster will be identified as deferrable except for the last one that has its library call generated. When the library receives a deferrable operation, it simply queues it for later processing. When the library receives a non-deferrable operation, it must then effect that operation and all previously deferred operations before returning to the compiled code.

This clustering analysis is performed for all C* communication types. Currently we only have run-time support for clustered grid communications. In our terminology a stencil computation is one in which clusters of grid communications can be found.

The Jacobi program of Figure 2 is a stencil computation since lines 28–29 contain a cluster of grid communications. Figure 3 illustrates the C code that would be generated by our compiler for these lines.

4   EFFICIENT RUN-TIME SUPPORT FOR OPTIMIZATION

A key problem that must be solved in our portable framework is the efficient generation of communication schedules at run time. A schedule specifies, for a given communication operation on a particular processor, which data items need to be shipped to which processor. Prior designs and implementations have taught us that it is important, when possible, to generate communication schedules in bigger units than on an individual virtual processor basis.

For a grid communication and a block distribution, a particular processor will send at most 2^{rank} messages, where $rank$ is the number of dimensions in the virtual processor grid. Each message will contain data from a contiguous block of virtual processors. The exact number of messages and their destinations can be quickly computed by examining the effect of the grid operation on the corners of the data stored on the particular processor. For each corner the shift amounts of the grid operation are applied to the coordinates of the corner. A target machine specific routine, which isolates all details of the data-to-processor mapping, is called to determine the destination of the corner's data. The communication schedule is then represented as a list of descriptors for contiguous virtual processor blocks (which we call *regions*) and their associated destinations (processor numbers).

The second key problem is the efficient use of the generated communication schedules. As discussed above, our run-time library queues deferrable communication operations until a non-deferrable operation is seen. What is actually queued for each operation is the region list obtained by examining the effect of the operation on the local corners of the data. When a non-deferrable operation is seen, all queued region lists are merged to form one general communication schedule for the cluster of grid communications. In this manner standard message aggregation is performed for a stencil communication.

Our optimization goes beyond standard message aggregation however. The standard method is to initiate on each processor as many messages as there are unique destination processors for the data on that processor. We use a multi-phase approach to combine messages when feasible to eliminate message-initiation costs. For example, when delivering a full nine-point stencil on a physical two-dimensional mesh of processors, we would use two phases. The first phase would move data along the north-south axis of the machine and second phase would move data east-west. Data moving along the diagonal would be decomposed into north-south and east-west components and each component would be combined with a message moving other data along that axis. This allows the data to be delivered with four messages rather than the eight messages required by the standard approach. This example is illustrated in Figure 4.

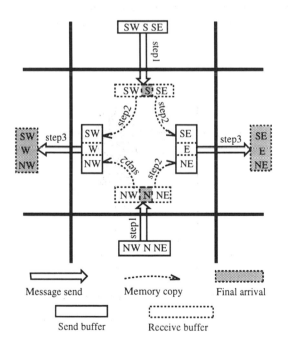

Figure 4   An improved stencil delivery algorithm on one node.

The trade-off in our approach is fewer messages for more data copying and a restriction on parallelism in message delivery. In the standard approach data is packed in a message once and all messages can be transmitted at the same time. In our approach we must pack the diagonal data twice into messages and we must send the messages in stages, not all at once.

The amount of data traveling along a diagonal in a stencil is typically small relative to the amount traveling along the virtual axes. In stencil computations most often a block mapping is used and a relatively high virtual processor to physical processor ratio is required to provide enough work per physical processor to justify parallel execution. For an access of shift offset one along the diagonal of the virtual processor mesh, only a single data item will move along the physical diagonal, while the amount of data moving on axis is two less than twice the square root of the number of data items stored locally. This is illustrated in Figure 5.

The conclusion is that the amount of additional copying required in our method is typically insignificant. Our experience to date is that the savings we obtain from fewer message initiates overshadows any loss we incur by performing staged delivery.

5   PRELIMINARY RESULTS

Figure 6 and Figure 7 contain performance data collected from executing, at various communication optimization levels, a C* version of the *shallow* benchmark   from

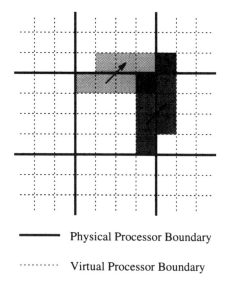

——————   Physical Processor Boundary

··········   Virtual Processor Boundary

Figure 5   Physical messages generated by a C* diagonal grid communication.

the National Center for Atmospheric Research. The *shallow* benchmark is a stencil computation that applies finite-difference methods to solve shallow-water equations. Two parallel computers were used: the Intel Touchstone Delta at Caltech and the Meiko CS-2 at Oregon State University (OSU). The Delta is a two-dimensional mesh of i860 processors. The CS-2 is a collection of Superscalar Sparc processors connected by Meiko's Elan network. The *shallow* problem sizes used were a 64 × 64 mesh for 1200 timestep iterations and a 256 × 256 mesh for 120 timestep iterations. Three communication optimization levels were measured: none, standard aggregation, and aggregation with our stencil delivery method (denoted as *stencil* in the figures). Figure 6 and Figure 7 display the additional improvement provided by each optimization.

$$improvement_{aggregation} = \frac{aggregation - none}{none}$$

$$improvement_{stencil} = \frac{stencil - aggregation}{none}$$

The *shallow* program presents a number of opportunities for aggregation and they are exploited by the optimizer. In addition, even though *shallow* never presents a full

machine	partition size	optimization level	time (sec)	additional improvement
Delta	4 × 4	none	27.9	
		aggregate	20.4	27%
		stencil	19.1	5%
	5 × 5	none	25.7	
		aggregate	17.9	30%
		stencil	16.9	4%
	6 × 6	none	20.9	
		aggregate	15.4	26%
		stencil	14.4	5%
	7 × 7	none	20.3	
		aggregate	14.9	27%
		stencil	13.7	6%
	8 × 8	none	19.2	
		aggregate	14.2	26%
		stencil	12.8	7%
CS-2	3 × 4	none	16.1	
		aggregate	12.9	20%
		stencil	12.6	2%
	4 × 4	none	14.6	
		aggregate	11.9	18%
		stencil	11.7	1%

Figure 6 Optimization results for the *shallow* benchmark on the Intel Delta and the Meiko CS-2. The problem size is 64 × 64, 1200 iterations.

stencil (at most six of the possible eight compass directions are used), a small but significant additional improvement is usually provided by our stencil delivery method.

For the smaller problem size (Figure 6) the communication optimizations are most effective. For the larger problem size (Figure 7), where better speedup is obtained relative to the best sequential program, the significance of the communication optimizations is diminished because of the decreasing importance of the communication time to the overall execution time.

Our stencil delivery method was motivated by the two-dimensional physical mesh topology of the Intel Delta. Messages moving logically along a diagonal of the physical mesh actually are moved in two stages along the physical axes of the machine. We decided to move this two stage delivery into the software in order to save message initiates.

However, our preliminary numbers indicate that the optimization can also be effective on the Meiko machine. The 16 node OSU Meiko CS-2 has two layers of switches with redundant connections in its Elan network. Saving message initiates still appears

machine	partition size	optimization level	time (sec)	additional improvement
Delta	4 × 4	none	13.2	
		aggregate	12.4	6%
		stencil	12.3	1%
	5 × 5	none	9.2	
		aggregate	8.4	9%
		stencil	8.2	2%
	6 × 6	none	6.8	
		aggregate	6.0	12%
		stencil	5.9	1%
	7 × 7	none	5.5	
		aggregate	4.8	13%
		stencil	4.7	2%
	8 × 8	none	4.6	
		aggregate	4.0	13%
		stencil	3.8	4%
CS-2	3 × 4	none	11.6	
		aggregate	11.5	1%
		stencil	11.2	3%
	4 × 4	none	8.2	
		aggregate	8.2	—
		stencil	8.1	1%

Figure 7 Optimization results for the *shallow* benchmark on the Intel Delta and the Meiko CS-2. The problem size is 256 × 256, 120 iterations.

to be worthwhile on this machine even though our two stage delivery method will not exploit all the wires in the machine.

We are essentially performing our optimizations considering the physical processors to be organized in a mesh configuration. (In Figure 6 and Figure 7 the size of the CS-2 partition used is given in terms of a logical mesh.) Since grid communications are inherently mesh oriented, we believe the optimizations can be effective even when the physical processors are connected in a different topology. (In fact, we actually assume the processors are organized as a logical torus. Since the Delta is strictly a mesh, without wrap-around connections, this means our logical model does not exactly match the Delta.)

Since the CS-2 message initiate cost is low in absolute terms, the improvement demonstrated by our stencil delivery method is modest for the *shallow* benchmark. To gauge the effectiveness of the optimization independent of an application's computation requirements, we also gathered performance data for a simple communication kernel. This kernel repeatedly executes on all processors the exchange of 128 bytes with all eight neighboring physical processors in a logical two-dimensional mesh (torus).

Figure 8 contains the performance results of executing the communication kernel on both the Delta and the CS-2. Numbers are reported for the normal point-to-point delivery and for our staged delivery. The staged delivery reduces the number of message initiates from eight to four and therefore the potential improvement of the method has an upperbound of 50%. The overhead of the our stencil delivery method (and the fact that the per-byte transmission cost does contribute to the overall communication cost) keeps us from fully realizing the potential improvement. The data does indicate that roughly a 35% improvement is realizable on the Delta and a 20%–40% improvement is realizable on the CS-2.

The running time of the communication kernel should be independent of the number of processors employed. On the Delta this is nearly true, but we believe the slight drift upwards reflects the fact the the Delta is not a torus and as the mesh increases in size it becomes marginally more expensive to emulate the wrap-around connections.

machine	partition size	point-to-point (sec)	staged (sec)	improvement
Delta	4×4	16.7	11.1	34%
	5×5	17.2	11.0	36%
	6×6	17.6	11.3	36%
	7×7	17.8	11.3	37%
	8×8	17.8	11.3	37%
Meiko	3×4	9.1	7.2	21%
	4×4	14.2	8.7	39%

Figure 8   Optimization results for a communication kernel on the Intel Delta and the Meiko CS-2. The kernel simulates the communication for a nine-point stencil.

Similarly, on the CS-2 the increase in running time as the number of processors grows is due to increasing contention in the Elan network. This contention makes the staged stencil delivery more valuable for larger numbers of processors.

6 RELATED WORK

There has been a large amount of work concerning optimizing stencil computations, e.g. [1], [8], [13]. A relatively recent comprehensive reference on optimizing data-parallel programs is Tseng's dissertation [14]. With our emphasis on portability and run-time support, our work is more closely related to the Syracuse HPF compiler [4].

Our approach was also motivated by our earlier experience optimizing irregular communications [12]. In this work we developed run-time routines for aggregating and delivering batches of logical messages generated at the C* virtual processor level. The efficiency and generality of these routines suggested their use in aggregating and delivering messages generated by stencil computations.

Our stencil delivery method was motivated in part by work that suggested that staged message delivery can sometimes be advantageous, depending on the capability of the hardware congestion control [2] [5]. Our staged message delivery along real or logical two-dimensional grid connections is reminiscent of the *Subway* software router that delivers unstructured communications on SIMD processor grids [3].

7 CONCLUSIONS

We have designed and implemented in the UNH C* system a portable optimizer for stencil computations. The optimizer performs the standard aggregation of messages as well as employing a specialized store-and-forward protocol that reduces the total number of messages initiated.

The system was originally developed for the Intel Touchstone Delta. Portability to other distributed-memory MIMD computers is provided by emulating on the new target the small number of Delta Node Executive (NX) calls used by our run-time system:

- **gsync** (global synchronization),

- **infocount** (get length of last send/recv),

- **iprobe** (probe for presence of message),

- **csend** (non-blocking send),

- **crecv** (blocking receive),

- **mynode** (get processor number),

- **numnodes** (get total number of processors),

- **mypart** (get dimensions of allocated processor mesh).

The optimizer proceeds as if always targeting the two-dimensional mesh provided by the Delta. When running on other machines, we believe this approach is still effective because the C* programmer is expressing communications in terms of a virtual grid of processors and because two-dimensional grids can be efficiently embedded in most other topologies.

We have demonstrated the effectiveness of our system by presenting performance results for the Intel Delta and the Meiko CS-2. Further ports of our system are in progress for the IBM SP-2, for the nCUBE-2, and for clusters of workstations or PCs.

Acknowledgements

This work is being supported by National Science Foundation grant ASC-9203971. Access to the Intel Delta is being provided by Caltech and the Concurrent Supercomputing Consortium. Access to the Meiko CS-2 is being provided by Oregon State University with partial support from the National Science Foundation through grant CDA-9216172. The UNH C* compiler was originally implemented by Herold and Lapadula [10].

REFERENCES

[1] M. Baber. Hypertasking: Automatic array and loop partitioning on the iPSC. In *Proceedings of the 24th Hawaii International Conference on Systems Sciences*, pages 438–447, January 1991.

[2] M. Barnett, R. Littlefield, D. Payne, and R. van de Geijn. Efficient communication primitives on mesh architectures with hardware routing. In *Sixth SIAM Conference on Parallel Processing for Scientific Computing*, March 1993.

[3] P. Bjørstad and R. Schreiber. Unstructured grids on SIMD torus machines. In *Proceedings of the 1994 Scalable High Performance Computing Conference*, pages 658–665, 1994.

[4] Z. Bozkus, A. Choudhary, G. Fox, T. Haupt, S. Ranka, and M. Wu. Compiling Fortran 90D/HPF for distributed memory MIMD computers. *Journal of Parallel and Distributed Computing*, 21:15–26, 1994.

[5] E. Brewer and B. Kuszmaul. How to get good performance for the CM5 data network. In *Proceedings of the 1994 International Parallel Processing Symposium*, April 1994.

[6] G. Chandranmenon, R. Russell, and P. Hatcher. Providing an execution environment for C* programs on a Mach-based PC cluster. Technical Report 94–20, University of New Hampshire, 1994.

[7] J. Frankel. A reference description of the C* language. Technical Report TR-253, Thinking Machines Corporation, Cambridge, MA, 1991.

[8] H. Gerndt. *Parallelization for Distributed-Memory Multiprocessing Systems*. PhD thesis, University Bonn, 1989.

[9] P. Hatcher and M. Quinn. *Data-Parallel Programming on MIMD Computers*. The MIT Press, 1991.

[10] A. Lapadula and K. Herold. A retargetable C* compiler and run-time library for mesh-connected MIMD multicomputers. Technical Report 92–15, University of New Hampshire, 1992.

[11] J. LaRosa and R. Russell. A dedicated network and streamlined protocol to support UNH C* programs in distributed environments. Technical Report 95–07, University of New Hampshire, 1995.

[12] J. Mason. Optimizing irregular communication in C*. Master's thesis, University of New Hampshire, 1994.

[13] D. Socha. An approach to compiling single-point iterative programs for distributed memory computers. In *Fifth Distributed Memory Computing Conference*, pages 1017–1027, 1990.

[14] C. Tseng. *An Optimizing Fortran D Compiler for MIMD Distributed-Memory Machines*. PhD thesis, Department of Computer Science, Rice University, Houston, TX, January 1993.

5

A COMPILER STRATEGY FOR SHARED VIRTUAL MEMORIES

François Bodin, Michael O'Boyle*

IRISA-INRIA, Campus de Beaulieu,
35042 Rennes Cedex,
* Department of Computer Science, University
of Manchester, Oxford Rd, Manchester M13 9PL

ABSTRACT

This paper describes a compiling strategy for SVM that exploits parallelism and minimises overheads when using an SPMD execution model. Our strategy integrates compiler techniques developed separately for data and control parallelism paradigms and integrates them into one approach. This strategy has been implemented in a prototype compiler, called MARS, currently running on the KSR-1 architecture. The technique is intended to be generic for all SVM systems. Initial results are encouraging.

1   INTRODUCTION

Shared Virtual Memory (SVM) architectures provide a single address space on distributed hardware with no physically shared memory. Instead, the distributed local memories collectively provide a virtual address space shared by all processors. SVM promises the benefit of the ease of programming found in shared-memory multiprocessors with the scalability of distributed memory multiprocessors. The compiler is relieved from the difficulties of producing optimised message-passing code, but must now be concerned with issues such as data locality and synchronisation overhead.

This paper describes a compiler strategy developed for SVM architectures and prototyped in MARS, an optimising compiler. A broad outline of the issues and costs involved is presented along with the rationale for our approach. This is followed by a brief description of successive compiler phases and samples of performance results.

1.1   Costs

The main issue in designing a parallelising compiler is the internal strategy. The major goal, for multi-processors, is to determine a set of transformations that minimise the

57

following cost, which is an approximation to the execution time:

$$Cost = \sum_S max_P(T_{co}) + \sum_S max_P(T_{ra}) + \sum_S (T_{sy}) + \sum_S (T_{la}) + \sum_S (T_{ov})$$

where P is the set of processors and S the set of statements, T_{co} the amount of time spent performing useful computation, T_{ra} the amount of communication between processors, T_{sy} the amount of synchronisation, T_{la} the amount of communication within a processors (between cache and main memory) and T_{ov}, the amount of extra computation due to parallelisation. In general, determining the execution time is undecidable at compile time and the number of transformations is infinite. However, for a large class of interesting programs, it is possible to statically estimate each overhead and hence execution time. Furthermore, in restricting our search space by making reasonable assumptions and applying them consistently throughout the strategy, we can optimise programs in an acceptable time. Unfortunately, the costs are not independent, therefore one of the most important characteristics of a successful strategy is to trade off competing overheads based on their relative costs which in turn depends on the target system.

1.2   SVM Characteristics

When designing a compiler strategy it is necessary to consider the main characteristics of the target platform. These characteristics determine the various costs the compiler must take into account. The main benefit of SVM is that no local/global address translation is necessary since it is provided by the OS/hardware. The page structure allows limited exploitation of locality within appropriately structured codes. However this benefit is at the price of a more complex memory model, where page movement is expensive, and characterises the issues that a compiler for SVM must consider.

There are three runtime phenomena which must be considered for efficient execution:

- **Locality of Reference:** Transformations that increase local accesses and reduce remote will reduce page movement. Once a page has been moved it is important that all it's elements are accessed before it is invalidated or replaced and will therefore determine the array access stride. Similarly, data re-use within the page should be exploited by restructuring so that re-use occurs before data is replaced.

- **False Sharing:** If two processors access a page and one of them is a writer, the page will oscillate between the two, serialising operations and greatly increasing the number of page faults. Therefore the compiler must schedule work and data in such a manner that false sharing is avoided.

- **Synchronisation:** Synchronisation is necessitated by the read/write access model of shared memory programming. This may be a considerable overhead in SVM systems [14]. An optimising compiler should place synchronisation only where necessary.

We assume a sequentially consistent memory system where optimising coherency traffic by the compiler is not directly possible and is not addressed further in this paper.

1.3 Assumptions

Certain choices are made to reduce the complexity of the compiler strategy. These assumptions are thought to give good program performance:

- **Execution Model:** The fork-and-join model allows nested parallelism but increases overhead. We use the SPMD model as it reduces overheads and enables the reduction of the synchronisation cost.

- **Data Distribution:** A knowledge of the data distribution allows remote data access optimisation. If we were to consider a model as general as HPF distribution, we may achieve an optimal solution but this will be at the expense of compiler complexity. We consider a restricted set of partition whose impact is easier to compute and simplifies later analysis such as determining cross-processor data dependence*.

- **Work Scheduling:** In SVM systems the way work is scheduled to processors will determine data layout. Scheduling of work, for instance, must trade off load balancing against communication. In our compiler we schedule work such that all write accesses are local throughout the program reducing to zero the communication overhead of writes, at the possible expense of more read accesses.

These assumptions allow successful exploitation of parallelism for programs whose behaviour is largely compile-time determinable. More dynamic programs may find these assumptions too restrictive, leading to degraded performance.

2 A COMPILER STRATEGY FOR SVM

Our compiler strategy splits naturally into two stages: global partitioning and local optimisation (called post-partitioning). The first stage makes global trade-off decisions to minimise execution time and is concerned with balancing the distinct requirements of different parts of the program. The second phase applies more aggressive optimisations once global trade-offs have been reconciled, but must trade off costs within each part of the processor program. Although distinct stages, both rely on the other making sensible choices; partitioning to minimise remote accesses depends on post-partitioning locality transformations to realise it. The post-partition stage, in turn, will try to optimise any given processor code but will only perform well if a sensible data partition is used. Hence, both stages must operate in a consistent manner.

The costs addressed by our compiler are in order of significance; parallel execution T_{co}, synchronisation T_{sy}, inter-processor communication T_{ra}, load imbalance T_{co},

---

* A dependence whose source and sink are executed on different processors.

intra-processor communication T_{la} and loop overhead T_{ov}. Throughout the compiler this ordering is honoured at all stages. The first four are global costs and are addressed in the global partitioning stage where an explicit trade-off is made. The last two (T_{la}, T_{ov}) are considered to be of less significance and can largely be managed once a local node program has been generated. Each compiler phase tries to reduce one or more costs. The phases of our compiler are shown in table 1 and are described in sections 3 and 4. The diagram in figure 1 shows which costs each phase attempts to reduce. Certain phases cooperate (shown by solid lines) while others require conflicting program transformations (shown by broken lines) which will trade off their associated costs.

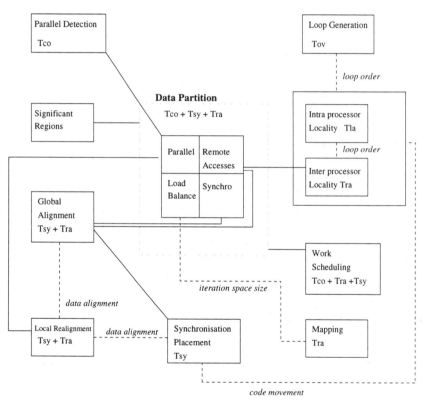

Figure 1   Relationships (solid lines) and conflicts between phases (broken lines).

3   GLOBAL PARTITIONING

At the core of the strategy is the global partitioning phase which determines the work and data distribution based on parallelism and SVM overheads. Although data cannot be physically allocated to processors at the program level, we can exploit the SVM to achieve this.

Pre-Partitioning	Parallel Detection
	Significant Regions
Partitioning	Global Alignment
	Global Data Partitioning
Post-Partitioning	Local Realignment
	Work Scheduling
	Synchronisation Placement
	Mapping
	Hierarchical Locality
	Loop Optimisation

Table 1 Compiler Phases

To simplify the data distribution selection, it is split into two phases: global alignment and data partitioning. To limit the search space we restrict the data distribution to orthogonal partitions of the arrays. Thus if an array has N dimensions, it may be partitioned in $2^N - 1$ different ways. Alignment has the property that corresponding array elements are always mapped to the same processor, i.e. if array element $X(6, 12)$ is mapped to processor 3, so will array elements $Y(6, 12)$, $Z(6, 12)$ etc. We can exploit this property in order to reduce communication. If in a given loop, $Y(6, 12)$, $Z(6, 12)$ are both referenced, and one reference is known to be local, the other will also be local.

3.1 Global Data Alignment for SVM

Alignment transformations are applied so as to globally maximise the number of references that will be local. We use a simplified version of the method described in [13] where global alignment is restricted to permutations. In addition, we use a variant of the index space alignment algorithm [12] in which only accesses in significant regions are considered. Data alignment reduces data sharing T_{ra} and synchronisation T_{sy}, but may trade off against parallelism T_{co}. If there is any conflict, this is addressed in the post-partitioning phase by doing local realignment of some arrays.

The alignment matrices for Loop Nests 1 are given in figure 2. For further details on their definition see [13].

Loop Nests 1

```
        DO I₁ = 2 TO N₁
          DO I₂ = 1 TO N₂
S₁ :          X(I₂, I₁) = X(I₂, I₁ − 1) + Y(I₁, I₂)
          END DO
        END DO
        DO J₁ = 1 TO N₁ − 1
```

$$S_1 : X(I_2, I_1) \qquad S_1 : Y(I_1, I_2) \qquad \mathcal{A} = \begin{bmatrix} 0 & 1 \\ 1 & 0 \end{bmatrix}$$

$$S_2 : Z(J_2 + 1, J_1 + 1) \quad S_2 : X(J_2 + 1, J_1) \quad \mathcal{A} = \begin{bmatrix} 1 & 0 \\ 0 & 1 \end{bmatrix}$$

$$S_2 : Z(J_2 + 1, J_1 + 1) \quad S_2 : Y(J_2, J_3) \qquad \mathcal{A} = \begin{bmatrix} 1 & 0 \\ 0 & 1 \end{bmatrix}$$

Figure 2   Alignment Affinity for Loop Nests 1.

```
          DO  J2  =  1  TO  N2 − 1
            DO  J3  =  1  TO  N3
S2 :              Z(J2 + 1, J1 + 1)    + = X(J2 + 1, J1) + Y(J2, J3)
            END  DO
          END  DO
      END  DO
```

The preferred alignment between arrays X and Y in statement S_1, for instance, matches two dimension in statement S_1 but only one in statement S_2. If we assume that the global alignment phase aligns X normal to the index space and Y permuted, then we have the the Loop Nests 2; where the new alignment on Y is shown by transposing the access to array Y.

Loop Nests 2

```
          DO  I1  =  2  TO  N1
            DO  I2  =  1  TO  N2
S1 :              X(I2, I1) = X(I2, I1 − 1) + Y(I2, I1)
            END  DO
          END  DO
          DO  J1  =  1  TO  N1 − 1
            DO  J2  =  1  TO  N2 − 1
              DO  J3  =  1  TO  N3
S2 :                Z(J2 + 1, J1 + 1)    + = X(J2 + 1, J1) + Y(J3, J2)
              END  DO
            END  DO
          END  DO
```

partition first dimension	$\mathcal{S}_1$	Exploit Parallelism on I_2
	$\mathcal{S}_2$	Exploit Parallelism on J_2
partition second dimension	$\mathcal{S}_1$	Sequential execution
	$\mathcal{S}_2$	Exploit Parallelism on J_1
partition both dimensions	$\mathcal{S}_1$	Parallelism on I_2 limited to $\sqrt{p}$
	$\mathcal{S}_2$	Exploit Parallelism on J_1 and J_2

Figure 3 Impact of Partitioning on Parallelism for Loop Nests 2. Variable p is the number of processors.

3.2 Global Data Partitioning for SVM

Global partitioning must trade off the conflicting requirements of different program regions. Once a decision has been reached, it is applied throughout the entire program. The approach is based on concentrating any cost analysis on the "most significant" parts of the program and determining whether a cost or transformation will have any significant impact. Given cost information provided by the following analysis, a global partitioning strategy is constructed.

Parallelism (T_{co}): Partitioning for parallelism is based on identifying array indices which can be evaluated in parallel. The parallel iterators surrounding a statement are readily available from the pre-partitioning phase. Those indices that are accessed by parallel iterators are candidates for partitioning. In Loop Nests 2, loops on I_2, J_1, J_2 are parallel and loop on J_3 is a reduction. The first index of X and the two indices of Z can be computed in parallel. Figure 3 illustrates the relationship between the partitioning and parallelism.

Load Imbalance (T_{co}): If partitioning takes place with respect to "work invariant" iterators the same amount of work will take place in each processor. A parallel iterator is work invariant if it does not refer to another iterator in its bounds and is not referenced in the loop bounds of another iterator or in a conditional expression. It is possible to transform for invariance but as this may skew the data space and increase the complexity at later stages, it is not considered in this scheme. In the Loop Nests 2 example all partitions give equally good load balancing.

Synchronisation (T_{sy}): If the source and sink of a dependence are scheduled to the same processor, no synchronisation is needed. This stage uses the alignment information to determine the dimension which, if partitioned, would incur the least number of cross-processor dependences and hence synchronisations. This analysis relies on an efficient post-partition synchronisation placement phase. Figure 4 shows the impact of the partitioning decision on the number of synchronisations executed for Loop Nests 2.

partition first dimension	$(\mathcal{S}_1 \delta \mathcal{S}_1)$	Local Dep	No Sync
	$(\mathcal{S}_2 \delta \mathcal{S}_2)$	Local Dep	
	$(\mathcal{S}_1 \delta \mathcal{S}_2)$	Local Dep	
partition second dimension	$(\mathcal{S}_1 \delta \mathcal{S}_1)$	Cross Dep	Sync: $O(p)$
	$(\mathcal{S}_2 \delta \mathcal{S}_2)$	Local Dep	
	$(\mathcal{S}_1 \delta \mathcal{S}_2)$	Cross Dep	$O(1)$
partition both dimensions	$(\mathcal{S}_1 \delta \mathcal{S}_1)$	Cross Dep	Sync: $O(\sqrt{p})$
	$(\mathcal{S}_2 \delta \mathcal{S}_2)$	Local Dep	
	$(\mathcal{S}_1 \delta \mathcal{S}_2)$	Cross Dep	$O(1)$

Figure 4   Synchronisation costs (number of synchronisations executed) for Loop Nests 2. Symbol δ denotes data dependences and symbol p the number of processors.

Remote Accesses (T_{ra}): This analysis determines an approximate value for the remote array sections referenced for a particular partition. It determines which dimensions the arrays are to be partitioned so as to minimise non-local accesses. This partitioning scheme depends on data re-use to remove redundant non-local accesses. Figure 5 gives, for Loop Nests 2, according to the partitioning, an approximation of the amount of remote accesses assuming temporal locality is exploited.

The indices to be partitioned must be parallel and as far as costs are concerned, it is assumed that synchronisation is more costly than remote accesses; this is based on experience with KSR-1 but may change with other systems. Minimising remote accesses is more important than load imbalance; this is based on the assumption that a non-local access costs more than one computation assuming no latency tolerance. This is simplistic and the dominant costs may vary. With current strategy, for Loop Nests 2, the partition of the first dimension on the arrays would be chosen.

4   POST-PARTITION STAGE

Determining a good data partition will not in itself provide a successful implementation. The post-partition phase is responsible for reducing synchronisation, communication and loop overheads according to previous decisions. This phase is concerned with minimising the costs of implementing parallelism:

Local Realignment: Data partitioning for significant regions may be at the expense of parallelism in other regions for lower dimensional arrays. If a lower dimensional array is aligned on non-partitioned indices of the template, then all accesses to it will be sequentialised. To limit the loss of parallelism, we realign lower dimensional arrays onto partitioned template indices if applicable. This allows exploitation of parallelism in non-significant regions at the possible expense of

partition first dimension	$S_1 : X(I_2, I_1 - 1)$	
	$S_1 : Y(I_2, I_1)$	
	$S_2 : X(J_2 + 1, J_1)$	
	$S_2 : Y(J_3, J_2)$	$\frac{N_3 N_2}{p}$
partition second dimension	$S_1 : X(I_2, I_1 - 1)$	N_1
	$S_1 : Y(I_2, I_1)$	
	$S_2 : X(J_2 + 1, J_1)$	N_1
	$S_2 : Y(J_3, J_2)$	$N_3 N_2$
partition both dimensions	$S_1 : X(I_2, I_1 - 1)$	$\frac{N_1}{\sqrt{p}}$
	$S_1 : Y(I_2, I_1)$	
	$S_2 : X(J_2 + 1, J_1)$	$\frac{N_1}{\sqrt{p}}$
	$S_2 : Y(J_3, J_2)$	$\frac{N_3 N_2}{\sqrt{p}}$

Figure 5 Remote access costs for Loop Nests 2. Variable p is the number of processors.

remote accesses and synchronisations. This tries to reduce T_{co} in certain instances, but trades off against global alignment and may increase T_{ra} and T_{sy}.

Work Scheduling: The scheduling of work to processors given a data distribution depends on machine costs and the statement structure. At present we only consider creation and reduction parallelism. This stage marks each statement with the form of parallelism (if any) to be exploited in each partitioned index. For many statements there is only one form of parallelism present, i.e. summing an array into a scalar only has reduction parallelism, while initialising an array may only exhibit creation parallelism. In those cases where both are present, by default we schedule for creation parallelism as reductions always incur at least one barrier. Future implementations will be more sophisticated in determining the appropriate schedule.

Synchronisation: Synchronisation points can be removed by detecting those dependences that are entirely local. Once we have computed the minimum number of cross-processor dependences (using alignment information), they are mapped on the control flow graph. We then try to find the best place to insert synchronisations so as to minimise the number executed at runtime [14]. The efficacy of this phase depends on the data distribution determined by previous alignment, partitioning and local realignment phases.

Mapping: Once the data partition and synchronisation points have been determined we generate the local iteration space and new program structure depending on the form of parallelism determined previously. Although the local iteration space is based on the data layout, in SVM systems it is the actual computation executed at runtime that determines the layout of data; data distribution is "virtual" since actual data allocation is automatically handled by the SVM. This stage can reduce false sharing , T_{ra}, by ensuring that data and work is partitioned on page boundaries. This may increase the work , T_{co}, performed in some processors.

Hierarchical Locality Optimisation: Communication cost and memory hierarchy usage is optimised at this stage [7, 15, 16]. Data re-use and spatial locality require a combination of strip-mining, skewing, interchange and the introduction of temporaries. Minimising cache to local memory traffic requires the same treatment as reducing remote accesses. As remote accesses are an order of magnitude more expensive, we minimise them first at the possible expense of more cache misses. The loop overhead optimisations interact with the locality optimisations since they may both require conflicting loop orders. However, in SVM systems we believe page faults to be more important than loop overhead and thus the loop optimisation transformations assume a fixed loop order.

Loop Optimisation: This step's goal is to reduce the loop management overhead that may have been introduced by previous steps. Partitioning work increases the number of loop bounds and conditionals to evaluate before executing the loop body. In certain programs this can be a significant overhead particularly if strip-mining has been used to exploit locality. This is the final optimisation as it is considered less important and is concerned with uni-processor performance rather than parallel performance. This stage only improves T_{ov} and may trade off against the hierarchical locality optimisation stage as they may have conflicting loop order requirements.

5   RESULTS

The MARS compiler implements the global strategy described above. It is built on top of Sage++ [4] and uses an augmented linear algebraic framework. The framework is designed to simplify and unify the implementation of the compiler phases. We applied our compiler strategy to two Fortran programs, Tred2 and the ADI fragment used in [8]. The resulting code was run on a KSR-1 and compared with the results of the auto-paralleliser KAP. Tred2 is a 148 lines Eispack routine, while the ADI fragment is 19 lines in length. Tred2 allows the compilers to be tested over a relatively complex program with many trade-offs. ADI on the other hand is much simpler, but requires a consistent parallelisation strategy. Our compiler outperforms KAP, by an order of magnitude for large data sizes for Tred2. This effect is largely due to

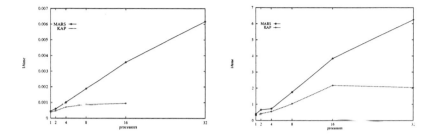

Figure 6   Performance for Tred2, $n=512$ (left). Performance for ADI, $n=512$ (right). The x-axis is the number of processors, the y-axis is 1/time.

excessive unnecessary synchronisations within loop bodies. The performance gap is less for the ADI program, as it is relatively trivial to parallelise. The differences are due to data movement, due to the opposing partitioning of two loop nests. The MARS compiler automatically determines a partition which requires no data movement or synchronisation.

6   RELATED WORK

Anderson et al. [1] proposed a global approach to optimise parallelism and locality. The approach is based on finding a data partition and the corresponding iteration space distribution over the processors. In this work the only costs considered are communication and parallelism; synchronisation and access stride are ignored. Furthermore exploiting locality is restricted to finding communication free partitions (which may not exist) rather than those that minimise remote accesses. Also, the relationship between data partitioning and post-partitioning transformations is not explored.

Appelbe et al. [2] approach relies on partitioning loop iteration space on processors. With the set of parallel loop a set of "distributed array references" is computed. Using a set of locality constraints, expressed in a graph which nodes are loops and arcs locality constraints the partitioning of the iteration spaces is decided. The code generation algorithm also consider array padding for eliminating false-sharing. Insertion of synchronisations happened only when locality constraints are not satisfied (i.e. cross-processor data dependences) and it is based on Kennedy/Callahan algorithm [18]. Our work differs in many aspects. First we exploit the properties of the owner computes rule for mapping computations and we consider both locality and synchronisation costs.

Gupta et al. [9] have proposed a system based on the Component Affinity Graph [12]. The partitioning decision is taken according to an approximation of the amount of communication. This approach has also the problem of not integrating other costs, such as synchronisation, when taking decision and considering the impact on post-partition transformations.

7 CONCLUSION AND FUTURE WORK

This paper describes an optimising compiler strategy for SVM systems. At present the compiler uses a static data partitioning approach to parallelism exploitation. However, internal compiler structure allows data to be redistributed at every statement and we are currently developing analysis to determine when redistribution (possibly by prefetching and post-storing) is worthwhile. There are occasions when loop based scheduling is preferable to a data based approach, particularly with regard to load balancing; we hope to address this issue in the future. Presently our strategy does not include interprocedural analysis, but this will be added shortly. We will also investigate how compile time knowledge can be used to relax memory coherence and how this may be integrated into a consistent compiler strategy.

REFERENCES

[1] Anderson J.M. and Lam M.S. Global Optimizations for Parallelism and Locality on Scalable Parallel Machines, *Proceedings of Programming Languages Design and Implementation,* ACM Press, 1993.

[2] Appelbe B. Doddapaneni S. and Hardnett C. A new Algorithm for Global Optimization for Parallelism and Locality, LNCS 892, *7th International Workshop on Languages and Compilers for Parallel Computing,* Ithaca, NY, August, 1994.

[3] Beckner S. Chapman B. and Zima H. Vienna Fortran 90, *Proceedings of Scalable High Performance Computing Conference,* 1992.

[4] Bodin F. Beckman P. Gannon D. and Srinivas J. Sage++: A Class Library for Building Fortran and C++ Restructuring Tools, *Second Object-Oriented Numerics Conference,* Oregon (USA), April 1994.

[5] Bodin F. Granston E. and Montaut T. Evaluating Two Loop Transformations for Reducing Multiple-Writer False Sharing, *LCPC,* Springer-Verlag in the Lecture Notes in Computer Science, August 1994.

[6] Bodin F. Eisenbeis C. Jalby W. and Windheiser D. A Strategy for Array Management in Local Memory, Special Issue of *Math. Programming B* on Applications of Discrete Programming in Computer Science, 1992.

[7] Callahan D. Carr S. and Kennedy K. Improving Register Allocation for Subscripted Variablesxe, *Proceedings of the Conference on Programming Language Design and Implementation,* 1990.

[8] Choudhary A. Fox G. Hiranandani S. Kennedy K. Koelbel C. Ranka S. and Tseng C. Unified Compilation of Fortran 77D and 90D, *ACM Letters on Programming Languages and Systems* Vol 2, N 1-4, March-December, 1993.

[9] Gupta M. and Banerjee P. Paradigm: A Compiler for Automatic Data Distribution on Multicomputers, *Proceedings of the International Conference on Supercomputing,* pp 87-96, 1993.

[10] Lahjomri Z. and Priol T. Koan : A Shared Virtual Memory for the iPSC/2 Hypercube, *Proceedings of CONPAR/VAPP92*, Lyon, September, 1992.

[11] Lam M. Rothberg E. and Wolf M.E. The Cache Performance and Optimizations of Blocked Algorithms, *Proceedings of the Fourth ACM ASPLOS Conference*, April 91.

[12] Li J. and Chen M. Index Domain Alignment: Minimizing Cost of Cross-Referencing between Distributed Arrays, *IEEE Proceedings of the Third Symposium on the Frontiers of Massively Parallel Computation*, October 1990

[13] O'Boyle M.F.P. and Hedayat G.A. Data Alignment: Transformations to Reduce Communication on Distributed Memory Architectures, *Scalable High Performance Computing Conference*, Williamsburg, April 1992.

[14] O'Boyle M.F.P. Kervella L. and Bodin F. Synchronisation Minimisation in a SPMD execution model, *to appear* in *Journal of Parallel and Distributed Computing* special issue on Distributed Shared Memory Systems.

[15] Wolf M.E. and Lam M. A Data Locality Optimizing Algorithm, *ACM Conference on Programming Language Design and Implementation*, June 26-28, 1991.

[16] Wolf M.E. and Lam M. A Loop Transformation Theory and an Algorithm to Maximize Parallelism, *IEEE Transactions on Parallel and Distributed Systems*, Vol 2, No 4, October 1991.

[17] Wolfe M.J. *Optimizing Supercompilers for Supercomputers*, PhD thesis, University of Illinois, October 1982.

[18] Zima H. and Chapman B. *Supercompilers for Parallel and Vector Computers*, ACM Press, 1991.

6

MACHINE-INDEPENDENT PARALLEL PROGRAMMING USING THE DIVIDE-AND-CONQUER PARADIGM

Santhosh Kumaran and Michael J. Quinn

Department of Computer Science
Oregon State University, Corvallis, Oregon 97331
USA

ABSTRACT

Parallel processing is facing a software crisis. The primary reasons for this crisis are the short life span and small installation base of parallel architectures. In this paper, we propose a solution to this problem in the form of an architecture-adaptable programming environment. Our method is different from high-level procedural programming languages in two ways: (1) our system automatically selects the appropriate parallel algorithm to solve the given problem efficiently on the specified architecture; (2) by using a divide-and-conquer template as the basic mechanism for achieving parallelism, we considerably simplify the implementation of the system on a new platform. There is a trade-off, however: the loss of generality. From a pragmatic point of view, this is not a major liability since our strategy will be useful in building domain-specific *problem solving environments* and *application-oriented compilers*, which are truly machine-independent. We give preliminary results from a case study in which our method is used to adapt the parallel implementations of the conjugate gradient algorithm on a multiprocessor and a workstation network.

1 INTRODUCTION

The most efficient parallel algorithm for solving a problem often depends on the target architecture. Thus, unless a parallel programming system has the ability to adapt the algorithm to the architecture, it will not be truly machine-independent.

In the traditional approaches to machine-independent parallel programming, the user encodes an algorithm as a parallel program using a high-level programming language. Using a combination of compilers and run-time systems, this program can be executed

71

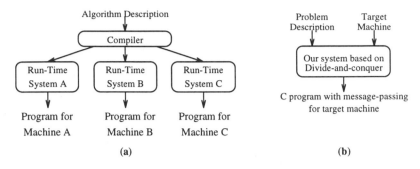

Figure 1 (a) Traditional algorithm-oriented approach to parallel processing. (b) Our problem-oriented approach to parallel processing.

on a variety of platforms, but the algorithm embedded in the program may not execute efficiently on all the platforms. Hence only limited machine-independence is achieved.

In this paper, we present a new scheme for machine-independent parallel programming. Our scheme is built on the following three key ideas: (1) the use of a problem solving paradigm—*divide-and-conquer*—for representing algorithmic templates; (2) frame-based representation of processing environments; and (3) the use of an analytical performance prediction tool for automatic algorithm design.

By automating the detailed design of an algorithm and the generation of a parallel program, our approach relieves the user from much of the burden of parallel programming. There is a trade-off, however: the set of problems that can be solved efficiently using a specific problem solving paradigm is a *subset* of the problems with efficient solutions. However, we believe our strategy will be useful in building domain-specific *problem solving environments* and *application-oriented compilers*, which are truly machine-independent. Figure 1 contrasts our approach with the traditional approach.

2   SOLUTION METHODOLOGY

We use the divide-and-conquer method of problem solving to map problem instances to the user-specified processing environment. The result of this mapping will be an efficient program to solve the problem on the specified platform. Assuming efficient implementations of a standard message-passing library are available on all target machines, this program can be coded in C with calls to the appropriate message-passing library.

We begin with a collection of divide-and-conquer templates for the problem and an abstract description of the architecture. The templates represent *methods* for solving the problem. The number of templates in the collection is problem-dependent—some will have only a single template, while others may have two or more. Our goal is to generate an efficient algorithm to solve the problem on the specified architecture.

To achieve this goal, we traverse the path from a generic method to an algorithm. This means customizing the template by adding details. We will invoke a number of procedures, accessible from the template, to make the decisions necessary for this customization. In weighing various options, an analytical performance prediction tool will play a dominant role [1].

What kind of details do we need to add to the template to make it an efficient algorithm? Here is a partial list:

- Structure of the divide-and-conquer tree: This will vary based on the processing environment for the same template.

- Mapping of the processing nodes to the leaves of the tree: The mapping that minimizes the communication overhead is desired.

- Depth of the tree: This determines the granularity of the resulting parallel program.

- Optimal subset mapping: Sometimes performance may be enhanced by using only a subset of the resources.

- Machine-specific data decomposition: There are several ways grid data can be decomposed, and based on the problem instance and the architecture, a particular decomposition may be superior.

- Machine-specific solution method: When there are several candidate templates, the one that maximizes the performance needs to be selected.

To accomplish the customization of the divide-and-conquer template, we allocate fields in the template to hold all the details. Each field will have a method attached to it to compute the detail it accounts for. By invoking these methods with the problem size and the architecture description as arguments, the generic template evolves into an efficient algorithm.

If there is more than one template for a problem, then each one of them will be customized and the best one selected using the performance prediction tool.

Our current design of the system uses a higher-order function to implement the template with the arguments of this function representing the fields of the template.

Converting the detailed template to a message-passing program can be accomplished using current compiler technology [2].

Figure 2 shows the method schematically.

It is important to note that *divide-and-conquer* is being used in this system merely as a methodology for designing the templates. Users do not write divide-and-conquer functions—they call higher-level functions like matrix-vector multiply or dot product. Emitted code is not a divide-and-conquer program. It is an SPMD program in which

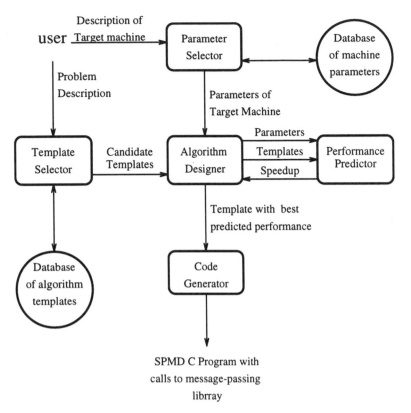

Figure 2   Schematic representation of our method for generating efficient parallel programs to solve a given problem on a specified architecture.

every processor is active throughout the execution of the program and doing useful work. Data distributions mentioned in the divide-and-conquer templates are converted by the code generator into initial data distribution conditions and message passing calls.

2.1   Divide-and-conquer template

Our template is based on the algebraic model of divide-and-conquer proposed by Mou and Hudak in [5]. The template encapsulates problem solving using divide-and-conquer in three phases: a divide phase, a conquer phase, and a combine phase. An overview of the template is given below.

Divide phase: Actions in this phase can be expressed using two functions:
1. Divide function: This explains how data points are distributed among the processing units for distributed memory machines; for shared-memory systems, this represents the logical division of data points among processing nodes. Using grid problems as

an example, row decomposition, column decomposition, and block decomposition can all be captured using appropriate divide functions.

2. Pre-adjust function: In addition to partitioning data, the divide phase may need to modify the partitioned data sets. This is accomplished using a pre-adjust function which is applied to the partitions *before* the subproblems contained in these partitions can be solved.

Conquer phase: We need to specify only a sequential base function and a base predicate in this phase since everything else reduces to recursive application of the previously defined template. The base predicate is used to specify the terminating condition of the recursion.

Combine phase: Similar to the divide phase, we need two functions to capture the actions in this phase:

1. Post-adjust function: Subproblem solutions are modified using this function.
2. Combine function: This function explains how to combine the modified subproblem solutions to form a solution to the original problem.

Below, we give an example template for matrix multiplication, $C = AB$. This is one of three templates we have for matrix multiplication in the system database.

Data Distribution:

      matrix A distributed row-wise among the processors

      matrix B distributed column-wise among the processors

      matrix C distributed row-wise among the processors

Divide function:

      Divide the processor pool into two equal partitions,

          a LEFT partition and a RIGHT partition.

      (In distributed-memory machines, this would automatically

      imply the division of data-structures as well.)

Pre-adjust function:

      None.

Base function:

      Sequential Matrix Multiplication.

Post-adjust function:

      Swap columns of B between partitions.

      Apply Matrix Multiplication Template to both partitions.

Combine function:

      Combine the LEFT and RIGHT partitions.

A *meta-template* can be developed by the composition of other templates. For example, an eigensolver template has matrix multiplication as one of its components. The system, while customizing the eigensolver template, will select the appropriate matrix multiplication template from the three available using the performance prediction tool.

2.2 Representation of the processing environment

The computing environment is described using a frame structure. The slots in the frame represent attributes, values of which may be represented by other frames. The collection of frames, thus formed, holds all the information we need to design a program that will execute efficiently on the represented environment. The information stored in the frame includes the number of processors, the processing power of the nodes, the inter-connection network, and the memory hierarchy. Figure 3 shows the frame representation of a typical high-performance computing environment.

2.3 Performance prediction

Performance prediction plays an important role in the development of a detailed algorithm from a generic template, as pointed out in section 2. Our analytical performance prediction tool is built on the model developed by Clement and Quinn [1]. It exploits the algebraic structure of divide-and-conquer algorithms to estimate their run time on the specified processing environment.

The performance prediction model for a message passing architecture is represented using the following set of equations:

TERMINOLOGY:

n	input size
c	base size; recursion stops here
p	number of processors
$D()$	time spent in the divide operation
$C()$	time spent in the combine operation
$f()$	sequential time
$S()$	speedup
T_{par}	parallel time
C_{comm}	communication time for combine phase
D_{comm}	communication time for divide phase
C_{comp}	computation time for combine phase
D_{comp}	computation time for divide phase
C_{mem}	memory access time for combine phase
D_{mem}	memory access time for divide phase
ϕ	normalized message startup time
M_c	messages in the combine phase
M_d	messages in the divide phase
τ	normalized cache miss penalty
η	input size factor

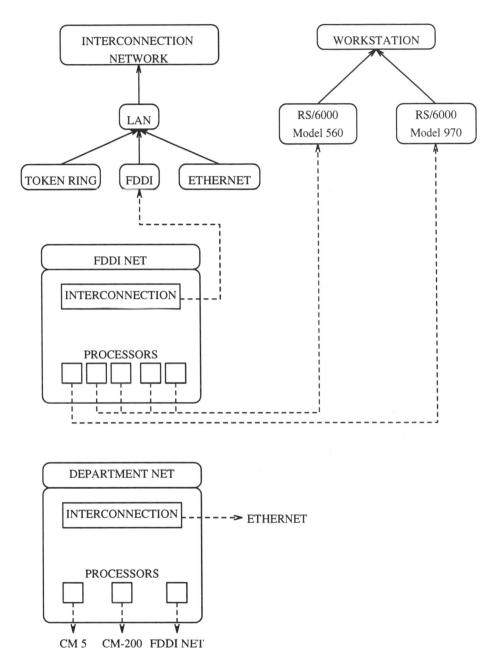

Figure 3 Frame representation of a typical processing environment.

χ cache size

$$
\begin{aligned}
(1) \quad T_{par}(n,p) &= \begin{cases} f(n) & \forall n \leq c \\ T_{par}(n/2, p/2) + D(n,p) + C(n,p) & \forall n > c \end{cases} \\
(2) \quad S(p,n) &= f(n)/T_{par}(n,p) \\
(3) \quad f(n) &= f_{comp}(n) + f_{mem}(n) \\
(4) \quad D(n,p) &= D_{comp}(n) + D_{mem}(n) + D_{comm}(n,p) \\
(5) \quad C(n,p) &= C_{comp}(n) + C_{mem}(n) + C_{comm}(n,p) \\
(6) \quad C_{comm}(n,p) &= \phi \times M_c \\
(7) \quad D_{comm}(n,p) &= \phi \times M_d \\
(8) \quad x_{mem}(n) &= \tau \frac{n \times n}{\chi} \quad x \in f, C, D
\end{aligned}
$$

A similar model exists for shared-memory machines. The tool is invoked with the algorithm template and the description of the processing environment as arguments.

3   A CASE STUDY USING THE CONJUGATE GRADIENT METHOD

In the remainder of the paper, we present an example in which the scheme described in the previous sections is used to develop efficient parallel implementations of the conjugate gradient (CG) method.

3.1   Mathematical description of the CG method

The conjugate gradient method is an iterative scheme for solving linear systems of equations. Given a symmetric, positive definite, coefficient matrix A, and a vector b, it computes the solution vector of the linear system $Ax = b$ using the following algorithm [6]:

$$i = 0; g_i = h_i = b - Ax_i;$$

while (not converged) do:
$$
\begin{aligned}
\lambda_i &= g_i^T h_i / (h_i^T A h_i) \\
x_{i+1} &= x_i + \lambda_i h_i \\
g_{i+1} &= b - A x_{i+1} \\
\gamma_i &= (g_{i+1} - g_i)^T g_{i+1} / (g_i^T g_i) \\
h_{i+1} &= g_{i+1} + \gamma_i h_i
\end{aligned}
$$

3.2   An algorithmic template for CG

Each CG iteration involves a matrix vector multiplication and a few dot products and SAXPYs. Each one of these operations can be expressed using a divide-and-conquer template. Thus the CG method is represented in our scheme by a composition of three different divide-and-conquer templates.

The template is parameterized using the following four parameters:

1. Processors used for matrix-vector multiplication (P1). The matrix vector multiplication is the most compute-intense task in the CG iteration. Hence it will be beneficial to use all the available processors for this operation. Thus, the size of the target platform essentially determines this parameter.

2. Processors used for the rest of the operations (P2). The poor granularity of dot product can affect the overall performance of the CG implementation. This parameter would let us improve the granularity by computing dot product on a subset of the available processors. The system uses performance prediction to decide the optimum granularity depending on the machine characteristics and problem size.

3. Decomposition of the coefficient matrix (MAT). The distribution of the coefficient matrix among the processors is an important parameter, since the adjust functions, the divide function, and the combine function will be determined by this distribution. We consider two different distributions:

   (a) Row-contiguous.
   (b) Column-contiguous.

4. Memory location (MEM). Physical memory could be either *centralized* or *distributed*, allowing us to differentiate between "shared memory" and "distributed memory" architectures.

We now present a parameterized template for CG using pseudo-code.

CG-Template(P1,P2,MAT,MEM)
    switch (**MAT**)
        case **Row-contiguous**:
            Invoke DC-Template for row-oriented
                matrix vector multiplication
                with **P1** as the number of processors to use.
        If (**MEM = Distributed**)
            Invoke DC-Template to distribute the product vector
                from one node to **P2** nodes.
        case **Column-contiguous**:
            Invoke DC-Template for column-oriented
                matrix vector multiplication
                with **P1** as the number of processors to use.

If (**MEM** = **Distributed**)

Invoke DC-Template to distribute the product vector

from **P1** nodes to **P2** nodes.

End *switch* (**MAT**).

Invoke a series of DC-Templates for dot product and SAXPY

with **P2** as the number of processors to use.

If (**MEM** = **Distributed**)

Invoke DC-Template to redistribute the result vector

from **P2** nodes to **P1** nodes.

End *If*

End **CG-Template**.

3.3   Generation of efficient programs on diverse platforms

The template is adapted to a specified target platform by tuning the values of the parameters described earlier. The *Algorithm Designer* module of the system will invoke the *Performance Predictor* several times to determine the set of parameters that maximizes the speedup. In this case study, we have considered two vastly different parallel processing environments as target platforms: an eight-processor Silicon Graphics Power Challenge shared memory machine and an FDDI network of four IBM RS/6000 model 560 workstations.

Processors	vector length			
	100	800	6400	51200
1	**1.00**	1.00	1.00	1.00
2	0.59	**1.00**	1.70	1.95
4	0.31	0.67	**2.13**	3.58
8	0.16	0.36	1.70	**5.38**

Table 1   Predicted speedups of dot product on SGI for varying vector lengths.

Adapting the template to a shared memory machine

The implementation that minimizes the synchronization points performs best on a shared memory machine. The performance prediction enables the system to choose *row-contiguous* as the value of the third parameter, since row-wise matrix vector multiplication requires no synchronizations at all. For the same reason, it is always advantageous to utilize all the available processors for matrix vector multiplication, another decision the system can easily make using the performance prediction. The granularity of the dot product computation that maximizes the performance is a function of the vector size as well as the machine parameters. Table 1 shows the predicted speedups for various problem and machine sizes. The system uses the results from the performance prediction to select an appropriate level of granularity. The observed speedups of CG scheme while solving a linear system of size 800, given in Table 2, validates the use of performance prediction for algorithm design. Best performance is obtained when using only two processors of the machine for dot product while using all eight processors for matrix vector multiplication.

Adapting the template to a workstation network

The decomposition of the coefficient matrix, the processors to be used for matrix vector multiplication, and the granularity of the dot product are all determined by the system using the performance predictor. Table 3 shows the predicted performance using row decomposition of the matrix for varying cluster sizes and dot product granularities. The problem size is kept the same as in the shared memory example—800 unknowns. Table 4 shows the same information when the matrix is decomposed column-wise. The predictions enable the system to arrive at the best implementation on the workstation network: column decomposition of the coefficient matrix along with single processor execution of the dot product. The observations, shown in Tables 5 and 6, mirror the predictions, validating our approach for the workstation network as well.

4 CONCLUSIONS FROM THE CASE STUDY

There are three key issues in parallel processing: performance, portability, and pro-grammability. We believe that our method addresses all three of them, at the expense of generality. The loss in generality is not a serious drawback if the expressibility of the system is sufficient enough to cover most problems of practical interest. By using the conjugate gradient method as an example, we have shown that an algorithm of significant practical interest can be represented using our system.

As detailed in the previous section, the case study corroborated our thesis that perfor-mance prediction along with the divide-and-conquer paradigm can provide architecture adaptability.

The case study shows that the algorithms generated by the system can have efficient implementations on diverse processing environments. There are two reasons for this. First, the system is able to search the parameter space exhaustively, since this space is relatively small. The other reason for good efficiency is the low overhead of our implementation of the DC templates [3].

We have seen similar results from another case study involving a finite element ocean circulation model [4].

5 FUTURE WORK

We plan to use this method to develop domain-specific **problem solving environments** (PSE) and **application-oriented compilers** targeted to linear algebra and partial differential equations (PDE). PSEs and compilers based on this method will be architecture-independent since the description of the processing environment is an independent parameter.

Most of the future work will be focused on three areas: performance prediction, the database of algorithm templates, and code generation. The performance prediction needs to be improved to take into account memory effects and automatic architecture linearization. Automatic generation of code for a specified target machine based on the template with best predicted performance is an area which requires further work.

The database of algorithm templates will be organized with a hierarchical structure. At the bottom, we will have basic linear algebra kernels, data distribution and communication primitives, and divide/combine functions. On top of this layer, non-trivial applications—such as *conjugate gradient method, two-dimensional FFT, banded-system solver*, and *eigensystem solver*—will be built. Numerical models and PDE solvers will form yet another layer. We believe this layered approach will have the expressibility to solve most problems in scientific computing, including the irregular and unstructured problems.

REFERENCES

[1] Clement, M. J., and M. J. Quinn. Analytical Performance Prediction on Multicomputers. *Proceedings of Supercomputing'93*, November 15–19, 1993, Portland, Oregon, pp. 886-894.

[2] Hatcher, P. J., and M. J. Quinn. *Data-Parallel Programming on MIMD Computers*, Cambridge, Mass.: The MIT Press (1991).

[3] Kumaran, S., and M. J. Quinn. Divide-and-Conquer Programming on MIMD Computers. *Proceedings 9th International Parallel Processing Symposium*, April 25–28, 1995, Santa Barbara, CA, pp 734-741.

[4] Kumaran, S., R. N. Miller, and M. J. Quinn. Architecture-Adaptable Finite Element Modeling: A Case Study using an Ocean Circulation Simulation, submitted to *Supercomputing'95*.

[5] Mou, Z. G., and P. Hudak. An algebraic model for divide-and-conquer algorithms and its parallelism. *The Journal of Supercomputing*, 1988, pp. 257-278.

[6] Polak, E. *Computational Methods in Optimization, A Unified Approach*, New York: Academic Press, (1971) pp. 44-66.

Processors	Option1	Option2	Option3	Option4
1	1.00			
2	2.06	**2.09**		
4	4.30	**4.44**	4.09	
8	8.64	**8.83**	7.77	0.26

Table 2   Observed speedups of the CG Method on SGI when solving a dense 800×800 linear system. Various options differ in the number of processors used for dot product. Option1 uses a single processor, option2 uses two processors, option3 uses four processors, and option4 uses eight processors.

Processors	Option1	Option2	Option3
1	1.00		
2	1.71	1.75	
4	1.92	1.98	1.85

Table 3   Predicted speedups of the CG Method on workstation network using row decomposition of the coefficient matrix. Various options differ in the number of processors used for dot product. Option1 uses a single processor, option2 uses two processors, and option3 uses four processors. The data is for solving a dense 800×800 linear system.

Processors	Option1	Option2	Option3
1	1.00		
2	1.79	1.71	
4	2.48	2.33	1.92

Table 4   Predicted speedups of the CG Method on workstation network using column decomposition of the coefficient matrix. Various options differ in the number of processors used for dot product. Option1 uses a single processor, option2 uses two processors, and option3 uses four processors. The data is for solving a dense 800×800 linear system.

Processors	Option1	Option2	Option3
1	1.00		
2	1.08	1.48	
4	1.52	1.72	1.52

Table 5 Observed speedups of the CG Method on workstation network using row decomposition of the coefficient matrix. Various options differ in the number of processors used for dot product. Option1 uses a single processor, option2 uses two processors, and option3 uses four processors. The data is for solving a dense 800 × 800 linear system.

Processors	Option1	Option2	Option3
1	1.00		
2	1.70	1.30	
4	2.15	1.47	1.12

Table 6 Observed speedups of the CG Method on workstation network using column decomposition of the coefficient matrix. Various options differ in the number of processors used for dot product. Option1 uses a single processor, option2 uses two processors, and option3 uses four processors. The data is for solving a dense 800 × 800 linear system.

7

LOAD BALANCING AND DATA LOCALITY VIA FRACTILING: AN EXPERIMENTAL STUDY[†]

Susan Flynn Hummel*,

Ioana Banicescu, Chui-Tzu Wang and Joel Wein

Department of Computer Science, Polytechnic University,
Six MetroTech Center, Brooklyn NY 11201

* and IBM T. J. Watson Research Center

ABSTRACT

In order to fully exploit the power of a parallel computer, an application must be distributed onto processors so that, as much as possible, each has an equal-sized, independent portion of the work. There is a tension between balancing processor loads and maximizing locality, as the dynamic re-assignment of work necessitates access to remote data. Fractiling is a dynamic scheduling scheme that simultaneously balances processor loads and maintains locality by exploiting the self-similarity properties of fractals.

Fractiling accommodates load imbalances caused by predictable phenomena, such as irregular data, and unpredictable phenomena, such as data-access latencies. Probabilistic analysis gives evidence that it should achieve close to optimal load-balance. We have applied fractiling to two applications, an N-body problem and dense matrix multiplication, running on shared-address space and on private-address space parallel machines, namely the Kendall Square KSR1 and the IBM SP1. Although the applications contained little or no algorithmic variance, fractiling improved performance over static scheduling due to systemic variance; however, artifacts of the memory subsystems of the two architectures impeded the scalability of the fractiled code.

1 INTRODUCTION

Loops are the most prevalent source of parallelism in numeric codes. When the iterate duration is variable and difficult to predict, the dynamic assignment of iterates is often

[†]Research supported by ARPA/USAF under Grant no. F30602-95-1-0008 and the New York State Science and Technology Foundation. The research was conducted using the resources of the Cornell Theory Center, which receives major funding from the National Science Foundation and New York State, additional funding comes from the Advanced Research Projects Agency, the National Institute of Health, IBM Corporation and other members of the center's Corporate Research Institute. Susan Hummel was also supported in part by NSF Grant CCR-9321424; Joel Wein by NSF Grant CCR-9211494. We thank Bob Walkup for his assistance in programming the SP1.

the best way to achieve load balancing. Variance can result from both algorithmic (e.g., if statements) and systemic (e.g., page faults and memory-access or message-passing latency) features [8].

To be efficient, dynamic scheduling schemes must achieve a tradeoff between the runtime cost of scheduling and good load balancing. For example, *factoring*, proposed by Flynn and Flynn Hummel, dynamically schedules iterates in decreasing size batches of P equal-sized chunks (where P is the number of processors) [8]. Scheduling chunks of iterates simultaneously reduces overhead, while decreasing the chunk size promotes load balancing. Factoring uses a probabilistic rule to choose the decreasing batch chunk sizes so that there is a high probability that the loop will complete by the optimal finishing time.

Most dynamic scheduling schemes, however, focus solely on load balancing and do not take data locality into account. On machines with complex memory hierarchies - both local and remote - additional performance can be achieved by placing iterates and data on the same processing unit. Many techniques for achieving this have been developed in the context of static scheduling. For example, in *tiling* [26], the iteration space of nested parallel loops is divided into per-processor tiles; the shape of the tile is chosen so that data reuse is maximized thereby minimizing inter-processor communication. When data are instead assigned to processors, then an "owner-computes" rule, wherein an iterate is executed by the processor that has been assigned the data element being updated, is often employed.

Hummel has proposed a scheme, *fractiling*, that combines factoring and tiling, to yield a dynamic scheduling method that exploits both spatial and temporal locality for nested loops [9]. Initially, iterate tiles and their associated data are placed on the same processor. The processor executes the iterates using the decreasing size chunking scheme developed in factoring to preserve load balance. If a processor exhausts its local iterates, it acquires work from other processors. The novelty of this approach is that fractiling enables the processor to acquire new work in the form of decreasing size subtiles, called *fractiles*, which conform to the shape specified by the tiling algorithm. The shape of the fractile can be any blocked/blocked-cyclic/cyclic parallelpiped subspace of the iterate/data space. The fractiles are computed in an efficient and elegant order, called shuffled row-major, by exploiting self-similarity properties like those found in fractals. This self-similar property allows fractiling to scale naturally to multidimensional problems, such as multiple nested loops accessing multidimensional arrays. In fractiling, multidimensional-tile iterates can be allocated in shuffled row-major order using a single counter; it is, thus, a self-similar extension of coalescing/de-coalescing [23], allocating the iterates in row-major order.

We describe our experience with implementing fractiling on two current generation parallel machines: a shared-address space machine, the Kendall Square Research KSR1 [11], and a message passing machine, the IBM SP1 [17]. Despite the superficial similarities of the architectures of these machines, processors with local storage connected to other processors via an interconnection network, the implementation of fractiling was orders of magnitude easier on the KSR1 than on the SP1 because of the KSR1's shared memory paradigm. More importantly, both storage management subsystems have features that limited the scalability of the implementations: the lack of control over data placement on the KSR1, and the lack of remote memory transfer operations on the SP1. Both of these deficiencies are correctable without major modifications to the machine architectures.

In the next two sections, we give an overview of loop scheduling schemes in general, and fractiling scheduling in particular. We then briefly describe the application of fractiling to dense-matrix multiplication on the SP1 and N-body codes on the KSR1. Since we only considered uniform distributions of bodies for the N-body problem, both applications little or no algorithmic variance; nonetheless, a remarkable amount of operating-system induced variance was observed, and fractiling was able to exploit this and produce good load-balance.

2 SCHEDULING SCHEMES

One way to assess the performance of scheduling schemes, is to model the time to process a unit of work (e.g., an iterate) as a random variable with mean μ and variance σ. A simple way to ensure (close to) even processor loads is to dynamically assign work one unit at a time—the resulting load imbalance will be proportional to μ. Such dynamic self-scheduling can be efficiently implemented with two shared counters: one for allocating work, and one for barrier synchronization at the loop end. So that they can allocated with two shared counters, perfectly nested parallel loops can be coalesced into a single loop (see figure 1) [23]. Unfortunately, the overhead of dynamic self-scheduling is proportional to N/P.

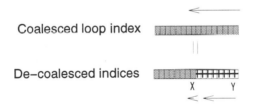

Coalesced loop index

De–coalesced indices

Figure 1   Inner loop grows faster than outer loop with row-major order.

At the other extreme to dynamic scheduling, work units can be initially assigned to processors in *chunks* of size N/P with very little overhead; however, the expected load imbalance of such static scheduling is proportional to $\sqrt{\sigma N/P}$ [18]. This load imbalance can severely degrade performance [8]. Schemes that dynamically schedule work in chunks of K units have also been investigated [18, 6]. Kruskal and Weiss derive a formula for calculating the optimal K based on μ, σ, N and P [18].

To better trade off scheduling overhead and load imbalances, work can be dynamically assigned to processors in decreasing-size chunks [18, 24, 29, 7, 8]. Decreasing the chunk size promotes load balancing. Factoring, for example, uses a probabilistic rule to choose the decreasing chunk sizes so that there is a high probability that the work will complete by the optimal finishing time $\mu N/P$ [7, 8]. Flynn and Flynn Hummel derive a distribution-free bound for selecting optimal batch chunk sizes K_i based on μ, σ, N and P.

Unfortunately, in practice, it is not possible to use the optimal chunk size formula derived by either Kruskal and Weiss (fixed size chunks) or Flynn and Flynn Hummel because the mean and variance of parallel work execution times depend not only on applications features, but on nondeterministic system effects as well. If characteristics of work execution times are unknown or hard to predict, then Flynn Hummel *et al.* suggest using a halving rule, wherein the size of each batch is half the remaining work [8]. The intuition for this choice is that the sums (chunk execution times) of random variables (work unit execution times) is itself a random variable with (close to) normal distribution; the expected finishing time of a batch of P chunks of K work units with a truncated normal distribution is $2\mu K$. Since the average processor finishing time is μK, this suggests that only half of the remaining work should be allocated per batch. In simulations [7], and experiments [8], factoring using the halving approximation consistently outperformed other chunking schemes on dense-matrix benchmark programs with a wide variety of characteristics (e.g., fine versus coarse grain, constant versus variable algorithmic work).

The above schemes focus solely on load balancing and do not exploit locality. On machines with complex memory hierarchies, additional performance can be achieved by placing work and data on the same processing unit. Many techniques for achieving this have been developed in the context of static scheduling. For example, *tiling* reduces communication time by statically partitioning the data/iterate space of nested parallel loops into tiles whose shape is chosen to maximize data reuse and locality. Much research has been done in this area [15, 16, 19, 26, 30, 4, 5].

In addition to fractiling, we know of two scheduling schemes that combine static techniques that exploit data locality with dynamic scheduling techniques that promote load balancing: Affinity Scheduling [21] and Locality-based Dynamic Scheduling (LDS) [20]. In these schemes, work units and their associated data are initially placed on the same processor. The processor executes its units using a decreasing size chunking scheme to preserve load balancing. If a processor exhausts its local work, it acquires decreasing size work from other processors.

These schemes are designed for one-dimensional loops, and do not address the more challenging problem of executing multidimensional tiles in decreasing subtiles of the same shape. Since the shape of a tile is initially selected to maximize reuse, it is desirable that subtiles be of the same shape (self-similarity) to better exploit locality. Self-similar subtile assignment is also important so that a complex history of executed subtiles need not be maintained: the space covered should be the same whether it was executed as 4 subtiles of size K or one of size $4K$ (see figure 2).

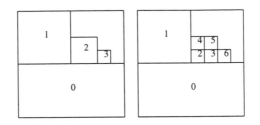

Figure 2   Illustration of self-similarity.

Flynn Hummel has developed a scheme, *fractiling* (discussed in §3), that combines factoring and tiling, to yield a dynamic scheduling method that exploits temporal and spatial locality for multidimensional problems [9]. Fractiling uses the factoring halving approximation discussed above to assign decreasing size chunks. A novelty of the fractiling approach is that processors acquire new work in the form of decreasing size subtiles, called *fractiles*, which conform to the optimal shape specified by the tiling algorithm. The fractile assignments are computed in an efficient and elegant way by exploiting self-similarity property of fractals, namely shuffle row-major [28]. This self-similar property allows fractiling to be efficiently applied to multidimensional problems.

3 FRACTILING SCHEDULING

As with factoring, we refer to P consecutively assigned fractiles (chunks) as a *batch* of fractiles, setting the size of the fractiles in a batch to be one half the size of the fractiles in the previous batch. The scheme has been shown to be very robust [8]. The tile shape can by any parallelpiped that is a blocked/blocked-cyclic/cyclic subspace of the iteration/data space. The two examples we discuss below, N-body simulations and matrix multiplication, use tiles with blocked dimensions. For concreteness, in our description of fractiling, we assume that the d-dimensional iteration space $S = S_1, ..., S_d$ is tiled into P $S_0/\sqrt[d]{P} \times ... \times S_d/\sqrt[d]{P}$ shaped tiles, and each is initially assigned to a processor. Our techniques can be applied to other distributions of processors and dimensions [9].

Our goal is to define a self-similar recursive tiling of the workspace, where by self-similar we mean a decomposition of a tile into smaller subtiles *of the same shape*. We also require that the next tile in the ordering can be computed efficiently. In general, it is not possible to divide a d-dimensional shape into two similarly shaped parts. It is, however, possible to divide a d-dimensional parallelpiped into 2^d similarly shaped parallelpipeds by geometrically bisecting each dimension. In a self-similar tiling the combination of consecutive fractiles will form a larger similarly shaped fractile. This self-similarity insures that the iterates that have been executed in a tile do not depend on the particular sizes of the fractiles that have been executed—only on the total number of iterates that have been executed. Thus, a complex history of executed fractiles need not be maintained, and as described below, fractiles can be efficiently allocated using per-tile counters.

Fractiling uses the fractal shuffled row-major numbering [28] to allocate tiles. A shuffle operation maps a number with bits $[n_7, n_6, n_5, n_4, n_3, n_2, n_1, n_0]$ to $[n_7, n_3, n_6, n_2, n_5, n_1, n_4, n_0]$, i.e., it "shuffles" the upper and lower halves, just as one shuffles the two halves of a deck of cards. An unshuffle is the inverse operation. To map from

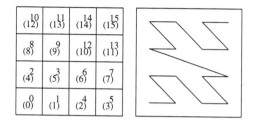

Figure 3   2-dimensional shuffled row-major numbering and its fractal.

a position on the shuffled row-major curve to one on the row-major curve, its x and y coordinates are concatenated (coalesced [23]) and unshuffled, and the result is split into two halves (de-coalesced) yielding the new x and y coordinates (see Figure 3).

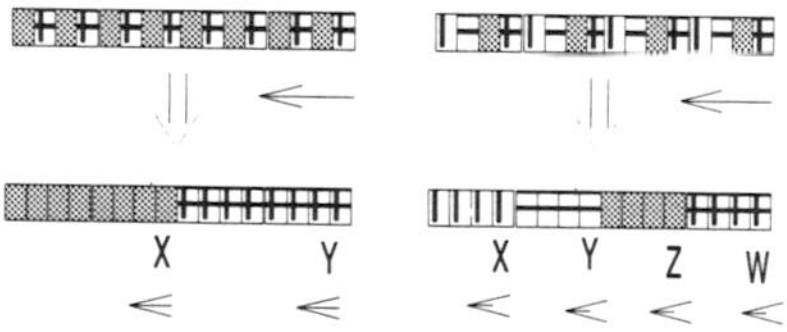

Figure 4   All dimensions grow at the same rate with shuffle row-major order.

Shuffled ordering naturally extends to higher dimensions: the bits are divided into d equal-size segments and a d-way shuffle performed. To use the card analogy, a deck is divided into d stacks and then shuffled back together by interleaving their cards. So, for instance, a four-way shuffle of $[n_7, n_6, n_5, n_4, n_3, n_2, n_1, n_0]$ yields $[n_7, n_5, n_3, n_1, n_6, n_4, n_2, n_0]$. To allocate fractiles in shuffled row-major order, the bits of a per-processor executed-iterate counter are divided into d segments and d-way unshuffled. The unshuffled integer is divided into d segments yielding coordinates in the d-dimensional parallelepiped. With shuffled row-major order, the lower bits are spread out evenly in all dimensions, so each grows at the same rate (see Figure 4). Unshuffle operations can be efficiently implemented using table-lookups, shifts and masks [9].

4 MATRIX MULTIPLICATION ON THE SP1

In this section we report on the application of fractiling to a dense-matrix multiplication code, $C = A \times B$, on the SP1. Dense-matrix multiplication contains no algorithmic variance; it was chosen because of its simplicity to use as a proof of concept and to gauge the overhead of a message passing implementation of fractiling. Future work involves experimentation with fractiling sparse-matrix multiplication, which can contain significant algorithmic variance.

The SP1 is a collection of RISC System/6000 processing nodes (each with disk, main memory and cache) connected by a high-speed switch. Processors communicate via explicit message passing. Several communications libraries run on the SP1 that support blocking and nonblocking send and receives [12]; the communication latencies of these packages are roughly 3000 cycles, and communication bandwidths 60 cycles per doubleword. The communication latency is due in a large part to the buffering of messages: there are user* and system buffers involved in the transfer of messages. The elapsed time of messages can differ by several orders of magnitude due to interference from operating systems daemons [25]

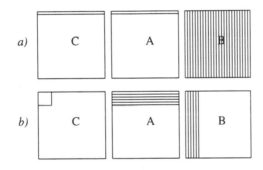

Figure 5 Rows of A and columns of B needed to calculate *a)* a row and *b)* a block tile of matrix multiplication $C = A \times B$.

The code was parallelized by assigning a block of $C(i,j)$s to each processor and adhering to an owner-computes rule. Only the first dimension of A and the second dimension of B were blocked. This tiling makes good reuse of the rows of A and the columns of B when the submatrices fit in memory (see figure 7).

Both the non-fractiled and fractiled codes were implemented with the MPI message passing library [22]. All matrices were evenly distributed among processors at the start, and processors exchanged the necessary data for computing their portion of the C matrix without explicitly sending requests. In order to reduce overhead, nonblocking receives were posted before blocking sends were issued.

The fractiled code used a designated processor to schedule fractiles. Having a single scheduler processor is a potential bottleneck that could affect scalability; however, in

---

* A nonblocking send or receive completes when the message has been copied out of the user buffer.

simulations of up to 256 processors this did not occur [10], so we opted for this simple strategy. To decrease the likelihood of the scheduler becoming a bottleneck, requests for fractiles were pipelined, so that the next fractile allocated would be waiting when the current one completes.

Since there are no remote memory transfer operations on the SP1, in the fractiled code, each processor had to poll for requests for its portion of the A and B matrices. Polling made the implementation of fractiling very complicated, and led to an uncomfortable tradeoff: if processors poll too infrequently, then other processors awaiting their data will be delayed; if processors poll too often, then overhead costs will be high. With suitable hardware support for remote memory transfer operations such as put and get, the implementation would have been much simpler.

In our implementation, a processor checks for requests for its data after a parameterized number of computations that determines the polling interval. When a processor replies to a request for data that it owns, it returns all the data it owns in one message. Sending long messages better amortizes communication overhead, and will be a win if the requesting processor executes additional fractiles from the sending processor (and a potential loss if it doesn't). It also reduces the overhead of storing the data on the receiving processor, since the received data is always of the same format.

After computing the entries of C assigned to it, a processor tries to help other processors with unexecuted work. When the processor requests the next fractile size from the scheduler processor, the scheduler processor, through the per-tile counters that it maintains, detects that the "helping" processor has completed its work, and returns the id and counter of the processor with the maximum unexecuted work. If the helping processor needs remote data for executing the fractile, it explicitly sends a request for the data. When the helping processor finishes a fractile, it returns the fractile to the helped processor before requesting another fractile to execute from the scheduler processor; this avoids the possibility of a processor "grabbing" some work to do and then incurring a significant delay before starting it while waiting to return the previous fractile to the helped processor.

To test the scalability of the fractiled code, experiments were run on 4 and 16 processors on different sized matrices. At least eight runs were made for each parameter combination; we report best, worst and average performance. For small problem sizes on 4 processors, the non-fractiled and fractiled code performed similarly. When the number of processors was 16, the fractiled code always performed better than the non-fractiled code by $11\% - 12\%$. Increasing the number of processors increases the probability of one being unlucky and running long. The apparent "superlinear" speedup for the 4096×4096 size problem is because on 4 processors the submatrices/buffers do not fit in memory; the fractiled code performs better than the non-fractiled code in the 4 processor case presumably because it masks variability in disk access times. Preliminary results on 64 processors indicate good scalability to that level, but we were not able to obtain full results by the closing of this version.

↘ Problem Algorithm ↘ Size	1024	2048	4096
Static 4 PEs	16.96	135.32	2235.78
Fractiled 4 PEs	18.04	144.58	1984.04
Static 16 PEs	6.59	51.09	352.81
Fractiled 16 PEs	5.56	46.59	339.20

Figure 6 Minimum Execution Times in Seconds for Matrix Multiplication.

↘ Problem Algorithm ↘ Size	1024	2048	4096
Static 4 PEs	19.53	153.78	2399.44
Fractiled 4 PEs	19.60	154.04	2271.68
Static 16 PEs	7.39	60.11	481.10
Fractiled 16 PEs	6.59	52.47	424.78

Figure 7 Average Execution Times in Seconds for Matrix Multiplication.

↘ Problem Algorithm ↘ Size	1024	2048	4096
Static 4 PEs	25.18	204.11	2639.84
Fractiled 4 PEs	23.17	216.53	2400.60
Static 16 PEs	8.73	68.39	608.40
Fractiled 16 PEs	7.79	60.41	501.32

Figure 8 Maximum Execution Times in Seconds for Matrix Multiplication.

5 N-BODY SIMULATIONS ON THE KSR1

The N-body problem is a much-studied example of a problem with potentially irregular-ly-distributed data that is challenging and important to parallelize. We therefore implemented parallel and fractiled N-Body simulations on a KSR1. A 2-d serial code [27] was parallelized and fractiled, and a 3-d parallel code [3] was fractiled. Recent efficient N-body algorithms find approximate solutions by recursively partitioning space into a hierarchy of finer grained cells resulting in a computation tree structure. At the lowest level cells contain bodies in their space, and at coarser levels, their summary effects on distant bodies. We chose to parallelize the Greengard Fast Multipole Algorithm (FMA) in two and three dimensions [13, 14]. Performance improvements were obtained by fractiling on both uniform and non-uniform distributions of bodies [1, 2]. We report here on the results of fractiling FMA on uniform distributions; since this reduces the potential algorithmic variance significantly, our results demonstrate the benefits of a scheduling scheme that accommodates systemic variance.

The KSR1 is a hardware-coherent cache-only multiprocessor. Its topology is a ring of rings, with processors distributed on the outer rings. The top level ring has a bandwidth of 4GB/sec., and the outer ones 1GB/sec. In the KSR1 there is no main memory in the conventional sense. Instead, each processor has a 32MB local cache and a 0.5MB split instruction and data subcache. The cache line (page) is 16KB, and the subcache cache line (subpage) is 128 bytes. A snoopy invalidate protocol is used to keep caches coherent. The relative data access latencies for local subcache, local cache, non-local cache same ring, and non-local cache different ring, are (2:18:150:500).

An advantage of the KSR1 architecture is that it was relatively easy to port a serial version of the N-body simulation code because of its shared address space. A disadvantage is that data access latency depends critically on its location, which is not easy to control, so performance tuning the parallel code was difficult.

The FMA makes an upward and a downward pass on the tree in each time step. The leaf-level of the downward pass was selected to be fractiled because it is the most computationally intensive step in the algorithm. In our implementation, space is discretized into P tiles, and each tile is assigned to a processor. Each tile is a dense array of cells containing pointers to the start and end of bodies belonging to the cell. A per-tile counter is used to indicate the amount of work already computed in the processor tile, and to dynamically decompose the tile into decreasing size fractiles.

To prevent fractiles from "ping ponging" between caches, they are aligned on cache-line boundaries. The additional cost of aligning the subtitles is approximately one sixth of the required fractile storage without aligning.

To test the effectiveness of fractiling, we ran the fractiled versions and non-fractiled versions of the parallelized 2-d and 3-d FMA on uniform distributions of bodies. All programs were run on the KSR1 with 1 to 32 processors. There was variance in the parallel execution times between runs, especially for the 2-d case, so we ran each program ten times on each distribution for the 2-d case, and 5 times for the 3-d case.

For the 2-d problems we report minimum, average, and maximum execution times in Figures 5, 6 and 7, and for the 3-d case, only the average in Figure 8, since the minimum and maximum are relatively closer.

The uniform distributions used in the 2-d experiment had 2K bodies, which resulted in a maximum of 4 bodies per cell. For 8 or more processors fractiling consistently ran faster than the non-fractiled code by 20% to 25%; on four processors its performance matched the performance of the non-fractiled code—the fewer the number of processors the smaller the amount of expected load imbalance. The fractiled version also scaled (slightly) better than the non-fractiled one; however, neither version is scaling well. This lack of scalability is due in part to the limited amount of parallelism in the 2-d FMA N-body algorithm. Neither version ran faster on 32 processors than it did on 16 processors, and only inconsistent gains were seen from 8 to 16 processors. Additional details about the implementations are described in [1, 2].

No. Procs	1	4	8	16	32
PFMA Uniform	29.5	10.2	8.5	8.0	8.0
Fract. Uniform		10.1	6.1	6.0	7.1

Figure 9   Minimum Execution Times in Seconds for 2-d Data.

No. Procs	1	4	8	16	32
PFMA Uniform	29.6	10.8	8.8	8.6	8.8
Fract. Uniform		10.8	6.5	6.8	8.1

Figure 10   Average Execution Times in Seconds for 2-d Data.

No. Procs	1	4	8	16	32
PFMA Uniform	29.8	11.3	9.1	9.4	9.8
Fract. Uniform		11.3	6.8	7.3	9.0

Figure 11   Maximum Execution Times in Seconds for 2-d Data.

The 3-d uniform distributions reported on here involved 10K bodies, with average densities of 20 bodies per cell. The average execution times of the non-fractiled and fractiled 3-d runs for the uniform distribution are given in figure 8. The 3-d algorithm contains more parallelism than the 2-d algorithm, and performance gains were obtained on up to 64 processors. The fractiled code results significantly outperform the non-fractiled code results in all cases. Increasing the number of processors led to greater improvements of the fractiled versus the non-fractiled code.

No. Procs	1	4	8	16	32	64
PFMA 10K Bodies	106.00	32.30	17.90	13.50	9.01	5.92
Fract. 10K Bodies		31.40	17.10	11.00	6.49	4.27
Fract. % Improvement		2.79	4.47	18.52	27.97	27.87
PFMA Speedup		3.28	5.92	7.85	11.76	17.91
Fract. Speedup		3.38	6.20	9.64	16.33	24.82

Figure 12 Average Execution Times in Seconds for 3-d Uniform Data.

Additional performance improvements could potentially be obtained on a shared-memory architecture that permits more control over data movement—the KSR1 has only limited facilities for controlling data placement.

6 CONCLUSIONS

Our experiments have demonstrated that systemic variance can degrade performance by causing unbalanced loads on parallel machines. Although our fractiled code has more overhead than static scheduling schemes, it outperformed the static schemes even on applications with little or no algorithmic variance. Systemic variance is due to the complex hardware and software subsystems of current parallel machines, which interact in unpredictable ways. In the the near term, such systemic variance is likely to be endemic as the life-span of current parallel machines does not allow their software environments to mature to the same level as that of current uniprocessors.

REFERENCES

[1] I. Banicescu and S. Flynn Hummel, Balancing Processor Loads and Exploiting Locality in Irregular Computations, IBM Research Report RC19934, Feb. 1995.

[2] I. Banicescu, Load Balancing in the Parallel Fast Multipole Algorithm Solution to the N-body Problem, PhD Thesis, Polytechnic University, Computer Science Dept., in preparation.

[3] J. A. Board, KSR implementation of Greengard's PFMA, email, Oct. 1994.

[4] Carter, L., J. Ferrante and S. Flynn Hummel, Efficient Parallelism via Hierarchical Tiling, Proc. of SIAM Conference on Parallel Processing for Scientific Computing, Feb. 1995

[5] Carter, L., J. Ferrante and S. Flynn Hummel, Hierarchical Tiling for Improved Superscalar Perfomance, Proc. of International Parallel Processing Symposium, Apr. 1995.

[6] M.D. Durand, T. Montaut, L. Kervella and W. Jalby, Impact of Memory Contention on Task Duration in Self-Scheduled Programs, *Int. Conf. on Parallel Processing*, Aug. 1993.

[7] L. E. Flynn and S. Flynn Hummel, The Mathematical Foundations of the Factoring Scheduling Method, IBM Research Report RC18462, Oct. 1992.

[8] S. Flynn Hummel, E. Schonberg, and L. E. Flynn, Factoring: A Practical and Robust Method for Scheduling Parallel Loops, *Comm. of the ACM* **35(8)** pp. 90-101, Aug. 1992.

[9] S. Flynn Hummel, Fractiling: A Method for Scheduling Parallel Loops on NUMA Machines, IBM Research Report RC18958, June 1993.

[10] S. Flynn Hummel, C. Wang, and J. Wein, Simulations of Fractiling in the logP Model, unpublished manuscript, 1994.

[11] S. Frank, H. Burkhardt and J. Rothnie, The KSR1: Bridging the Gap between Shared Memory and MMPs, *Proc. Compcon '93*.

[12] H. Franke, C. E. Wu, M. Riviere, P. Pattnaik, and M. Snir, MPI Programming Environment for IBM SP1/SP2, unpublished manuscript, 1995.

[13] L. Greengard, *The Rapid Evaluation of Potential Fields in Particle Systems*, ACM Distinguished Dissertaion Series, MIT Press, 1987.

[14] L. Greengard and W. D. Gropp, A Parallel Version of the Fast Multipole Algorithm, *Computers Math. Applic.* **20(7)** pp. 63-71, 1992.

[15] M. Gupta and P. Banerjee, Demonstration of Automatic Data Partitioning Techniques for Parallelizing Compilers on Multicomputers, *IEEE Tran. on Parallel and Distributed Systems*, **3(2)** pp. 179-193, Mar. 1992.

[16] F. Irigoin and R. Triolet, Supernode Partitioning, *Proc. 15th ACM Symp. Principles of Programming Languages* pp. 319-329, Jan. 1988.

[17] G. Khermouch, *Technology 1994: large computers*, IEEE Spectrum **31(1)** pp. 46-49, 1994.

[18] C. Kruskal and A. Weiss, Allocating Independent Subtasks on Parallel Processors, *IEEE Trans. Software Eng.* **SE-11(10)** pp. 1001-1016, Oct. 1985.

[19] F. F. Lee, Partitioning of Regular Computation on Multiprocessor Systems, *Journal of Parallel and Distributed Computing* **9** pp. 312-317, 1990.

[20] H. Li, S. Tandri, M. Stumm, K. C. Sevcik, Locality and Loop Scheduling on NUMA Machines, *Int. Conf. on Parallel Processing*, Aug. 1993, to appear.

[21] E. P. Markatos and T. J. LeBlanc, Using Processor Affinity in Loop Scheduling on Shared-Memory Multiprocessors, *Proceeedings of Supercomputing '92* pp. 104-113, Nov. 1992.

[22] MPI Furum, *Document for a standard message passing interface*, Tech Rep. CS-93-214, University of Tennessee, Nov. 1993.

[23] C. Polychronopoulos, Loop Coalescing: A Compiler Transformation for Parallel Machines, *Int. Conf. on Parallel Processing* pp. 235–242, 1987.

[24] C. Polychronopoulos and D. Kuck, Guided Self-Scheduling: A Practical Scheduling Scheme for Parallel Computers. *IEEE Transactions on Computers* **C-36(12)** pp. 1425-1439, Dec. 1987.

[25] R. Mraz, Reducing the Variance of Point-to-Point Transfers for Parallel Real-Time Programs, *Parallel and Distributed Technology* **2(4)** pp. 20-31, Winter 1994.

[26] D. A. Reed, L. M. Adams, and M. L. Patrick, Stencils and Problem Partitionings: Their Influence on the Performance of Multiple Processor Systemn, *IEEE Tran. on Computers* **C-36(7)** pp.845-858, July 1987.

[27] S. Talla, C implementation of Greengard's FMA, email, June 1994.

[28] C. D. Thompson and H. T. Kung, Sorting on a Mesh-Connected Parallel Computer, *Comm. of the ACM* **20(4)** pp. 263–271, 1977.

[29] T. H. Tzen and L. M. Ni, Dynamic Loop Scheduling for Shared-Memory Multiprocessors, *Proc. Int. Conf. on Parallel Processing*, Vol. II, pp. 247-250, 1991.

[30] M. E. Wolf and M. S. Lam, A Data Locality Algorithm, *Proc. of the ACM SIGPLAN '91 Conference on Programming Language Design and Implementation* pp. 30-44, June 1991.

8

A PATH TO SCALABILITY *AND* EFFICIENT PERFORMANCE

Charles K. Shank, Gary Craig*, and Doug Lea**

*Department of Computer Engineering, Rochester Institute
of Technology, Rochester, New York 14623*

* Department of Computer Science, Syracuse University, Syracuse New York
** Department of Computer Science, State University of New York at Oswego

ABSTRACT

We have developed a programming and execution environment for the implementation of highly flexible applications. Applications in our environment are structured so as to be able to take advantage of their maximum intra-application parallelism, while still being able to be run when fewer resources are available. Furthermore, our environment is machine independent and so are the applications that it supports.

In most systems the cost for this high degree of scalability and flexibility is a constant overhead in terms of generality. Our system is structured to allow dynamic optimization of both code and communications, leading to context specialized performance. Our work contributes both a framework for location based optimization and an examination of the optimizations possible within that framework.

This paper first presents background material on the nature and context of our research. It then focus on the framework and structures that allow for the support of scalability with performance, including the dynamic optimization of communications and code.

1 INTRODUCTION

We have developed a system for end-to-end software engineering of object oriented software, targeted towards distributed systems *. This system, Diamonds, incorporates support for design, development and execution of object oriented applications in a distributed setting [9].

Among the salient features of Diamonds are:

■ The use and support of a fine-grained active object model.

---

*This work has been support in part by Rome Laboratory Contract #F-30602-93-C0108

- The use of *message passing* as the basic communications mechanism between all objects in the system.

- *No limit* on algorithmic concurrency.

- Static and dynamic support for scaling applications with resources.

Among the primary design goals of Diamonds as a system has been the support for both scalability and performance. We define scalability as

> The transformation and mapping of the same basic algorithmic/code structures to varying resources.

This sort of scaling can be expressed in several ways, including on a per program instantiation, and/or as needed during program execution. In either case the same code is used to adapt to changes in the execution environment. There is no need for programmer to make design or language modifications, nor is there any need for explicit configuration by the end user. The typical cost for this sort of flexibility in other systems comes in runtime performance. In Diamonds however, this is not the case. Within Diamonds flexibility brings with it the opportunity for performance.

Our work is unique in that we have designed and structured a parallel computing environment that addresses both scalability and performance. This approach features the flexible use of varying number of resources. An application is able to adapt and make use of more or fewer resources when its needs change, as well as when the resources within the system change. To obtain performance in the presence of such flexibility Diamonds allows for a range of performance enhancements to be applied, throughout the static and dynamic life of an application.

The Diamonds system provides a distinctive solution to the dual problems of scalability and performance. In this paper we will look at our approach to these problems: follows:

- We first lay out what we believe is necessary for true support of scalable applications.

- We then describe some of the optimizations that are possible that allow our scalable environment to also be a high-performance one.

2 SCALABILITY

So how do we address scalability? We believe that any *complete* solution to the scalability problem must overcome obstacles in three areas:

Languages Problem solutions must be specified and structured so that they do not limit scalability. Ideally this sort of specification is not intimately directed by the programmer, rather it should be more of a by-product of the environment.

Compilers Static analysis and compilation can either preserve and express language and algorithmic concurrency, or ignore it.

Runtime Systems We must structure execution environments and language runtime systems that deliver concurrency and scalability to the customer, the application program and end users.

The three areas are of course not independent, but rather intertwined in terms of what can happen in each. Overall however, the design goal for each in terms of scalability must be to forestall tempting premature optimizations that would limit scalability. In the following sections we present our approach to these obstacles.

2.1 Language

If the user interface (front-end) to the whole system does not adequately express problems in a scalable manner, then the scalability battle is lost before it has even been fought.

We make use of a fine grain active object (FGAO) model for our language. In this sort of model,

- *everything* is an object (*potentially*),

- and there is unlimited parallelism (*potentially*)

This is much different than the traditional decompositional approach to parallelism and concurrency. In the decompositional approach concurrency is treated as an orthogonal issue, something to be addressed once the whole (*sequential*) entity is designed.

Our FGAO approach to the design and development of concurrent applications leaves us in a somewhat peculiar position with respect to most other approaches. In Diamonds, everything is an object and every object is potentially active (i.e., a stand-alone process). A straightforward development model would leave us looking for thousands or millions of processors on which we could run our applications. So, rather than trying to find concurrency in applications, we are left with a need to constrain the concurrency in ours.

An important point to keep in mind about a FGAO is that the characteristics of everything is an object and unlimited parallelism are language features, not necessarily runtime ones. In section 3 we show how we can maintain these characteristics from the design and modeling perspective, but loosen their demands at runtime to allow for an easier path to performance. The details of our language interface (called ODL) are addressed in [8].

2.2 Compilation

Our compiler transforms ODL into a byte-coded interpretable intermediate format (SIRF). SIRF is a simple RISC-like language that is very similar to Hennessy and

Patterson's DLX [7]. The target of the code is a heterogeneous distributed virtual machine. No assumptions are made during compilation about the actual hardware that may execute the code.

Our flexibility goals demand that we do not produce a compiled image at this point. Here a compiled image would, hamper scalability and *limit* performance. It would lock us in to producing architecture specific binary forms for each machine we might encounter, and limit performance because we would be forced to be conservative in our optimizations.

2.3 Runtime

A well structured and flexible execution environment is the key to delivering on the promise of scalability and performance.

The Diamonds runtime environment, focuses on:

■   support for execution on tens or several hundreds of workstations

■   A distributed runtime environment for the execution of SIRF, featuring,

–   Heterogeneity

–   No a priori limits on concurrency

–   Adaptive object placement

–   Facilities for object migration [†]

A unique feature of the runtime is its support for what we call, "Threadless Threads". One of the major challenges in creating an environment for a fine-grained active object language is the management of both true and pseudo concurrency. In any ODL program we have the potential for both types. There is true concurrency when we are able to utilize two or more CPUs for the same application, and clusters are active simultaneously on the multiple CPUs. There is pseudo concurrency in any application when multiple clusters reside in a single ensemble, and that ensemble is mapped to a single CPU. There can also be pseudo concurrency within a cluster itself when multiple objects have messages sent to them.

Ultimately, if we are going to run an ODL application on today's hardware, we will have to come up with some scheme for accurately and efficiently simulating the active object model. This is because we are unable to assign either a CPU or a "process" to every object. It is also likely that due to the resource waste that would occur if we were able to do this, we would not want to.

What we have done within Diamonds is to design a thread sharing protocol among computing Agents. Our use of the term *thread* here is in its most abstract definition,

---

[†] we really only migrate *groups* of objects, we call *clusters*

as nothing more than a thread of control. Whether there is an actual operating system thread abstraction is orthogonal to the design discussed here.

Our thread sharing protocol takes advantage of the hierarchical relationship between the agents: `Program`, `Ensemble` and `Cluster`. For each `Agent`, we specify a *unit of work* to be,

$$unitOfWork == processAMsg + handleAMsg + shareThread$$

where the distinction between processing a message and handling it is one of acceptance and removal from the buffer while the later is a scheduling decision.

This heirachical model of an application is shown in figure 1. In the figure the partitions

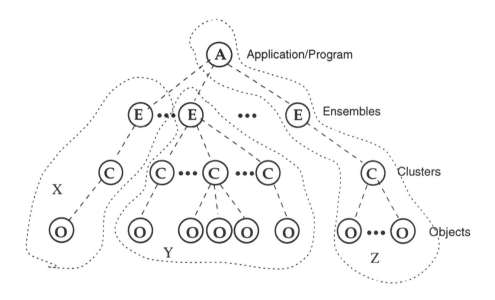

Figure 1   Runtime Application Hierarchy

X, Y and Z all represent valid assignment of runtime components to processors (3 in this case). The assignment of all elements to a single processor would also be valid.

With this model of threading we can support:

■   True concurrency, either

    1. with multiple workstations

    2. within an expressly parallel machine

    3. any combination of 1 and 2.

■   pseudo/simulated concurrency

■   any combination of both true and pseudo-concurrency.

This, we believe, is true scalability support.

3   PERFORMANCE

Scalability is only one half of the promise we must fullfil. The other part is performance. We have designed the structures within Diamonds with both scalability and performance in mind. We will examine these issues from the same perspectives as we have for scalability: languages, compilers, and runtime systems.

3.1   Language Driven Performance

The over-arching theme or goal of most of our optimizations is an effort to enhance locality. This is especially true for objects. We allow programmers to provide placement *hints*, that are to be used when an object is to be created. The hint indicates desired placement relative to other objects.

The form of the hints is,

■   closeTo(objRefX1, ..., objRefXN)

■   farFrom(objRefY1, ..., objRefYM)

While it is possible for a programmer to specify these hints, we do not require it. The compiler itself, is able through static analysis techniques, to add these hints to a program which does not have them.

Scalability demands that these be hints, rather than absolute directives.

3.2   Compiler Performance Issues

We push our compiler and static analysis tools to remove much of the overhead that may be inherent in our language model.

A significant part of what our static analysis tools contribute towards performance is a pseudo-static grouping of program "objects". We statically analyze program code in an effort to determine which objects are candidates for true parallelism and which ones interact sequentially with others. The result of this analysis is the closeTo and farFrom hints discussed previously as well as an indication for object creation asSeed. The asSeed specification hints that the object should be given a new processor, if possible.

We said previously that a FGAO has the potential for all objects to be separate autonomous entities. In any real system however it is unlikely that all object *need* to have this level of autonomy. Instead a great many objects will be completely hidden to others, playing a synchronous helper role with another object or two. For these objects we can relax the runtime expression of the FGAO model and completely encapsulate (nest) one object within another. This can be done statically, so that the contained object no longer needs to be named or have its space allocated separately from its container.

3.3 Runtime Performance Issues

At this point we have to account for several accommodations/decisions we have made in order to be scalable. The issues involved,

- fine-grained active objects

- interpreted code

- placement independent communications

We will address these in the following sections.

3.4 Object Clusters

We are able to make use of several fundamental characteristics of active object models that allow us to bridge the gap between potential concurrency and actual concurrency. First, not all objects are active, or active enough, to warrant first class status as concurrent entities. When one considers the character objects that make up a string of text, it seems highly wasteful (to say the least) to assign a processing element to each character, when all they do is occasionally print themselves. This fundamental observation leads to the use of *clusters* as a means of introducing coarser grained units for runtime management without any loss of algorithmic expression.

A cluster is a grouping of objects whose primary inter-object relationship is that they can share a thread of control with little loss of potential concurrency. Clusters are *hinted* at statically via analysis of program text but are dynamically created and mapped on to resources.

3.5 Context Dependent Optimizations

One of the goals of our research is the development of language and runtime environments that can adapt to varying levels of underlying parallelism, and do so without a constant overhead cost in the form of generality. By generality we refer to a possible implementation approach of designing for the greatest common denominator in terms of communications and computation facilities in network of workstations and parallel machines. The price for this generality is the use of less than optimal structures on any given machine (assuming that any sort of common denominator can even be found).

The approach that we have taken is to use the compiler to translate object oriented program code to a runtime environment where context dependent optimization is always possible. We do this by applying sound object oriented design principles at every step in the code generation process and in the structure of the dynamic runtime entities.

Statically, code is developed in terms of the most abstract interfaces, allowing for dynamic substitution of more specialized (in our case *faster*) versions. We will illustrate these basic principles in the next two sections, discussing communications and computation.

Communications

Our model of interaction between objects is via message passing. This approach allows for decisions about *where* objects are to be placed in the network to be deferred until runtime without cluttering the algorithmic or language interface with these details. However, compiling code for this sort of flexible execution environment, where the actual topological arrangement of all components is not known statically (at compile time) is certainly difficult. We attack the problem at several levels.

First, at the cluster level we are able to substitute *statically* highly efficient communication mechanisms such as inlined access or procedure calls for many messages within the cluster. These messages are from local objects to local "contained" or helper objects. The overhead of these other objects can be fully removed through an optimization process we call *attribute subsumption* [9]. In this process we identify simple, local objects whose existence and identity is completely controlled and encapsulated by another object. This basic technique removes much of the potential overhead of our active object model.

In order to allow for further optimizations we route other object to object messages through their containing clusters. This allows for substitution of communication mechanisms between clusters that are tuned for their relative locations. This is a new and unique form of communications optimization in object oriented distributed systems where the communication structure is dynamically substituted based on the *location* of the receiver. This can be viewed as an extension to the normal type based message dispatch in object oriented systems. In our model *receiver type* selects the possible set and form of messages that might be sent, while *receiver location* selects the mechanism used to transmit the message. In the case of clusters:

sharing a process – we use procedural calls.

running on the same node – we might use fast local call techniques such as LRPC [1].

running on different nodes – we use the best network or operating system communications primitives *for that environment*.

These communications optimizations are dynamic, with selection and use based on the current *actual* location of the clusters involved in the computation. Cluster migration is allowed, but rare, which allows us to cache communication structures and amortize the setup cost over many uses.

Built into **Diamonds** is an object naming structure that allows for quick and efficient determination of relative location information such as that specified above. The details of this naming system are discussed in [9].

Computation

Efficient and flexible communications structures are only part of the solution in our environment. The other part is the ability to tune code based on actual use. Our work in this area can be viewed as an extension of the optimization techniques pioneered in the Deutsch-Shiffman Smalltalk compiler [5], or in the work done with Self [6, 4, 2], into the realm of distributed and concurrent systems.

We start with an interpreted form for the generated code. This form can be interpreted at any node in our network. As need and performance measures indicate, we perform compilation of the interpreted code on a method by method basis. When a compiled form of a method is available, then it will be dispatched to service a message in favor of an interpreted version. The interpreted version will still remain. The interpretable version of the code can be viewed as the persistent backing store of an application's code. If a cluster is unable to locate a compiled image of a method, the interpreted code can be used.

The dynamic compilation of code allows for a wide variety of optimizations to be made that range from the traditional techniques such as those used within any C or Fortran compiler, to newer techniques allowing for the removal of much of the overhead of both object orientation and distribution. For example, customization and message splitting have been shown in Self [3] to be effective means for lowering the overhead of object orientation, we also consider receiver location in our application of these techniques.

3.6 Resources and Performance

In a highly scalable framework like **Diamonds**, resource utilization needs to be driven by application demands. Applications naturally exploit available resources (as permitted by current system-wide allocation policy), configuring themselves to make intelligent use of those resources.

As an application *grows*, and requests additional pseudo-processors (clusters), the **Diamonds** run-time is able to determine whether or not the current resource allocation is sufficient for the application's degree of concurrency. If the current concurrency level is sufficient, the run-time will determine which of the already allocated resources is best suited the new cluster. This determination is based on application placement hints and current application performance measures.

Locality continues to be a critical item with regard to application performance. The run-time is frequently able to detect when pseudo-concurrency is not optimally configured. This can happen when there are multiple clusters per ensemble and tightly coupled clusters reside on different nodes, thus creating larger than necessary communication overhead. Under these circumstances the **Diamonds** run-time may elect to call upon the cluster migration services available within the framework to ameliorate the imbalance. Such cluster migrations do not involve requests to change resource allocations. Thus the application run-time can still autonomously make such decisions.

This organization permits the system resource management facilities to concentrate on policy. Such a facility is free to accept or reject an application's resource request. Further, the run-time provides an interface whereby a resource manager may reclaim resources currently in use by an application.

4 CONCLUSION

Why do we have to push so much off to the runtime?

Scalability : Doing any of our dynamic optimizations earlier would limit or fix the resources the application could use.

Performance : Doing any of our dynamic optimizations earlier would not allow many of the optimizations:

- Clustering
- Context based communication structures

We have developed a programming and execution environment that supports machine independent parallel programming, primarily via the use of networks of hetcrogeneous workstations. Diamonds utilizes a fine grained active object model for programming expressiveness, and a set of runtime abstractions that allow the overhead of this model to be ameliorated.

In addition to the efficient support of this programming model we have also developed a model for the optimization of communications structures based on dynamic placement and not on the more common static *potential* placement of objects.

Our communications optimizations are complemented by a set of code optimizations that take advantage of a framework for dynamic compilation.

A running prototype version of Diamonds is available for use or experimentation. The code can be accessed via WWW/html tools at

$$\texttt{http://www.cat.syr.edu/diamonds\_home.html}$$

REFERENCES

[1] Brian N. Bershad, Thomas E. Anderson, Edward D. Lazowska, and Henry M. Levy. Lightweight remote procedure call. In *Proceedings of the Twelfth ACM Symposium on Operating System Principles*, pages 102–113, Litchfield Park, Arizona USA, December 1989. ACM.

[2] Craig Chambers and David Ungar. Customization: Optimizing Compiler Technology for SELF, a Dynamically-Typed Object-Oriented Programming Language. In *Proceedings of the SIGPLAN '89 Conference on Programming Language Design and Implementation*, pages 146–160. Published as SIGPLAN Notices 24(7), 1989.

[3] Craig Chambers and David Ungar. Making pure object-oriented languages practical. In *Proceedings of the 1991 Conference on Object Oriented Programming Systems, Languages and Applications (OOPSLA '91)*, pages 1–15, November 1991. Published as ACM SIGPLAN Notices, volume 26, number 11.

[4] Craig Chambers, David Ungar, and Elgin Lee. An efficient implementation of SELF – a dynamically-typed object-oriented language based on prototypes. In *Proceedings of the 1989 Conference on Object Oriented Programming Systems, Languages and Applications (OOPSLA '89)*, pages 49–70, October 1989. Published as ACM SIGPLAN Notices, volume 24, number 10.

[5] L. Peter Deutsch and Allan M. Schiffman. Efficient Implementation of the Smalltalk-80 System. In *Proceedings of the 11th Annual ACM Symposium on the Principles of Programming Languages*, pages 297–302, 1983.

[6] Urs Hölzle, Craig Chambers, and David Ungar. Optimizing dynamically-typed object-oriented languages with polymorphic inline caches. In P. America, editor, *Proceedings ECOOP '91*, LNCS 512, pages 21–38, Geneva, Switzerland, July 1991. Springer-Verlag.

[7] John L. Hennessey and David A Patterson. *Computer Architecture: A Qualitative Approach.* Morgan Kaufmann Publishers, Inc., 1990.

[8] Doug Lea and Charles K. Shank. Odl: Language report. Technical Report 9409, NYS CASE Center, Syracuse University, December 1994.

[9] Charles K. Shank. *A Computing Framework for Open Distributed Systems.* PhD thesis, Syracuse University, August 1994.

9

RUNTIME SUPPORT FOR PORTABLE DISTRIBUTED DATA STRUCTURES

Chih-Po Wen, Soumen Chakrabarti, Etienne Deprit, Arvind Krishnamurthy, Katherine Yelick

Computer Science Division, Department of EECS
University of California, Berkeley, California 94720
USA

ABSTRACT

Multipol is a library of distributed data structures designed for irregular applications, including those with asynchronous communication patterns. In this paper, we describe the Multipol runtime layer, which provides an efficient and portable abstraction underlying the data structures. It contains a thread system to express computations with varying degrees of parallelism and to support multiple threads per processor for hiding communication latency. To simplify programming in a multithreaded environment, Multipol threads are small, finite-length computations that are executed atomically. Rather than enforcing a single scheduling policy on threads, users may write their own schedulers or choose one of the schedulers provided by Multipol. The system is designed for distributed memory architectures and performs communication optimizations such as message aggregation to improve efficiency on machines with high communication startup overhead. The runtime system currently runs on the Thinking Machines CM5, Intel Paragon, and IBM SP1, and is being ported to a network of workstations. Multipol applications include an event-driven timing simulator [1], an eigenvalue solver [2], and a program that solves the phylogeny problem [3].

1 INTRODUCTION

Multipol is a library of distributed data structures for irregular applications such as discrete event simulation [1], symbolic computation [4], and search problems [3]. These applications have conditional control constructs and dynamic data structures that produce unpredictable communication patterns and computation costs. Multipol has data structures for both bulk-synchronous applications with irregular communication patterns and asynchronous applications, but in this paper we focus on the latter. Compiler analysis and runtime preprocessing, such as that used in PARTI [5], are not effective in asynchronous applications, since the computation patterns change dynamically. An

APPLICATIONS

REUSABLE
DATA STRUCTURES

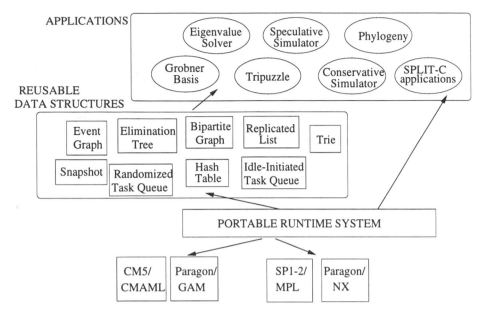

Figure 1 The Multipol architecture. The runtime layer is used to write the data structures, but can also be used directly by the applications.

overview of the Multipol library with its underlying runtime layer and example applications is depicted in Figure 1. In this paper, we explore the issues in developing irregular parallel applications and present the design of the Multipol runtime layer. We use example applications to highlight the design tradeoffs and justify our approach to latency hiding, scheduling, load balance, and communication.

The Multipol runtime system contains a thread system and a simple producer-consumer synchronization construct called a *counter* that can be used to express dependencies between threads. The threads also create opportunities for overlapping communication latency with computation, and for aggregating multiple remote operations in large physical messages to reduce communication overhead. In addition to threading support, the runtime system also provides a set of portable communication primitives for bulk-synchronous communication and asynchronous communication. Like TAM [6] and Nexus [7], the runtime system can be used as a compilation target, but it is primarily designed for direct programming by library and application programmers.

Our design and implementation targets distributed memory architectures, including the Thinking Machines CM5, Intel Paragon, IBM SP1, and future networks of workstations. Such machines typically have high communication latency and overhead for variable-size messages, due to buffer allocation, copying, and on some machines kernel crossing. On these machines, it is common in bulk-synchronous applications to pre-allocate message buffers and pack many values into a single message, taking advantage of global communication information at compile time or at synchronization points at runtime. The Multipol runtime system takes this idea one step further, and aggregates messages "optimistically," even when there is no information about future messages going to the same processor. The runtime system is compact and has a universal interface across distributed memory platforms, which makes Multipol easy to port.

The rest of the paper is organized as follows. Section 2 describes the thread system for hiding latency and introduces *atomic threads* and *split-phase* interfaces, which are the basic programming abstractions in Multipol. Section 3 describes our support for application-specific schedulers. Section 4 explains our approach to load balance. Section 5 presents *dynamic message aggregation*, our solution to efficiently support asynchronous communication. Section 6 compares the Multipol runtime system with other runtime systems. Section 7 summarizes the paper and reports on the current status of the runtime system.

2 MULTIPOL THREADS

In this section, we describe the Multipol thread support for latency hiding and concurrent programming. The simple design of the thread system makes it extremely easy to port. The entire thread system is written in C, and can run on most machines without modification.

2.1 Latency Hiding

A typical Multipol application resembles a shared-memory parallel program, which consists of processes communicating via shared data structures. However, the logically shared data structure is physically distributed among the processors, and the distribution is explicitly controlled by the programmer for better locality and load balance. Since distributed memory architectures do not support a shared address space, accessing remote data requires communication with the remote processor, and is inherently more expensive than local accesses.

To save communication costs, the data structure designers usually adopt an *owner computes* rule , which often involves computation migration. For example, to perform a remote look-up operation on a distributed hash table, it is typically more efficient to migrate the operation to the processor where the bucket resides, than to fetch the data items of the bucket and perform local search. Although migrating computation saves communication overhead, each individual operation may have longer latency, since it turns shorter remote read and write operations into longer remote computation operations. The overall latency of a remote operation contains not only the network transport latency, but also the remote scheduling and computation delays. Therefore, it is essential for the runtime system to provide latency hiding mechanisms.

Operations on distributed data structures seldom have substantial local computation to hide the communication latency. For example, a hash table lookup cannot proceed locally without waiting for the reply. Therefore, the latency must be overlapped with the caller's computation, which requires breaking the traditional abstractions, since a data structure operation must return before it is complete. This is accomplished by providing *split-phase interfaces* for operations that may require communication. A split-phase operation returns after doing whatever local computation is necessary, but never waits for communication to complete. The caller is required to explicitly check for completion of the operation using other synchronization mechanisms. If the operation does not require communication, it behaves like a normal procedure call. Otherwise, it creates a separate thread of control and passes its local state to the new thread which awaits the reply from the remote processor.

Synchronization can be accomplished with continuation passing, which explicitly passes the continuation thread handle to the remote processor, or with synchronization data structures such as *counter*. A counter maintains a list of threads waiting for the counter to exceed certain values. Upon completion, a split-phase operation increments the counter, which starts all threads that become eligible for execution after the increment. Counters are usually used to synchronize threads that pipeline multiple operations, where the issuing threads need to know if some number of operations have taken effect on the data structure.

Multipol supports a simple thread system which requires the programmer to specify what local state to save. The programmer can use knowledge of the data structures or the application to reduce the state saving overhead. Without knowledge from the compiler or the programmer, the runtime system would have to make conservative assumptions and save the entire processor state and the stack frame.

2.2   Invoking Remote Computation

Communication layers such as active messages [8] provide mechanisms for implementing computation migration. Direct use of active messages as remote request handlers, however, presents three major problems for implementing general data structures other than simple memory cells:

- Most active message layers either assume a fixed number of arguments (e.g., 4 words [8, 9]), whose size is tailored to the network packet size, or require the programmer to pre-allocate remote memory for holding arguments [10]. The lack of flexibility makes it difficult to express dynamic communication patterns.

- Because active messages do not implement any flow control, they usually require the programmer to follow a request/reply protocol to avoid network level deadlock. For example, request handlers can only send reply messages, which severely restricts the code that can run as a handler. The protocol causes problems for data structures which may need to re-migrate computation, such as hash table lookups that require re-hashing.

- Active message handlers may execute whenever the network is serviced (by polling or interrupt). Therefore, a local thread loses atomicity whenever the network is touched. To guarantee atomicity, the programmer must either explicitly lock all data structures touched by the thread, which is overly general for short operations, or disable interrupt and polling. Disabling network service may cause congestion. It is also hard to enforce when modules or data structures are composed in a program that has no knowledge of their implementations. Finally, the programmer has no control over how the operations are scheduled (they always execute upon reception).

In our experience, asynchronous applications require higher level programming abstractions than a SPMD model (one thread per processor) with active messages. The Multipol runtime system provides *atomic threads* as the basic programming abstraction, and unlike active message handlers, messages from the network can be accepted without affecting atomicity. Atomic threads run to completion without preemption or suspension. Except for a non-blocking restriction, which forbids the atomic threads from spinning on a condition and requires that each thread terminates in finite time, they are completely general computation constructs and can be created by remote processors. We use atomic threads as building blocks for higher-level programming constructs in Multipol data structures as well as applications. A restricted subset of active messages are used by the runtime system to send data over the network or to create remote atomic threads. Above the runtime level, all communication is done using the runtime system primitives, and not through direct access to active messages or other message layers.

The overhead of scheduling and thread management can be reduced when lack of atomicity does not affect the correctness of the program. For such applications, the programmer can use a preemptive scheduler (see Section 3) for selected threads. Such threads may preempt the running computation when the network is serviced.

3 SCHEDULING

There are many applications where the scheduling policy has a significant impact on performance. In the Gröbner basis application, for example, there are two types of tasks, one of which must be scheduled at a higher priority to keep the memory utilization and total work low [4]. In this discussion, we use Parswec, a speculative timing simulator [11] and Tripuzzle, a state space search program that counts the number of unique solutions for the tripuzzle problem [12].

In Parswec, a digital circuit is decomposed into subcircuits that are distributed among the processors, and the simulation proceeds speculatively using an algorithm similar to Timewarp [13]. A separate thread is created for each subcircuit to simulate its state. These threads are ready to start any time (subject to storage constraints), since they can speculate on the input values. However, some threads are more likely to lead to redundant work than others. Therefore, it is imperative to give higher priorities to threads that are more likely to be useful work. Also, the thread scheduling priorities must change as the simulation progresses. For example, a subcircuit that is rolled-back in time due to incorrect speculation should be given higher priority to avoid an avalanche of roll-backs. If these scheduling policies are not properly enforced, the overall running time can easily increase by more than two-fold. Therefore, applications such as Parswec not only require sophisticated control over scheduling, but also require access to the scheduler's data structure.

In contrast, in the Tripuzzle application a simple scheduling policy is sufficient, and being less complicated, it has lower scheduling overhead. The performance of Tripuzzle improves by 20% to 30% if we use a cheap scheduler that sacrifices atomicity with respect to the hash table operations, which is not required by Tripuzzle.

To accommodate application-specific scheduling policies, our runtime system allows the programmer to use customized schedulers, which are data structures with two operations: *deposit* and *select*. When a thread is ready for execution, the runtime system invokes the designated *deposit* operation to store the thread in the scheduler's internal data structure. The programmer also registers the *select* operation with the runtime system, which periodically executes the operation to choose the next thread to dispatch. In addition to the user-written schedulers, Multipol also provides common schedulers such as a FIFO and a priority queue.

Separating out schedulers as independent data structures also eases performance tuning, because scheduling decisions are localized to the implementation of the schedulers. Scheduling decisions are some of the hardest design decisions to make in advance, and by separating the scheduling abstraction we allow application programmers to select a scheduler or write their own very late in the development process. The runtime system guarantees that each registered deposit operation is executed exactly once within finite time of being registered, and the frequency of call can be configured by the programmer. The scheduling of different modules or data structures can then be tuned separately without affecting other parts of the program.

4 LOAD BALANCE

Many irregular applications can be naturally decomposed into parallel tasks. These applications include the phylogeny problem [3], which uses a parallel branch and bound algorithm to search for the largest character subset that forms a perfect phylogeny tree, a divide-and-conquer eigenvalue algorithm, and the Gröbner basis problem, which reduces sets of polynomials in parallel with respect to a growing basis.

Runtime systems such as Cilk [12] adopt a built-in load balancer and treat threads not only as a latency-hiding mechanism, but also as units of load balance which can be migrated freely. This approach suffers the same problem as providing fixed scheduling policies – different applications require different load balancing policies. For example, the phylogeny program observes a 5-fold increase in running time if tasks are migrated randomly for load balance. The significant increase in running time is due to the loss of locality, which is important for effective pruning of the search space. There are also applications where the loss of locality incurs additional communication overhead.

It is infeasible to build a general load balancer in the runtime system, since it is very difficult to predict the impact of locality on performance. We separate out load balancing policies from the Multipol runtime system and put the functionality in data structures such as a distributed task queue [14]. The programmer can then select different data structures or implement new ones to tailor the load balancing policy to a particular application. Furthermore, Multipol threads do not migrate, because they are used only for latency hiding or message aggregation (described in the next section).

5 EFFICIENT COMMUNICATION

Besides the thread system, the Multipol runtime system also provides a communication layer that is portable across a variety of distributed memory architectures. Two types of communication are supported: bulk-synchronous and asynchronous. The bulk synchronous communication primitives include *put* and *get* operations, which are split-phase versions of remote read and write. Asynchronous communication primitives include *remote threads*, which start a thread on a remote processor with a variable number of arguments, and *store*, which is similar to remote threads except that it requires the user to pre-allocate buffer space for holding the arguments.

Many irregular applications have unknown numbers of concurrent operations, each taking some arbitrary number of arguments. Such communication patterns have low bandwidth characteristics on distributed memory architectures, which perform better for pre-allocated or large messages. The Multipol runtime system dynamically aggregates small, asynchronous messages to improve communication performance. For example, asynchronous remote thread calls are copied into a message buffer, which is sent to the destination processor in bulk when the accumulated size exceeds a certain threshold, or when the local processor runs out of work. The extent of aggregation depends on the available concurrency in the application. To allow more aggregation, the application may need to increase its level of multithreading beyond what is sufficient for latency hiding.

Message aggregation amortizes the communication startup overhead over large volumes of data. However, it introduces copying overhead, and increases the latency of remote operations. Increase in the latency may increase idle time because of the additional delay in synchronization, which is demonstrated by Tripuzzle (Figure 2). Tripuzzle enumerates the states in the state space, and its execution consists of constructing a series of hash tables that record all the possible states of a particular depth. The results showed that aggregating up to 4K bytes improves performance due to the sharp reduction in the number of physical messages. However, the benefit is offset by the increase in idle time, when the processors wait for all updates to a hash table to complete. The tradeoff results in a optimal aggregation size at about 4K byes.

The increase in latency may also generate more redundant work for speculatively parallel applications such as Parswec, which is illustrated in Figure 3. Figure 3 shows that a moderate aggregation size (1K bytes) reduces the running time by more than 20% due to the reduction in the number of physical messages. However, the running

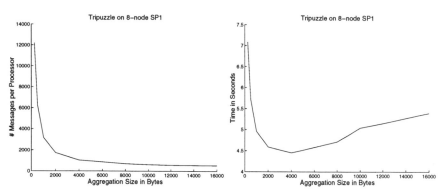

Figure 2 Effect of aggregation on Tripuzzle. The running time of Tripuzzle first decreases due to better communication efficiency, and then increases due to synchronization delay.

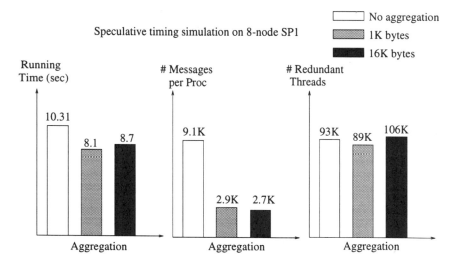

Figure 3 Effect of aggregation on Parswec. The running time of Parswec first decreases due to better communication efficiency, and then increases due to redundant work.

time increases by 7% when the aggregation size changes from 1K bytes to 16K bytes due to a proportional increase in redundant work.

6 RELATED WORK

Past research has produced a variety of runtime systems such as TAM [6], the Chare kernel [15] Cilk [12], and Nexus [7]. TAM threads are similar in spirit to the Multipol atomic threads in that they are used to hide latency. However, since TAM is designed as a compilation target, the threads are statically allocated within the scope of an activation frame, and a fixed scheduling policy is used to maintain locality of threads in the same frame. The threads in Cilk are also atomic, but unlike the Multipol threads, they can be migrated for load balance. Both Cilk and Chare kernel have built-in load balancers. Nexus is designed to support heterogeneous computing, and is built on top of standard thread packages, which are more heavy weight. TAM and Cilk programs are synchronized in a data-flow fashion, while most Multipol programs communicate and synchronize via shared data structures. PARTI [5] performs runtime message aggregation, but it does not handle dynamic communication patterns where runtime preprocessing techniques cannot be applied. We have not found any runtime system that allows customized schedulers, or performs dynamic message aggregation.

7 CONCLUSIONS AND CURRENT STATUS

The design of the Multipol runtime system is motivated by our experiences in parallelizing irregular applications. Specifically, we have identified the following important features:

- Split-phase interfaces for latency hiding.

- Atomic threads as the basic programming abstraction.

- Customized schedulers for application-specific scheduling.

- Dynamic message aggregation for better communication performance.

Currently, the runtime system exists for CM5, Paragon, and SP1. Ports to network of workstations and tools for performance tuning are currently being developed.

Acknowledgements

This work was supported in part by the Advanced Research Projects Agency of the Department of Defense monitored by the Office of Naval Research under contract DABT63-92-C-0026, by the Department of Energy grant DE-FG03-94ER25206, by the National Science Foundation Grants CCR-9210260 and CDA-8722788, The information presented here does not necessarily reflect the position or the policy of the Government and no official endorsement should be inferred.

REFERENCES

[1] Chih-Po Wen and Katherine Yelick. Portable parallel asynchronous simulation on distributed memory architectures. In *Internation Conference on Parallel Processing*, 1995. To appear.

[2] Soumen Chakrabarti and Abhiram Ranade and Katherine Yelick Randomized Load Balancing for Tree Structured Computation In *IEEE Scalable High Performance Computing Conference*, 1995.

[3] Jeff Jones. Exploiting parallelism in the perfect phylogeny computation. Master's thesis (TR-95-869), University of California, Berkeley, Computer Science Division, December 1994.

[4] Soumen Chakrabarti and Katherine Yelick. Distributed data structures and algorithms for Gröbner basis computation. *Lisp and Symbolic Computation*, 1994.

[5] H. Berryman, J. Saltz, and J. Scroggs. Execution time support for adaptive scientific algorithms on distributed memory multiprocessors. *Concurrency: Practice and Experience*, pages 159–178, June 1991.

[6] D. Culler, A. Sah, K. Schauser, T. von Eicken, and J. Wawrzynek. Fine-grain parallelism with minimal hardware support: A compiler-controlled threaded abstract machine. In *Proc. of 4th Int. Conf. on Architectural Support for Programming Languages and Operating Systems*, Santa-Clara, CA, April 1991.

[7] Ian Foster, Carl Kesselman, Robert Olson, and Steve Tuccke. Nexus: An interoperability toolkit for parallel and distributed computer systems. Technical Report ANL/MCS-TM-189, Argonne National Laboratory, 1991.

[8] Thorsten von Eicken, David E. Culler, Seth Copen Goldstein, and Klaus Erik Schauser. Active messages: a mechanism for integrated communication and computation. In *International Symposium on Computer Architecture*, 1992.

[9] Eric A. Brewer and Robert D. Blumofe. Strata: A multi-layer communication library. To appear as a MIT Technical Report, February 1994.

[10] David Culler, Kim Keeton, Lok Tim Liu, Alan Mainwaring, Rich Martin, Steve Rodrigues, and Kristin Wright. The generic active message interface specification. Unpublished, 1994.

[11] Chih-Po Wen and Katherine Yelick. Parallel timing simulation on a distributed memory multiprocessor. In *International Conference on CAD*, Santa Clara, CA, November 1993. An earlier version appeared as UCB Technical Report CSD-93-723.

[12] Robert D. Blumofe, Christopher F. Joerg, Bradley C. Kuszmaul, Charles E. Leiserson, Keith H. Randall, and Yuli Zhou. Cilk: An efficient multithreaded runtime system. In *Principles and Practice of Parallel Programming*, 1995.

[13] D.R. Jefferson. Virtual time. *ACM Transactions on Programming Languages and Systems*, 7(3), July 1985.

[14] Chih-Po Wen. The distributed task queue user's guide. Unpublished, 1994.

[15] Wei Shu and L.V. Kalé. Chare kernel – a runtime support system for parallel computations. *Journal of Parallel and Distributed Computing*, 11:198–211, 1991.

USER DEFINED COMPILER SUPPORT FOR CONSTRUCTING DISTRIBUTED ARRAYS

Matt Rosing

Pacific Northwest Laboratory
m_rosing@pnl.gov

ABSTRACT

This paper describes a preprocessor developed for supporting distributed arrays on parallel machines. The goal is to support Fortran90 like array operations on arrays that have been distributed using general, user defined mappings. To support both general mapping functions and efficient implementation of array operations, the user programs applications at two distinct levels. There is both a high level view where the programmer does most of the programming, and a low level where the user defines how the high level code is to be implemented on a specific target machine. The key to generating efficient runtime code while keeping flexible support for different types of data distributions is to incorporate the low level code into the high level code at compile time. This paper describes the operations performed by the preprocessor and how the user defines mapping functions.

1 INTRODUCTION

This paper describes a preprocessor developed for supporting distributed arrays on parallel machines. The goal is to support Fortran90 like array operations on arrays that have been distributed using general, user defined mappings. These mappings are much more general than typical distributions, such as block and cyclic, yet are still efficiently implemented. To support both general mapping functions and efficient implementation of array operations, the user programs applications at two distinct levels. There is both a high level view where the programmer does most of the programming, and a low level where the user defines how the high level code is to be implemented on a specific target machine. Thus, the low level view is a description of how the preprocessor will translate high level array constructs into code that is efficiently executed on the target machine. The main emphasis of this work is to support user defined translations of array constructs, and have considerable flexibility in specifying these transformations.

Furthermore, the resulting code should run efficiently on a wide range of parallel machines.

In the high level view, arrays are viewed as large global objects that reside in a flat memory. Operations on arrays include typical Fortran90 array operations, dynamic allocation of arrays, the Fortran90 where clause, CM-Fortran index shifting, and a construct similar to the HPF forall [4].

In the low level view, a NUMA memory hierarchy is assumed and the programmer must specify address translation, communication, and how to iterate through the local part of a distributed array. These low level details are associated with each distributed array in the form of a "mapping function". A mapping function is a user defined type and is associated with each array. In this manner, mapping functions and arrays are similar to objects in object oriented languages.

The key to generating efficient runtime code while keeping flexible support for different types of data distributions is to incorporate the low level code into the high level code at compile time. At compile time there is relatively little need for efficient execution and the typical tradeoff between flexibility and efficiency found in many runtime systems is of little concern. At this time, the compiler can interpret a rich set of commands and generate code that runs efficiently. An example is a parameter describing how to translate global addresses into local addresses. If this is done at run time then flexibility is added at the expense of efficiency. By using a preprocessor, however, the interpretation is done at compile time and the added flexibility does not result in less efficient code.

This technique of having the user specify compile time operations for implementing distributed arrays is the basis for how mapping functions are used to translate high level code. A mapping function consists of code fragments that describe how to implement various aspects of the high level model. For example, expressions can be specified that translate global, high level indices, into local, low level indices. The preprocessor operates by replacing such high level constructs by the code fragments specified in the mapping function. The fragments can, in turn, generate code based on the high level code being replaced and other static information about the distributed array. Other types of fragments and the way in which they generate code are described in Section 3.

There are several goals in this project that are driven by the needs of our users. The first of these is to support a wide range of data distributions. For example, many languages that have been developed for supporting distributed data structures have fairly limited data distributions. These are primarily based on operators such as block, cyclic, shift, and combinations of these. Unfortunately, for many real applications, this is limiting. One example of this is the need for having a block distribution where blocks are irregularly sized. Another example is a block distribution used on globally addressable machines like the KSR2, that puts pads on the edge of a processor's block to prevent false sharing. While this might be treated as a compiler optimization, it is fairly easy to specify within the context of the preprocessor.

Another need is to support portability of the high level code across many machines. This is a natural consequence of breaking the code into both a high and low level. An example of how this has been achieved is that we have easily ported code originally written for the CM-5 to both a KSR-2, a shared memory machine, and networks of workstations by only modifying 100 lines of code. Both versions use the native hardware very efficiently and the same 100 lines of code have also been used to translate other programs. This is considerably easier than rewriting the CM-Fortran compiler and also allows us to add support for features not available in CM-Fortran.

This multi level approach also supports another user need, namely extensibility. By giving the user full control over the translation, the user can define a wider range of data distributions. Complete control also implies that the system is not hiding the low level details, but is helping the user manage these details. This has the advantage that the user has control over the code generated, yet is not mired in implementation details.

Section 2 of this paper describes the language for the high level constructs. Section 3 describes the low level constructs and the basic operation of the preprocessor. Section 4 describes related work and Section 5 is the conclusion.

2 HIGH LEVEL CONSTRUCTS

The high level view is derived from a subset of CM-Fortran but differs in many important aspects. Instead of being a data parallel SIMD model, it follows a MIMD model that is intended to be loosely synchronous. Within this model the number of processes is fixed at the time the program is executed, and all variables that are not distributed arrays are replicated on every node. The major difference between the high level model and a language such as CM-Fortran is that the distribution of arrays is defined by the user.

The syntax for declaring a distributed array is

```
DARRAY( [Dims,] [Dynamic,] [Mapping]) decl block
   array-decls
   endblock
```

where DARRAY, decl, block, and endblock are keywords. Dims is an optional integer specifying the number of dimensions if the array is to be dynamically allocated, and Dynamic is an optional keyword indicating that the array is dynamic. Mapping is an optional identifier that corresponds to a previously declared mapping function. Mapping functions are described in Section 3. Between the keywords block and endblock is a list of normal fortran array declarations. All of these arrays will be distributed using the mapping function specified. If the array is to be dynamically allocated then the dimension information in the declaration is not required and will be ignored. An example of declaring distributed arrays is

```
DARRAY( news) block
   integer mask(-1:nx+2, -1:ny+2)
```

```
real A(-1:nx+2, -1:ny+2)
real B(-1:nx+2, -1:ny+2)
endblock
```

Operations on darrays include scalar access, and array operations. Scalar access is specified the same as in Fortran, the name of the array followed by a list of indices. Array operations include Fortran90 like array operations using triplet notation or operations on entire arrays. There is also support for the Fortran90 `where` clause, the CM-Fortran `shift` operator, and a modified version of the HPF `forall` construct. To support dynamic arrays, the Fortran90 `allocate` and `deallocate` constructs are also supported. There is also support for intrinsics that operate on arrays including `max`, `min`, and `abs`. There is support for doing I/O on subranges of distributed arrays but this is limited to having at most one array per record.

The `where` clause is nearly identical to the fortran90 `where` construct except that any statement can be within the body as opposed to only assignment statements. This includes other `where` and `forall` statements. The `forall` clause can also operate over any statement but there are further differences. Instead of specifying a list of indices and ranges, a section of some array is specified, along with expressions that are used to replace the index expressions within arrays that the `forall` statement will operate over. Furthermore, within the body of the `forall`, triplet notation is used to specify the ranges to be operated on. This has been done to simplify the translation process and appears to be as flexible as the `forall` statement found in HPF. An example of a `forall` statement is

```
forall( A(:,:), ix,jx)
  sum = sum + A(:,:)
  maxval = max( A(:,:), B( :,:))
endforall
```

Another difference between high level programs using this tool and that of languages such as fortran90 is that the preprocessor will not insert temporary arrays to follow the usual array semantics found in fortran90. The result of this is that users should not write statements of the form

```
A(2:N) = A(1:N-1)
```

but should instead write

```
temp(2:N) = A(1:N-1)
A(2:N) = temp(2:N)
```

This is an example of the tradeoff between using a compiler with a fixed set of distributions that might be able to hide the details of how this should be translated, and a preprocessor that helps the user manage details but does not recognize these problems.

3 MAPPING FUNCTIONS

The low level view of array operations is described within the mapping function. The mapping function contains both declarations and code fragments that are used to translate code written at the higher level. Just for nomenclature, the combination of declarations and code fragments are called translation fragments.

Translation fragments are used by the preprocessor to modify the high level program in the following manner. Each translation fragment is one of a fixed type. Each type corresponds to some high level construct found in the main part of the program. For each high level construct corresponding to a translation fragment, it is replaced by the code specified in a fragment. The actual translation fragment used depends on the array that is associated with the high level construct.

In order to make this process of transforming the high level code viable, the translation fragment needs to make use of various types of information found in the high level code. As an example, when translating indices, the new expression will probably be a function of the global index. To support this, there are different compile time functions that a translation fragment can call to get information about the associated array and how it is used. These functions return code fragments and are described in Section 3.1.

A mapping function, syntactically, is of the form

```
MAP name block
    translation-fragments
    end block
```

`MAP`, `block`, and `endblock` are keywords, `name` is the name of the resulting mapping function, and everything between the `block` and `endblock` define the translations fragments.

Translation fragments belong to one of three categories. This includes declaration and initialization, array element access, and I/O. A summary of the functions is given in Table 1.

Within the first category, there are two types of declarations associated with a mapping function. The first is the declaration of the physical array, given a logical array. For example, on a distributed memory machine, the physical array will probably be declared smaller than the logical array, as only part of the array is mapped onto each processor. This mapping is done via a translation fragment called `Declare`. The general form of this specification is

```
Declare ( listof expression)
```

This fragment takes a list of expressions as parameters and each parameter corresponds to the eventual size of each dimension of the physical array. The parameter can be a function of the sizes of the logical array, via the `Size(i)` function, where `i` is the number of the dimension of interest. The function `Size` is an example of

Translation Fragments	High Level Construct Replaced
LocalAddress	Scalar index translation
\<declarations\>	Variables local to an array
Initialize	Initialization code
Declare	Array size translation
LocalIterator	Array statement, where, and forall translation
IoRead	Read statement translation
IoWrite	Write statement translation
ReadArray	Code associated with every read
WriteArray	Code associated with every write
ReadArrayBlock	Code associated with unique reads
WriteArrayBlock	Code associated with unique writes

Table 1   Translation fragments and the high level constructs they replace.

how translation fragments can make use of the high level constructs being translated. Table 2 in Section 3.1 briefly describes other types of information that can be accessed.

An example of how to declare an array mapped by panels might use

```
MAP panel block
    Declare( Size(1), Size(2)/NPROCS + 2)
    endblock
```

The extra elements in the second dimension are used to specify one column of ghost cells on either side of each panel. Then, a global declaration of

```
DARRAY(panel) decl block
    real A(100,100)
    endblock
```

would be translated into the declaration

```
    real A(100, 100/NPROCS+2)
```

Obviously, more complex expressions involving runtime variables and functions can be used if the array is dynamically allocated. In such a case, the preprocessor different data structures are declared and the array is allocated off of a heap managed by the preprocessor.

The second type of declaration is used to create variables that are useful in the support of other aspects of the mapping function. These variables are declared at the top of a mapping function much like variables are declared at the top of a normal function. For each instantiation of a mapping function, each such variable is given a unique name. This is similar to private variables in object oriented languages. An example of the mapping function that contains the `Declare` fragment and declaration of local variables is

```
ADT MAP panel block
    integer offset
    Declare( Size(1), Size(2)/NPROCS + 2)
    end block
```

A mapping function can also specify a set of statements, associated with the distributed array, that are to be run before any other statements in a procedure. Typically this is used to initialize any variables associated with the array. This is done with the `Initialize` translation fragment. An example of this is

```
Initialize block
    offset = -mynode()*(Size(2)/NPROCS)
    endblock
```

The next classification of translation fragments is used to translate array element access. Of these, there is support for accessing a single element at a time, and support for array operations. To support scalar element access of distributed arrays there needs to be support for translating global indices into local indices. This is done similarly to how declarations are translated. A translation fragment called `LocalAddress` is called with a set of expressions. Each expression, after it is evaluated, is used as an index into the physical array. The expression can be a function of the global array size, any local variable associated with the array, or the logical indices provided in the high level computation (using the `Index` function). As an example, if the translation is

```
LocalAddress( Index(1), Index(2)-offset),
```

and the high level code contains a reference such as A(i, j), then this would be translated into

```
A(i,j-offset_1)
```

where `offset` is declared to be a local variable in the mapping function. The number appended to the name of `offset` is generated by the preprocessor to ensure uniqueness of the variable and will vary depending on the total number of private variables and distributed arrays.

This ability to specify the translation of indices makes it possible to specify general mapping functions and does not limit the user to a fixed set of mappings. Not only can more general mappings be defined, but other abstractions can also be supported, such as generating lower or upper triangular arrays. Because these translations are implemented in the preprocessor, the resulting code is as efficient as if it were hand coded.

3.1 Compiler Functions Accessible to Translation Fragments

As translation fragments are used by the preprocessor to replace high level constructs in the user's code, there needs to be a mechanism to access information about the high level code. This method of parameterization adds flexibility to how code is generated. To further increase flexibility, there also needs to be mechanisms for doing such things as conditional code generation. This flexibility is provided through a set of compile time functions that can be called from translation fragments. Table 2 summarizes these fragments.

The first set of fragments, `Size`, `ArrayType`, `ArrayName`, and `IsParam` generate code based on static information about the associated array. `Size` returns the declared size of the dimension specified in the parameter. `ArrayType` returns an integer indicating the type of the array. This is one of TYPEINT, TYPEREAL, TYPEDOUBLE, etc. `ArrayName` returns the name of the array. `IsParam` returns a boolean indicating whether the array is declared as a parameter.

The next set of functions return dynamic information about how the array is being accessed. This includes the expression of a specified dimension, `Index`, triplet information `IndexLo` and `IndexHi`, and whether a dimension is accessed as a scalar value or a triplet operator, `IsRange`. It is also possible to get unit and format information from an IO read or write statement using `IoControl`. One obvious compiler function that is missing from this is one that returns the third, or stride value, in a triplet operator. This will be added in a future version of the preprocessor.

The next set of functions are used when translating array statements and are described in Section 3.2. Finally, there is a control function used for optionally generating code. An example of using the `CIF` function is

```
CIF( IsParam .eq.  0) block
    call init_array( ArrayName, Size(1), Size(2))
    endblock
```

Where this construct is invoked, the call to `init_array` would be generated if the array is not a parameter to the enclosing routine.

3.2 Array Statement Translation

The next type of abstraction supported is for translating array operations. An array operation is specified, at the high level, using Fortran90 like array operations, possibly in conjunction with the `where` statement, `forall` statement, and the `shift` operator. The preprocessor takes statements involving arrays and translates them using the translation fragment `LocalIterator`, associated with the mapping function of one of the arrays. The array that drives the translation is the left most array in an array assignment, or the array specified in the outermost `where` or `forall` construct.

Compiler Function	Return Fragment
Size(i)	The global declared size of dimension i
ArrayType	Enumerated type of declared array
ArrayName	Name of array
IsParam	Whether the array is a parameter
Index(i)	Scalar expression of dimension i
IndexLo(i)	Low value of triplet operator
IndexHi(i)	Hi value of triplet operator
IsRange(i)	Whether dimension i is a range or scalar
IoControl	Unit and format from IO
Body	Body of array statement
PlaceRead	Code associated with every read
PlaceWrite	Code associated with every write
PlaceReadBlock	Code associated with unique reads
PlaceWriteBlock	Code associated with unique writes
CIF	Compile time if statement

Table 2   Compiler functions callable from within translation fragments.

It is important to note that the translation of statements containing array operations is done at the statement level, and not at the array operation level. At this level it is possible to generate more efficient code than working on each array operation independently. For example, there is no need to generate temporary arrays, and intermediate values can be stored in registers instead of put back in memory. Operating at this level is challenging as it requires a very flexible abstraction that can operate on an entire statement, as opposed to one operator. At the same time it is desirable to give a large degree of flexibility in specifying synchronization, communication, and how to iterate over an array.

There are several assumptions that have been made in the construction of the preprocessor related to the translation of array operations. While it is not required that the user follow these as concrete rules, they define the practical limit of the tool. The first assumption is that all arrays in a statement have similar distributions. They do not have to be identical bu the closer they are the easier it will be to generate code. Thus, it will be fairly easy to generate code for matrices distributed by, say, columns. On the other hand, operations on matrices distributed by blocks of columns and matrices having a block cyclic distribution of rows will be difficult, if not impossible, to implement. A compiler working with a fixed set of distributions will also have problems with such nonconforming distributions, so it is not clear that hiding such details from the user is always beneficial.

The next assumption is that all data operated on is within the arrays specified in the array statements. In other words, there must be room, usually in the form of ghost cells in each array ro any remote data that is operated on and remote values can not be operated on from temporary buffers. Therefore, communication before or after any computation will update these "ghost cells". In the future, this limitation will be removed.

The translation of array statements is handled in the same manner as the translation of other high level fragments, the array statement is replaced by a list of statements specified in the mapping function. The same construct used to translate an array statement is also used to translate the `where` and `forall` constructs, and this use is described in Section 3.3. The statement list used to replace the array assignment, `where`, or `forall` constructs is defined in the `LocalIterator` translation fragment.

The translation of array statements can be decomposed into a set of issues that are described here. The first is to specify, for each array in the statement, what data is to be operated on. In the current version of the preprocessor, this must be the array being accessed. As described above, this limitation will be removed and it will be possible to specify a temporary buffer.

The next issue is the specification of the loops that iterate over the data. There should be one loop for each non-scalar dimension to be iterated over. The bounds on each loop is derived from the distribution of the "controlling" array, as described above. It may be unknown, at the declaration of the mapping function, which dimensions of an array might be non scalar. In such a case, the loops can be built using the conditional if (`CIF`) statement and the `IsRange` compiler function.

The next issue is the specification of the loop body. The general form of the loop body is derived from the array statement, but the placement of the body within the loop nest and the construction of the indices for each array is controlled by the mapping function. The placement of the loop body is specified by a call to the `Body` compiler function. The `Body` function takes, as parameters, a list of expressions that are used to translate range indices. The generation of indices is the next issue.

The generation of indices is done for each dimension of each array. If the index is a scalar index then it is replaced by the corresponding expression in the `LocalAddress` fragment associated with the array. If the index specifies a range then the index is replaced by one of the parameters to the `Body` function call. The parameter selected is chosen based on the controlling array; the nth non-scalar dimension will be replaced by the expression corresponding to the nth non-scalar dimension of the controlling array. This complexity ensures that, for example, the statement

```
A(i,:)  = x(:)
```

is easity translated in a manner that sets row i of A to x.

It should be noted that the parameters to the `Body` function can contain calls to other compiler functions, like expressions in the `LocalAddress` function used to translate indices. These functions are evaluated in the context of the array being operated on and add flexibility to how array statements can be translated. For example, a call to `Body` of the form

```
Body(ix+IndexLo(1)-off1, jx+IndexLo(2)-off2)
```

when applied to the statement

```
A(p:q,:)  = B(:,m:n)
```

might generate the code

```
A(ix+p-off1_1,jx+1-off2_2) =
          x(ix+1-off1_3,jx+m-off2_4)
```

In this example, the loop variables `ix`, and `jx` are indices that iterate over the elements operated on, and the terms `IndexLo(1)-off1`, and `IndexLo(2)-off2` represent the start of each segment on each processor.

The final issue involved in the translation of array statements is the generation of communication. The specification of communication involves two parts. The first is the specification of what code is generated. The second is the specification of where the code is placed within the `LocalIterator` fragment. Both of these specifications are further split into two cases to increase the flexibility in what code can be generated. In the first case code can be generated and placed for every read and write of an array in an array statement, `where` or `forall` clause. In the second case, a single block of code can be generated for each array, irrespective of the number of times it is accessed. The first case is used to collect information about individual elements to be accessed and the second is used to combine information from the first case and generate the communication. The first case might be skipped it is easier to generate communication for every element that can be potentially accessed. Furthermore, it could be the only communication code if message latency is sufficiently low.

There are two translation fragments used to generate statements for each array access in the statements translated by the `LocalIterator` fragment. These include `ReadArray` and `WriteArray`. For each read (write) of an array, the statement list defined in `ReadArray` (`WriteArray`) will be generated based on the mapping function of the array being read (written). This code can be placed in the code defined in `LocalIterator` with a call to the `PlaceRead` (`PlaceWrite`) compiler function. Analogous fragments and functions can be defined for unique access with `ReadArrayBlock`, `WriteArrayBlock`, `PlaceReadBlock`, and `PlaceWriteBlock`.

An example of translating an array using the panel mapping described above is now given. This mapping function makes the simplifying assumption that all arrays in an array statement have the same distribution and that all arrays in the array statement specify, relative to the start of the array, the same data. Furthermore, communication is generated for each write to update ghost cells on neighboring nodes. The code to translate array operations is

```
LocalIterator block
  jlo = max(2,IndexLo(2)+offset)
  jhi = min(Size(2)/NPROCS-1,IndexHi(2)+offset)
  do jx= jlo, jhi
    do ix= IndexLo(1), IndexHi(1)
      Body(ix,jx)
      enddo
    enddo
  PlaceWriteBlock
  endblock
WriteBlock block
  CIF( ArrayType .eq.  REALTYPE) block
    call update_border_real( ArrayName)
    endblock
  CIF( ArrayType .eq.  INTTYPE) block
    call update_border_int( ArrayName)
    endblock
  endblock
```

In this example, jlo and jhi are set to the low and high indices along the second dimension of the data that the executing processor is responsible for iterating over. This is a function of the compiler functions IndexLo and IndexHi, functions that return the low and high expressions from the triplet notation, respectively. These indices are translated from the global reference to a local reference by the summation with offset. The min and max functions assure that, in the case of a subrange, a processor only iterates over data within a subrange. The do-loops following this initialization execute over the appropriate bounds. Within the do-loops, there is a call to the Body compiler function to place the loop body within the loop nest. Finally, communications for all writes are placed after the loops with the PlaceWriteBlock compiler function. The WriteBlock definition generates a call to a function, based on the type of each array being written.

Thus, the full translation of the array operation

```
A = shift(B+C,2,-1)
```

is translated, using the above mapping function, into

```
jlo = max(2,1+offset)
jhi = min(100/NPROCS-1,100+offset)
do jx= jlo, jhi
  do ix= 1, 100
    A(ix,jx) = B( ix, jx-1) + C(ix,jx-1)
    enddo
```

```
      enddo
   call update_border_real( A)
```

3.3   Where and Forall Translation

The translation of the where clause is automatically handled by the preprocessor
and uses the same mapping function constructs as the translation for array assignment
statements. The LocalIterator function is used to replace the entire where
clause. In this case the Body compiler function returns a conditional statement that
in turn contains all of the statements within the where clause. Thus the high level
program, using the above LocalIterator,

```
   where( B .neq.  0)
     A = A/B
   elsewhere
     A = C
   endwhere
```

would be translated into

```
   jlo = max(2,1+offset)
   jhi = min(100/NPROCS-1,100+offset)
   do jx= jlo, jhi
     do ix= 1, 100
       if( B(ix,jx) .neq.  0) then
         A(ix,jx) = A(ix,jx)/B(ix,jx)
       else
         A(ix,jx) = C(ix,jx)
       endif
     enddo
   enddo
   call update_border_real( A)
```

The translation of the forall construct is similar except that the Body function does
not generate conditional statements. In the case of where statements being nested,
only the outermost one will be translated using the LocalIterator translation
fragment. All others will be replaced by the corresponding if statements. All nested
forall statements are expanded but the indices of an outer forall can not be
used within a nested forall.

3.4   I/O

Fortran read and write statements can operate on arrays in the high level program.
However, to simplify the preprocessor, a read or write statement can only operate on
a single array. To translate these statements in the high level code, the two translation

fragments `IoRead` and `IoWrite` can be used. Within these fragments, all of the static and dynamic compiler functions (the first two sets of functions in Table 2) can be called. This includes the function `IoControl`, which returns unit and format information.

3.5   Miscellaneous Constructs

There are a few constructs added to the preprocessor that are neither translation fragments or compiler functions. The first of these allows the user to replace, in the high level code, the mapping function used. The name of the construct is `Use` and specifies a mapping function name along with a list of statements. The list of statements are then translated using the specified mapping function. An example of this construct is

```
Use( newsNoComm) block
  mask = 0
  mask( -2:0, :  )  = 1
  mask( n+1:n+2, :  )  = 1
  mask( :, -2:0 ) = 1
  mask( :, n+1:n+2 ) = 1
  endblock
```

In this example, all of the array operations are implemented based on the mapping function `newsNoComm`. This is an example of tuning the high level code.

Within high level code, a program can also specify a variable that has been declared to be local to a specific distributed array. This is done with the `LocalVar` function. This function takes two parameters, the first is the array name and the second is the name of the variable specified in the mapping function. This compiler function generates the name of the variable associated with the distributed array.

The last two constructs are used to insert declarations and statements within routines. The first, `DarrayRoutineHook`, inserts declarations and statements at the top of every subroutine or function that contains at least one distributed array. The second, `RoutineHook`, inserts declarations and statements at the top of every routine, and is quite similar to adding `include` statements.

4   RELATED WORK

The idea of user defined mapping functions was first discussed in [1]. These mapping functions are interpreted at run-time and therefore do not run very efficiently.

User defined mapping functions can be built with object oriented languages such as C++. For example, index translation and array size translation can be embedded within overloaded operators. The efficiency of how well index translation can be generated depends on the compiler and whether it implements inlined code. If it does not, and generates a function call for every array element access then the resulting code will be very inefficient. A bigger problem with efficiency arises with the translation of array statements. In an object oriented language, where only operators can be overloaded, the implied execution order will generate more memory accesses than probably required. For each operator there will be one memory read and write times the number of elements covered by the operator. In a system that translates entire statements, these memory accesses can be circumvented, given a reasonable number of registers.

A fixed set of mapping functions were first used in DINO [3] and Kali [2], and subsequently incorporated into many other languages, including HPF [4]. The advantage of having a fixed number of mapping functions is that a compiler can do all of the translation. With this, various optimizations can also be done, including communication placement. A compiler can also have stricter semantics that allow, for example, a SIMD model be followed. A programmable preprocessor has the advantage that there is no limitation on the types of mapping functions that can be generated. Another distinction is that a compiler is designed to hide details and a programmable preprocessor is designed to separate low level details from the high level code. This difference manifests itself in making it difficult for a programmer to understand how long it takes for a particular construct to execute. This is not an issue when the compiler generates good code but is a problem when the compiler generates poor code. This is usually due to the complexity of a construct or a failure in the optimizer to recognize a pattern.

5 CONCLUSION

A preprocessor has been built to support the implementation of user defined mapping functions with respect to array operations. This is done by allowing the user to specify, via a mapping function associated with each array, a set of code fragments that describe the translation process. A fundamental aspect of this system is that the user defines abstractions that execute at compile time, resulting in highly efficient code.

Preliminary results indicate that the tool is very flexible with respect to the types of mapping functions that can be supported. Furthermore, the addition of more flexibility will not hinder the efficiency of the resulting code. Addition of more flexibility is also quite feasible as the preprocessor is only 3500 lines long and is built on top of a programmable preprocessor.

REFERENCES

[1] Rogers, A. and Pingali, K. Process Decomposition Through Locality of Reference. *Proceedings of the SIGPLAN Conference on Programming Language Design and Implementation*, Jun 1989, pp. 69-80.

[2] Koelbel, C., Mehrotra, P., and Van Rosendale, J. Supporting Shared Data Structures on Distributed Memory Architecture. *Conf. on Principles and Practice of Parallel Processing*, Mar. 1990.

[3] Rosing, M., Schnabel, R., and Weaver, R. The DINO Parallel Programming Language. *Journal of Parallel and Distributed Computing*, Sep 1991, 13(9), pp 30-42.

[4] High Performance Fortran Forum. High Performance Fortran Language Specification. *Scientific Programming*, 2, 1993, pp 1-170.

11

COMPILING FOR MULTITHREADED MULTICOMPUTER

Balaram Sinharoy

IBM Corporation
Poughkeepsie, NY 12601
USA
balaram@vnet.ibm.com

ABSTRACT

Over the last decade processor speed has increased dramatically, whereas the speed of the memory subsystem improved at a modest rate. To balance this mismatch of speed, Multithreaded (or Multiple Context) Processors have been proposed. In this paper, we present a novel compiler optimization method to create threads suitable for Multithreaded Processors and Multicomputers based on such processors. The method is based on loop transformation theory and optimizes both spatial and temporal data reference locality. The created threads exhibit high level of intra-thread and inter-thread data locality which effectively reduces the cache miss rate and total execution time of numerically intensive computation.

1 INTRODUCTION

Most high performance multiprocessor systems are built using sophisticated microprocessor at each node of a large processor interconnection network. Most applications exhibit some amount of data sharing between the nodes in a multicomputer (also known as distributed memory multiprocessor). The scalability of a multiprocessor system is usually sublinear and the higher the data sharing among the processing nodes, the worse the scalability of the system. To cope with the sublinear scalability and still provide high performance, it is important to use the most powerful processors at each node of the multiprocessor system and take necessary steps to increase the utilization of these processors.

Recent developments in microprocessor technology have improved the processor performance by more than two orders of magnitude over the last decade. However the memory subsystem speed and the speed of the processor interconnection network did not improve nearly as fast. Not only the cycles per instruction (CPI) of the microprocessors are increasing, the processor cycle time is also improving and it is improving much faster than the memory cycle time. Recent studies show that the number of processor clock cycles required to access main memory doubles approximately every 6.2 years [4]. This divergence in the memory access latency limits the performance of each node in a multicomputer. It is not unusual to find that as much as 60% of a task's execution time is spent loading the cache, while the processors idle [9].

As the latency gap between the processor and memory cycle time continues to increase, the reliance on compiler optimization techniques will increase to alleviate the problem. Compiler optimization can help in at least three different ways.

1. *Program restructuring:* use program control flow structure (perhaps with added information from execution profiles of earlier runs), to determine code transformation that can increase the spatial and temporal locality of the program to reduce the cache miss rates [10].

2. *Software prefetching:* use data flow and control flow information to insert cache load instructions well ahead of the time when the cache line is needed [12].

3. *Multithreading:* attempt to hide the memory latency by switching, in a few processor cycles, to a new thread of execution whenever an event occurs that stalls the processor for a number of cycles (e.g., cache miss or TLB miss) [1].

Of all these methods compiler support for multithreading is the least understood, even though it does not suffer from some of the disadvantages that other methods do. Designing software prefetching algorithms with low rates of inaccurate fetches are difficult. Inaccurate fetches pollute the cache and puts unnecessary burden on the memory subsytem and the processor interconnection network, which can potentially increase both the memory access latency and communication latency in a multicomputer. For many applications, to be more accurate prefetching needs to be done close to the point of execution where it is needed. However this approach does not leave enough time for the cache line to be brought in early enough so that the processor does not stall. For prefetching algorithms to be effective the program should have predictable reference patterns that can be detected well ahead of the time when the reference is actually made.

Multithreading (or Multiple Context Processor) has been proposed in the literature to partially hide the increasingly higher memory access latency (in terms of the number of processor cycles). Multithreading is a mechanism in which states of multiple threads of execution is saved on the processor (various registers, condition codes, etc.). When one thread stalls for some reason (say cache miss, TLB miss or pipeline stall due to data or control dependency, etc.), instead of waiting for the thread to become active again, the processor switches to one of the other available threads with very little switch penalty (a few processor cycles). All the threads running on a processor share the same cache and TLB. For high efficiency, multithreading requires that a large number of threads be available at all time during execution to keep the processors busy.

Several techniques have been developed to partition the loops in a program so that each partition can run on separate processors in a multicomputer with low communication overhead [13, 5, 15]. When processors share data, data communication – an expensive step in a multicomputer – takes place and optimizing program transformations, such as data alignment, need to be performed to reduce the communication cost [16].

If the processors in a multicomputer are multithreaded, the system will be called multithreaded multicomputer (MTMC) in this paper. In an MTMC, some of the threads (or loop partitions) share the same processor. This introduces new constraints on the parallelizing compiler on how it partitions the loop nests to generate the threads, how it keeps the execution of different threads synchronized and how it helps the processor in deciding which thread to schedule next in order to reduce the congestion on the processor interconnection network.

Example 1.1 Suppose we want to execute the loop nest at the top of figure 1 on an MTMC with p processors and t threads on each processor. Figure 1 shows the t threads that are created from the loop nest for execution on processor k, where $\alpha = (k-1)N/p$ and $\beta = N/(p * t)$ (assume $p * t$ divides N). Let the execution of the innermost two loops be a *step*. Each thread evaluates a subarray of array A of size $5 \times \beta$ at each step.

Due to data dependency constraints among the threads, threads need to synchronize at the end of each step. Let the running thread be t_r and let it be data dependent on thread t_d (i.e., t_r uses data element(s) computed by t_d). When t_r finishes step n, it cannot proceed with step $n + 1$ unless t_d has finished step n. Since the threads run asynchronous of each other during the execution of a step, either of t_r or t_s can finish step n before the other. If the running thread, t_r, is blocked, it disables itself by setting a bit in the Thread Execution Mask (TEM) on the processor (subsequently t_r will be enabled by t_d when t_d finishes its step n). When t_r is disabled or when there is a thread switching event during the execution of t_r, the processor switches to an enabled thread (thread whose corresponding bit in TEM is zero) with the highest priority, if there is any.

In this implementation, threads T_1 and T_t are special. These are the only threads that cause inter-processor communication at the end of processing the innermost two loops. T_1 sends a packet to processor p_{k-1} and T_t receives a packet from processor p_{k+1}. Since these are the only threads on the processor that have data dependency on threads on a different processor, they should be given the highest priority. This allows the threads on the communicating processors to run as early as possible. It also reduces the buffer contention at the I/O ports of the communicating nodes. No other synchronization operations are needed for the execution of the loop nest and the loop nest is now optimized to run on the MTMC.   □.

The example in figure 1 elucidates various compilation issues in an MTMC. It is still important to map threads in a manner so that inter-processor communication cost is low. Since threads mapped to the same processor share the same cache and TLB, data and instruction sharing among the local threads increase the utilization of these resources. The optimum number of threads to be run on a processor depends on the data dependence vectors, cache configuration and available parallelism. Some optimization steps such as array replication and array privatization [3] are still important but in a modified form.

ORIGINAL LOOP NEST

for $i = 1, N$
    for $j = 1, 5 * N$
        $A[i, j] = A[i, j - 5] + A[i - 4, j - 6]$;
    endfor

MULTITHREADED LOOP NEST

T_l
for $1 \leq l \leq t$

for $j1 = 1, \ N$
    if ($l == t$) receive ($A[\alpha + t * \beta + 1 \ldots \alpha + (t - 1) * \beta$,
                    $(j1 - 2) * 5 + 1 \ldots (j1 - 1) * 5])$;
    for $j2 = (j1 - 1) * 5 + 1, \ j1 * 5$
        for $i = \alpha + 1 + (l - 1) * \beta, \ \alpha + l * \beta$
            $A[i, j] = A[i, j - 5] + A[i - 4, j - 6]$;
        endfor
    endfor
    if ($l == 1$) send ($A[\alpha + 1 \ldots$
                    $\alpha + \beta, \ (j1 - 1) * 5 + 1 \ldots j1 * 5])$;
    $step[l] = step[l] + 1$;
    if ($l \neq t \ \&\& \ step[l] > step[l + 1]$) disable ($T_l$);
    if ($l \neq 1$) enable (T_{l-1});
endfor

Figure 1 Partitioning of the original loop nest that are mapped onto the processor $k, 1 \leq k \leq p$, in a p processor system where each processor has t threads, T_1 to T_t.

Since the threads run asynchronously for the most part, it is important to generate synchronizing instructions, such as enable and disable threads, in a manner similar to generating send and receive primitives in a distributed memory machine. The compiler can help in reducing the network latency and I/O buffer conflict by identifying the threads that participate in inter-processor communication to the processor, for higher priority.

The paper is organized as follows. In section 2, we discuss various latency hiding techniques and their relative merits and demerits. Section 3 gives a brief overview of program transformation method. Section 4 describes the program transformation method to improve locality of reference. Algorithm to improve spatial locality is presented in subsection 4.1 and the algorithm to improve temporal locality is described in subsection 4.2.

2 LATENCY HIDING

Microprocessor speed is often measured in terms of the average number of processor cycles required to execute an instruction, known as cycles per instruction (CPI). Ignoring disk and communication network latency, CPI has two major parts: CPI_∞ (that is, CPI under the assumption that there is no TLB or Cache miss) and storage CPI (average number of cycles lost per instruction due to the processor waiting for a cache or TLB miss to be resolved). Today's high-end processors has low CPI_∞ and it is decreasing dramatically due to various innovations in the microprocessor technology. However, the storage CPI has decreased only modestly. Execution time of an application depends on the total CPI, that is, the sum of the CPI_∞ and storage CPI.

To improve the overall system speed, CPI_∞ and storage CPI need to be properly balanced. Obviously, one can always improve the bus bandwidth by increasing the bus width, number of memory ports, number of memory banks, etc. These increases the memory bandwidth, but the memory access latency does not decrease significantly. Besides, all these increases the cost of the system. To reduce the effective memory latency two major techniques has been proposed in the literature, *Prefetching* and *Multithreading*, which are discussed next.

2.1 Prefetching

Prefetching has been studied extensively in the literature [11, 14]. Prefetching is the method in which a cache line is fetched from a lower level to a higher level in the memory hierarchy, before it is needed by the processor during execution. Prefetching can be implemented through hardware (usually following a simple algorithm) or software (by inserting "prefetch" instructions appropriately in the program). Prefetching does not necessarily mean a cache hit, because the line may get evicted due to collision or cache invalidation. Beside the cache interference, prefetching can also reduces the effective memory bandwidth by prefetching lines that are never used. Alternatively, it can cause unnecessary ILP overhead when the data is actually available in the higher level. Although for many scientific computation with regular loop strides, it is possible to predict which data cache line will be needed next, in general the optimum prefetch distance depends on the dynamic behavior of the system [7] and is hard to predict by software or hardware.

2.2 Multithreading

Another approach to reduce the effective memory access latency is by saving contexts of multiple threads on the processor and switching from one thread to another in only a few cycles whenever the running thread faces a long latency event (such as cache miss or TLB miss). The concept is very similar to task switching performed by most operating systems when the running task faces a long latency operation (such as disk access, lock contention, etc.). Processors which can save contexts of multiple

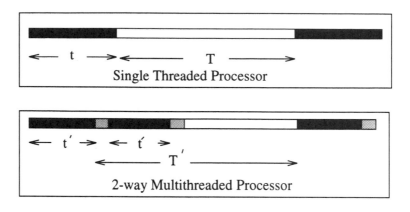

Figure 2 Two way processor multithreading. White area indicates that the processor is stalled, black area indicates that the processor is executing and shaded area indicates that the processor is switching from one thread to another. T (T') is the average number of cycles to resolve an L1 cache miss and t (t') is the number of cycles between misses for the single-threaded (multithreaded) processor. Multithreading attempts to reduce the processor stall time (the white area).

threads that it can switch to are called, *Multiple Context* or *Multithreaded* processors [1]. Figure 2 shows the timing diagram of processor states for a single threaded and a two-way multithreaded processor. Multithreading saves on processor cycles that would have been wasted otherwise just waiting on cache miss, TLB miss or other long latency operation for which the processor switches task (some of the other long latency operation when switching is useful are, *send* and *receive* operation, lock contention to access critical section, etc.).

A non-multithreaded processor has at most one thread that can put a memory transaction request to the memory subsystem, whereas a multithreaded processor with m threads can put at most m requests. So multithreading potentially require higher memory bandwidth. Since more than one threads' footprint occupies the cache for a multithreaded processor, the effective size of the cache available to each thread may become smaller, especially if there is no sharing of data or instruction among the threads. In this case, each thread will have more cache misses per instruction, causing extra pressure on the memory bandwidth. To exploit the full benefit of multithreading, the memory subsystem should allow multiple-issue, multi-ported memory.

Cache misses can be classified into three categories: *compulsory misses* (the first time a cache line is referred it must be a miss), *capacity misses* (cache misses because the cache is not big enough to hold the working set size of the application) and *conflict misses* (cache miss because of not having high enough associativity). Multithreading hides the memory access latency for compulsory cache misses as long as there is another thread available and ready to switch to and the cost of thread switch is significantly lower than the average latency to satisfy a cache miss. However since more than one threads' footprint occupies the cache the conflict and capacity misses could potentially be higher with multithreading, unless the threads are created carefully with data sharing among the threads. Methods to create threads and perform loop transformation to improve the intra-thread and inter-thread locality of references are described in section 4.

3 PROGRAM TRANSFORMATION

To reap the full benefit of multithreading, the threads should be created in a manner so that there is data sharing among the threads. Compiler optimization can help by performing loop transformation that improves cache reuse by the references within a thread and by creating threads with inter-thread locality. Compiler also needs to generate the necessary synchronization primitives as discussed in section 1.

Given a dependence matrix $D_{n \times k} = [\bar{d}_1 \ \bar{d}_2 \ \ldots \ \bar{d}_k]$, where $\bar{d}_i$'s are the dependence vectors, any non-singular matrix $T_{n \times n}$ is valid for transformation if and only if

$$T \cdot \bar{d}_i > 0 \qquad i \in \{1, 2, \ldots, k\} \qquad (11.1)$$

Once a tranformation matrix T is determined that optimizes the required criterion, the process of loop tranformation involves two steps: (1) change the subscript expressions to reflect the new loop variables and (2) determine the bounds of the new loop variables.

The loop variables, $\bar{i}$, in the original loop nest is related to the loop variables, $\bar{i}'$, in the transformed loop nest by the equation

$$\bar{i} = T^{-1} \cdot \bar{i}'$$

If an m dimensional variable is referred by the expression $A \cdot \bar{i} + \bar{c}$ in the original program (where $A_{m \times n}$), then the same reference is made by the expression $A \cdot T^{-1} \cdot \bar{i}' + \bar{c}$ in the tranformed program.

To determine the bounds of the new loop variables, *Fourier-Motzkin* elimination process can be used [19]. Example 2 explains the method. The time complexity of the Fourier-Motzkin method is exponential, however the depths of the loop nests in most applications are small and the method has been found to be useful [17].

4 IMPROVING LOCALITY OF REFERENCE

In this section, we discuss methods of determining the transformation matrix T, that increases the locality of reference of a thread and also helps in creating threads with inter-thread data sharing. Our objective is to determine transformation matrix, T, such that once a cache line is fetched, it is reused as many times as possible before it is evicted from the cache due to capacity misses.

There are two different transfomations that can increase the locality of reference by increasing the reuse of a fetched cache line:

■   Improving spatial locality: transform the innermost loops such that successive iterations use the same data cache line (for the same reference to the same array).

■   Improving temporal locality: transform the outermost loops such that the temporal distance between the iterations that reuse the same memory locations (by a different reference to the same array) is reduced.

4.1 Spatial Locality

Spatial locality can be improved by transforming the innermost loops in a way such that the likelyhood of the next iteration to make reference to the same cache line is increased. The exact tranformation depends on the layout of the arrays in the memory. For an array B of size $N \times M$, the reference $B[i,j]$ maps to the memory location

$$B[i,j] \rightarrow \text{offset} + i + (j-1) * N$$

in a column major layout and to

$$X[i,j] \rightarrow \text{offset} + (i-1) * M + j$$

in a row major layout. For our analysis we assume row major layout. Similar results can be obtained for column major layout.

The distance between the memory locations that a given reference to an array refers to in two successive iterations is called *spatial reuse distance*. *Spatial reuse fraction* is the conditional probability that a given array reference will refer the same cache line in the $(i+1)$-th iteration given that in the i-th iteration the reference is made to a byte within the cache line at random.

For more general references, $X[A.\bar{I} + \bar{c}]$, with unit loop strides the spatial reuse distance can be obtained as

$$[A \cdot \bar{I} + \bar{c}] - [A \cdot (\bar{I} + \bar{e}_n) + \bar{c}] = A \cdot \bar{e}_n = \bar{A}_n = \begin{bmatrix} a_{1n} \\ \dots \\ a_{mn} \end{bmatrix}$$

where $\bar{A}_n$ is the n-th column of A. If the array X is of size $M_1 \times M_2 \dots \times M_n$ and the stride of the innermost loop is Δ_n, then we define the *stride vector* as

$$\text{Stride vector} = \bar{u} = \begin{bmatrix} u_1 \\ \dots \\ u_{n-1} \\ u_n \end{bmatrix} = \begin{bmatrix} M_2 M_3 \dots M_n \\ \dots \\ M_n \\ \Delta_n \end{bmatrix}$$

The k-th element of the stride vector denotes the number of array elements a reference to X is advanced by in the next iteration if a_{kn} is 1, for $2 \leq k \leq n$.

For each reference $X[A \cdot \bar{I} + \bar{c}]$, the same cache line is reused in next iteration only if

$$\bar{A}_n^T \cdot \bar{u} < \text{cache line size}$$

Example 4.1 In two successive iterations, $[i, j]$ and $[i, j + 1]$, the reference $X[i + 2j + 2, i + j + 3]$ in figure 3 refers to the memory locations (assuming array X of size $M \times N$, and row major mapping of the array)

$$X[i + 2j + 2, i + j + 3] \rightarrow (i + 2j + 2) * N + (i + j + 3)$$
$$X[i + 2(j+1) + 2, i + (j+1) + 3] \rightarrow (i + 2(j+1) + 2) * N + (i + (j+1) + 3) \text{ So}$$

the spatial reuse distance between successive iterations is $2N + 1$. In matrix notation, the spatial reuse distance can be expressed as

$$\bar{e}_2^T \cdot [A]^T \cdot \bar{u} = \bar{e}_2^T \cdot \begin{bmatrix} 1 & 2 \\ 1 & 1 \end{bmatrix}^T \cdot \begin{bmatrix} N \\ 1 \end{bmatrix} = [2 \ 1] \cdot \begin{bmatrix} N \\ 1 \end{bmatrix} = 2N + 1$$

If the cache line size is 128 bytes, the spatial reuse fraction is only 21% for $N = 50$ and 0 for $N \geq 64$ (using equation 11.4).

```
for (i = 1; i <= m; i++)
    for (j = 1; j <= n; j++)
        X[i+2j+2, i+j+3] = .......
```

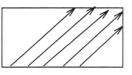

(a)

```
for (k = -2n-m; k <= -3; k++)
    for (l = max (-n-k, (1-k/2) );
         l <= min(-1-k, (m-k)/2); l++)
        X[-k+2, l+3] = .......
```

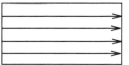

(b)

Figure 3 Spatial locality transformation. The program in (a) is transformed into the program in (b), with the corresponding change in the access pattern of the successive array elements, which reduces cache misses when the array is mapped to the memory in row-major order.

Applying the transformation in equation (11.2),

$$T = \begin{bmatrix} -1 & -2 \\ 1 & 1 \end{bmatrix} \tag{11.2}$$

the reference $X[i + 2j + 2, i + j + 3]$ changes to $X[-k + 2, l + 3]$, as shown in figure 3 and the resulting spatial reuse distance is 1. If the cache line size is 128 bytes, the spatial reuse fraction is $127/128 \approx 99\%$ □

Spatial Locality Transformation

To determine the spatial reuse transformation, we first determine all the references to the array elements in the loop nest and prioritize them. If profile directed feedback is not available to prioritize the references, heuristics such as [2] can be used, which has been shown to provide branch predictions reasonably well for SPEC benchmarks.

Input: Ordered set of reference matrices $S = \{A_1, A_2, ...\}$.
$\qquad\qquad$ Priority order $P = \{p_1, p_2...\}$.
$\qquad\qquad$ Set of dependence vectors $D = \{\bar{d}_1, \bar{d}_2, ...\}$.
$\qquad\qquad$ Set of stride vectors $\{\bar{u}_1, \bar{u}_2....\}$.
Output: Transformation matrix M for Spatial reuse.
$M = $ Identity matrix;
$d = n;$ $\qquad\qquad\qquad$ /* loop depth */
while $(S \neq NULL)$ {
$\qquad$ Find largest i for which spatial reuse condition holds.
$\qquad\qquad\qquad\qquad$ /* determines the last column of $T^{-1} = [t_{n1}...t_{nd}]^T$ */
$\qquad$ Delete A_j from S for $j > i$. If $(i == 0)$ terminate.
$\qquad$ $k = rank[A_1\ A_2\ ...\ A_i]^T$
$\qquad$ If $(k < d)$ express $t_1, ...t_k$ in terms of $t_{k+1}, ..., t_d$
$\qquad$ Find smallest $|\gamma_j|$ in the priority order of A_j for $1 \leq j \leq i$
$\qquad$ If $((u_d)_j * |\gamma_j| > line\_size)$ delete A_j from S.
$\qquad$ Expand last column of T^{-1} to n.
$\qquad$ Complement T^{-1} to full rank and find T.
$\qquad$ If $T \cdot \bar{d}_i > 0$ for all $\bar{d}_i \in D$ then $M = T \cdot M$
$\qquad$ else delete A_i from S and continue with next iteration
$\qquad$ Compute spatial reuse fractions, f_j for $1 \leq j \leq i$
$\qquad$ Order A_j in increasing order of $p_j = p_j * f_j$ for $1 \leq j \leq i$
$\qquad$ Order entries in S in the priority order.
$\qquad$ $d = d - 1$ }
return (M)

Figure 4 Spatial Transformation Algorithm.

For each reference matrix, A_i, we want to determine a non-zero column vector $\bar{t}'_n$ so that

$$A_i \cdot \bar{t}'_n = [0\ 0\ ...\ \gamma]^T$$

where γ is such that $\Delta_n| \cdot \gamma| <$ cache line size. To increase the likelyhood of spatial reuse, we choose γ as small as possible.

We define the *spatial reuse condition* for reference A_i as

$$[A_i]_{row\ k} \cdot \bar{t}'_n = 0 \quad \text{for } 1 \leq k \leq n - 1 \qquad\qquad (11.3)$$

The spatial reuse fraction for A_i is

$$\text{Spatial reuse fraction } = \left\langle \frac{\text{cache line size} - u_n * |\gamma|}{\text{cache line size}} \right\rangle \qquad (11.4)$$

where $\langle x \rangle = x$ when x is positive and zero otherwise.

Figure 4 shows the algorithm to determine the spatial transformation matrix. The algorithm first tries to determine the best transformation for the innermost loop and then successively moves to the outermost loop until there is no reference matrix available which satisfies the spatial reuse condition, or the spatial reuse fraction is zero for all the reference matrices. At each iteration, the algorithm determines the last column of the transformation matrix, T, which is then expanded to the full rank.

The values of the smallest $|\gamma_j|$, as referred in line 9 of the algorithm, can be determined using the euclidean algorithm to find the GCD. For example, let $n = 5$ and after applying the spatial reuse conditions we can express t_1 and t_2 in terms of t_3, t_4 and t_5. Assume that there are two references and that

$$\gamma_1 = 5t_3 + 10t_4 + 15t_5 \tag{11.5}$$

and

$$\gamma_2 = 9t_3 + 3t_4 \tag{11.6}$$

Since γ_1 and γ_2 must be multiples of 5 and 3 respectively, for the smallest values of γ_1 and γ_2 we must have

$$t_3 + 2t_4 + 3t_5 = 1 \tag{11.7}$$

and

$$3t_3 + t_4 = 1 \tag{11.8}$$

From equations (11.7) and (11.8), we can write

$$-5t_3 + 3t_5 = -1 \tag{11.9}$$

Since the gcd of the coefficients at the left hand side divides the constant in the right hand side, there is a solution to equation (11.9), which can be obtained from the euclidean algorithm. The final solution for $[t_3\ t_4\ t_5]$ that minimizes γ_1 and γ_2 is [2 -5 4].

4.2 Temporal Locality

So far we have discussed the transformation that will increase the reuse of the same cache line in the next iteration. To increase the temporal locality, we look for a tranformation that decreases the distance between the iterations that make reference to the same memory location. Thus this transformation has the effect of reducing the footprint of a loop nest in the data cache.

Let us consider the program in figure 5. Variable $A[i, j]$ is referenced in three different iterations: $[i, j], [i + 3, j + 1]$ and $[i + 6, j + 2]$ by the three references $A[i, j], A[i - 3, j - 1]$ and $A[i - 6, j - 2]$ respectively.

The distance between the two iterations in which reference to the same memory location is made is called *reuse vector*. For the example in figure 5, there are three reuse vectors

```
for (i = 6; i <= m; i++)
    for (j = 2; j <= n; j++)
        B[i,j] = B[i-3, j-1]+B[i-6, j-2];
```

Figure 5   Simple program with three temporal reuses.

which forms the reuse matrix

$$R = \begin{bmatrix} 3 & 6 & 3 \\ 1 & 2 & 1 \end{bmatrix}$$

For more general array reference, let us consider two references to array X, $X[A\cdot\bar{i}+\bar{c}_1]$ and $X[A\cdot\bar{i}+\bar{c}_2]$, where $A = [\bar{\alpha}_1\ \bar{\alpha}_2\ ...]^T$. Iterations $\bar{i}_1$ and $\bar{i}_2$ refer to the same memory location when

$$A \cdot \bar{i}_1 + \bar{c}_1 = A \cdot \bar{i}_2 + \bar{c}_2$$

The *temporal reuse distance* vectors between the two iterations, $\bar{r} = \bar{i}_1 - \bar{i}_2$, can be found by solving

$$A \cdot [\bar{i}_1 - \bar{i}_2] = A \cdot \bar{r} = \bar{c}_2 - \bar{c}_1 \tag{11.10}$$

that is,

$$\bar{r} = \text{null space}(A) + \bar{s} = span\{\bar{a}_1, \bar{a}_2, ...\bar{a}_k\} + \bar{s} \tag{11.11}$$

where $k = n - rank(A)$, $\{\bar{a}_1, \bar{a}_2, ...\bar{a}_k\}$ is the set of basis vectors of the null space of A and $\bar{s} = [s_1\ s_2...]^T$ is a special solution of equation (11.10).

To increase the temporal reuse, the transformation matrix should be chosen in a way so that the higher dimensional elements of the vector $T \cdot \bar{r}$ are zero or very small. To reduce the number of reuse vectors, we choose one vector $\bar{r}$, that incorporates the maximum of all the reuse distances in equation (11.11) as

$$\bar{r} = [r_1\ r_2\ ...\ r_n]^T$$

where $r_l = s_l$ if the l-th element of $\bar{a}_j$, $a_{jl} = 0$ for all j, $1 \le j \le k$
      = range of $[\bar{\alpha}_l\cdot\bar{i}_1 - \bar{\alpha}_l\cdot\bar{i}_2 + c_{1k} - c_{2k}]$ for $\bar{i}_1, \bar{i}_2 \in$ Iteration Space, otherwise.

For more general array references, let us consider the references $X[A.\bar{i} + \bar{c}_1]$ and $X[B.\bar{i} + \bar{c}_2]$, where $A = [\bar{\alpha}_1\ \bar{\alpha}_2\ ...]^T$ and $B = [\bar{\beta}_1\ \bar{\beta}_2\ ...]^T$. Same memory location will be referred to in iterations $\bar{i}_1$ and $\bar{i}_2$ by these two references if and only if

$$A \cdot \bar{i}_1 + \bar{c}_1 = B \cdot \bar{i}_2 + \bar{c}_2 = \bar{x}\ (\text{say})$$

Again to keep the number of reuse vectors small and still capture the maximum reuse distance, we choose

$$\bar{r} = [r_1\ r_2\ ...\ r_n]^T$$

where $r_k = c_{2k} - c_{1k}$,   when $\bar{\alpha}_k = \bar{\beta}_k = \bar{0}$
      = range of $[\bar{\alpha}_k\cdot\bar{i}_1 - \bar{\beta}_k\cdot\bar{i}_2 + c_{1k} - c_{2k}]$ for $\bar{i}_1, \bar{i}_2 \in$ Iteration Space, otherwise.

Input: Reuse matrix $R_{n \times m} = [\bar{r}_1 \ \bar{r}_2...]$ in priority order $P = \{p_1, p_2...\}$.
Set of dependence vectors $D = \{\bar{d}_1, \bar{d}_2, ...\}$.
GCD of the elements of each vector $\bar{r}_i$: $\bar{g} = [g_1 \ g_2 \ ...]$.
Output: Transformation matrix T for Temporal reuse.
$q = 1$
while $(R \neq empty \| q \neq n)$ {
     if $(r_{qj} == 0)$ for all $1 \leq j \leq n$ continue with next iteration.
     Construct m linear equations
$$\bar{t}^T \cdot \bar{r}_j = x_j g_j \quad \text{for } 1 \leq j \leq m$$
     If $(q \neq 0)$ do singular value decomposition of
$$T = W\Sigma V^T$$

     Replace t_j by $y_q v_{qj} + y_{q+1} v_{(q+1)j} + ... y_n v_{nj}$ to obtain
$$[f_1(\bar{y}) \ ... \ f_n(\bar{y})] \cdot \bar{r}_j = x_j g_j \quad \text{for } 1 \leq j \leq m$$
     Solve for $\bar{y}$ in terms of $\bar{x}$. Find minimum $|x_i|$'s in lexicographical order so that
$$\bar{t}^T \cdot \bar{d}_i = [f_1(\bar{y})...f_n(\bar{y})] \cdot \bar{d}_i = [h_1(\bar{x})...h_n(\bar{x})] \cdot \bar{d}_i > \bar{0} \qquad \text{for all } \bar{d}_i \in D$$

     If no such $\bar{x}$ or $\max_j(|x_j g_j|)$ is too large, choose one alternatives.
     Delete $\bar{d}_i$'s for which $\bar{t}^T \cdot \bar{d}_i > 0$.
     Adjust m.
     $q = q + 1$ }
If $(q \neq n)$ complement T to full rank.

Figure 6 Temporal Locality Transformation Algorithm.

Temporal Locality Transformation

To improve the temporal data locality for a loop nest, we construct the transformation matrix T, by adding rows $\bar{t}_i$ successively for $1 \leq i \leq n$ to it. The new rows should be determined using the following three criteria:

1. $\bar{t}_i$ is linearly independent of rows already in T

2. $\bar{t}_i \cdot \bar{d}_i > 0$ for all $\bar{d}_i \in D$

3. Minimize

$$\left| \bar{t}_i \cdot \begin{bmatrix} r_{j1} * u_1 \\ r_{j2} * u_2 \\ .... \end{bmatrix} \right| \qquad (11.12)$$

for all reuse vectors, $\bar{r}_j$. $\bar{u} = [u_1, u_2, ... u_n]$ is the unit iteration vector, where $u_k, 1 \leq k \leq n$, denotes the number of times the innermost loop body is executed when the k-th loop index is incremented by 1.

Condition 1 guarantees that the transformation is non-singular. Condition 2 guarantees that the transformation is a legal transformation and condition 3 finds the best transformation for temporal locality. However it is not possible to evaluate condition 3, because the unit iteration vector $\bar{u}$ that results after the loop nest have been transformed is not known until the transformation matrix T is fully known. The best that can be done is to try to minimize $|\bar{t}_i \cdot \bar{r}|$. So condition 3 is modified to

3'. Minimize $|\bar{t} \cdot \bar{r}|$.

The temporal locality transformation algorithm is shown in figure 6. At the q-th iteration the algorithm attempts to add the q-th row, $\bar{t}^T$, to the partially built tranformation matrix $T_{(q-1) \times n}$, such that the new row is linearly independent of the existing rows of T and the new temporal reuse distance along the q-th dimension, $\bar{t}^T \cdot \bar{r}_j$, is minimized. Since g_j is the gcd of the elements of $\bar{r}_j$, we have

$$\bar{t}^T \cdot \bar{r}_j = x_j g_j \quad \text{for } 1 \leq j \leq m \qquad (11.13)$$

To guarantee that $\bar{t}^T$ is linearly independent with the existing rows of T, singular value decomposition* theorem [6] can be used which decomposes matrix $T_{m \times n}$ to $W \Sigma V^T$, where $W_{m \times m}$ and $V_{n \times n}$ are orthogonal matrices and $\Sigma_{m \times n}$ is a diagonal matrix. If the rank of T is $q - 1$, it can be shown that the last $(n - q + 1)$ column vectors of V, $\{\bar{v}_q, \bar{v}_{q+1}, \ldots, \bar{v}_n\}$ spans the null space of T. Since an element, $y_q \bar{v}_q + y_{q+1} \bar{v}_{(q+1)} + \ldots y_n \bar{v}_n$, in the null space of the column vectors of T also belongs to the space orthogonally complement to the row vectors of T (hence linearly independent of the rows of T), $\bar{t}$ can be written as

$$\bar{t} = y_q \bar{v}_q + y_{q+1} \bar{v}_{(q+1)} + \ldots y_n \bar{v}_n \qquad (11.14)$$

Replacing $\bar{t}$ in equation (11.13) we get

$$[f_1(\bar{y}) \ldots f_n(\bar{y})] \cdot \bar{r}_j = x_j g_j \quad \text{for } 1 \leq j \leq m \qquad (11.15)$$

Equations (11.15) is a system of linear equations with $(n - q + 1)$ unknown variables y_j's and m equations. If it has one or more solutions, we can express y_j, $q \leq j \leq n$ in terms of x_j, $1 \leq j \leq m$. Using these values of y_j's in equation (11.14), we can search for the minimum values (in the lexicographical order) of $|\bar{x}|$ within the valid transformation space

$$\bar{t}^T \cdot D = [f_1(\bar{y}) \ldots f_n(\bar{y})] \cdot D = [h_1(\bar{x}) \ldots h_n(\bar{x})] \cdot D > \bar{0} \qquad (11.16)$$

This can be accomplished by successively solving the set of linear inequalities

$$[h_1(\bar{x}) \ldots h_n(\bar{x})] \cdot D \geq e_i$$

for unit vectors $\bar{e}_i, i = \{n, n-1, \ldots, 1\}$ by Fourier-Motzkin elimination process and determining the minimum $x_j, 1 \leq j \leq m$ in the priority order for each set.

---

*Alternatively, matrix T can be transformed into row echeleon form, by elementary row operations, to determine the unit row vectors that span the set of vectors linearly independent of the row vectors of T.

If equation (11.15) does not have any solution or equation (11.16) does not have any solution or $\max_j(|x_j g_j|)$ is too large compared to the cache size, one of the following alternatives can be chosen (based on the underlying architecture) in the following order.

1. Tile and distribute the loop over Multicomputer, if the loop has not already been distributed. We try to maximize $|\bar{t}_i \cdot \bar{r}|$'s (in priority order), so that the distance between communication step is long.

2. Multithread the loop being processed by strip mining the loop with step size equal to the level of multithreading that the processor supports. The threads thus created will have significant data sharing. This alternative is next in priority (that is, this alternative is applied towards the outermost loops) so that the synchronization among the threads occur less frequently.

3. Tile the loop with tiles of size between the minimum and the maximum reuse distance on the dimension.

4. Discard the last reuse vector and recompute the step.

5 CONCLUSION

A novel compiler optimization method based on loop transformation theory to reduce the data cache misses for a uniprocessor by increasing the temporal and spatial locality of reference has been discussed in this paper. The algorithms presented work for general array references. The method helps in creating threads in a multithreaded processor with increased intra and inter-thread locality. The method can also be extended for partitioning and mapping loop nests on a multicomputer so that the number of iterations between communication steps is large. This reduces the total communication and synchronization cost on a multicomputer.

REFERENCES

[1] A. Agarwal, "Performance Tradeoffs in Multithreaded Processors," *IEEE Transactions on Parallel and Distributed Systems*, Vol 3, No 5, pp. 525-539, 1992.

[2] T. Ball and J. R. Larus, "Branch prediction for free," SIGPLAN Notices Vol.28, No.6 pp. 300-13, June 1993.

[3] W. Blume, et. al., "Automatic Detection of Parallelism: A Grand Challenge for High-Performance Computing," *IEEE Parallel and Distributed Technology: Systems and Applications*, Vol 2, No 3, pp. 37-47, 1994.

[4] K. Boland and A. Dolles, "Predicting and Precluding Problems with Memory Latency," *IEEE Micro*, Vol.14, No.4, August 1994, pp 59-67.

[5] P. Boulet, A. Darte, T. Risset and Y. Robert, "(Pen)-ultimate Tiling," *Proc. of Scalable High Performance Computing Conference*, Knoxville, TN, pp. 568-576, May 1994.

[6] G. H. Golub and C. F. Van Loan, *Matrix Computations*, The Johns Hopkins University Press, 1989.

[7] S. F. Hummel, I. Banicescu, C.-T. Wang and J. Wein, "Load Balancing and Data Locality via Fractiling: An Experimental Study," in *Languages, Compilers and Run-time Systems for Scalable Computers* by B. Szymanski and B. Sinharoy (eds.), Kluwar Academic Publishers, 1995.

[8] W. Kaplow and B. K. Szymanski, "Impact of Memory Hierarchy on Program Partitioning and Scheduling," *Proc. 28th Hawaii Int. Conf. on System Sciences*, Maui, Hawaii, vol. II, pp. 93-102, Jan. 1995.

[9] E. Markatos, *Scheduling for Locality in Shared-Memory Multiprocessors*, Ph.D. Thesis, University of Rochester, Rochester, New York, 1993.

[10] S. McFarling, "Program Optimizations for Instruction Caches," *Proc. of 3rd Int. Conf. on Arch. Support for Prog. Lang. and Op. Sys.*, pp. 183-191, April 1989.

[11] T. C. Mowry, S. Lam, A. Gupta, "Design and evaluation of a compiler algorithm for prefetching," Fifth International Conference on Architectural Support for Programming Languages and Operating Systems (ASPLOS V) Boston, MA, USA 12-15 Oct. 1992.

[12] T. C. Mowry, *Tolerating Latency Through Software-Controlled Data Prefetching*, Ph.D. Thesis, Stanford University, March 1994.

[13] J. Ramanujam and P. Sadayappan, "Tiling Multidimensional Iteration Spaces for Multi-computers," *Journal of Parallel and Distributed Computing*, Vol 16, pp. 108-120, 1992.

[14] R. H. Saavedra, W. Mao and K. Hwang, "Performance and Optimization of Data Prefetching Strategies in Scalable Multiprocessors," *Journal of Parallel and Distributed Computing*, Vol 22, No 3, 1994, 427-448.

[15] B. Sinharoy and B. K. Szymanski, "Finding Optimum Wavefront of Computation," *Parallel Algorithms and Applications*, Vol 2, pp. 5-26, 1994.

[16] B. Sinharoy and B. K. Szymanski, "Data and Task Alignment in Distributed Memory Architectures," *Journal of Parallel and Distributed Computing*, Vol 21, pp. 61-74, 1994.

[17] R. P. Wilson, et al, "SUIF: an infrastructure for research on parallelizing and optimizing," SIGPLAN Not. (USA) Vol.29, No.12, pp. 31-7, December 1994.

[18] M. E. Wolf and M. S. Lam, "A Data Locality Optimizing Algorithm," *ACM SIGPLAN Conf. on Prog. Lang. Design and Implementation*, pp. 30-44, June 26-28, 1991.

[19] J. Xue, "An algorithm to automate non unimodular transformations of loop nests," Proceedings of the Fifth IEEE Symposium on Parallel and Distributed Processing, pp. 512-19, December, 1993.

12

ENABLING PRIMITIVES FOR COMPILING PARALLEL LANGUAGES

Seth Copen Goldstein, Klaus Erik Schauser*, David Culler

Computer Science Division, University of California at Berkeley
{sethg,culler}@cs.berkeley.edu
*Department of Computer Science, University of California at Santa Barbara
schauser@cs.ucsb.edu

ABSTRACT

This paper presents three novel language implementation primitives—lazy threads, stacklets, and synchronizers—and shows how they combine to provide a parallel call at nearly the efficiency of a sequential call. The central idea is to transform parallel calls into parallel-ready sequential calls. Excess parallelism degrades into sequential calls with the attendant efficient stack management and direct transfer of control and data, unless a call truly needs to execute in parallel, in which case it gets its own thread of control. We show how these techniques can be applied to distribute work efficiently on multiprocessors.

1 INTRODUCTION

Many modern parallel languages provide methods for dynamically creating multiple independent threads of control, such as forks, parallel calls, futures [15], object methods, and non-strict evaluation of argument expressions [17, 12]. Generally, these threads describe the logical parallelism in the program. The programming language implementation maps this dynamic collection of threads onto the fixed set of physical processors executing the program, either by providing its own language-specific scheduling mechanisms or by using a general threads package. These languages stand in contrast to languages with a single logical thread of control, such as Fortran90, or a fixed set of threads, such as Split-C. There are many reasons to have the logical parallelism of the program exceed the physical parallelism of the machine, including ease of expressing parallelism and better utilization in the presence of synchronization delays [16, 25], load imbalance, and long communication latency. Moreover, the semantics of the language or the synchronization primitives may allow dependencies to be expressed in such a way that progress can be made only by interleaving multiple threads, effectively running them in parallel even on a single processor.

A parallel call is fundamentally more expensive than a sequential call because of the storage management, data transfer, scheduling, and synchronization involved. This cost has been reduced with a combination of compiler techniques and clever run-time representations [7, 19, 23, 16, 25, 20, 18], and by supporting fine-grained parallel execution directly in hardware [13, 2]. These approaches, among others, have been used in implementing the parallel programming languages Mul-T [15], Id90 [7, 19], CC++ [5], Charm [14], Cilk [3], Cid [18], and Olden [4]. In many cases, the cost of the parallel call is reduced by severely restricting what can be done in a thread.

In earlier approaches, the full cost of parallelism is borne for all potentially parallel calls, although the parallelism is neither needed nor exploited in most instances. For example, once all the processors are busy, there may be no need to spawn additional work, and in the vast majority of cases the logic of the program permits the child to run to completion while the parent is suspended. The goal of this work is to make the cost of a potentially parallel call as close as possible to that of a sequential call unless multiple threads of control or remote execution are actually needed. We also produce a very fast parallel call when it is needed.

The key idea is that we fork a new thread as if it were a sequential call and elevate it to a true fork of a local thread only if the child actually suspends. This concept, which we call *lazy threads*, builds upon work on lazy task creation [15]. In the best case our system eliminates all the run-time bookkeeping costs associated with forking a thread or creating a future. In the worst case it requires only three instructions to create a future. Similarly, we can defer generating work for other processors until a request for work is received from another processor. If all the processors have plenty to do, potential parallel work is simply assumed by the current thread of control. Our experience is that potentially parallel calls frequently degenerate into the simple, local, sequential case and that handling the simple case very well has a significant impact on performance.

Our current experimental results focus on two prototype implementations on the CM-5: a direct implementation in C and a compiler for the fine-grained parallel language Id90. The C implementation was used to write some kernels and shows that these primitives introduce little or no overhead over sequential programs. The Id90 implementation shows that for complete programs we achieve a substantial improvement over previous work. Our work is applicable to many other systems as well. For example, our techniques could be applied to other programming languages [5, 26], thread packages [8], and multithreaded execution models. Our work relies extensively on compiler optimizations; lazy threads cannot simply be implemented with a function call in a user-level threads library without substantial loss of efficiency. Because the synthesis between compiler and run-time system is key to obtaining efficiency, these ideas must be evaluated in the context of an actual compiler.

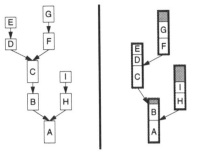

Figure 1 How individual activation frames of a cactus stack are mapped onto stacklets. Only parallel calls or stacklet overflows require allocation of a new stacklet. (The arrows point back to the parent; in the above example, A calls B and H in parallel.)

1.1 Overview

In this work a *thread* is a locus of control on a processor which can perform calls to arbitrary nesting depth, suspend at any point, and fork additional threads. Threads are scheduled independently and are non-preemptive.* We associate with each thread its own unbounded stack.

Before considering the parallel call, observe that the efficiency of a sequential call derives from several cooperating factors. Storage allocation on call and return involves merely adjusting the stack pointer, because the parent is suspended upon call and the child and its children have completed upon return. Data and control are transferred together on the call and on the return, so arguments and return values can be passed in registers and no explicit synchronization is involved.

To realize a parallel-ready sequential call—i.e., one that creates a sequential task that can be elevated gracefully into an independent thread of control—we proceed in four steps.

First, in Section 2, we address storage allocation. Since threads can fork other threads and each requires a stack, a tree of stacks, a *cactus stack*, is required. We realize this cactus stack using *stacklets* (see Figure 1). A stacklet is a fixed-size region of storage which can contain multiple call frames, is cheap to allocate, and is managed internally like a sequential stack. Allocation of a new stacklet occurs when a new thread is created or when a stacklet overflows. *Stacklet stubs* are used to handle many special cases, including underflow and remote return, without the sequential call needing to perform tests on return. This provides a naive parallel language implementation with conventional local and remote forks.

Next, in Section 3, we address control and data transfer when a thread is forked on the local processor. A *lazy thread fork* is performed exactly like a sequential call; control

---

* This is similar to what is provided in many kernel threads packages. Our threads, however, are stronger than those in TAM [7] and in some user-level threads packages, e.g. Chorus [21], which require that the maximum stack size be specified upon thread creation so that memory can be preallocated.

and data are transferred to the child and the call is made on the parent stack. However, if the child suspends, the parent is resumed with its stack extended, so it gives up its own stacklet to the new thread and uses a new stacklet for its subsequent children. We generate code so that the child can suspend and resume the parent by doing a jump to a simple offset of the return address. Thus, control is transferred directly to the parent on either return or suspension.

Third, in Section 4, we show how to perform synchronization cheaply between the parent and child, should they become independent threads. The only flexibility we have in the sequential call is the indirect jump on the return address. The key idea, implemented by *synchronizers*, is that the parent and the child share the return address, which by our code generation technique represents multiple return addresses. The return entry points can be adjusted to reflect the synchronization state. The optimizations outlined so far are required to support many logical threads on a single processor.

Finally, in Section 5, we extend the use of multiple return addresses to allow the parent to generate additional parallel work *on demand*, in response to a work-stealing request from another processor. We call this concept a thread *seed* because it allows potential threads to be held dormant very cheaply until they are either assumed by the local processor or stolen and planted in another processor. Growing a thread seed into a full thread requires executing a piece of code in the context of the function that created it. On the other hand, the overhead for creating and assuming a thread seed is minimal.

In Section 6 we give empirical data to show that these concepts can be combined to efficiently implement excess logical parallelism. Underlying our optimizations is the observation that in modern microprocessors, a substantial cost is paid for memory references and branches, whereas register operations are essentially free. Since stacklets are managed like a sequential stack, arguments and results can be passed in registers, even in the potentially parallel case. By manipulating the existing indirect return jump, conditional tests for synchronization and special cases can be avoided.

1.2   Related Work

Attempts to accommodate logical parallelism have include thread packages [8, 21, 6], compiler techniques and clever run-time representations [7, 19, 16, 25, 23, 20, 10], and direct hardware support for fine-grained parallel execution [13, 2]. These approaches have been used to implement many parallel languages, e.g. Mul-T [15], Id90 [7, 19], CC++ [5], Charm [14], Cilk [3], Olden [4], and Cid [18]. The common goal is to reduce the overhead associated with managing the logical parallelism. While much of this work overlaps ours, none has combined the techniques described in this paper into an integrated whole. More importantly, none has started from the premise that all calls, parallel or sequential, can be initiated in the exact same manner.

Our work grew out of previous efforts to implement the non-strict functional language Id90 for commodity parallel machines. Our earlier work developed a *Threaded Abstract Machine* (TAM) which serves as an intermediate compilation target [7]. The two key differences between this work and TAM are that under TAM calls are always parallel, and due to TAM's scheduling hierarchy, calling another function does not immediately transfer control.

Our lazy thread fork allows all calls to begin in the same way, and creates only the required amount of concurrency. In the framework of previous work it allows excess parallelism to degrade efficiently into a sequential call. Many other researchers have proposed schemes which deal lazily with excess parallelism. Our approach builds on *lazy task creation* (LTC) which maintains a data structure to record previously encountered parallel calls [16]. When a processor runs out of work, dynamic load balancing can be effected by stealing previously created lazy tasks from other processors. These ideas were studied for Mul-T running on shared-memory machines. The primary difference is that LTC always performs extra work for parallel calls, whether they execute locally or remotely. Even the lazy tasks that are never raised to full fledged tasks are "spawned off" in the sense that they require extra bookkeeping. In addition, in order to avoid memory references and increase efficiency our work uses different primitives from LTC. LTC also depends on a garbage collector, which hides many of the costs of stack management. Finally, while earlier systems based on LTC relied on shared-memory hardware capabilities, our implementation works on both distributed- and shared-memory systems.

Another proposed technique for improving LTC is *leapfrogging* [25]. Unlike the techniques we use, it restricts the behavior of the program in an attempt to reduce the cost of futures.

We use stacklets for efficient stack-based frame allocation in parallel programs. Previous work in [10] developed similar ideas for handling continuations efficiently. Olden [4] uses a "spaghetti stack." In both systems, the allocation of a new stack frame always requires memory references and a garbage collector.

The way thread seeds encode future work builds on the use of multiple offsets from a single return address to handle special cases. This technique was used in SOAR [22]. It was also applied to Self, which uses parent controlled return continuations to handle debugging [11]. We extend these two ideas to form synchronizers.

Building on LTC, Olden [20, 4] applies similar techniques for the automatic parallelization of programs using dynamic data structures. Of the systems mentioned so far, Olden's integration is closest to ours.

Finally, user-level thread packages are still not as lightweight as many of the systems mentioned above. Since the primitives of thread packages are exposed at the library level, the compiler optimizations we present are not possible for such systems.

2   STORAGE MANAGEMENT: STACKLETS

Stacklets are a memory management primitive which efficiently supports cactus stacks. Each stacklet can be managed like a sequential stack. A stacklet is a region of contiguous memory on a single processor that can store several activation frames (see

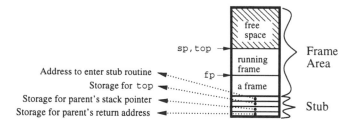

Address to enter stub routine

Storage for top

Storage for parent's stack pointer

Storage for parent's return address

Figure 2   The basic form of a stacklet.

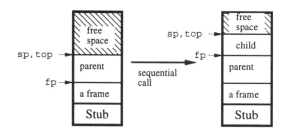

Figure 3   The result of a sequential call which does not overflow the stacklet.

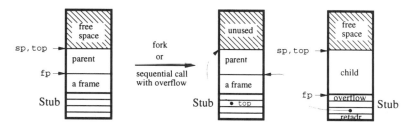

Figure 4   The result of a fork or of a sequential call which overflows the stacklet.

Figure 2). Each stacklet is divided into two regions, the stub and the frame area. The stub contains data that maintains the global cactus stack by linking the individual stacklets to each other. The frame area contains the activation frames. In addition to a traditional stack pointer (sp) and frame pointer (fp), our model defines a *top pointer* (top) which—for reasons presented in the next section—points to the top of the currently used portion of the stacklet, or, in other words, to the next free location in the stacklet. These three pointers are kept in registers.

We recognize three kinds of calls—sequential call, fork, and remote fork—each of which maps onto a different kind of allocation request. A sequential allocation is one that requests space on the same stack as the caller. The child performs the allocation; therefore, it determines whether its frame can fit on the same stacklet. If so, sp, fp, and top are updated appropriately (see Figure 3). If not, a new stacklet is allocated and the child frame is allocated on the new stacklet (see Figure 4). This also happens for a fork, which causes a new stacklet to be created on the local processor. We could

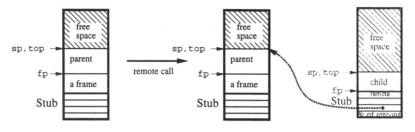

Figure 5 A remote fork leaves the current stacklet unchanged and allocates a new stacklet on another processor.

either run the child in the new stacklet immediately or schedule the child for later execution. In the former case, fp, sp, and top would point to the child stacklet (see Figure 4). In the latter case, they would remain unchanged after the allocation. For a remote fork there are no stacklet operations on the local processor. Instead, a message is sent to a remote processor with the child routine's address and arguments (see Figure 5).

In our current naive implementation, the overhead in checking for stacklet overflow in a sequential call is two register-based instructions (an AND of the new sp and a compare to the old) and a branch (which will usually be successfully predicted). If the stacklet overflows, a new stacklet is allocated from the heap. This cost is amortized over the many invocations that will run in the stacklet.

2.1 Stacklet Stubs

Stub handlers allow us to use the sequential return mechanism even though we are operating on a cactus stack. The stacklet stub stores all the data needed for the bottom frame to return to its parent. When a new stacklet is allocated, the parent's return address and frame pointer are saved in the stub and a return address to the stub handler is given to the child. When the bottom frame in a stacklet executes a return, it does not return to its caller; instead it returns to the stub handler. The stub handler performs stacklet deallocation and, using the data in the stacklet stub, carries out the necessary actions to return control to the parent (restoring top, and having sp and fp point to the parent).

In the case of a remote fork, the stub handler uses indirect active messages [24] to return data and control to the parent's message handler, which in turn has responsibility for integrating the data into the parent frame and indicating to the parent that its child has returned.

2.2 Compilation

To reduce the cost of frame allocation even further we construct a call graph which enables us to determine for all but the recursive calls whether an overflow check is needed. Each function has two entry points, one that checks stacklet overflow and another that does not. If the compiler can determine that no check is needed, it uses the latter entry point. This analysis inserts preventive stacklet allocation to guarantee that future children will not need to perform any overflow checks.

2.3   Discussion

In summary, stacklets provide efficient storage management for parallel execution. In the next section we will see that potentially parallel calls can use the same efficient mechanism as regular sequential calls, because each stacklet preserves the invariants of a stack. Specifically, the same call and return mechanisms are used; arguments and results can be passed in registers. These benefits are obtained at a small increase to the cost of sequential calls, namely checking whether a new stacklet needs to be allocated in the case of an overflow or parallel call. The extra cost amounts to a test and branch along with the use of an additional register. This overhead is required only when the compiler cannot statically determine that no check is needed. Stubs eliminate the need to check for underflows. This contrasts with previous approaches which always require some memory touch operations or a garbage collector.

3   CONTROL TRANSFER: THE LAZY THREAD CALL

Our goal is to make a fork as fast as a sequential call when the forked child executes sequentially. Using stacklets as the underlying frame-storage allocation mechanism gives us a choice as to where to run the new thread invoked by the fork. The obvious approach is to explicitly fork the new thread using the parallel allocation explained in the previous section. However, if the child is expected to complete without suspending—i.e., if it behaves like a sequential call—we would rather treat it like a sequential call and invoke the child on the current stacklet.

This section introduces a *lazy thread fork* (tfork) which behaves like a sequential call unless it suspends, in which case—in order to support the logical parallelism implied by the fork it represents—it directly resumes the parent and behaves like an eagerly forked thread. tfork behaves like a sequential call in that it transfers control (and its arguments) directly to the new thread. Further, if the new thread completes without suspending, it returns control (and results) directly to its parent.

If the child suspends, it must resume its parent in order to notify its parent that the tfork really required its own thread of control. Thus, the child must be able to return to its parent at either of two different addresses: one for normal return and one for suspension. Instead of passing the child two return addresses, the parent calls the child with a single address from which it can derive both addresses. At the implementation level, this use of multiple return addresses can be thought of as an extended version of continuation passing [1], where the child is passed two different continuations, one for normal return and one for suspension. The compiler ensures that the suspension entry point precedes the normal return entry point by a fixed number of instructions.

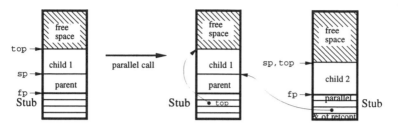

Figure 6 A parallel call creates a new stacklet.

A normal return will continue execution after the `tfork`. In the case of suspension, the compiler uses simple address arithmetic to calculate the suspension entry point.

In the case where the child suspends, the parent will not be the topmost frame in the stacklet—i.e., `sp` will not equal `top` (the situation shown in Figure 6). To maintain the sequential stack invariant, we do not allocate future children of the parent on the current stacklet. Instead, while there is a suspended child above the parent in the current stacklet, we allocate future children, sequential or parallel, on their own stacklets (see Figure 6). As a result, the translation for a call must first compare `sp` and `top`. If they are equal, the call occurs on the current stacklet (as in Figure 3). If they are different, it starts a new stacklet (as in Figure 6). As a result, regardless of the children's return order, no stacklet will ever contain free space between allocated frames. This simplifies memory management.

In summary, `tfork` allows a potentially parallel thread to be executed sequentially and still have the ability to suspend and get its own thread of control. A child that needs its own thread of control takes over its parent thread, causing its parent to allocate subsequent work on other stacklets. Using stacklets and compiler support we have created a multithreaded environment in a single address space which gives each thread a logically unbounded stack.

3.1 Parent Controlled Return Continuations

To reduce the cost of parallel calls, we always want a child which terminates to return directly to its parent. If the child terminates without suspension it can use its original return address. But if it suspends, is later resumed, and finally terminates, it generally cannot return to the same point: Once the child has suspended, the child and parent are truly separate threads and the parent may have already carried out the work immediately following the `tfork` that created the child.

If we want the child to return directly to the parent we need some way to modify the child's return continuation so that the child will return to a location of the parent's choosing. Since we are using stacklets, both the parent and the child know where the child's return address is located in the stack. If the parent is given permission to change the return continuation, it can change it to reflect the new state of the parent's

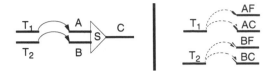

Figure 7   Example of a two-way join, illustrating synchronizers.

computation. The new return continuation will return the child to the point in the parent function that reflects that the child, and any work initiated after the child suspended, have been carried out. We call this mechanism *parent controlled return continuations* (PCRCs).

4   EFFICIENT SYNCHRONIZATION: SYNCHRONIZERS

The ideas found in PCRCs can be extended to efficiently implement synchronization. We minimize the synchronization cost due to joins by extending the use of PCRCs with judicious code duplication and by exploiting the flexibility of the indirect jump in the return instruction. The basic idea is to change the return continuation of a child to reflect the synchronization state of the parent. In this way, neither extra synchronization variables nor tests are needed. The amount of code duplicated is small since we need to copy only the code fragments that deal with returned results. This allows us to combine the return with synchronization at no additional run-time cost. For full details see [9].

Figure 7 illustrates synchronizers. As indicated in the left part of the figure, assume that we have two threads, T_1 and T_2, which return to the code fragments A and B, respectively, in the parent. There they synchronize, before starting the code C.[†] The key observation is that modifying the contents of the return address lets us encode synchronization information. PCRCs allow the parent to perform this modification.

The resulting situation, which relies on code duplication, is shown in the right part of Figure 7. Depending on the synchronization state, each of the two threads returns directly to the code for synchronization failure (AF or BF) or success (AC or BC). If both threads are explicitly forked, the return addresses for both initially point to their respective failure entry points (AF and BF). Whichever returns first executes its return code fragment (A or B) followed by a piece of code for synchronization failure. If the first thread was invoked with `tfork`, its initial failure entry point will invoke the second thread. The failure entry point will also modify the other thread's return address to point to the code for synchronization success. Synchronizers and PCRCs provide the mechanisms to efficiently combine the return and synchronization.

[†]Each of the three pieces of code is fairly short. A and B usually handle only taking the results and depositing them into the parent's frame, while C includes only one basic block.

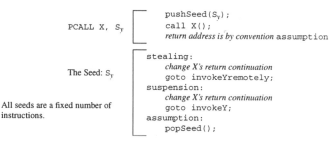

Figure 8   How `pcall` and thread seeds are implemented.

5   REMOTE WORK: THE LAZY PARALLEL CALL

So far we have shown how to reduce the overhead of potential parallelism when it actually unfolds sequentially on the local processor. Here we extend these ideas to generate work for remote processors. We introduce *thread seeds*, which allow us to represent the potential work in the system so that it may be distributed efficiently among multiple processors. Our goal is to allow work to be distributed remotely, but pay the cost only when there is an actual need to do so.

Thread seeds are a direct extension of the multiple return addresses we introduced to handle the suspension of children invoked by a t fork. As shown in Figure 8, a thread seed is a code fragment with three entry points: one for child return, one for child suspension, and one for an external work-stealing request. At the implementation level, a thread seed can be thought of as an extended version of continuation passing [1], where the child is passed three different continuations, one for each of the three cases. When the compiler determines that there is work that could be run in parallel, it creates a thread seed which represents the work. For example, with two successive forks, the t fork for the first thread will be associated with a thread seed representing the fork of the second thread.

We combine seed generation and tfork into a single primitive, pcall X, S_Y, where X is the function to call and S_Y is a thread seed that will, when executed in the context of the parent, cause the function Y to be invoked. Upon execution of the pcall, a seed is created and control is transferred to X, making the current (parent) frame inactive. The newly created seed remains dormant until one of three things happens: the child returns (the seed is inlined), the child suspends (the seed is activated), or a remote processor requests work (the seed is stolen). All three cases require the intervention of the parent. If the child returns, the parent picks up the seed and inlines the new thread of control into its own, i.e.Y executes on the parent's stacklet, just as if it had been called sequentially. If the child suspends, the parent activates the seed by spawning Y off on its own new stacklet; the seed becomes a new thread concurrent with the first, but on the same processor. If a remote processor requests work, the parent executes a remote call of Y, which becomes a new thread running concurrently with the current thread, but on another processor.

The model described above is a direct extension of the multiple return addresses used to implement the lazy thread fork. In addition to two continuations for handling the "return" and "suspension," we need a third for "finding work." If a remote work request is received, the run-time system must somehow find the thread seed (the third continuation) to initiate the creation of remote work. Here we consider two approaches to finding such work: an implicit seed model and an explicit seed model.

In the implicit model, the remote work request interrupts the child, which then continues execution at the work-stealing entry point of its parent. If there is no work, the entry point contains a code fragment to jump to the parents ancestor on the stack. The search continues until either work is generated or no work is found because no excess parallelism is present. For the implicit model, the `pushSeed` and `popSeed` macros in Figure 8 turn into nops and the planting of a seed is an abstract operation. The advantage of this model is that when a `pcall` is made no bookkeeping is required. Instead, the stack frames themselves form the data structure needed to find work. The disadvantage is that finding work is more complex.

In the explicit model, when a seed is planted a special continuation is pushed onto the top of a *seed queue*. The continuation is a pointer to the return address in the frame. The calling convention is such that the return from the child will default to the assumption point. If a child suspends, it saves the top pointer in the stacklet stub, pops the top seed off the queue, sets the `sp` as indicated by the seed, and jumps into the suspension entry point of the seed.

The explicit queueing of seeds allows us to find work with just a few instructions. For instance, if a child suspends, it can find its ancestor, which has more work to perform, merely by popping off the top seed. Or, more importantly, if a remote processor requests work, we can determine if there is work by simply comparing the top and bottom pointers to the seed queue. We can also spawn off that work by jumping through the work-stealing entry point of the seed at the bottom of the queue. The parent, invoked through the seed, will execute the work-stealing routine, placing any appropriate seed on the bottom of the queue. The drawback of this scheme is that even when a seed is inlined into the current thread (the sequential case) there is an extra cost of two memory references over the previously described implicit scheme.

6   EXPERIMENTAL RESULTS

In this section we present preliminary performance results for our techniques on both uni- and multiprocessors. Our uniprocessor data were collected on a SparcStation 10. Our multiprocessor data were collected on a CM-5.

We have produced a parallel version of C for the CM-5 which incorporates the techniques presented in this paper. To evaluate these techniques we begin by comparing the performance of four different implementations of the doubly recursive Fibonacci function. Fib, being fine-grained, is a good "stress test" of function invocation. As shown in Table 1, the C version is significantly slower than either the synchronizer or

Compilation Method	Runtime (secs)
gcc -O4 fib.c	2.29
Assembly version of Fib	1.22
Fib with stacklets, lazy threads, and synchronizers	1.50
Fib as above with explicit seeds	1.86

Table 1 Comparing runtimes of fib 31 on a SparcStation 10.

Program	Short Description	Input Size	TAM	Lazy Threads
Gamteb	Monte Carlo neutron transport	40,000	220.8	139.0
Paraffins	Enumerate isomers of paraffins	19	6.6	2.4
Simple	Hydrodynamics and heat conduction	1 1 100	5.0	3.3
MMT	Matrix multiply test	500	70.5	66.5

Table 2 Dynamic run-time in seconds on a SparcStation 10 for the Id90 benchmark programs under the TAM model and lazy threads with multiple strands using explicit seeds. The programs are described in [7].

the seed version. The reason is that our stacklet management code does not use register windows, which introduce a high overhead on the Sparc. For a fair comparison we wrote an assembly version of Fib that also does not use register windows. This highly optimized assembly version runs only 18% faster than the synchronizer version, which incorporates all the mechanisms for multithreading support.

Further evidence that lazy threads are efficient is presented in Table 2, where we compare our lazy thread model with TAM for some larger programs on the Sparc. At this time our Id90 compiler uses a primitive version of explicit seed creation. In addition to the primitives described so far, the compiler uses strands, a mechanism to support fine-grained parallelism within a thread [9]. We see a performance improvement ranging from 1.1 times faster for coarse-grained programs like blocked matrix multiply (MMT) to 2.7 times faster for finer-grained programs. We expect an additional benefit of up to 30% when the compiler generates code using synchronizers.

Next, we look at the efficiency of work-stealing combined with seeds on a parallel machine by examining the performance of the synthetic benchmark proposed in [16] and also used in [25]. Grain is a doubly recursive program that computes a sum, but each leaf executes a loop of g instructions, allowing us to control the granularity of the leaf nodes. We compare its efficiency to the sequential C code compiled by gcc. As shown in Figure 9, using stacklets we achieve over 90% efficiency when the grain size is as little as 400 cycles. Compare this to the grain size of an invocation of fib, which is approximately 30 cycles. Most of the inefficiency comes from the need to poll the CM-5 network. The speed-up curve in Figure 9 shows that even for very fine-grained programs, the thread seeds successfully exploit the entire machine.

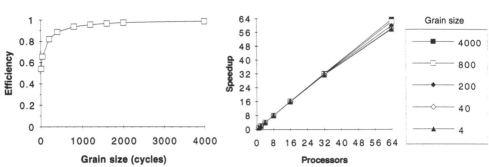

Figure 9   Efficiency of lazy threads on the CM-5 compared to the sequential C implementation as a function of granularity. We use the synthetic benchmark Grain [16, 25].

7   SUMMARY

We have shown that by integrating a set of innovative techniques for call frame management, call/return linkage, and thread generation we can provide a fast parallel call which obtains nearly the full efficiency of a sequential call when the child thread executes locally and runs to completion without suspension. This occurs frequently with aggressively parallel languages such as Id90, as well as more conservative languages such as C with parallel calls.

The central idea is to pay for what you use. Thus, a local fork is performed essentially as a sequential call, with the attendant efficient stack management and direct transfer of control and data. The only preparation for parallelism is the use of bounded-size stacklets and the provision of multiple return entry points in the parent. If the child actually suspends before completion, control is returned to the parent so that it can take appropriate action. Similarly, remote work is generated lazily. When a thread has work that can be performed remotely, it exposes an entry point, called a thread seed, that will produce the remote work on demand. If the work ends up being performed locally, it is simply inlined into the local thread of control as a sequential call. We exploit the one bit of flexibility in the sequential call, the indirect jump on return, to provide very fast synchronization and to avoid explicit checking for special cases, such as stacklet underflow.

Empirical studies with a parallel extension to C show that these techniques offer very good parallel performance and support fine-grained parallelism even on a distributed memory machine. Integrating these methods into a prototype compiler for Id90 results, depending on the frequency of parallel calls in the program, in an improvement by nearly a factor of two over previous approaches.

Acknowledgements

We are grateful to the anonymous referees and participants at the workshop for their valuable comments. We would also like to thank Manuel Faehndrich, Urs Hölzle,

Martin Rinard, Nathan Tawil, and Deborah Weisser for their comments. Computational support at Berkeley was provided by the NSF Infrastructure Grant number CDA-8722788. Seth Copen Goldstein is supported by an AT&T Graduate Fellowship. Klaus Erik Schauser received research support from the Department of Computer Science at UCSB. David Culler is supported by an NSF Presidential Faculty Fellowship CCR-9253705 and LLNL Grant UCB-ERL-92/172.

REFERENCES

[1] A. W. Appel. *Compiling with continuations*. Cambridge University Press, New York, 1992.

[2] Arvind and D. E. Culler. Dataflow architectures. In *Annual Reviews in Computer Science*, volume 1, pages 225–253. Annual Reviews Inc., Palo Alto, CA, 1986.

[3] R. D. Blumofe, C. F. Joerg, B. C. Kuszmaul, C. E. Leiserson, P. Lisiecki, K. H. Randall, A. Shaw, and Y. Zhou. *Cilk 1.1 reference manual*. MIT Lab for Comp. Sci., 545 Technology Square, Cambridge, MA 02139, September 1994.

[4] M.C. Carlisle, A. Rogers, J.H. Reppy, and L.J. Hendren. Early experiences with Olden (parallel programming). In *Languages and Compilers for Parallel Computing. 6th International Workshop Proceedings*, pages 1–20. Springer-Verlag, 1994.

[5] K.M. Chandy and C. Kesselman. Compositional C++: compositional parallel programming. In *Languages and Compilers for Parallel Computing. 5th International Workshop Proceedings*, pages 124–44. Springer-Verlag, 1993.

[6] E. C. Cooper and R. P. Draves. C-Threads. Technical Report CMU-CS-88-154, Carnegie-Mellon University, February 1988.

[7] D. E. Culler, S. C. Goldstein, K. E. Schauser, and T. von Eicken. TAM — a compiler controlled threaded abstract machine. *Journal of Parallel and Distributed Computing*, 18:347–370, July 1993.

[8] J.E. Faust and H.M. Levy. The performance of an object-oriented threads package. In *SIGPLAN Notices*, pages 278–88, Oct. 1990.

[9] S. C. Goldstein, K. E. Schauser, and D. E. Culler. Lazy Threads, Stacklets, and Synchronizers: Enabling primitives for compiling parallel languages. Technical report, University of California at Berkeley, 1995.

[10] R. Hieb, R. Kent Dybvig, and C. Bruggeman. Representing control in the presence of first-class continuations. In *SIGPLAN Notices*, pages 66–77, June 1990.

[11] U. Hölzle, C. Chambers, and D. Ungar. Debugging optimized code with dynamic deoptimization. In *SIGPLAN Notices*, pages 32–43, July 1992.

[12] P. Hudak, S. Peyton Jones, P. Walder, B. Boutel, J. Fairbairn, J. Fasel, M.M. Guzman, K. Hammond, J. Hughes, T. Johnsson, D. Kieburtz, R. Nikhil, W. Partain, and J. Peterson. Report on the programming language Haskell: a non-strict, purely functional language (version 1.2). *SIGPLAN Notices*, vol.27 (no.5): Ri–Rx, Rl–R163, May 1992.

[13] H. F. Jordan. Performance measurement on HEP — a pipelined MIMD computer. In *Proc. of the 10th Annual Int. Symp. on Comp. Arch.*, Stockholm, Sweden, June 1983.

[14] L.V. Kale and S. Krishnan. CHARM++: a portable concurrent object oriented system based on C++. In *SIGPLAN Notices*, pages 91–108, Oct. 1993.

[15] D.A. Kranz, R.H. Halstead Jr., and E. Mohr. Mul-T: a high-performance parallel Lisp. In *SIGPLAN Notices*, pages 81–90, July 1989.

[16] E. Mohr, D.A. Kranz, and R.H. Halstead Jr. Lazy task creation: a technique for increasing the granularity of parallel programs. *IEEE Transactions on Parallel and Distributed Systems*, vol.2 (no.3): 264–80, July 1991.

[17] R. S. Nikhil. Id (version 88.0) reference manual. Technical Report CSG Memo 284, MIT Lab for Comp. Sci., March 1988.

[18] Rishiyur S. Nikhil. Cid: A parallel, "shared memory" C for distributed-memory machines. In *Languages and Compilers for Parallel Computing. 7th International Workshop Proceedings*. Springer-Verlag, 1995.

[19] R.S. Nikhil. A multithreaded implementation of Id using P-RISC graphs. In *Languages and Compilers for Parallel Computing. 6th International Workshop Proceedings*, pages 390–405. Springer-Verlag, 1994.

[20] A. Rogers, J. Reppy, and L. Hendren. Supporting SPMD execution for dynamic data structures. In *Languages and Compilers for Parallel Computing. 5th International Workshop Proceedings*, pages 192–207. Springer-Verlag, 1993.

[21] M. Rozier, V. Abrossimov, F. Armand, I. Boule, M. Gien, M. Guillemont, F. Herrman, C. Kaiser, S. Langlois, P. Leonard, and W. Neuhauser. Overview of the CHORUS distributed operating system. In *Proceedings of the USENIX Workshop on Micro-Kernels and Other Kernel Architectures*, pages 39–69. USENIX Assoc, 1992.

[22] David M. Ungar. *The design and evaluation of a high performance Smalltalk system*. ACM distinguished dissertations. MIT Press, 1987.

[23] M.T. Vandevoorde and E.S. Roberts. WorkCrews: an abstraction for controlling parallelism. *International Journal of Parallel Programming*, vol.17 (no.4): 347–66, Aug. 1988.

[24] T. von Eicken, D. E. Culler, S. C. Goldstein, and K. E. Schauser. Active Messages: a mechanism for integrated communication and computation. In *Proc. of the 19th Int'l Symposium on Computer Architecture*, Gold Coast, Australia, May 1992.

[25] D.B. Wagner and B.G. Calder. Leapfrogging: a portable technique for implementing efficient futures. In *SIGPLAN Notices*, pages 208–17, July 1993.

[26] Akinori Yonezawa. *ABCL– an object-oriented concurrent system* . MIT Press series in computer systems. MIT Press, 1990.

13

INTEGRATING DATA AND TASK PARALLELISM IN SCIENTIFIC PROGRAMS[†]

Ewa Deelman, Wesley K. Kaplow,
Boleslaw K. Szymanski, Peter Tannenbaum, Louis Ziantz

Department of Computer Science,
Rensselaer Polytechnic Institute,
Troy, NY 12180 USA

ABSTRACT

Functional languages attract the attention of developers of parallelizing compilers because of the implicit parallelism of functional programs and the simplified data dependence analysis of functional statements. A major drawback of functional languages is that naive translation of functional programs results in code that requires excessive memory. In this paper we explore the connection between the memory optimization and communication optimization of parallel codes generated from functional languages. We also show how a functional language can be used as an intermediate form in the translation from FORTRAN to customized, architecture-specific parallel code.

1 INTRODUCTION

FORTRAN is a common language used in engineering and scientific computing. Recent versions of the language (*e.g.*, Fortran90 and High Performance Fortran) allow programmers to embed special directives for running their programs in parallel. However, many currently used programs are written in older dialects of FORTRAN and cannot benefit from faster parallel computers; these programs run strictly sequentially.

We are developing a system that automatically transforms serial FORTRAN into parallel C, performing memory optimization and introducing data and task parallelism (see Figure 1). The core of the system is a new version of the EPL compiler (the original version of EPL is described in [12]) with a FORTRAN front-end. EPL is a functional language and therefore obeys the single-assignment rule. As such, data dependencies in EPL are readily visible. We exploit this characteristic in the construction of a detailed data-dependency graph called an *array graph*. The array graph represents

---

[†] This work was partially supported by ONR Grant N00014-93-1-0076 and NSF Grant CCR-9216053.

both data and control flow in a single structure. From the array graph we generate a *schedule graph* that represents the minimal constraints on the execution order of a computation.

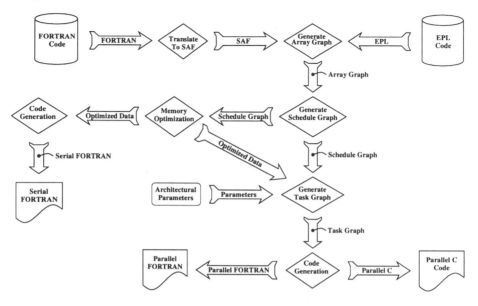

Figure 1 Overview of EPL System

The scheduled program is then optimized for memory usage and communication by finding optimal loop arrangements and variable representations. The schedule graph defines an initial task parallelism. Architectural parameters of the target machine are used both to tune the task parallelism and to extract data parallelism from the program. The new parallel schedule, called a *task graph*, is finally sent to the *code generator*.

Many scientific computations include iterative solvers, where an approximate result is repeatedly refined. In FORTRAN, each iteration writes the new values over the previous result. When such a solver is converted to a single assignment form, each successive result must be written to a new data location. This is one example of the excessive memory requirements inherent in functional languages.

Fortunately, analysis of array assignments and references can often show that each iteration step through a loop uses only a fixed number of adjacent elements of a data structure. This allows the object code to allocate a "window" large enough for only this fixed number of elements, not the entire dimension of the structure[13]. As with the original FORTRAN, the elements in the window are overwritten in each iteration.*

Programmers use variable windows intuitively, often with the intension of maintaining code readability. This approach may discount several more efficient (but counter-intuitive) windowing opportunities. Likewise, loops are the main source of task

---

*There is no reason for the optimized code to obey the single-assignment rule.

partitioning that enables data or pipeline parallelism. The scope of loops and their arrangements are crucial for parallelization of a program. We employ a systematic approach to windowing and parallelization in order to find an efficient solution. In general, new windows are formed by merging two or more loops found in the schedule graph. Large mergers, incorporating many loops, can potentially provide several windowing and pipelining opportunities. However, special care must be taken to preserve data dependencies.

In this paper we briefly present the major steps of FORTRAN to parallel C transformation and focus on loop transformations for both memory optimization and data and pipeline parallelization for distributed memory machines.

2   FORTRAN FRONT-END

The FORTRAN front-end is a procedural to functional language converter. Its purpose is to rename variables such that each variable is assigned exactly once. The result of this transformation is Single Assignment Fortran (SAF). SAF is still valid FORTRAN, but, as with EPL, the single-assignment rule exposes data dependencies. (Each assignment statement in SAF uniquely defines a variable, and so we will refer to EPL and SAF statements as equations.) A correct translation from FORTRAN into SAF centers on two major issues. First, each translated assignment must be guaranteed to bind a value to a unique variable. This requires a renaming scheme for variables that are multiply-assigned. The second issue is to ensure that every reference actually refers to the proper (renamed) variable. These two problems are intimately related, and are best addressed simultaneously.

As a first step in renaming, the line number of each assignment is appended to each assigned variable. FORTRAN allows only one assignment per line, and so the appended numbers are guaranteed to be unique. To find and rename variable references, we use def-use chaining: for each assignment, we find all uses of the renamed variable and rename the references accordingly. As a result of this first step, each basic block in the program, when considered independently, is in SAF. Any variable that was assigned repeatedly inside a basic block is now represented by new assignments, differentiated by line number.

The second step in renaming translates basic blocks from loops and subroutines; these blocks are executed iteratively. Each multiply-assigned variable assigned in these blocks is promoted in dimension: scalars become one dimensional arrays; one dimensional arrays become two dimensional arrays, *etc.* This new dimension, sometimes called a "temporal" dimension, is guaranteed to have a unique value for each iteration through the basic block. An iteration through a basic block that would have reassigned a variable in the original code will now make an assignment to a unique element in that variable's array. Note that assignments to two distinct array elements are valid in SAF; repeated assignments to the same array element are not valid. To determine whether assignments are made to the same array elements, we use various dependence tests (cf. [6, 7]). If the results of the dependence tests are negative within a loop, then no two elements are reassigned in the loop, and no temporal dimension is needed.

The temporal dimension is so named because it represents a time-stamp for each iteration. In the case of loops, its value can be simply the loop control variable. In subroutines, it can be an activation counter, automatically incremented each time the subroutine is called.[†] This additional dimension means that SAF programs require significantly more memory to execute than the original FORTRAN. Fortunately, memory optimization can reclaim this added space.

3   INTERNAL DATA STRUCTURES

Array Graph   The array graph is one of the fundamental structures used by the EPL compiler. It represents control-flow and data dependence constraints on program execution in the form of dependencies between data elements in the program. The basic components of the array graph are nodes, edges, and edge attributes. The nodes of the graph represent different activities associated with the data elements and equations of a program. Data nodes indicate that a variable should receive its value, and equation nodes imply that an equation should be evaluated. The array graph has one node for each variable that is not a subscript and one for each equation.[‡] The edges in the graph indicate dependencies between nodes, and paths through the graph show an implied partial ordering of the computations associated with the equation nodes. Edge attributes list subscripting expressions and other information related to a particular dependency.

Formally, the array graph is defined as: $G_A = (N, E, M)$ where $N = \{n_1, \ldots, n_p\}$ is a set of nodes, $E \subseteq N \times N$ is a set of edges, and $M : L = \{l_1, \ldots, l_m\} \to N \cup E$ is a labeling function. E^* represents the standard transitive closure of the edge relation E. The labeling function M defines a label for each node and edge in the graph. The node label $l_i = M(n_i)$ includes information on the type and class of the node, its dimensionality, ranges of the dimensions, and subscripts associated with these dimensions. The edge label $l_{i,k} = M(e_{i,k})$ includes the type of the dependence and subscripting information.

A list of trees is created representing the equations in a program, and from this list the subgraphs for the equations are built. Each equation node is augmented with a list of the subscripts used in the corresponding equation — this is referred to as the node subscript list and is used in code generation. A dimension attribute node list is a sequence of indexing expressions associated with a dependency. One such list is attached to each edge based upon the array access that generated the edge. These lists are used in scheduling the computation.

[†] Strictly speaking, these counters do not obey the Single Assignment rule, and therefore they behave like subscripts in EPL. However, all other variables in the program are in SAF.

[‡] A variable of type subscript in EPL would correspond to a loop-control variable in an SAF program.

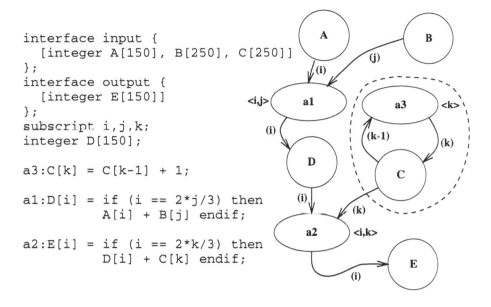

```
interface input {
   [integer A[150], B[250], C[250]]
};
interface output {
   [integer E[150]]
};
subscript i,j,k;
integer D[150];

a3:C[k] = C[k-1] + 1;

a1:D[i] = if (i == 2*j/3) then
          A[i] + B[j] endif;

a2:E[i] = if (i == 2*k/3) then
          D[i] + C[k] endif;
```

Figure 2 Example EPL code and corresponding Array Graph

Figure 2 shows an example array graph. The circles represent data nodes, and equation nodes are represented by ovals. The bracketed variables correspond to node subscript lists, and the variables enclosed by parentheses are dimension attribute node lists. Note that equation one (**a1**) represents the assignment of values to D, equation two (**a2**) represents the assignment to E, and equation three (**a3**) represents the assignment to C. The dotted line in Figure 2 encloses a strongly connected component (SCC).[§]

Schedule Graph The scheduler recursively traverses the array graph, storing a feasible program ordering in the (directed, acyclic) schedule graph. Nodes in the schedule graph represent loops, assignments, and I/O. One edge class represents temporal dependence: the action at the source of the edge must complete before the action at the destination begins execution. The other edge class, called a *zoom* edge, represents a loop nesting: the source of a zoom edge is always a loop node, and the subgraph at the destination is nested inside the loop. This subgraph can itself contain loop nodes and zoom edges, representing multiply nested loops.

Formally, the schedule graph is a refinement of the array graph in which nodes represent disjoint subsets of array graph nodes and edges include the additional class of zoom edges.

A major function of the scheduler is to find and break SCCs in the array graph. (Cycles in the array graph occur when variables are defined recursively.) If a component

---

[§] An SCC is a maximal subgraph of the array graph with the property that for any pair of its vertices v, w there are directed paths in the SCC from v to w and from w to v.

contains more than one node, it will be scheduled inside a loop. The components are then interconnected based on the dependencies present in the array graph. Each SCC is searched for cycles formed by edges containing the same subscript. Under certain conditions, the scheduler can form a loop over that subscript and mark the edges forming a subscript as resolved. For example, if a cycle contains edges labeled with indexing expressions k and $k - 1$, then scheduling a loop over k will enforce a dependency represented by the edge labeled $(k - 1)$.¶ This edge is redundant and can be removed, thus breaking the cycle and decomposing the SCC.

Each newly formed loop has associated with it a direction: ascending, descending, or either. In the case above, the dependencies dictate that the loop over k must be ascending. A loop that calculates $B[k] = A[k]$ could proceed in either direction.

Code Generation   The C code generator traverses the task graph in a topological order. For each loop node, a corresponding C *for* loop is formed. Then all the zoom edges emerging from the loop node are traversed, and the code generation is performed on the subgraph. As the zoom edge is traversed, the loop subscript is remembered by placing it into an *active subscript* list. The code for an equation node is constructed as follows: first the loops for the subscripts present in the equation and not present in the *active subscript* list are formed, and then the code for the equation itself is emitted. After the code for all the subgraphs reachable via the zoom edges has been generated, other nodes dependent on the loop node are generated. If an equation is not reached via some zoom edge, loops will be emitted for all the subscripts present in the equation's node subscript list.

4   MEMORY OPTIMIZATION

The scheduler produces loops with the smallest possible scope for a correct schedule. This means that each loop defines a minimal number of variables. Loop merging expands the scope of loops to define several variables at once. As a simplification, we only consider merging loops that iterate over equivalent ranges. (An alternative would be to consider merging a loop over range n with a loop over range $m \subset n$; this would require special guards to avoid defining or referencing invalid values. For a special class of subscripts, called sublinear subscripts in EPL [12], this is a straightforward extension and it will be included in the next version of the EPL compiler.) Variable definitions are characterized by their *range-sets*.

Definition 4.1 *A range-set defines the iteration space for a single dimension of a variable's defining equation. An n-dimensional variable will thus have n (possibly distinct) range-sets. Two range-sets are equivalent if they define the same iteration space.*

To illustrate our algorithm for merging loops, we use a refined version of the schedule graph, called a *variable graph* (see Figure 3): $G_V = (N, E, M)$ where $N =$

¶The value of the $(k - 1)^{st}$ iteration will be preserved for the kth iteration.

$\{n_1, \ldots, n_p\}$ is a set of nodes, $E \subseteq N \times N$ is a set of edges, and $M : L = \{l_1, \ldots, l_m\} \rightarrow N \cup E$ is a labeling function. Here, the defining node for each variable (called the equation node) is shown explicitly in the graph only when the defined variable has a lower dimensionality than any of its constituent variables. If the defined variable has at least as many dimensions as its constituents, then the equation node is merged with the data node. This distinction is useful in defining loops as described below. Edges in the graph point to nodes in which variables are referenced. The edge label $l_{i,k} = M(e_{i,k})$ includes a *dependence bound*.

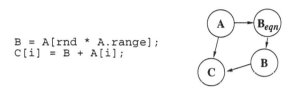

```
B = A[rnd * A.range];
C[i] = B + A[i];
```

Figure 3 Example of EPL equations and resulting variable graph. Note that B is a scalar, but its assignment requires iterating through potentially all elements of A.

The dependence bound gives an indication of how many new elements of a variable are created before the current element is used. It is calculated for each variable graph edge as follows:

Let an edge $e \in E$ correspond to an equation of the form,

$$B[\ldots, se_0, \ldots] = f(A[\ldots, se_1, \ldots], \ldots, A[\ldots, se_k, \ldots])$$

where each se_j is a sub-expression on i. The bound on the range-set i for this edge is given by:

$$\max_{1 \leq i \leq i.range} \max_{1 \leq m \leq k} se_0 - se_m$$

For the current version of the EPL compiler, we assume that the bound is the full range of i except when $se_0 = i$ and all se_j have the form $i \pm c$, where c is a constant. If the bound is a compile-time constant, then i is written as $i_<$ for an ascending loop and $i_>$ for a descending loop. If the bound is not known at compile time, or is known to be the full range of i, then i is written as $i_\perp$. Future versions will include deeper subscript analysis.

Two sets are easily built from the variable graph: the set of windowable variables and the set of distinct range-sets. From these, four more sets are also easily created: the set of variables referenced and/or defined in each node, the set of nodes in which each variable appears, the range-sets associated with each node, and the nodes associated with each given range-set.

Definition 4.2 *Let* $V = \{v_1, v_2, \ldots, v_q\}$ *be the set of all variables in the variable graph that are potentially windowable. A variable is potentially windowable iff:*

1. *For at least one dimension, its dependence bound is defined at compile-time and is known to be less than the full range of that dimension.*

2. *All its successors in the variable graph have at least one range-set in common.*

Definition 4.3 *Let $R = \{r_1, r_2, \ldots, r_s\}$ be the set of all range-sets in the variable graph.*

Definition 4.4 *For each $n_i \in N$ let $W_{n_i} = \{w_1, w_2, \ldots, w_p\}$ be the set of variables associated with n_i, and $J_{n_i} = \{j_1, j_2, \ldots, j_r\}$ be the set of range-sets associated with n_i. For each $v_i \in V$ let $M_{v_i} = \{n_j \in N : v_i \in W_{n_j}\}$. M_{v_i} is the set of all nodes in the variable graph that are associated with variable v_i. For each range-set $r \in R$, let $P_r = \{n_k \in N : r \in J_{n_k}\}$. P_r is the set of all nodes that are associated with range-set r.*

The objective of merging loops is to create valid windowing opportunities. A variable window is valid only when the definition and all references to the variable are enclosed in the same loop. To see this, consider a one-dimensional variable $A[n]$. If A is windowed, then in the ith iteration of its loop $A[i]$ will be defined and referenced. In a later iteration, the same memory location will be re-defined. If a reference to $A[i]$ appears outside the loop, the resulting value will be undetermined.

Another concern in merging loops is the preservation of data dependencies. Consider the EPL equation $B[i] = A[i]$. If A is windowed, then each iteration through the loop will assign an element[||] of A and then will reference that element in the assignment to the corresponding element of B. However, consider the slightly modified equation $B[i] = A[i] + A.last$ (where $A.last$ refers to the final element of the array A). The value of $A.last$ depends on the array A. If A is windowed, then the first iteration through its loop will define an element of A and will try to assign it, plus $A.last$, to the corresponding element of B. But, $A.last$ will not be defined until the final iteration of the loop. This is an instance where merging loops violates dependencies.

4.1 Well-Formed Loops

To address these three considerations: existence of a common range-set, presence of completely enclosed variables, and preservation of data-dependencies, we have developed the concept of *well-formed loops*. A well-formed loop is a subset of variable graph nodes with certain properties. Informally, nodes in the loop must all have at least one range-set in common (*i.e.*, they must all share at least one range-set in the source program). For at least one variable, the loop must contain all nodes associated with that variable. If any node inside the well-formed loop is dependent upon a node outside the loop, then the outside node cannot be dependent upon any nodes inside the loop. Finally, the loop cannot contain nodes that are not needed to satisfy the above constraints.

[||] This element can come from an equation or be read from an input port.

These properties can be defined in terms of functions over subsets of nodes in the variable graph.

Definition 4.5 *Let the <u>iterators</u> of a set of nodes in a variable graph, denoted $I(X)$, be defined as:* $I(X) = \prod_{n \in X} J_n$

Definition 4.6 *Let the <u>core</u> of X over r, denoted $C(X, r)$, where $X \subseteq N$, and $r \in R$, be defined as:* $C(X, r) = (\bigcup_{v \in V : M_v \subseteq (X \cap P_r)} M_v) \cap (\{n \in X : \forall n_1 \in X, (n, n_1) \in E \to r \in J_{n_1} \text{ and the bound of } (n, n_1) < r.range\})$

Definition 4.7 *Let the <u>closure</u> of a set of nodes in a variable graph, denoted $Cl(X)$, be defined as:*
$$Cl(X) = X \cup \{n \in N : (\exists p_0 \in X : (p_0, n) \in E^*) \wedge (\exists p_1 \in X : (n, p_1) \in E^*)\}$$

Iterators are similar to loop control variables in FORTRAN, with the associated loop direction; the core represents the minimal subset of variable graph nodes needed to completely enclose a windowable variable; the closure enforces preservation of dependencies. The following definition formalizes the concept of a well-formed loop:

Definition 4.8 *A non-empty subset $L \subseteq N$ of nodes in a variable graph is called a <u>well-formed loop</u> iff:*

1. *The set of iterators over L is non-empty. $(I(L) \neq \emptyset)$*

2. *The closure of the core of L is equal to L. $(Cl(C(L)) = L)$*

The algorithm for finding well-formed loops uses a slightly different definition:**

Definition 4.9 *A non-empty subset $L \subseteq N$ of nodes in a schedule graph is called a <u>well-formed loop</u> iff: $I(L) \neq \emptyset$, $Cl(L) = L$, and $Cl(C(L)) \supseteq L$.*

4.2   Generating and Merging Well-Formed Loops

Well-formed loops are constructed and merged one range-set at a time. The first step in the algorithm creates the lowest rank well-formed loops for each variable in the range-set; rank refers to the number of variables enclosed in a loop. Then, where possible, the loops are iteratively merged. For n variables in a given range-set, there are potentially 2^n loop mergers. Fortunately, certain loops will be incompatible with other loops; this feature can greatly reduce the algorithm's search space. A loop is incompatible with another loop, for example, if it is only partially enclosed in the second loop. (A similar rule applies to loops in procedural languages.)

**The proof that the two definitions are equivalent is straightforward but somewhat lengthy, and is not included here.

As the algorithm merges loops, it stores its results in a *loop graph*. Nodes in this graph represent well-formed loops, and edges (called exclusion edges) connect pair-wise incompatible loops. In addition to the rule above, two loops are marked incompatible if they are mutually dominated by a third loop. A loop dominates two other loops if it has a higher rank than the two smaller loops and its set of exclusion edges is the union of the exclusion edges of the smaller loops. When two loops are found to be dominated by a third, the two loops are removed from the list of loops to use in future mergers; only the dominator is retained. In this way, each domination reduces the search space by one.

Once the loop graph is fully constructed, the final step is to choose the most memory efficient, feasible (*i.e.*, compatible) set of well-formed loops. Memory efficiency is based on the window sizes for each loop as calculated in [9]. The results of the memory optimization are either read by the code generator for serial output, or parallelized as described in the next section.

Definition 4.10 *For the pair consisting of the subset of nodes $U \subseteq N$ and a range-set $r \in I(U)$, the* <u>*loop over r generated by U*</u>, *designated $L(U, r)$, is defined as $L(U, r) = Cl(\overline{C(U)})$ if $Cl(C(U)) \subseteq P_r$ and $L(U, r) = \emptyset$ otherwise.*

Definition 4.11 *The* <u>*rank*</u> *of a loop $L(U, r)$ is defined as:*
$|\{v_j \in V : M_{v_j} \subseteq L(U, r)\}|.$

The construction incorporates the three rules in the definition of well-formed loops. Recall the distinction between the schedule graph and the variable graph. In the example shown in Figure 3, a well-formed loop containing the three nodes A, B_{eqn}, and C will be augmented to contain B by the closure requirement. However, B does not share a range-set with the other three nodes, and therefore the loop containing all four nodes is not a well-formed loop. If B did share a common range-set with the other nodes, then this would not be an issue, and there would be no reason to treat B's data node separately from its equation node. The general algorithm for generating the loop graph is then:

1. $\forall r \in R$:

    (a) $\forall v_j \in V : M_{v_j} \subseteq P_r$, create $L(\{ev_j\}, r)$, where ev_j is the equation node that defines v_j. This creates the initial set of seed loops.

    (b) Loops are iteratively joined as follows:
    For any two seed loops $L(U_j, r)$ and $L(U_k, r)$, if $Cl(C(u_j \cup u_k)) \neq \emptyset$ then create $L(u_j \cup u_k, r)$. If $L(u_j \cup u_k, r)$ dominates $L(U_j, r)$ and $L(U_k, r)$, draw an exclusion edge from $L(U_j, r)$ to $L(U_k, r)$, remove the two dominated loops from the set of seeds, and replace them with the dominator.

2. For all pairs of loops, $L(U_j, i)$ and $L(U_k, l)$, if $L(U_j, i) \cap L(U_k, l) \neq \emptyset$ and $L(U_j, i) \not\supseteq L(U_k, l)$ and $L(U_j, i) \not\subseteq L(U_k, l)$ then draw an exclusion edge

from $L(U_j, i)$ to $L(U_k, l)$. In other words, draw an exclusion between any two overlapping loops where one loop is not completely enclosed in the other.[††]

5 PARALLELIZATION

The semantics of EPL allow for a trivial parallelization of an EPL program on a dataflow machine. Every instance of each equation could be a separate thread enabled for execution when the data it requires becomes available [14, 1, 4]. Such synchronization would enforce a valid order of EPL program execution. However, this form of parallelization is not efficient on current dataflow machines, such as the Monsoon[5], because all synchronization is done at run-time, increasing the overhead incurred by token communication and matching.

A more efficient approach is to recognize at compile time which threads must execute sequentially relative to each other and then to merge them. This is the motivation behind creating the EPL schedule graph, introduced earlier, in which equations that are cyclically dependent on each other are clustered together. The nodes of the schedule graph constitute the smallest unbreakable tasks of computation in EPL parallelization.

The schedule graph nodes that are data dependent are clustered further at the time of memory optimization when the well-formed loops (WFL) are created. As discussed below, to explore pipeline parallelism such clustering can be extended beyond the boundaries of the well formed loops. An essential observation motivating this clustering is that the bodies of the pipeline loops can be parallelized in two ways. If the input to the pipeline loop can be provided in parallel, a data parallelization can be used in which an instance (or a range of instances) of the loop body is assigned to a separate processor. Regardless of the way the input arrives, the loop body can be pipelined, *i.e.*, several processors can be assigned to different parts of the loop body. The second method, pipelining of EPL programs, is discussed below. It should be noted that the object code created by pipelining invokes different parallel tasks executing together, and therefore such parallelization reaches beyond the SPMD model.

The goal of pipeline loop optimization is to enable the compiler to adjust the *granularity* [3] of the resulting computation to match the architectural parameters of a target architecture. This can be done by first adjusting the size of the pipeline stages to balance the computational load of each resulting cluster. Then, the pipeline communication message size can be selected to reduce the overhead incurred by inter-cluster communication based on the communications performance of the target.

5.1 Creation of Pipeline Loops

The objective of this stage of EPL parallelization is to create the largest clusters of schedule graph nodes that are amenable to pipelining. We refer to those clusters as Pipeline Loops (PLs). As in the case of well-formed loops (WFLs), nodes in such

---

[††]Note that these exclusion edges go both within and across range-sets.

clusters must share the same or equivalent range set[‡‡] and the closure of the cluster must be equal to itself. Unlike the well-formed loops, there is no need for a PL to cover all references to variables associated with the nodes. As a result, for each PL there is a WFL such that PL $\supseteq$ WFL, so WFLs are a good starting point for building PLs. Because of this looser restriction on the variable coverage, several well-formed loops can be clustered together into a pipeline loop.

Definition 5.1 *A non-empty subset $L \subseteq N$ of nodes in a variable graph is called a* *pipeline loop iff:*

1. *The set of iterators over L is non-empty. $(I(L) \neq \emptyset)$*

2. *The closure of L is equal to L. $(Cl(L) = L)$*

Any clustering of the schedule graph nodes defines an equivalence relation between those nodes. Therefore, there exists a corresponding refinement graph which we will refer to as a Clustered Schedule Graph (CSG). To determine the largest pipeline loops of a computation, we will consider only maximal clusterings and their corresponding graphs. Initially, each node of the CSG is a well-formed loop, and each edge describes the communication requirements between each pair of well-formed loops. Using this information we are able to enumerate all of the pipelines of a computation. Figure 4 shows an example CSG, illustrating the two possible maximal pipeline loop arrangements.

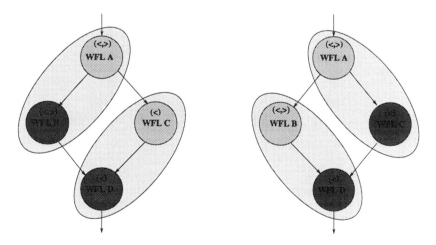

Figure 4   Two Candidate Dominant Pipeline Loop CSGs

In a CSG, each node is labeled with its directed iterators. The edges are labeled with the minimum delay.

[‡‡]Equivalence is defined over the relation in terms of subscript sublinearity (see [12]).

The graph in Figure 5 is a CSG where each node represents a well-formed loop, except for WFL C which also exposes its component schedule graph nodes. For example, consider WFL C and WFL E; the latter depends on values created by T ordered by the range set i in ascending order. We can easily see why a component of WFL E could not be merged into WFL C. This is due to the fact that WFL G uses the same values from T, but in a different order (descending). Thus, the windowing could not be extended. However, this does not mean that a pipeline loop could not be extended. In particular the pipeline loop could be extended to include both WFL E and WFL F. In the backward direction, we could extend the pipeline loop to include WFL A as well.

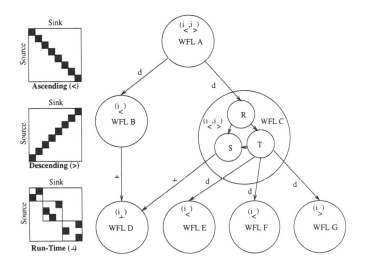

Figure 5   Example of a Clustered Schedule Graph

In our example CSG, WFL A and WFL C are labeled with $i_<, i_>$, indicating that the nodes are pipelineable in either direction. Therefore, another pipeline can be formed, one that includes WFL A, WFL C and WFL G. However, this is an exclusive-or in that it excludes the previously formed pipeline loop (*i.e.*, WFL A, WFL C, WFL E, and WFL F). To determine the compatibility for each node in the CSG we will use an algorithm described in [10], for *internal* data dependency propagation.

5.2   Optimizing Pipelines for Target Architectures

Pipeline Optimization Process   The following steps are used to optimize the execution of pipeline loops on a given target architecture:

1. Apply algorithm in Section 4.2, replacing Definition 4.8 with Definition 5.1. This creates an exclusion graph of the *dominant* pipeline loops.

2. For each candidate dominant pipeline loop CSG, optimize for a given architecture:

    (a) Determine the number of processors that can be effectively used for each dominant pipeline loop.

    (b) Determine the optimal pipeline communication size.

3. Cluster dependent pipeline loops.

The first step is performed by the process described in the previous section. Figure 4 shows a CSG with the two possible pipeline loop configurations where optimization can be explored.

For parallelization and pipeline optimization, only the boundaries of the pipeline loops are significant. Thus, each schedule graph node in a pipeline loop can potentially be scheduled on a separate processor as a pipeline stage. However, as shown in [8, 3] this may lead to a parallelization with too fine a granularity. Moreover, a pipeline's throughput is limited by its *worst* stage. Because of the regular communication patterns within a pipeline loop, Step 2a in the process is free to *cluster*, or *internalize* the communication between stages in the pipeline to increase the granularity to match target architecture parameters, while not reducing the potential speedup due to pipeline execution. Thus, Steps 2a and 2b are executed iteratively. Starting with n processors, Step 2a partitions the pipeline into n equal pipeline stages. Once this is done, the optimal block size (discussed in the next subsection) is chosen. If the resultant efficiency is lower than a serial execution, then the number of processors is decreased, and the pipeline is again repartitioned and communication optimized. If a binary search method is used, then the execution time is $O(Nlog(P_n))$ where N is the number of schedule graph nodes in the pipeline loop, and P_n is the maximum number of processors that can be assigned.

For the final step, we are investigating how known clustering techniques, *e.g.*, reducing the makespan [2], or increasing throughput [11], apply to this environment.

Determining the Pipeline Parameters   The following is a simple analytical model that is used to illustrate how optimal parameters of a pipeline can be determined. The base case of the model assumes that we have a pipeline loop which consists of a sending node E_1 with C_1 instructions executing on processor with S_1 instruction rate, and a receiving node, E_2, with C_2 and S_2 defined similarly. For simplicity, we assume a linear cost model for inter-processor communications, $C = \alpha + n \times \beta$, where α is the startup message overhead, β is the time to transfer one element over the communication channel, and n is the number of elements to transfer. The minimum number of elements required for a pipeline stage is given by d.

The cost of executing the pipeline loop with blocking factor k is:

$$kS_1C_1 + (n/k - 1)max(kS_1C_1, kS_2C_2, \alpha + kd\beta) + \alpha + kd\beta + kS_2C_2$$

If we assume that the computation of the pipeline can be balanced, that is: $A = S_1C_1 = S_2C_2$, then to find k that minimizes the cost, consider two cases: $k \geq \alpha/(A - d\beta)$, so $A \geq d\beta + \alpha/k$, and therefore, $k = \alpha/(A - d\beta)$, is the minimum. In the opposite case: $k < \alpha/(A - d\beta)$, and therefore $A < d\beta + \alpha/k$, so the derivative of the cost is: $2A - (n\alpha)/k^2$, and $k = \sqrt{n\alpha/2A}$, hence,

$$k_{opt} = min \left(\sqrt{\frac{n\alpha}{2A}}, \frac{\alpha}{A - d\beta} \right)$$

We can further observe that,

$$k_\infty \equiv \lim_{n\to\infty} k_{opt} = \frac{\alpha}{A - d\beta}$$

In fact, if

$$n \geq \frac{2A\alpha}{(A - d\beta)^2} \approx 2\frac{\alpha}{A} \text{ , then } k_{opt} = k_\infty$$

This formula helps to define the proper granularity for the pipeline for a given architecture. As long as the pipeline executes more than n repetitions, then it achieves optimum performance. Also, for a given n and latency α, the granularity of A can be adjusted by clustering.

6 CONCLUSIONS

This work shows how a uniform representation of fine-grain parallelism can be used for both the memory optimization and parallelization processes. We have presented a common formal basis for memory optimization and task creation. This method can be incorporated into a compiler to determine optimum pipelines based on a model of target architecture parameters. Much research remains, and we intend to incorporate these ideas into the EPL compilation system.

REFERENCES

[1] J. L. Gaudiot and L. Bic. *Advanced topics in dataflow computing.* Prentice Hall, New Jersey, 1991.

[2] A. Gerasoulis and T. Yang. Comparison of clustering heuristics for scheduling directed acyclic graphs on multiprocessors. *Journal of Parallel and Distributed Computing,* (16):276–291, 1992.

[3] A. Gerasoulis and T. Yang. On the granularity and clustering of directed acyclic task graphs. *IEEE Transactions on Parallel and Distributed Systems,* 4(6):686–701, 1993.

[4] B. Lee and A. R. Hurston. Dataflow architectures and multithreading. *IEEE Computer,* pages 27–39, August 1994.

[5] G. M. Papadopoulos. *Implementation of a general-purpose dataflow multiprocessor.* Research Monographs in Parallel and Distributed Computing. MIT Press, 1991.

[6] K. Psarris, X. Kong, and D. Klappholz. The direction vector I test. *IEEE Transactions on Parallel and Distributed Systems,* 11(4), November 1993.

[7] W. Pugh and D. Wonnacott. Nonlinear array dependence analysis. In B. K. Szymanski and B. Sinharoy, editors, *Languages, Compilers and Run-Time Systems for Scalable Computers*, pages 1–14. Kluwer Academic Publishers, Boston, 1995.

[8] V. Sarkar. *Partitioning and scheduling parallel programs for multiprocessors.* Research monographs in parallel and distributed computing. MIT Press, Cambridge, MA., 1989.

[9] B. Sinharoy and B. K. Szymanski. Memory optimization for parallel functional programs. *Computer Systems in Engineering.* To appear; abstract published in "Abstracts: International Meeting on Vector and Parallel Processing," CICA, Porto, Portugal, 1993, p. 36.).

[10] K. L. Spier and B. K. Szymanski. Interprocess analysis and optimization in the equational language compiler. In Burkhart, editor, *CONPAR 90-VAPP, Joint International Conference on Vector and Parallel Processing, Zurich, Switzerland,* Lecture Notes In Computer Science. Springer-Verlag, September 1990.

[11] J. Subhlok, D. R. O'Hallaron, T. Gross, P. A. Dinda, and J. Webb. Communication and memory requirements as the basis for mapping task and data parallel programs. In *Proceedings of SuperComputing 1994.* ACM, 1994.

[12] B. K. Szymanski. EPL–parallel programming with recurrent equations. In B.K. Szymanski, editor, *Parallel Functional Languages and Compilers.* ACM Press/Addison Wesley, New York, 1991.

[13] B. K. Szymanski and N. S. Prywes. Efficient handling of data structures in definitional languages. *Science of Computer Programming,* 10(3):221–245, 1988.

[14] A. H. Veen. Dataflow machine architecture. *ACM Computing Surveys,* 18(4), 1986.

14

COMMUNICATION GENERATION FOR CYCLIC(K) DISTRIBUTIONS[†]

Ken Kennedy,
Nenad Nedeljković,
and Ajay Sethi

Department of Computer Science
Rice University, Houston, TX 77005, USA

ABSTRACT

Communication resulting from references to arrays with general $cyclic(k)$ distributions in data-parallel programs is not amenable to existing analyses developed for *block* and *cyclic* distributions. The methods for communication generation presented in this paper are based on exploiting the repetitive nature of array accesses. We represent array access patterns as periodic sequences and use these sequences for efficient communication analysis and code generation. Our approach allows us to incorporate message coalescing optimization and to use overlap areas for shift communication. Experimental results from our prototype implementation demonstrate the validity of the proposed techniques.

1 INTRODUCTION

High Performance Fortran (HPF) is designed for portable high-level programming of parallel computers. It supports the data-parallel programming style in which Fortran 90 statements are combined with data layout directives that specify how arrays should be mapped to processors. The most general regular data distribution in HPF is the $cyclic(k)$ (or *block-cyclic*) distribution; array elements are first divided into blocks of size k, and these blocks are then assigned to processors cyclically. Two major tasks in compiling programs with references to block-cyclically distributed arrays are the enumeration of local addresses for array accesses performed by each processor and the generation of interprocessor communication. In our related work, we describe efficient methods for computing each processor's local addresses for array references with arbitrary affine subscripts [7]. In this paper, we present methods for computing

---

[†] This work was supported in part by ARPA contract DABT63-92-C-0038, NSF Cooperative Agreement Number CCR-9120008, and NSF/NASA grant# ASC-9213821. The content of this paper does not necessarily reflect the position or the policy of the Government and no official endorsement should be inferred.

communication sets and optimizations that improve the efficiency of the generated code.

The starting point for our work are the results by Chatterjee et al. [1]. By visualizing the layout of an array as a two-dimensional matrix, with each row containing pk elements, where p is the number of processors and k is the block size, they show that the local memory sequence corresponding to a regular array section can be described by a finite state machine (FSM) with at most k states. The FSM method is then applied to communication generation for array assignment statements. In the sending phase, each processor makes a single pass over its local data, determining the destination for each array element and building messages that consist of (address, value) pairs; message sending is followed by the execution of local iterations, after which each processor enters a receive-execute loop, receiving data items from other processors and performing non-local iterations. While this technique may lead to good data locality, especially during message packing, its disadvantage, as Stichnoth [7] points out, is that one ownership computation is required for each array access, and expensive integer divisions can incur substantial overhead.

Our techniques improve on Chatterjee et al.'s FSM approach in several ways. We take advantage of the repetitive memory access patterns to significantly reduce the number of required index translations. Using an idea previously applied in communication generation for irregular problems [2], we allocate overflow areas for non-local array elements which simplifies the generated code. Furthermore, this allows us to execute all loop iterations in the order specified by the original program. We also show how message coalescing can be applied to statements with multiple right-hand-side (rhs) references to the same array, in order to reduce the number of messages. Finally, we discuss the applicability of overlap areas, previously used only with $block$ distributions, for a common special case of shift communication.

2   COMPUTING COMMUNICATION SETS

We first consider the following normalized loop with the arrays A and B having $cyclic(k_A)$ and $cyclic(k_B)$ distributions:

$$\mathbf{do}\ i = 0,\, u$$
$$A(i\, s_A + l_A) = f(B(i\, s_B + l_B))$$
$$\mathbf{enddo}$$

Chatterjee et al. show that for each reference, the sequence of array elements accessed by any given processor can be computed using a table of local memory gaps whose size does not exceed the block size of the array's distribution [1]. In a related work, we present an improved algorithm for constructing the table in time linearly proportional to its size [8]. The algorithm is based on finding the basis vectors ($\mathbf{R} = (x^R, y^R)$ and $\mathbf{L} = (x^L, y^L)$) for the integer lattice corresponding to the accessed array elements, such that for any given array element and its offset within the block to which it belongs

Processor 0				Processor 1				Processor 2			
☐0	1	2	3	4	☐5	6	7	8	9	☐10	11
12	13	14	☐15	16	17	18	19	☐20	21	22	23
24	☐25	26	27	28	29	☐30	31	32	33	34	☐35
36	37	38	39	☐40	41	42	43	44	☐45	46	47
48	49	☐50	51	52	53	54	☐55	56	57	58	59
☐60	61	62	63	64	☐65	66	67	68	69	☐70	71
72	73	74	☐75	76	77	78	79	☐80	81	82	83
84	☐85	86	87	88	89	☐90	91	92	93	94	☐95

Figure 1 Elements of array A with $cyclic(4)$ distribution on 3 processors. The squares mark the array elements accessed by $A(5i)$ $(i \geq 0)$.

$(0 \leq offset < k)$, the next element accessed by the same processor is at the distance R (if $offset + x^R < k$), L (if $offset + x^R \geq k$ and $offset + x^L \geq 0$), or $L + R$ (otherwise). Using these vectors, we can construct the sequences of accessed array elements in both the local and the global index space (LOCAL and GLOBAL, respectively), as well as their corresponding iteration numbers (ITER).

As an example, we consider the arrays A and B distributed onto $p = 3$ processors with the block sizes $k_A = 4$ and $k_B = 8$. In Figure 1 we show the elements of array A that are accessed due to the reference $A(5i)$ $(s_A = 5, l_A = 0)$. Similarly, Figure 2 depicts the access pattern for the reference $B(7i + 2)$ $(s_B = 7, l_B = 2)$. The basis vectors of the lattice corresponding to array accesses in Figure 1 are $R_A = (x_A^R, y_A^R) = (3, 1)$ and $L_A = (x_A^L, y_A^L) = (-2, 1)$; the distance between indices 0 and 15 is R_A, the distance between 15 and 25 is L_A, and the distance between 25 and 50 is $L_A + R_A$. In Figure 2 we have $R_B = (7, 0)$ (the distance between indices 72 and 79), $L_B = (-3, 1)$ (the distance between 79 and 100), and $L_B + R_B = (4, 1)$ (the distance between 2 and 30).

Processor 0								Processor 1								Processor 2							
0	1	②2	3	4	5	6	7	8	⑨9	10	11	12	13	14	15	⑯16	17	18	19	20	21	22	㉓23
24	25	26	27	28	29	㉚30	31	32	33	34	35	36	㊲37	38	39	40	41	42	43	㊹44	45	46	47
48	49	50	㊿51	52	53	54	55	56	57	㊽58	59	60	61	62	63	64	㋫65	66	67	68	69	70	71
⑦72	73	74	75	76	77	78	⑲79	80	81	82	83	84	85	㊊86	87	88	89	90	91	92	㊽93	94	95
96	97	98	99	⑩100	101	102	103	104	105	106	⑩107	108	109	110	111	112	113	⑭114	115	116	117	118	119
120	⑫121	122	123	124	125	126	127	⑫128	129	130	131	132	133	134	⑬135	136	137	138	139	140	141	⑭142	143
144	145	146	147	148	⑭149	150	151	152	153	154	155	⑮156	157	158	159	160	161	162	⑯163	164	165	166	167
168	169	⑰170	171	172	173	174	175	176	⑰177	178	179	180	181	182	183	⑱184	185	186	187	188	189	190	⑲191

Figure 2 Elements of array B with $cyclic(8)$ distribution on 3 processors. The circles mark the array elements accessed by $B(7i + 2)$ $(i \geq 0)$.

We can now compute the global index spacing corresponding to the vector R_A as $global(R_A) = y_A^R \times pk_A + x_A^R = 1 \times 12 + 3 = 15$, the local index spacing as $local(R_A) = y_A^R \times k_A + x_A^R = 1 \times 4 + 3 = 7$, and the iteration distance as $iter(R_A) = global(R_A)/s_A = 15/5 = 3$. In the same way, we have $global(L_A) = 1 \times 12 - 2 = 10$, $local(L_A) = 1 \times 4 - 2 = 2$, and $iter(L_A) = 10/5 = 2$), and in Figure 2, $global(R_B) = 0 \times 24 + 7 = 7$, $local(R_B) = 0 \times 8 + 7 = 7$, and $iter(R_B) = 7/7 = 1$; and $global(L_B) = 1 \times 24 - 3 = 21$, $local(L_B) = 1 \times 8 - 3 = 5$, and $iter(L_B) = 21/7 = 3$.

In order to compute the sets of data that processor 0 must send to other processors, using the vectors R_B and L_B we first find the sequence of accesses to array B (in the global index space) that processor 0 owns, $\text{GLOBAL}_B(0) = [2, 30, 51, 72, 79, 100, 121, 149]$ with the period 168, and the iteration sequence $\text{ITER}_B(0) = [0,4,7,10, 11,14,17,21]$ with the period 24. After multiplying the iteration numbers by the stride s_A, we get the global index sequence of corresponding left-hand-side (lhs) accesses, $\text{IMAGE}_{lhs}(0) = [0, 20, 35, 50, 55, 70, 85, 105]$ with the period 120. Assuming that the computation is partitioned using the *owner computes* rule, the sequence of processors that processor 0 sends data to is $\text{PSEND}(0) = [0,2,2,0,1,2,0,2]$. (For any index j in the GLOBAL_B on a given processor, the corresponding entry in PSEND is $Owner_A(((j - l_B)/s_B) \times s_A + l_A)$, where $Owner_A(x) = (x \text{ div } k_A) \bmod p$.) For example, processor 0 owns the elements $B(30)$, $B(51)$, $B(100)$, and $B(149)$ referenced by processor 2, and the set of data that processor 0 needs to send to processor 2 is $\text{DSEND}(0 \to 2) = B[30, 51, 100, 149]$ with the period 168, which corresponds to $B[30, 51, 100, 149, 198, 219, \ldots]$.

The sets of data that processor 0 must receive from other processors are computed similarly; using the basis vectors R_A and L_A we build the table of global indices for accesses made by processor 0, $\text{GLOBAL}_A(0) = [0, 15, 25, 50]$ with the period 60 and $\text{ITER}_A(0) = [0, 3, 5, 10]$ with the period 12. Since the iteration periods of ITER_A and ITER_B are different, we expand the ITER_A sequence so that its period is equal to the period of ITER_B. (In general, it may be required to expand both sequences so that the resulting iteration period is the least common multiple of $pk_A/\text{GCD}(pk_A, s_A)$ and $pk_B/\text{GCD}(pk_B, s_B)$, but in practice we do not expect the length of the expanded sequence to exceed the larger of the two block sizes.) After expansion, we get $\text{ITER}_A(0) = [0,3,5,10,12,15,17,22]$ with the period 24, and the sequence of corresponding rhs accesses is $\text{IMAGE}_{rhs}(0) = [2, 23, 37, 72, 86, 107, 121, 156]$ with the period 168. By computing the owners of the elements of array B with these indices we can construct the table $\text{PRECV}(0) = [0,2,1,0,1,1,0,1]$, as well as DRECV sets, for example, $\text{DRECV}(0 \leftarrow 1) = B[37, 86, 107, 156]$ with the period 168.

Not all the tables shown here need to be actually allocated and assigned values. The initial array access sequences for either reference can be traversed using the demand-driven address generation based on the vectors R and L [7]. The only table essential for packing outgoing messages is PSEND since it eliminates the need for computing the owner processor for every array reference. In addition, this table can be used to compute the lengths of the DSEND sequences. Similarly, the PRECV table is needed to generate the efficient code at the receiving end and find the lengths of the DRECV sequences.

3   CODE GENERATION

When generating communication for irregular problems, Das et al. allocate buffers for the non-local data immediately following the space for local array elements and translate the off-processor references to point to buffer addresses [2]. Using a similar idea, we allocate the space for the local and non-local rhs references contiguously, but we have a separate, appropriately sized buffer for each processor in PRECV∪PSEND. Each overflow segment is used to both pack the outgoing message and receive the incoming message from the corresponding processor. If this imposes unacceptable constraints on the communication schedule, we can pack messages into temporary buffers and exploit the overflow segments only in the receiving phase. The size of each overflow area can be computed using the length and the period of the DRECV (DSEND) sequence and the loop upper bound. If the necessary information is not available at compile time, the compiler can try to estimate the required space and let the run-time system resize the segments if needed.

Chatterjee et al. show that only one pass over the locally owned elements of array B is needed to build all outgoing messages [1]. However, an ownership computation involving integer divisions is performed for each array access, in order to determine the destination processors for the accessed elements. We reduce the number of required computations to the length of the access cycle for the rhs reference by using the PSEND table when packing messages. In the code for processor m shown below, *buffer* is an array of pointers to overflow segments for all destination processors. Processor m scans the elements of B it owns using the *NextIndex* function, which can be implemented using either the table of the local memory gaps between consecutive array accesses [1] or our demand-driven address generation method [7].

```
index_B = start_B; count_P = 0
while (index_B < end_B) do
    if (PSEND[count_P] ≠ m) then
        *(buffer[PSEND[count_P]])++ = B[index_B]
    endif
    count_P = (count_P + 1) mod Length(PSEND)
    index_B = NextIndex(index_B)
endwhile
```

Although expensive integer divisions are eliminated (the mod operation is shown only for simplicity and would, in practice, be replaced by a simple wrap-around test), the message-packing code can be further improved. Firstly, when computing the access sequence for the rhs reference, we can separate the elements that are to be sent to other processors from those that are used locally; in this way the PSEND table for processor m can be compressed to contain only the entries that are different from m, which, in turn, allows us to eliminate the **if** statement test from the loop. Secondly, by strip-mining the loop based on the length of the PSEND sequence, we can significantly reduce the number of the **while** loop tests, since they will be necessary only in the epilog of the strip-mined loop.

After all the messages are packed, the interprocessor communication takes place. We do not consider the issue of communication scheduling, but instead focus on the code generation at the receiving end. Contiguous memory allocation for non-local array elements allows each processor to receive data directly into the appropriate overflow segment, thereby eliminating the overhead of unpacking messages. However, in order to preserve the original execution order, the non-local references need to be converted to access the appropriate memory locations in the overflow region.

The repetitive access pattern is exploited once again for efficient mapping function generation. Since the local and non-local elements of B are stored contiguously, we can construct the ΔM_B table that contains the memory gaps between consecutive rhs accesses (this table is of the same size as PRECV). Its entries are computed in a linear scan of the IMAGE$_{rhs}$ sequence by taking into account the sizes of the local array area and the non-local overflow segments.

Since the lengths of the DRECV sequences corresponding to different processors may vary, the memory gap between two fixed consecutive accesses in the rhs sequence is not necessarily constant across different cycles; in the example shown in Figure 3, the gap between $B(2)$ and $B(23)$ is 70, while the gap between the corresponding accesses in the next cycle, $B(170)$ and $B(191)$, is 15. The *correction* to the access gaps is equal to the difference between the local cycle lengths corresponding to the consecutive accesses, 1 for $B(23)$ and 56 for $B(2)$ (the local memory gap between $B(2)$ and $B(170)$, which starts the next cycle, is 56, while the cycle length for elements received from processor 2 is 1). These gap corrections are stored in the ΔC_B table and applied at every rhs access.

$$
\begin{aligned}
&index_A = start_A; index_B = start_B; i_A = 0; i_B = 0 \\
&\textbf{while } (index_A < end_A) \textbf{ do} \\
&\quad A(index_A) = f(B(index_B)) \\
&\quad index_A = index_A + \Delta M_A[i_A] \\
&\quad i_A = (i_A + 1) \bmod Length(\Delta M_A) \\
&\quad index_B = index_B + \Delta M_B[i_B] \\
&\quad \Delta M_B[i_B] = \Delta M_B[i_B] + \Delta C_B[i_B] \\
&\quad i_B = (i_B + 1) \bmod Length(\Delta M_B) \\
&\textbf{endwhile}
\end{aligned}
$$

In the loop shown above, which each processor executes after receiving all the messages, the original non-local references are converted to accesses into the overflow region where the received data is stored. Since we assume the *owner computes* rule, the lhs accesses are traversed using the ΔM_A table of local memory gaps, as described by Chatterjee et al. In order to simplify the code, the access gap tables can be expanded

Proc. 0 - Array A			
[0]	1	2	3
12	13	14	[15]
24	[25]	26	27
36	37	38	39
48	49	[50]	51
[60]	61	62	63
72	73	74	[75]
84	[85]	86	87
96	97	98	99
108	109	[110]	112
[120]	121	122	123
132	133	134	[135]
144	[145]	146	147

$A(0) = B(2)$
$A(15) = B(23)$
$A(25) = B(37)$
$A(50) = B(72)$
$A(60) = B(86)$
$A(75) = B(107)$
$A(85) = B(121)$
$A(110) = B(156)$

$A(120) = B(170)$
$A(135) = B(191)$
$A(145) = B(205)$

$\Delta M_A = [7, 2, 9, 2]$

$\Delta M_B = [70, -8, -40, 41, 1, -25, 26, -9]$

$\Delta C_B = [-55, 3, 52, -52, 0, 52, -52, 52]$

Proc. 0 - Array B							
0	1	(2)	3	4	5	6	7
24	25	26	27	28	29	30	31
48	49	50	51	52	53	54	55
(72)	73	74	75	76	77	78	79
96	97	98	99	100	101	102	103
120	(121)	122	123	124	125	126	127
144	145	146	147	148	149	150	151
168	169	(170)	171	172	173	174	175

(37) (86) (107) (156) (205)

(23) (191)

Figure 3 Layout of array elements after communication and assignments performed by processor 0 for the statement $A(5i) = B(7i + 2)$, $(i \geq 0)$.

to be of the same size, in which case a single index is sufficient to traverse all three tables. If this is done, then the strip-mining, as described for the message-packing loop, is also applicable and will result in the more efficient code.

4 MESSAGE COALESCING

It is not unusual for assignment statements to have multiple *rhs* terms referencing the same array, as in

$$\textbf{do } i = 0, u$$
$$A(5i) = f(B(7i + 2), B(7i + 5))$$
$$\textbf{enddo}$$

Although it is possible to repeat the communication step for each term, significant savings in communication time can be achieved by grouping the data corresponding to different references so that each processor sends only one message to any other processor. Neither Chatterjee et al. [1] nor Gupta et al. [4] deal with this issue. Stichnoth [7] indicates that combining communication steps would be profitable, but he does not describe the necessary analysis. In contrast, we show how our approach can support message coalescing optimization [5] to reduce the communication cost.

In order be able to pack the messages corresponding to different *rhs* terms in a single pass over the array, we must find the union of PSEND sequences corresponding to different *rhs* references. In Section 2, we have seen that $\text{GLOBAL}_{B(7i+2)}(0) = [2,30,51,72,79,100,121,149]$ with the period 168 and also that $\text{PSEND}_{B(7i+2)}(0) = [0,2,2,0,1,2,0,2]$. Similarly, for $B(7i + 5)$ we can compute $\text{GLOBAL}_{B(7i+5)}(0) = [5,26,54,75,96,103,124,145]$ with the period 168, which results in $\text{PSEND}_{B(7i+5)}(0) = [0,0,2,0,1,2,0,2]$. By merging the two GLOBAL sequences we get $\text{GLOBAL}_B = [2,5,26,30,\ldots,124,145,149]$ with the period 168, and the unioned $\text{PSEND}_B(0) =$

[0,0,0,2,2,2,0,0,1,1,2,2,0,0,2,2]. From this we can compute the sets of elements that a processor needs to send for both rhs references, for example, $\text{DSEND}_B(0 \to 2) =$ [30,51,54,100,103,145,149] with the period 168. Using the PSEND_B set, the messages can be packed in a single scan over the array B, as described in Section 3. This scheme interleaves the elements corresponding to the two rhs references in the packed message and allows the possibility of reducing message sizes by eliminating multiple occurrences of an element in the GLOBAL_B sequence.

However, before merging the two GLOBAL sequences, we may have to replicate them so that they have the same period. If the strides of the two rhs references are s_{B_1} and s_{B_2}, then the sequence period after expansion is the least common multiple of $pk_B s_{B_1}/\text{GCD}(pk_B, s_{B_1})$ and $pk_B s_{B_2}/\text{GCD}(pk_B, s_{B_2})$, and based on our experiments, the increased sequence length significantly increases the overhead. Even without the sequence replication, we can pack the messages in a single pass by effectively merging the GLOBAL sequences on the fly, but the control overhead associated with merging has to be incurred for each element packed in the message.

An alternative to interleaving of array elements from two messages into a single coalesced message is to pack the messages for different rhs references in separate areas of the same contiguous buffer. Although this precludes the possibility of eliminating redundancies, we choose this method because it keeps the construction of access gap tables for the rhs references simple. Since the messages are packed in a contiguous buffer, we still reduce the number of the messages by sending a single message for multiple rhs references. Moreover, as described in Section 3, we allocate contiguous overflow regions to directly receive the message and avoid the unpacking overhead.

For code generation we construct an access gap table for each rhs reference. Since the non-local array elements for two references are received and buffered in separate overflow regions, the access gap tables (ΔM_{B_1} and ΔM_{B_2}) and the correction tables (ΔC_{B_1} and ΔC_{B_2}) for the two rhs references can be computed in exactly the same way as described in Section 3.

5 SHIFT COMMUNICATION

Shift communication occurs when the lhs and rhs arrays have identical distributions and access strides but different offsets. If the arrays are $block$-distributed, the code can be significantly improved by using the overlap areas [3]. The same idea can be applied to the $cyclic(k)$ distribution, but this requires an overlap region for every block of size k. In order to restrict the size of the additional memory allocated, we assume that overlaps are used only when the shift offset is smaller than the block size k (or perhaps a small fraction of k). This assumption implies that the communication takes places only between logically adjacent processors, which greatly simplifies the analysis and code generation. We illustrate this with the following example in which array B has the same distribution as shown in Figure 2:

Processor 0 - Array B								
⓪	1	2	3	4	⑤	6	7	
24	㉕	26	27	28	29	㉚	31	32
48	49	㊿	51	52	53	54	㊺	56 57
72	73	74	㊆	76	77	78	79	
96	97	98	99	⑩	101	102	103	
⑫	121	122	123	124	⑫	126	127	

Figure 4   Elements of array B with $cyclic(8)$ distribution on 3 processors that are owned by processor 0. Each block of size 8 is extended with an overlap region of width 2 where non-local elements needed to execute the statement $B(5i) = f(B(5i + 1), B(5i + 2))$ $(i \geq 0)$ are received.

$$\textbf{do } i = 0, u$$
$$B(5i) = f(B(5i + 1), B(5i + 2))$$
$$\textbf{enddo}$$

Since the shift offsets (1 and 2) are both positive and smaller than the block size (8), for each processor m, $\text{PSEND}_B(m) = [(m - 1) \bmod p]$ and $\text{PRECV}_B(m) = [(m + 1) \bmod p]$. DSEND sets for processor 0 are $\text{DSEND}_{B(5i+1)}(0 \to 2) = \{B(5i + 1)|\textit{Offset}(B(5i + 1)) < 1\} = B[96]$ and $\text{DSEND}_{B(5i+2)}(0 \to 2) = \{B(5i + 2)|\textit{Offset}(B(5i + 2)) < 2\} = B[72, 97]$, both with the period 120. After coalescing, we get $\text{DSEND}_B(0 \to 2) = B[72, 96, 97]$ with the period 120. The DSEND_B table is used in the message packing so that processor 0 visits only those array elements that it must send to processor 2, and not all the elements referenced by $B(5i + 1)$ and $B(5i + 2)$ that it owns. DRECV sets are computed similarly: $\text{DRECV}_{B(5i+1)}(0 \gets 1) = \{B(5i + 1)|\textit{Offset}(B(5i)) \geq 7\} = B[56]$ and $\text{DRECV}_{B(5i+2)}(0 \gets 1) = \{B(5i + 2)|\textit{Offset}(B(5i)) \geq 6\} = B[32, 57]$, both with the period 120, which results in $\text{DRECV}_B(0 \gets 1) = B[32, 56, 57]$ with the period 120.

Although these sets are shown here in global indices, each processor uses its local addresses when packing and unpacking messages. Conversion from global to local indices must take into account the width of the overlap area. Since we need two overlap cells for each block (Figure 4), for the purpose of local addressing, we take $8 + 2 = 10$ as the block size; for example, the local address of $B(32)$ on processor 0 is 18, and the local period for $\text{DRECV}_B(0 \gets 1)$ is 50.

The loop that will be executed after the messages are received, as shown below, is much simpler than that described in Section 3.

$$index_B = start_B; i = 0$$
while $(index_B < end_B)$ **do**
$\quad B(index_B) = f(B(index_B + 1), B(index_B + 2))$
$\quad index_B = NextIndex(index_B)$
endwhile

Each processor scans local elements referenced on the lhs $(B(5i))$ using the $NextIndex$ function described earlier, but it does not perform any additional table lookups for the rhs accesses, since the non-local elements referenced by $B(5i + 1)$ and $B(5i + 2)$ now lie in the overlap area.

6   EXPERIMENTAL RESULTS

In order to validate the previously described methods we implemented a prototype system for computing communication sets and generating code for array assignment statements. This allowed us to evaluate the overheads incurred by our techniques, as well as compare them with other existing methods, in particular the virtual processor approach by Gupta et al. [4]. Their solution is based on treating a *block-cyclic* distribution as either a *block* or *cyclic* distribution of data onto virtual processors, and mapping of the virtual processors to the physical processors in either a *cyclic* or *block* fashion. Depending on how arrays are distributed on the virtual processors, the scheme is called either virtual-block or virtual-cyclic, and each array can be visualized under either of the two views.

Table 1 gives the table generation, message packing, communication, and loop execution times for 160,000 iterations of the normalized loop described in Section 2 for our method and the virtual processor approach. (The code that implements the virtual processor scheme was provided by S.D. Kaushik [6].) The experiments were performed on 32 processors of an Intel iPSC/860 hypercube, using the *icc* compiler with –O4 optimization level and *dclock* timer. The parameters l_A and l_B were kept constant at 0 since the lower bounds have little effect on the execution times, while the parameters k_A, k_B, s_A, and s_B were varied to compare our technique against all possible virtual views adopted by the virtual processor approach. Reported times, shown in milliseconds, represent maximums over all 32 processors.

Since we used the identical complete exchange algorithm as in the virtual processor implementation, the communication times were similar for both schemes and we report them only for our method. The execution times for the virtual processor approach correspond to the best visualization view selected separately for each parameter set. The last column shows the virtual views for the rhs and lhs arrays that were chosen to minimize the estimated indexing overhead, where vb and vc correspond to virtual-block and virtual-cyclic.

Table 1 shows that the table construction overhead of our technique is consistently and significantly smaller than that incurred by the virtual processor approach. We construct all the tables in time linearly proportional to their sizes and take advantage of the repetitiveness of array accesses. While Gupta et al. derive closed-form expressions for the communication sets of virtual processors, the mapping of these sets onto physical processors can incur a substantial overhead.

Although our table generation is in most cases at least one order of magnitude faster than in the virtual processor scheme, with the increase in the block size the time needed to construct the tables may represent a sizable overhead relative to the time spent in the interprocessor communication. However, the table generation time is independent of the number of iterations executed in the loop, and thus, for larger data sets the overhead would be less significant.

In the virtual processor scheme, each processor performs a separate pass over its portion of the rhs array for each message that it must build. With our approach, all outgoing array elements are packed into corresponding messages in a single pass over the array, which results in the shorter message packing time. During the execution of loop iterations in the virtual processor approach non-local rhs array elements are simply unpacked from the receive buffers. In contrast, we do not need to unpack the received messages, but our approach requires table lookups in the loop. Since the overheads due to indirect addressing are small [8], the loop execution in our scheme is faster than with the virtual processor method, except in the case when virtual-cyclic view was selected at both the sending and the receiving side.

In order to evaluate the proposed method for shift communication that is based on using the overlap regions we compared this special case technique with the our general communication scheme; the results of this comparison are given in Table 2. Although the simplified code decreases the loop execution time, a significant portion of this improvement is offset by the message unpacking overhead. However, in the presence of multiple rhs references that require shift communication, a simple message coalescing with overlap regions, as described in Section 5, can result in greater performance gains.

k_A	k_B	s_A	s_B	Table Generation		Message Packing		Loop Execution		Comm.	View
				Rice	OSU	Rice	OSU	Rice	OSU		
64	256	3	11	3.70	47.63	4.04	5.04	2.51	2.93	30.11	vb-vb
		5	5	3.69	59.18	3.32	4.04	2.77	2.68	43.64	vb-vb
		7	3	3.70	72.71	2.78	4.19	2.42	3.52	26.84	vb-vb
1000	5	1	1	11.43	89.86	2.61	4.56	2.98	3.74	25.02	vb-vc
		1	3	11.51	91.83	3.06	5.12	3.06	3.76	24.75	vb-vc
		1	7	11.45	93.10	3.82	6.12	3.11	3.82	24.95	vb-vc
16	15	2	3	0.89	8.86	2.62	3.08	2.32	1.68	31.57	vc-vc
		3	5	0.95	11.57	3.04	3.78	2.37	1.69	29.36	vc-vc
		4	4	1.07	10.98	2.99	3.73	2.33	1.73	27.56	vc-vc
4	1200	1	1	13.42	56.25	3.26	4.28	3.17	3.45	30.35	vc-vb
		3	2	7.29	160.68	2.86	6.40	2.78	5.42	26.06	vc-vb
		5	3	5.25	313.03	2.91	8.02	2.66	7.41	25.53	vc-vb

Table 1   Breakdown of execution times in milliseconds for the array assignment $A(0 : 160000s_A - 1 : s_A) = B(0 : 160000s_B - 1 : s_B)$ obtained on a 32 processor Intel iPSC/860 hypercube using our method (Rice) and the virtual processor approach (OSU).

Block Size	Access Stride	Shift Offset	Table Generation		Message Packing		Loop Execution	
			Overflow	Overlap	Overflow	Overlap	Overflow	Overlap
8	3	1	0.511	0.530	0.732	0.720	2.992	2.877 (2.484)
16	5	2	0.587	0.630	0.638	0.629	3.160	3.300 (3.013)
32	7	3	0.726	0.637	0.500	0.509	3.712	3.523 (3.289)
64	5	1	1.108	0.313	0.202	0.157	3.360	3.045 (2.970)
128	10	2	1.105	0.316	0.220	0.178	4.167	3.894 (3.804)

Table 2 Execution times in milliseconds for shift communication on a 32 processor Intel iPSC/860 hypercube using the general method with overflow buffers and the specialized scheme with overlap regions. Numbers in parentheses are the loop execution times without the message unpacking overhead.

7 SUMMARY

We have described a general and efficient communication generation approach for $cyclic(k)$ distributions and shown how it can support the message coalescing optimization. We have also presented the experimental results to show that the low overheads incurred by our method compare favorably to those of an already existing technique, the virtual processor approach. We have discussed the use of overlap areas for $cyclic(k)$ distributions and shown that this can be an efficient way for handling the special case of shift communication. Although not described in this paper, alignments with non-unit strides can also be incorporated in our analysis.

REFERENCES

[1] S. Chatterjee, J. Gilbert, F. Long, R. Schreiber, and S. Teng. Generating local addresses and communication sets for data-parallel programs. In *Proceedings of the Fourth ACM SIGPLAN Symposium on Principles and Practice of Parallel Programming*, San Diego, CA, May 1993.

[2] R. Das, M. Uysal, J. Saltz, and Y-S. Hwang. Communication optimizations for irregular scientific computations on distributed memory architectures. Technical Report CS-TR-3163, Dept. of Computer Science, Univ. of Maryland, College Park, October 1993.

[3] M. Gerndt. Updating distributed variables in local computations. *Concurrency: Practice and Experience*, 2(3):171–193, September 1990.

[4] S.K.S. Gupta, S.D. Kaushik, C.-H. Huang, and P. Sadayappan. On compiling array expressions for efficient execution on distributed-memory machines. Technical Report OSU-CISRC-4/94-TR19, Department of Computer and Information Science, The Ohio State University, April 1994.

[5] S. Hiranandani, K. Kennedy, and C.-W. Tseng. Compiler optimizations for Fortran D on MIMD distributed-memory machines. In *Proceedings of Supercomputing '91*, Albuquerque, NM, November 1991.

[6] S. D. Kaushik. Private communication, April 1995.

[7] K. Kennedy, N. Nedeljković, and A. Sethi. Efficient address generation for block-cyclic distributions. In *Proceedings of the 1995 ACM International Conference on Supercomputing*, Barcelona, Spain, July 1995.

[8] K. Kennedy, N. Nedeljković, and A. Sethi. A linear-time algorithm for computing the memory access sequence in data-parallel programs. In *Proceedings of the Fifth ACM SIGPLAN Symposium on Principles and Practice of Parallel Programming*, Santa Barbara, CA, July 1995.

[9] J. Stichnoth. Efficient compilation of array statements for private memory multicomputers. Technical Report CMU-CS-93-109, School of Computer Science, Carnegie Mellon University, February 1993.

15

POINT-TO-POINT
COMMUNICATION USING
MIGRATING PORTS

Ian T. Foster, David R. Kohr, Jr., Robert Olson,
Steven Tuecke, and Ming Q. Xu

Mathematics and Computer Science Division
Argonne National Laboratory
Argonne, IL 60439
{foster,kohr,olson,tuecke,mqxu}@mcs.anl.gov

ABSTRACT

We describe and evaluate an implementation of a port-based communication model for task-parallel programs. This model permits tasks to communicate without explicit knowledge of the location or identity of their communication partners, which facilitates modular programming and the development of programs that consist of multiple communicating tasks per processing node. We present the protocols used for point-to-point communication and port migration, expressed in terms of portable abstractions for naming, threading, and asynchronous communication provided by the Nexus runtime system. Experimental results on an IBM SP allow us to quantify the performance costs of the functionality associated with port-based communication. We conclude that task-to-task communication via ports can be achieved efficiently even using standard system software, but that improvements in the integration of threading and communication mechanisms would improve performance significantly.

1 INTRODUCTION

Compilers for data-parallel languages such as Fortran D [9] and Vienna Fortran [3] have proven capable of synthesizing efficient single program multiple data (SPMD) code for a variety of regularly structured problems. However, there exist many problems whose solution on a multicomputer may be more efficient if one can employ *task parallelism*, that is, simultaneous execution of logically distinct tasks on the same or different processing nodes. Classes of problems for which task parallelism is particularly appropriate include pipelines for signal and image processing, task farms, and multidisciplinary simulations. For such problems, it is often desirable for the programmer to retain control over the definition and creation of tasks, the placement of tasks on nodes, and communication between tasks.

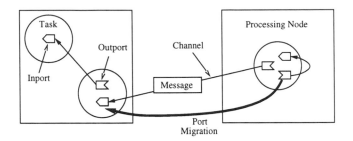

Figure 1   Collection of tasks communicating via ports.

Communication in a task-parallel computation can be specified in a variety of ways. In the *message passing* approach, programmers use send and receive operations to transfer data from a sending task to a designated recipient task. This approach is supported by libraries such as MPI [7] and PVM [12]. It is relatively simple to implement and can be mapped efficiently to a wide range of multicomputer architectures. However, it is not in general a satisfactory solution for a high-level task-parallel programming language. Because message passing does not hide details about the physical location of recipients, development of modular programs becomes difficult. Also message passing does not provide direct support for point-to-point communications between specific tasks when several such tasks are mapped to a single node. Finally, the user is burdened with the management of message "type tags", which organize messages by logical function.

An alternative approach is for tasks to communicate by operating on abstract data types called *ports*. A sending task writes messages to an *outport*, while a receiving task reads messages from an *inport* (see Figure 1). A connection over which messages may pass from an outport to an inport is called a *channel*. This scheme provides direct support for task-to-task communication: we can communicate with a specific task by sending or receiving on a port associated with that task. Another advantage is that a task can send or receive on a port without needing to know the location or identity of the corresponding receiver or sender task. Finally, multiple channels can be created between tasks to group messages by logical function.

Because ports decouple the identities of the sender and receiver of a communication, it is possible to transfer the ability to communicate through a port from one task to another. In other words, we can *migrate* a port from one task to another task—possibly located on a different node—with complete transparency to the task using the channel's other port. Several situations motivate this port migration mechanism; some are illustrated in Figure 2. In (a), an entire task, including its ports, migrates to another node to balance the computational load. In (b), tasks from a user program call tasks from a parallel library to operate on a distributed array; after transposing the array to perform the operation, the library tasks use migrated ports to return the array to the user tasks and restore the original data distribution. In (c), the set of communicating tasks shrinks and grows over time. Some task A may not know the identity or location of another task B, but A may still communicate with B if an appropriate port migrates to A.

In this paper, we describe techniques that we have developed to realize port-based communication and port migration for task parallel programs. These techniques address such crucial issues as the following: message delivery and buffering, the relationship between communication and task scheduling, and a correct and efficient protocol for port migration. We have implemented these mechanisms in a runtime system for the task-parallel language Fortran M (FM), which provides high-level constructs for port-based communication [1]. We present performance results that enable us to quantify the effectiveness of our techniques.

The rest of this paper is organized as follows. In Section 2, we elaborate on the semantics of port-based communication. Section 3 points out the difficulties of implementing these semantics in a non-shared-memory environment with multitasked nodes. Section 4 sketches our design for point-to-point communications and discusses the performance of the FM implementation. In Section 5, we describe our protocol for performing port migration in the most general instances, and discuss its performance. Section 6 presents techniques for reducing the overhead of migration and shows when they are applicable. Finally, we compare our work with related projects, evaluate the effectiveness of our techniques, and map out directions for future work.

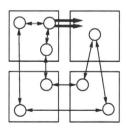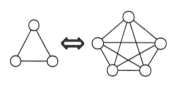

| a. Load balancing | b. Parallel libraries | c. Process dynamism |

Figure 2   Situations that motivate a mechanism for port migration.

2 SEMANTICS OF PORTS

We provide a brief, somewhat simplified review of the semantics of the port operations considered in this paper, focusing on those properties with significant implications for an implementation.

■   A computation comprises a set of tasks, each with a private address space and the ability to communicate with other tasks only via shared channels.

■   A message source (outport) can be connected to a sink (inport) to form a channel. Channels can be created and destroyed dynamically, and a port may be part of different channels at different times. Ports may be part of at most one channel at a time, however.

■   The send operation is nonblocking: a sending task may continue execution as soon as it is safe to modify the variables whose values were being transmitted, whether or not the message has been received yet. In contrast, a receiver always blocks until a message has arrived.

■   Channels guarantee message ordering: messages will always be read from the inport in the order in which they were written to the outport, even if one or both of the ports migrates.

■   A task may transmit a port value in a message, without affecting any channel to which the port is connected. The sending task yields to the recipient ownership of the capability for transmitting messages over the channel—that is, the port migrates from the sending task to the recipient.

An important consequence of the single-writer, single-reader property of channels is that FM can guarantee deterministic execution [1]. The same property can often be exploited to optimize certain port operations (see Section 6).

3 IMPLEMENTATION ISSUES

The port-based communication semantics described in the preceding section imposes several major requirements upon an implementation:

■   The asynchronous nature of the send operation implies a need for buffering.

■   Because multiple inports may be located on a single node, it must be possible to select an incoming message based on its destination port.

■   Because multiple tasks may execute on a single node, it is desirable that a task awaiting a message not consume processing resources. The task should be rescheduled for execution when the message arrives.

- Because inports and outports may reside on different nodes, a channel is an inherently distributed data structure that must be maintained in a consistent state when its constituent ports migrate.

It is difficult to meet these requirements in an implementation based on the SPMD model supported by many existing message-passing libraries. One reason is the need to distinguish between messages intended for different members of a dynamically varying collection of ports. Another is the inherently *synchronous* nature of the SPMD model: in general, both the sending and receiving node must be aware that a communication is to take place. Yet in task-parallel programs in which multiple tasks are executing on each node, communications are often asynchronous and unpredictable.

Our approach is to rely instead on a model that includes abstractions for both a global name space and asynchronous invocation of operations on objects in that name space. More specifically, we structure our implementation of port mechanisms in terms of three abstractions provided by the Nexus [5] runtime library:

- *Global pointers,* which furnish a global name space, even in distributed-memory execution environments;

- *Lightweight threads,* which facilitate mapping of multiple tasks to a single node and efficient switching between tasks; and

- *Remote Service Requests* (RSRs), which asynchronously invoke a designated handler function on an object referenced by a global pointer. The object may be nonlocal, in which case a message is sent that causes the handler to execute on the object's node. The request may specify arbitrary additional arguments for the handler.

We have found that use of the Nexus abstractions greatly simplifies the structure of the FM runtime: an early prototype based on the SPMD model was significantly more complex. In addition, the portability of Nexus enhances the portability of our runtime system. A potential disadvantage of the approach is that the Nexus abstractions may introduce unnecessary overhead. This issue is addressed in the next section.

4 POINT-TO-POINT COMMUNICATIONS

In this section, we describe our implementation of message-passing operations over ports. We also present measurements of communications latency and bandwidth, both for our implementation and for the underlying software layers on which it is based. We analyze the overheads imposed by our approach, placing particular emphasis on tradeoffs between functionality and performance.

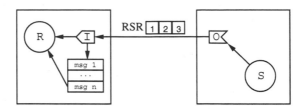

Figure 3 Using Nexus abstractions to implement port communication. Task S uses an RSR to send a message from outport O to inport I, from which task R will receive it.

4.1   Implementation Sketch

Our runtime system uses Nexus abstractions to implement point-to-point communication over a channel as follows (refer to Figure 3):

- FM tasks are represented by threads. Local variables within a task hold references to its ports.

- Ports are data structures that contain global pointer references to other ports. An inport also contains both a message queue and state fields that indicate whether a task is blocked waiting to receive from it.

- The distributed data structures representing channels are constructed by means of global pointers: the inport has a global pointer to the outport (for migration), and the outport has a global pointer to the inport (for communication and migration).

- Sending a message over a channel corresponds to sending an RSR to the inport by using the global pointer contained in the outport. The RSR incorporates the message contents as its additional arguments, and invokes a "send" handler that either buffers or delivers the message, as appropriate. If no receiving task is waiting on the inport, the message is buffered in the queue for later receipt. Otherwise, the message data is copied directly to memory locations previously specified by the waiting receiver, and the receiver is scheduled for execution.

4.2   Communications Performance

Compared with traditional message-passing systems such as MPI and PVM, the port-based communication mechanisms of FM provide substantial additional functionality, such as location transparency, the ability to discriminate among several tasks on a single node, and determinism. However, this added functionality introduces additional costs.

To enhance portability, the FM runtime is designed as a layered system, with each higher layer of software providing communications primitives with increased functionality. Therefore, it is possible to determine the approximate cost of each major piece of functionality by measuring the performance achieved by each successive layer, and then comparing the layers with each other. This is the methodology we employ for determining the costs incurred by our implementation of port mechanisms.

We measured latency and bandwidth using a simple synthetic "ping-pong" benchmark in which both short (one byte) and long (one megabyte) messages were exchanged between two different nodes of Argonne's IBM SP multicomputer. This machine is equipped with an SP2 network switch and SP1 nodes running version 3.2.5 of the AIX operating system. The FM runtime was layered atop a version of Nexus that used IBM's MPL message-passing library for communications and IBM's DCE Posix threads implementation for multithreading. All code was compiled with the most effective optimization options of the `xlf` and `xlc` Fortran and C compilers.

Table 1 contains the latency measurements for each layer of software. Because a detailed performance analysis of the first three layers has been provided elsewhere [5], here we discuss only the functionality provided by these layers. The lowest layer, the MPL message-passing library, provides transport of data between the memories of different nodes. The next layer is the RSR mechanism of Nexus, which provides the ability to invoke a handler function asynchronously when a message is received. At the next highest layer, Nexus threads on different nodes exchange messages through the RSR mechanism. The use of threads makes it possible for multiple tasks to run on each node.

For the highest layer, we measured FM tasks exchanging messages through ports. At this layer, the full semantics of ports becomes available, including message buffering, deterministic execution, in-order message arrival, and transparency of the locations of senders and receivers. We believe that the increase in latency to 25 μsec. more than the previous layer is chiefly due to the cost of acquiring locks for exclusive access to port data structures and to management of inport components such as the message queue.

The data in Table 1 indicate that, compared with the underlying message-passing library on the SP, our implementation of port-based communications has a latency about 2.5 times greater, with an absolute increase of about 100 μsec. To put this cost into perspective, we also measured the performance of IBM's RCVNCALL message driven processing facility. When a message arrives at a node, RCVNCALL interrupts the node and invokes a handler function defined by the programmer. Hence this facility provides functionality similar to the Nexus handler-to-handler layer, with the addition of pre-emption, yet it increases latency to 3.3 times, which is appreciably more than the entire additional cost imposed by our implementation of port-based communication.

Table 1 also contains bandwidth measurements for each layer. The data clearly show that the thread-to-thread and task-to-task layers add negligible costs in bandwidth, while the Nexus handler-to-handler layer adds a significant per-byte cost that reduces bandwidth to about half that of MPL. In other work [5], it was shown that most of

Software Layer	Latency (μsec.)	Bandwidth (Megabytes/sec.)
Native message passing (MPL)	66.8	32.2
Handler-to-handler (Nexus)	97.0	15.4
Thread-to-thread (Pthreads)	148.7	15.4
Task-to-task (FM)	173.6	15.4
Interrupt receive (RCVNCALL)	219.8	31.0

Table 1   Point-to-point communication performance for each software layer.

this bandwidth reduction was due to the fact that, for large messages, Nexus does not post receive buffers in advance. By switching to a multiple-message protocol for large messages, in which the length is sent in advance of the data so that a receive of the appropriate size can be posted ahead on the destination node, the bandwidth achieved by Nexus approached that of the underlying message-passing library. We believe that a similar technique can be used to reduce greatly the gap in bandwidth between our runtime system and the underlying MPL layer.

5   PORT MIGRATION

This section describes our runtime system's protocol for migrating ports between tasks. We also present data for the protocol's performance on a synthetic benchmark and discuss factors that contribute to its execution time.

5.1   Migration Protocol

Port migration must preserve any invariant properties of channel data structures needed to guarantee proper semantics for point-to-point communication, such as message ordering along channels and exclusive ownership of a port by at most one task. Figure 4 illustrates how the distributed data structure representing a channel changes as its inport migrates from one node to another. In this example, source task S on node N_S transfers inport I to destination task D on node N_D over channel $Ch_{S,D}$. Remote task R owns an outport O, and I and O together form a channel $Ch_{R,S}$.

In general, a protocol for migrating a port P must do the following:

■   Create a new data structure for P at the destination node.

■   Update global pointer references of any ports connected to P by a channel.

■   Forward any messages queued at P to the new data structure, taking care that message order is correct when migration completes.

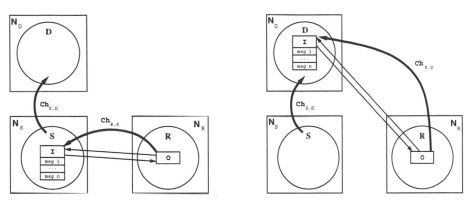

a. Before migration   b. After migration

Figure 4 Channel data structure before and after migration. Thick curved lines denote channels; thin straight lines denote references via global pointers.

■   Transfer ownership of P from the sending task to the receiver.

Performance considerations demand that a port migration protocol exploit parallelism where feasible and minimize message passing and synchronization. In designing the protocol described here, we struck a balance between performance and complexity: we parallelize steps that typically dominate execution time, but adopt simple solutions for cases that are expected to occur rarely. For example, we reduce the complexity inherent in simultaneously migrating both ends of a channel by serializing the two migrations.

We illustrate the operation of the protocol by describing the major steps that occur during its execution. Figure 5 contains a graphical depiction. Our example is the same as that of Figure 4:

1. S sends an RSR to node N_D requesting creation of a new data structure for I. S also sends an RSR to N_R to "lock down" O so that it will not migrate or send further messages to I.

2. O becomes "locked down", and an acknowledgment message is sent to S.

3. A new data structure for I is created on N_D, and a reply message containing a global pointer to the data structure is sent to S.

4. S waits until the messages sent in Steps 2 and 3 have arrived.

5. S sends an RSR to N_R to release the lock on O and update O's pointer to I.

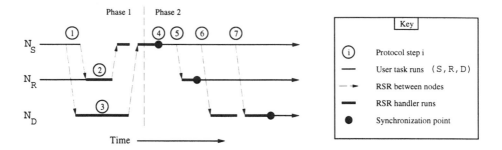

Figure 5 Timeline of execution of migration protocol for example of Figure 4. Timelines for each node are stacked vertically to show partial ordering of events.

6. S forwards all messages queued at I to the new data structure on N_D.

7. S sends to N_D an RSR which transfers ownership of I to D. If D had been blocked waiting for I, it is now unblocked.

Note that there are two round-trip exchanges of messages between S and R and between S and D in steps 1 through 4. We expect that in many cases, these round trips will dominate execution time. Hence in our protocol they are performed in parallel. Moreover, the portion of the protocol executed by S can be usefully split into two distinct phases: steps before 4, and steps from 4 onward. After S has completed its portion of the first phase (Step 1), it can fill the idle time spent waiting for Steps 2 and 3 to complete with other computation, then continue with the second phase at Step 4.

5.2   Migration Performance

We measured the performance of our protocol using a synthetic "ping-pong" benchmark that repeatedly migrates an inport in a manner identical to that shown in Figure 4. Table 2 shows the average execution time for each migration. The last column compares our protocol with a more conservative implementation that does not parallelize the two round-trip exchanges described above.

If these round trips in fact did dominate execution time, we would expect our protocol to be about twice as fast as the conservative one, and the ratio of migration time to latency to be close to but greater than 2. Yet under MPL, our protocol falls far short of that mark. We surmise that thread switching and poor thread scheduling are among the major factors causing this.

To test our hypothesis, we repeated these measurements, this time using the TCP/IP protocol over the SP's diagnostic Ethernet for communications. Latency was 1,413 μsec., about an order of magnitude higher than for MPL. As the table shows, round-trip

Communication Protocol	Raw Time (μsec.)	Ratio to Latency	Compared with Conservative
MPL	1,105	11.4	~2% faster
TCP/IP	5,571	3.9	~29% faster

Table 2   Execution times for port migration. Column 3 is Nexus handler-to-handler latency.

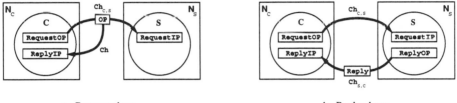

a. Request phase   b. Reply phase

Figure 6   Request and reply phases of client-server interaction.

latency then dominated execution time, and our parallel protocol gained significantly over the conservative one. The results of this experiment imply that if we can minimize overheads from sources such as threading, our protocol's performance under MPL should improve dramatically.

6   MIGRATION OPTIMIZATIONS

In many instances of port migration, it can be determined *a priori* that the ports affected by the migration will be used in only limited ways. Figure 6 illustrates one example that we commonly encounter in FM programs: A client task C sends a message to a server task S. The message includes both information about processing to be performed on behalf of C, and an outport ReplyOP through which S sends a reply message containing the results. Because the client needs the results produced by the server, it will not cause inport ReplyIP to migrate. Among other examples, this paradigm for task interaction appears when implementing both remote memory accesses of elements of distributed arrays and task farms in which slave tasks request work from a master task, as depicted in Figure 7.

In Figure 6, because ReplyIP does not migrate, it has no need for the global pointer to ReplyOP used by the general port migration protocol. Therefore migration of ReplyOP can become as simple as a single RSR from N_c to N_s. This RSR causes a new data structure for ReplyOP to be created and transfers ownership of ReplyOP to S. We expect that such an optimized migration protocol will be only slightly slower than the point-to-point communication latency and therefore considerably faster than the general migration protocol.

Opportunities for employing such an optimization can in principle be detected by a compiler, if appropriate analyses are performed. Alternatively, the programmer can supply annotations which indicate when to use the optimization. We plan to modify the FM compiler to process such annotations, and will extend our runtime system to include this optimized protocol.

7   RELATED WORK

Channel-based communication in task-parallel programs was introduced in Communicating Sequential Processes [10], and implemented in occam [11]. Our port-based communication mechanisms are significantly more general, supporting, for example, the dynamic creation of tasks and channels and reconfiguration of channels via port migration. In this respect, an FM channel has similarities to shared logical variables in concurrent logic programming languages [6]. An important difference is FM's guarantee of determinism.

Communication ports in FM are similar in certain respects to those of the Mach operating system, in that the physical location of ports is transparent to tasks, and capabilities to access ports may be passed through ports [4]. Yet Mach permits both reading and writing on the same port, while FM distinguishes between inports and outports. In addition, multiple writers may utilize a Mach port, whereas FM permits only a single writer at a time for each inport.

The port-based communication model described in this paper separates the concepts of communication endpoint and task, hence allowing a message to be sent to a specific task, without knowledge of the identity or location of that task. An alternative approach

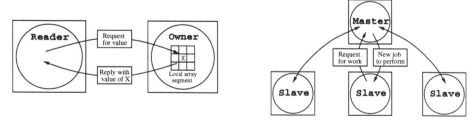

a. Remote access of distributed array element.   b. Task farm.

Figure 7   Examples of client-server interaction paradigm.

to intertask communication, adopted in Chant [8], is to augment traditional message-passing libraries with task identifiers. A send operation then specifies not only a destination node but also a destination task on that node.

8 CONCLUSIONS

We have found port-based communication useful for solving a number of interesting parallel programming problems. Our implementation of point-to-point communication and port migration mechanisms proved particularly natural when expressed in terms of the Nexus asynchronous invocation and global name space abstractions. Performance analysis of this implementation indicates that the cost of message delivery to individual threads need not be excessive compared to traditional message passing, but nevertheless could be improved by a tighter integration of threading and communication. Our implementation of general port migration still suffers from relatively large overheads, despite a significant design and tuning effort. Fortunately, we have discovered many instances in which faster special-case migration protocols can be employed instead.

Most of the techniques described in this paper have been incorporated in the Fortran M compilation system developed at Argonne, which is available at the World Wide Web URL http://www.mcs.anl.gov/fortran-m/. The parallelized version of port migration will be incorporated shortly. In future work, we will use more substantial task-parallel applications to evaluate port communication and migration performance and to investigate the utility of special-case protocols. We also wish to explore interoperability through port-based communication between FM and other parallel languages such as Compositional C++ [2].

Acknowledgments

This work was supported in part by the National Science Foundation's Center for Research in Parallel Computation under Contract NSF CCR-8809615 and by the Mathematical, Information, and Computational Sciences Division subprogram of the Office of Computational and Technology Research, U.S. Department of Energy, under Contract W-31-109-Eng-38. We are grateful to members of the Nexus development team for their assistance with the Nexus software.

REFERENCES

[1] K. M. Chandy and I. Foster. A deterministic notation for cooperating processes. *IEEE Trans. Parallel and Distributed Syst.*, 1995. To appear.

[2] K. M. Chandy and C. Kesselman. CC++: A declarative concurrent object-oriented programming notation. In *Research Directions in Concurrent Object-Oriented Programming*. MIT Press, 1993.

[3] B. Chapman, P. Mehrotra, and H. Zima. Programming in Vienna Fortran. *Scientific Programming*, 1(1):31–50, 1992.

[4] M. Young et al. The duality of memory and communication in Mach. In *Proc. of the 11th Symposium on Operating Systems Principles*, 1987.

[5] I. Foster, C. Kesselman, and S. Tuecke. Portable mechanisms for multithreaded distributed computations. Mathematics and Computer Science Division Preprint P494-0195, Argonne National Laboratory, 1995.

[6] I. Foster and S. Taylor. *Strand: New Concepts in Parallel Programming*. Prentice-Hall, 1989.

[7] W. Gropp, E. Lusk, and A. Skjellum. *Using MPI: Portable Parallel Programming with the Message Passing Interface*. MIT Press, 1995.

[8] M. Haines, D. Cronk, and P. Mehrotra. On the design of Chant: A talking threads package. In *Proc. of Supercomputing 94*, November 1993.

[9] S. Hiranandani, K. Kennedy, and C. Tseng. Preliminary experiences with the Fortran D compiler. In *Proc. of Supercomputing 93*, Portland, November 1993.

[10] C. A. R. Hoare. *Communicating Sequential Processes*. Prentice Hall, 1984.

[11] G. Jones. *Programming in occam*. Prentice Hall International, 1987.

[12] V. Sunderam. PVM: A framework for parallel distributed computing. *Concurrency: Practice & Experience*, 2(4):315–339, 1990.

[13] T. von Eicken, D. Culler, S. Goldstein, and K. Schauser. Active Messages: A mechanism for integrated communication and computation. In *Proc. 19th Int'l. Symposium on Computer Architecture*, May 1992.

THE PERFORMANCE IMPACT OF ADDRESS RELATION CACHING[†]

Peter A. Dinda
David R. O'Hallaron

School of Computer Science
Carnegie Mellon University
Pittsburgh, PA 15213
{pdinda,droh}@cs.cmu.edu

ABSTRACT

An important portion of end–to–end latency in data transfer is spent in address computation, determining a relation between sender and receiver addresses. In deposit model communication, this computation happens only on the sender and some of its results are embedded in the message. Conventionally, address computation takes place on–line, as the message is assembled. If the amount of address computation is significant, and the communication is repeated, it may make sense to remove address computation from the critical path by caching its results. However, assembling a message using the cache uses additional memory bandwidth.

We present a fine grain analytic model for simple address relation caching in deposit model communication. The model predicts how many times a communication must be repeated in order for the average end–to–end latency of an implementation which caches to break even with that of an implementation which doesn't cache. The model also predicts speedup and those regimes where a caching implementation never breaks even. The model shows that the effectiveness of caching depends on CPU speed, memory bandwidth and the complexity of the address computation. We verify the model on the iWarp and the Paragon and find that, for both machines, caching can improve performance even when address computation is quite simple (one instruction per data word on the iWarp and 16 instructions per data word on the Paragon.)

To show the practical benefit of address relation caching, we examine the performance of an HPF distributed array communication library that can be configured to use caching. In some cases, caching can double the performance of the library. Finally, we discuss other benefits to caching and several open issues.

[†]This research was sponsored in part by the Advanced Research Projects Agency/CSTO monitored by SPAWAR under contract N00039 93-C-0152, in part by the National Science Foundation under Grant ASC-9318163, and in part by a grant from the Intel Corporation.

1 INTRODUCTION

A basic communication operation for applications running on distributed memory machines is a *point-to-point communication*, where the *sender* transfers data, in the form of a *message*, from various locations in its memory to various locations in the memory of the *receiver*. Because each communication represents overhead to the application, it is important to perform this operation as quickly as possible. This task is complicated by the fact that applications do not always keep the data they need to communicate in convenient contiguous memory locations.

In general, point-to-point communication with conventional message passing systems like PVM [13], NX [6], and MPI [14] involves three basic steps on the sender: (1) *address computation*, which determines the local addresses of the data items to be transferred, (2) *message assembly*, which copies the data items into a contiguous buffer, and (3) *message transfer*, which copies the message from the buffer to the wire. The receiver performs a symmetric set of steps. The performance measure of interest is *end–to–end latency*, which is the time to perform all three steps on both the sender and receiver.

A different and typically more efficient approach, known as *deposit model message passing* [10, 12], combines the address computation steps on the sender and the receiver into a single step on the sender. The result of the address computation step on the sender is an *address relation* that associates addresses on the sender with addresses on the receiver. The sender performs the same steps as above, but passes the receiver addresses along with the data. The receiver uses these addresses to scatter the data to the correct memory locations. Other properties of the deposit model make it possible for sophisticated implementations to assemble and disassemble to and from the wire, possibly via specialized hardware. In this paper, we concentrate on a simple implementation that stages data in memory at both the sender and receiver.

In any implementation of deposit model message passing, and in conventional message passing systems, address computation is in the critical path of data transfer. Address relation caching decouples address computation and data transfer by doing address computation off-line, storing the address relation in memory, and doing message assembly using the stored address relation. A primary motivation is to amortize the address computation cost of communications that are repeated (for example, an HPF array assignment statement in a loop.) A similar approach is used by the CHAOS system [2] to improve the performance of irregular collective communications.

To determine the effectiveness of address relation caching, we develop a simple analytic model for predicting the performance tradeoffs between cached and uncached point–to–point communications for a simple representation of the address relation. The model shows that there are regimes where caching is always ineffective, as well as regimes where caching becomes effective after the communication has been repeated a sufficient number of times. For these latter regimes, the model predicts the number of times the communication must be repeated in order for caching to break even, as well as speedup. Speedup is bounded only by the complexity of the address relation computation.

We validate the simple model on both the Intel Paragon and Intel iWarp systems. The model's predictions closely match our measurements. Because of iWarp's higher ratio of memory bandwidth to instruction issue rate, caching becomes effective with far simpler address computations than on the Paragon. However, in both cases, even if only a small number of instructions are executed per tuple of the address relation, caching is effective.

To demonstrate the practical benefit of caching, we compare the cached and uncached performance of an HPF [12] communication library on the Paragon. We find that caching becomes more effective as the distribution of the data becomes more irregular, and thus the address relations become harder to compute.

We conclude with discussion about other issues and benefits of caching.

2 DEPOSIT MODEL COMMUNICATION

In a conventional communication system, such as PVM [13], NX [6], or MPI [14], the sender computes a binary relation S between local addresses and addresses offset into the *message* that is transported between it and the receiver. If $(s, m) \in S$ then the data item at local address s is copied into the message at offset m. The receiver computes a binary relation R between addresses offset into the message and local addresses. If $(m, r) \in R$, then the data item at offset m in the message is copied to local address r. No actual address information is contained in the message.

In deposit model communication, the sender computes a binary relation SR between local addresses at the sender and local addresses at the receiver – if $(s, r) \in SR$ then the data item at address s will be transported to address r at the receiver. We refer to SR as the *address relation*. The sender uses the address relation to *assemble* a message that conceptually consists of 2-tuples (r, d) where data item d (read from address s) is to be written to, or deposited at address r on the receiver. The receiver runs a simple *deposit engine* which receives the message and *disassembles* the message, writing each d to its corresponding local address r. If the message actually contains 2-tuples, it is in the *address-data pair* format. Often, the format of the message can be optimized so that the overhead of including addresses in the message is very low. One such format is referred to as *address-data block*. In this format, the message consists of 3-tuples (r, l, D), where D consists of l data items that are deposited at consecutive addresses starting at r. Obviously, other optimizations are also possible, depending on the properties of the address relation.

Strictly speaking, including addresses in the message is a variant of deposit called *direct deposit*. Other properties of the deposit model make it possible for sophisticated implementations to eliminate in memory staging of the message, possibly by using specialized hardware. We concentrate on a simple implementation that stages the message in memory and uses a simple address-data pair message format. Further details of deposit model communication can be found in [12].

3 ANALYTIC MODELS

This section presents models for the average end–to–end latency of a point-to-point communication using uncached and cached implementations of deposit model message passing. We consider the simplest (and least efficient) message format and cache structure and derive expressions for the average latency for both uncached and cached communication. We compare these expressions to provide some insight into the effect of caching.

3.1 Algorithm properties

Clearly, the time spent computing the address relation depends on the algorithm and its implementation. We model computing the address relation as instruction execution limited and as delivering the address relation in an on-line manner. We assume that all computation is done in registers, so we concentrate on the parameter n_g, the number of instructions executed per element of the relation.

3.2 Machine properties

Since computing the address relation is instruction execution limited, we must know r_i, the number of instructions the machine can execute per second. We also need to know r_c, the communication bandwidth between the two nodes. The memory system is parameterized by four values. The first two values, r_{rc} and r_{wc}, are the read and write bandwidths for unit–stride accesses, respectively. The other two values, r_{rr} and r_{wr}, are the read and write bandwidths for random memory accesses.

3.3 Uncached communication

The time for an uncached point-to-point communication has four components: t_g, the time to compute the address relation; t_{au}, the message assembly time; t_c, the message communication time; and t_d, the message disassembly time at the receiver. The total time for the communication is

$$t_{uncached} = t_g + t_{au} + t_c + t_d$$

In this simple model, we assume that the message format is address-data pair.

The time to compute the address relation is largely determined by the complexity of algorithm used, its implementation, and the instruction execution rate of the machine. Thus for an n word message, the time required is

$$t_g = \frac{n n_g}{r_i}$$

The code that computes the address relation presents tuples (s, r) in registers in an on-line manner. For each of these tuples, we read the data word at address s, write r to the message buffer, then write the data word to the message buffer. Note that the writes to the message buffer are to consecutive addresses, so their performance can be captured by r_{wc}, the contiguous write bandwidth of the machine. On the other hand, the sender side addresses of the tuples may not be contiguous, so we capture their performance with r_{rr}, the random read bandwidth of the machine. Furthermore, we capture the loop overhead as a number of instructions, n_{au}. Thus the time to assemble the message is

$$t_{au} = n \left(\frac{1}{r_{rr}} + \frac{2}{r_{wc}} + \frac{n_{au}}{r_i} \right)$$

Note that this expression does not take into account cache thrashing between the reads and writes. An implementation will probably optimize access patterns by reading several data items at a time. This will bring it close to the above expression.

After the message has been assembled, we use the communication hardware to transport it to the receiver. The message communication time is

$$t_c = \frac{2n}{r_c}$$

Note that r_c is really a function of $2n$, but we assume that n is sufficiently large that we can use a fixed value for r_c. Further, this value is the same without and with caching and becomes irrelevant in comparing them.

On the receiving node, each word of the message is read consecutively and each address-data pair results in one random write to memory. Additionally, n_d loop overhead instructions are executed for a total disassembly time of

$$t_d = n \left(\frac{2}{r_{rc}} + \frac{1}{r_{wr}} + \frac{n_d}{r_i} \right)$$

Note that this expression does not take into account cache thrashing between the reads and writes. Again, an implementation will probably improve performance by writing several data items at a time, bringing it close to the expression.

Substituting into the expression for $t_{uncached}$, we see that an n word communication between two nodes requires time

$$t_{uncached} = n \left(\frac{n_g + n_{au} + n_d}{r_i} + \frac{1}{r_{rr}} + \frac{2}{r_{wc}} + \frac{2}{r_c} + \frac{2}{r_{rc}} + \frac{1}{r_{wr}} \right) \qquad (16.1)$$

3.4   Cached communication

The average time for a cached point-to-point communication has five components: t_g, the time to compute the address relation; t_o, the time to store the address relation in the cache, t_{ac}, the message assembly time from the cached address relation; t_c, the message communication time; and t_d, the message disassembly time at the receiver. The average time for the communication is

$$t_{cached} = \frac{t_g + t_o}{n_i} + t_{ac} + t_c + t_d$$

Note that the first two components are amortized over the number of times the communication is performed, n_i. t_g, t_c, and t_d are the same between the uncached and cached schemes and were determined in the preceding section. We continue the assumption that the message format is address-data pair. Further, we choose the simplest possible cache data structure: an array of 2-tuples that represent the relation.

For the simple model, as each tuple of the address relation is generated, we write it to an array. Thus storing the address relation in the cache involves two contiguous writes for each in-register tuple produced by the address relation computation. In addition, we execute n_o loop overhead instructions, so

$$t_o = n \left(\frac{2}{r_{wc}} + \frac{n_o}{r_i} \right)$$

When assembling the message from the cached address relation, for each tuple in the message, we first perform two consecutive reads to read a tuple of the cached address relation. Then, we perform a random read to read the data word. Finally, we perform two consecutive writes to write the data word and the receiver address into the message buffer. We also execute n_{ac} loop overhead instructions, thus the time to assemble a message with n data words is

$$t_{ac} = n \left(\frac{2}{r_{rc}} + \frac{1}{r_{rr}} + \frac{2}{r_{wc}} + \frac{n_{ac}}{r_i} \right)$$

Note that this expression does not take into account cache thrashing between the reads and writes, but, again, a good implementation will perform several data word reads at a time and thus approach this performance.

Substituting into the expression for t_{cached}, we see that an n word communication between two nodes requires time

$$t_{cached} = n \left(\frac{(n_g + n_o)/r_i + 2/r_{wc}}{n_i} + \frac{n_{ac} + n_d}{r_i} + \frac{2}{r_{rc}} \right.$$
$$\left. + \frac{1}{r_{rr}} + \frac{2}{r_{wc}} + \frac{2}{r_c} + \frac{2}{r_{rc}} + \frac{1}{r_{wr}} \right) \qquad (16.2)$$

3.5   Effects of caching

Equations 16.1 and 16.2 provide insight into the following questions: For a point–to–point communication that occurs multiple times at run–time, can a cached implementation ever outperform an uncached implementation? If so, how many times must the communication be repeated before the cached implementation wins? For a large number of iterations, what is the speedup in message assembly time of the cached implementation over the uncached implementation?

Caching can only be effective if we can assemble the message faster using the cache than without using the cache, i.e.,

$$t_{ac} < t_g + t_{au}$$

or

$$n_g > \frac{2r_i}{r_{rc}} + n_{ac} - n_{au} \qquad (16.3)$$

The right hand side of equation 16.3 is a machine–specific threshold below which caching is ineffective. Notice that it is largely determined by the ratio of instruction issue rate and memory read bandwidth.

If 16.3 is true, then we can also predict how many times cached address relation must be used in order to fully amortize the cost of caching the relation. This break even point is found by setting $t_{cached} = t_{uncached}$ and solving for n_i. In doing this we find that the break even point for caching is

$$n_i = \left\lceil \frac{r_{rc}}{r_{wc}} \left(\frac{(n_g + n_o)r_{wc} + 2r_i}{(n_g + n_{au} - n_{ac})r_{rc} - 2r_i} \right) \right\rceil \qquad (16.4)$$

It is important to point out that as n_g moves away from the threshold, the break even point decreases sharply because the n_g terms in the fraction begin to dominate.

Finally, the speedup in message assembly time for the cached implementation over the the uncached implementation is

$$\frac{t_g + t_{au}}{t_{ac}} = \frac{r_{rc}r_{wc}r_{rr}(n_g + n_{au}) + r_i r_{rc}(r_{wc} + 2r_{rr})}{r_{rc}r_{wc}r_{rr}n_{ac} + r_i r_{rc}(r_{wc} + 2r_{rr})} \qquad (16.5)$$

The speedup is linear in n_g, so is bounded only by the complexity of the address computation.

4 MODEL VALIDATION

In this section we validate the models from Section 3 for point–to–point communications on an iWarp system and on a Paragon. To test the predictive power of the models, we use (16.4) to predict the number of iterations necessary for the average cached message assembly time to break even with the uncached message assembly time as a function of n_g, and we use (16.5) to predict the speedup of cached over uncached message assembly, also as a function of n_g. In each case, the address relation that is generated is the identity relation, and n_g, the number of instructions to compute the relation, is varied by inserting nops into the code stream. The predictions are compared to actual measured running times on the hardware.

n_g	Act	Pred-Stat	Pred-Dyn
1	13	INF	13
2	7	12	7
3	5	7	5
4	4	5	4
5	4	4	4
6	3	4	3
7	3	3	3
8	3	3	3

(a)

n_g	Act	Pred-Stat	Pred-Dyn
1	1.05	1.00	1.07
2	1.12	1.09	1.15
3	1.22	1.16	1.23
4	1.28	1.25	1.32
5	1.35	1.33	1.39
6	1.43	1.41	1.47
7	1.49	1.49	1.54
8	1.59	1.59	1.61

(b)

Figure 1 Model validation on iWarp: (a) Iterations required to break even (Eqn. 16.4), (b) Speedup in message assembly (Eqn. 16.5)

4.1 iWarp

On the iWarp [1] system, $r_{rc} = r_{rr} = r_{wc} = r_{wr} = 10^7$ words/second, and a node can execute $r_i = 2 \times 10^7$ instructions/second. The memory system parameters were derived directly from the iWarp specification. Specifically, the iWarp clock speed is 20 MHz and all memory operations complete in two cycles. There is no cache and we assume no dual dispatch of loads and stores.

The implementation parameters (n_{au}, n_o, and n_{ac}) can be estimated *statically* by simply counting the number of instructions in each loop, or *dynamically* by accounting for bypass stalls that arise in the loops. The static estimates for iWarp are $n_{au} = 5$, $n_o = 6$, and $n_{ac} = 2$. The dynamic estimates are $n_{au} = 7$, $n_o = 8$, and $n_{ac} = 3$.

Figure 1(a) shows the measured and predicted number of iterations needed on iWarp for cached assembly to break even with uncached assembly for different n_g. The predictions made using the dynamic measurements are exact. The predictions made using the static measurements are pessimistic for small n_g, but quickly converge to the actual numbers as n_g increases.

Figure 1(b) compares the actual and predicted speedup of cached over uncached message assembly on iWarp. As in Figure 1(a), the dynamic predictions are quite close for all n_g and the static predictions are pessimistic for small n_g. However, it is important to note that even with static measurements, the predictions only become inaccurate when n_g approaches the minimum number of instructions where the cached implementation can outperform the uncached implementation. Another important point is that the purpose of Figure 1(b) is to help validate the models when n_g is small, and not to highlight impressive speedups. In fact, the speedups grow arbitrarily large as n_g increases (see Equation 16.5.)

4.2 Paragon

A Paragon node contains a 50 MHz pipelined, multiple issue RISC processor [5, 4] We estimated the instruction issue rate by noting that we do not use the floating

n_g	Act	Pred-Stat
14	NONE	NONE
15	NONE	NONE
16	19	NONE
17	11	41
18	9	20
19	7	14
20	6	11
21	5	9
22	5	7
23	4	7
24	4	6
25	4	5

(a)

n_g	Act	Pred-Stat
14	NONE	NONE
15	NONE	NONE
16	1.03	NONE
17	1.06	1.01
18	1.09	1.02
19	1.12	1.03
20	1.15	1.04
21	1.17	1.05
22	1.20	1.06
23	1.22	1.07
24	1.24	1.08
25	1.26	1.09

(b)

Figure 2 Model validation on Paragon: (a) Iterations to break even (Eqn. 16.4), (b) Speedup in message assembly (Eqn. 16.5)

point pipeline. Therefore we can issue at most $r_i = 5 \times 10^7$ instructions/second. We directly measured the memory parameters and found $r_{rc} = 9 \times 10^6$ words/second, $r_{wc} = 8.2 \times 10^6$ words/second, and $r_{rr} = r_{wr} = 0.9 \times 10^6$ words/second. Only a static measurement (instruction counting) of the implementation properties was performed, which found $n_{au} = 6$, $n_o = 7$, and $n_{ac} = 11$.

Figure 2(a) shows the measured and predicted number of iterations needed for cached assembly to break even with uncached assembly for different n_g. The predictions are pessimistic, but quickly converge to the actual values with increasing n_g. Notice that n_g must be much larger to permit break even on the Paragon than on the iWarp. This is not surprising given that the Paragon's instruction issue rate is much higher than its memory bandwidth, while the iWarp's issue rate is well matched to its memory bandwidth.

Figure 2(b) compares the actual and predicted speedup of cached message assembly over uncached message assembly on the Paragon. Notice that speedup does not increase as quickly with n_g as on the iWarp (Figure 1(b).) This is the result of the lower memory bandwidth relative to instruction issue rate on the Paragon. The predictions are not as accurate as for the iWarp, reflecting the fact the Paragon's memory system is more complex. However, the predictions are pessimistic and converge to the correct values.

5   CACHING IN HPF

This section investigates the impact of caching on the performance of array assignments in task parallel HPF programs. In a task parallel array assignment statement, the source and destination arrays are distributed over disjoint sets of processors. The test cases presented are written in Fx [3] (a dialect of HPF that integrates task and data parallelism) and compiled and run on an Intel Paragon. Communication is performed

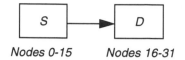

Nodes 0-15   Nodes 16-31

Figure 3   Experimental setup

with an enhanced version of the Fx run–time library that supports cached and uncached message assembly. The appropriate library function is invoked on each source node, with the distributions of the source and destination arrays passed in as arguments. Address computation is performed using the algorithm in [9]. The library can either cache the results of this computation, or use them to directly assemble a message.

We measured the performance of the library, with and without caching, for a variety of test cases. As shown in Figure 3, each test case consists of two data parallel tasks that repeatedly assign a 512×512 *source array S*, distributed over 16 nodes in the *source task*, to a *destination array D*, distributed over a disjoint set of 16 nodes in the *destination task*. Each test case is characterized by the distributions of the source and target arrays.

The results indicate that the effectiveness of caching depends on the source and destination distributions, and thus on the complexity of address computation. In some cases caching is worse, in other cases it is marginally better, and in other cases it is significantly better. Three of the Paragon test cases (Figure 4) illustrate this point quite clearly:

Case 1: S(:,BLOCK) → D(:,BLOCK). In this case, the distributions of the source and destination arrays are identical. The address computation for a block–to–block assignment of this sort is a common case that is highly optimized in the library. Because address computation is very inexpensive, caching is not helpful in this case. In fact, although it is hard to see in the figure, even after 1000 iterations the average end–to–end latency for the cached version is marginally higher than that of the uncached version. For this case, cached message assembly is slightly slower than uncached message assembly.

Case 2: S(BLOCK,:) → D(:,BLOCK). This example assigns a source array that is distributed by rows, to a destination array that is distributed by columns. Because of the additional computation involved (compared to Case 1), as well as the small number of address-address blocks necessary to represent the address relation, caching proves to be a marginal win. Ultimately, it improves average latency by about 20%.

Case 3: S(:,CYCLIC(5)) → D(:,CYCLIC(20)). This example assigns a source array with a small block size of 5 to a destination array with a block size of 20. The library does not have an optimization for this case, and, in fact, the inner loop of the address computation only generates one tuple each time it is entered. Despite this, there is a fair amount of contiguity in the address relation, so there are few address–address

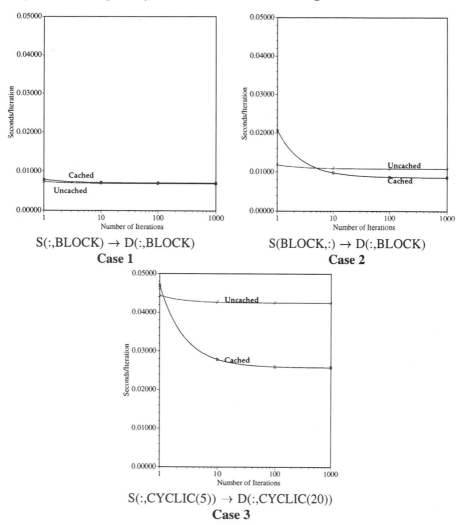

Figure 4 Effectiveness of caching for HPF on Paragon. Each graph plots the average end–to–end latency versus the number of iterations for cached and uncached message assembly.

blocks in the cache. As a result, the communication is ultimately a factor of two faster if message assembly is performed from the cache.

In general, as distributions become more irregular, address computation becomes more time expensive because it becomes increasingly difficult for the the communication library to provide special–case optimizations. In these cases, such as case 3 of Figure 4, caching can have a significant impact.

6 DISCUSSION

In this section, we comment on other issues in address relation caching. We begin by noting the benefits of decoupling address computation and message assembly in the communication system. Next, we discuss where to make the decision to cache an address computation, pointing out that compilers play a key role. Continuing, we comment on cache data structures and replacement policy. Finally, we point out that the cache provides an opportunity for optimizations.

6.1 Decoupling address computation and message assembly

By taking address computation out of the critical path of data transfer, address relation caching decouples address computation and message assembly. One advantage of this is that it makes it easier to achieve reasonable communication performance without a large number of special–case optimizations in the compiler and run–time library. Instead of optimizing each address computation algorithm for each architecture, only message assembly from cache needs to be optimized for each architecture in order for all data transfers to benefit.

Address relations are an ideal interface to the communication system because they are implementation neutral. This permits communication systems to be highly specialized for the available hardware while still presenting the same interface to the programmer or compiler. However, to best utilize the hardware, it may be necessary to change the representation of the address relation before using it. For example, the relation may be transformed into a DMA gather map on the sender to make best use of a network adapter such as the one described in [8]. Because transforming the relation may be expensive, it is desirable for the communication system to cache the (transformed) relation instead of the application.

6.2 Deciding to cache

Our analytical model and HPF results show that caching can sometimes be ineffective and that the number of times a cached address relation must be reused to break even depends on the complexity of address generation. Given this, where should the decision to cache or not be made? One option is to make this decision in the compiler. This is almost certainly the right place if the distributions and machine characteristics and the number of times the communication is performed are known at compile–time. If this is not the case, the decision can be made at run–time, where at least the distributions and machine characteristics are known. However, the number of repetitions may be data dependent and unknown until after the communication has been performed. To deal with this case, the library could keep track of the number of times a particular communication is performed uncached, and switch to a cached approach after some number of repetitions.

6.3   Cache data structures

There is a continuum of cache data structures that ranges from individually storing each tuple of the address relation in memory to simply performing the original address computation. The cache data structure should be chosen to minimize the time spent accessing the cache given memory constraints. The structure should be implementation dependent in order to make best use of available hardware.

6.4   Replacement policy

The cache replacement policy should make use of compile–time knowledge. The HPF library described above uses a strictly direct–mapped policy at run–time, but the cache entry tags are selected by the compiler, which knows the run–time policy. This means the compiler can assure that useful address relations remain in the cache. What to do when there is insufficient memory to hold even one address relation in cache is unclear.

6.5   Cache optimizations

The cache is an intermediate layer between address computation and message assembly. As such, it presents opportunities for optimization. For example, since the entire address relation is known to the cache, it could optimize it for memory locality on the sender, receiver, or both. As shown in [11], the choice is architecture–dependent. If the distributions, machine characteristics, and repetition count are known at compile–time, it is reasonable to perform address generation at this point, "pre-cache" the results, and always assemble from cache when running the program.

7   CONCLUSIONS

Address relation caching at the communication system level is an effective strategy for facilitating high bandwidth, low latency data transfer. Because address computation is removed from the critical path, its cost can not determine communication performance. Our results show that address relation caching is effective even when the cost of address computation is very low, even on the order of a few instructions. Further, the overhead of caching can be generally be quickly amortized if the communication is repeated. Although our analysis was in the context of deposit model communication, address relation caching is not limited this model.

ACKNOWLEDGEMENTS

We would like to thank Thomas Stricker for illuminating the finer points of deposit model communication, James Stichnoth for endless patience in explaining the details of performing HPF array assignment statements, and Ed Segall for helping to debug the HPF library.

REFERENCES

[1] S. Borkar, R. Cohn, G. Cox, S. Gleason, T. Gross, H. T. Kung, M. Lam, B. Moore, C. Peterson, J. Pieper, L. Rankin, P. S. Tseng, J. Sutton, J. Urbanski, and J. Webb. iWarp: An integrated solution to high-speed parallel computing. In *Supercomputing '88*, pages 330–339, November 1988.

[2] High Performance Fortran Forum. High Performance Fortran language specification version 1.0 draft, January 1993.

[3] T. Gross, D. O'Hallaron, and J. Subhlok. Task parallelism in a High Performance Fortran framework. *IEEE Parallel & Distributed Technology*, 2(3):16–26, 1994.

[4] *i860 Microprocessor Family Programmer's Reference Manual*. Intel Corporation, 1992.

[5] Intel Corp. *Paragon X/PS Product Overview*, March 1991.

[6] P. Pierce and G. Regnier. The Paragon implementation of the NX message passing interface. In *Proc. Scalable High Performance Computing Conference*, pages 184–190, Knoxville, TN, May 1994. IEEE Computer Society Press.

[7] J. Saltz, , S. Petiton, H. Berryman, and A. Rifkin. Performance effects of irregular communication patterns on massively parallel multiprocessors. *Journal of Parallel and Distributed Computing*, 13:202–212, 1991.

[8] P. Steenkiste, B. Zill, H. Kung, S. Schlick, J. Hughes, B. Kowalski, and J. Mullaney. A host interface architecture for high-speed networks. In *Proceedings of the 4th IFIP Conference on High Performance Networks*, pages A3 1–16, Liege, Belgium, December 1992. IFIP, Elsevier.

[9] J. Stichnoth. Efficient compilation of array statements for private memory multicomputers. Technical Report CMU-CS-93-109, School of Computer Science, Carnegie Mellon University, February 1993.

[10] J. Stichnoth, D. O'Hallaron, and T. Gross. Generating communication for array statements: Design, implementation, and evaluation. *Journal of Parallel and Distributed Computing*, 21(1):150–159, April 1994.

[11] T. Stricker and T. Gross. Optimizing memory system performance for communication in parallel computers. In *Proc. 22nd Intl. Symp. on Computer Architecture*, Portofino, Italy, June 1995. ACM/IEEE. to appear.

[12] T. Stricker, J. Stichnoth, D. O'Hallaron, S. Hinrichs, and T. Gross. Decoupling synchronization and data transfer in message passing systems of parallel computers. In *Proc. Intl. Conf. on Supercomputing*, page accepted, Barcelona, July 1995. ACM.

[13] V. S. Sunderam. PVM : A framework for parallel distributed computing. *Concurrency: Practice and Experience*, 2(4):315–339, December 1990.

[14] D. Walker. The design of a standard message passing interface for distributed memory concurrent computers. *Parallel Computing*, 20(4):657–673, April 1994.

17

THE DESIGN OF MICROKERNEL SUPPORT FOR THE SR CONCURRENT PROGRAMMING LANGUAGE†

Gregory D. Benson and Ronald A. Olsson

Department of Computer Science
University of California, Davis, California 95616
{benson,olsson}@cs.ucdavis.edu

ABSTRACT

In general, networked and distributed operating systems are still programmed using a sequential language like C, even though the underlying programming model is that of multithreaded programs that communicate using some form of message passing. In a distributed environment it is more natural to program using a distributed programming language. In addition, distributed languages do not map well to traditional operating systems. The new, minimal kernel, or microkernel, operating systems provide an opportunity to efficiently support distributed languages. This paper explores different ways to provide support for the SR concurrent programming language on the Mach microkernel.

1   INTRODUCTION

Our goal in this research is to make it not only feasible, but practical to write system-level and user-level distributed programs in a distributed programming language. Although such languages are well-suited for these tasks, the performance of their implementations is hampered by a mismatch between their needs and the primitives provided by the underlying operating systems [14]. Efficient support for distributed programming languages would make it easier to write distributed operating system services (e.g., files systems) and higher-level programming models such as distributed shared memory. It is reasonable to expect that one could write distributed language programs that will perform just as well as programs written in C that use library calls for concurrency and synchronization.

---

†This work is partially supported by the United States Department of Defense University Research Program.

Many languages are implemented on UNIX because it is widely available, therefore such implementations are very portable. An implementor could develop a custom kernel that runs on top of the bare hardware, but this solution limits the usability of the implementation. The concept of a minimal kernel, or microkernel , appears to offer an attractive platform for supporting distributed programming models. The microkernel advances operating system design by increasing system modularity, scalability, protection, and processor utilization. Unlike traditional operating systems, microkernels support only a few key abstractions, including multithreaded processes, communication, and memory management.

Our effort toward reaching our goal is based on an experimental implementation called SRMach, in which SR [4, 3] will be implemented on top of the Mach microkernel [1]. We have designed several RTS (run-time support) systems that take advantage of the Mach primitives, and we are currently implementing one of them. We intend to quantitatively evaluate each design to assess the efficiency of our RTS algorithms. SRMach will serve to explore the utility of a microkernel such as Mach for supporting distributed programming languages, and give insight into the implementation cost of several concurrency mechanisms. In addition, this work attempts to gain further understanding of the language/kernel boundary. This paper presents the rationale behind our designs, a brief introduction to the SR programming language and to the Mach microkernel, and our current SRMach RTS designs.

2   DESIGN RATIONALE

The foundation for our work is based on two basic assumptions. First, distributed programming languages have many desirable properties in contrast to sequential languages used for distributed programming. Second, microkernel-based systems significantly advance operating system design and offer a platform for efficient and portable distributed language implementations. Given these assumptions, this section focuses on the main issues surrounding microkernel support for distributed programming languages. For an in depth discussion of the design issues presented in this section see [7].

2.1   Programming Views

Microkernels present a significant change in structure from traditional operating system kernels. Most notably, microkernels redefine the kernel/user boundary and facilitate both multiprocessing and distributed computing. A consequence of the microkernel architecture is a radical change in the way operating systems are implemented. This consequence also affects the general notion of system-level programming versus user-level programming.

Microkernel-based systems necessitate revisions to the conventional view of programming. Kernel code now implements only a minimal set of abstractions, rather than high-level operating system objects. System programs define a much broader class than found in the conventional view. Using the microkernel primitives, system-level programs can implement many traditional operating system abstractions, or even entire operating systems. In addition, system-level programs can also provide support for different programming languages. In the context of an operating system running on top of a microkernel, the conventional view of a system program still holds. Figure 1 summarizes the microkernel view of programming.

Code Level	Purpose
Kernel	Basic abstractions (e.g., processes)
System	Programming language support
	Operating system abstractions (e.g., users and files)
	Operating system services
User	Application programs

Figure 1   The Microkernel View of Programming

Kernel, system, and user code can be further categorized as sequential, distributed, or parallel. Distributed programs are characterized by processes that communicate through message passing, while parallel programs are characterized by processes that communicate through shared memory [2]. Often, parallel programs have small grain sizes as found in many numerical and scientific applications*. This paper focuses on distributed programs.

Target Programs

In light of the programming view presented above, our work focuses on utilizing distributed programming languages for writing operating system abstractions, operating system services, and user-level applications. In a networked environment for example, a distributed language can simplify the development of distributed operating systems or distributed operating system services. In particular, a distributed language could be used to implement a distributed file system, or a distributed capability system. At the application level, distributed languages can aid the development of programs such as distributed databases, mail programs, and groupware.

2.2   Efficiency

High performance is usually an implied goal for many software systems. However, it is not always the primary goal for distributed programming languages. For example, other desirable properties such as ease of use or reliability may have a higher priority than efficiency. This section briefly describes efficiency problems associated with distributed languages and defines how our research will handle the efficiency issue.

---

*The *granularity* of a concurrent program refers to the number of sequential instructions executed by a process before it must communicate with other processes

Sources of Inefficiency

Distributed programming languages lack efficient implementations for several reasons:

- Inappropriate operating system interfaces

- Complex language mechanisms

- Prototype implementations

Efficient Language Implementation

If a language is to be implemented from scratch, where do efficiency problems manifest themselves? For a given language and operating system, two general places to improve efficiency are:

- The generated code (GC) (i.e., product of a compiler)

- The language/kernel interface (i.e., run-time support)

Our work focuses on the language/kernel interface. All languages require some form of run-time support. In distributed programming languages the run-time support usually implements the mechanisms for communication and synchronization by providing an interface to the underlying operating system kernel. Therefore, the design of the run-time support is critical to the performance of distributed mechanisms. The restrictive model imposed by traditional operating systems may limit the way in which run-time support is designed. As previously mentioned, microkernels are much less restrictive, therefore offer a very flexible platform for designing run-time support. Our work explores the wide spectrum of design possibilities for run-time support on microkernel-based systems.

2.3   Design Feedback

As discovered in systems such as Cedar [15] and Eden [10], the cooperative develop-ment of an operating system and the supported programming language is beneficial to both components. Our research is concerned with distributed programming languages and microkernels. As such, the implementation process will provide insight into both distributed language and microkernel design.

Language mechanisms, particularly concurrent mechanisms, have an associated im-plementation cost. As mentioned in Section 2.2, some language mechanisms may require complex implementations that lead to low run-time performance. For some applications, poor performance might be an acceptable trade off for extremely expres-sive language mechanisms. For many operating system services, good performance is critical to the overall performance of the operating system and applications. Exam-ining different language mechanisms and their associated run-time costs will provide constructive feedback to language designers.

In a similar vein, rigorous experimentation with different language implementations will yield useful analysis of the microkernel primitives and abstractions. If new language paradigms are to be supported by future operating systems, it is important to provide operating system designers with a critical evaluation of current interfaces. Without this information, operating systems will continue to exclusively support sequential languages.

2.4 The SR Programming Language and its Implementation

SR is a language for writing concurrent programs. The main language constructs are resources and operations. Resources encapsulate processes and variables they share; operations provide the primary mechanism for process interaction. SR also provides the concept of an address space, called a virtual machine or simply VM; processes that execute within the same address space can share variables and operations. Resources and virtual machines are dynamically created and destroyed with the **create** and **destroy** statements respectively.

An operation can be considered a generalization of a procedure: it has a name, and can take parameters and return a result. An operation is serviced in one of two different ways—by a **proc** or by **in** statements—and can also be invoked in two ways—by **call** and **send**. A **proc** resembles a conventional procedure in having parameters and a body, but invoking a **proc** causes a new process to be created to service that invocation. The **in** statement allows an existing process to accept operation invocations from other processes. The effects of executing the various combinations of **call/send** and **proc/in** are summarized as follows:

Invocation	Service	Effect
call	**proc**	procedure call (possibly remote or recursive)
call	**in**	rendezvous
send	**proc**	dynamic process creation
send	**in**	asynchronous message passing

The UNIX-based SR RTS implements a light-weight threads package so that multiple SR processes can execute within a single UNIX process. The RTS also contains primitives for semaphores and several additional operations such as timing functions. The RTS manages operation invocations, as well as the dynamic allocation of resources and globals. The RTS also provides coordinated access to I/O devices and files. In addition, the RTS supports distributed program execution by implementing the virtual machine abstraction and by hiding network access (UNIX sockets).

Another version of the SR implementation, called MultiSR, exists for shared-memory multiprocessors running UNIX, allowing true parallel execution of SR processes. MultiSR runs a job server on each real processor. Job servers allow multiple light-weight threads to execute simultaneously. Two processes can enter the RTS simultaneously, requiring the MultiSR RTS to synchronize access to its internal data structures. In addition, it uses a separate I/O server to process I/O operations.

Unfortunately, the SR model of computation — and models used by most other distributed languages — do not map well to the model supported by UNIX. This mismatch complicates the RTS because it must implement the functionality lacking in the UNIX kernel, thereby resulting in poor scalability and inefficient interprocess communication.

2.5   The Mach Microkernel

The Mach microkernel supports a small number of powerful abstractions including tasks, threads, ports, messages, and memory objects. Tasks contain threads and threads communicate with each other by sending messages through ports. In fact, all kernel requests are sent as messages from a thread to the kernel. The only real system calls are the ones used to send and receive messages.

In order to manipulate the Mach kernel abstractions, the programmer is given a set of interfaces and tools. The host language used to write Mach programs and servers is C or C++. However, C and C++ do not support the notion of multiple threads of execution, thus a library package called C Threads is required to write multithreaded programs. Although Mach supports asynchronous message passing, the syntax and semantics associate with the system calls to send and receive messages is quite complex. Therefore, a tool called MIG (Mach Interface Generator) is used to create client and server stubs for RPC (remote procedure call).

3   SRMACH — DESIGN AND IMPLEMENTATION

The experimental effort of our work centers around a prototype system, SRMach. The prototype type will serve as a vehicle for exploring language support issues — efficiency and design feedback — discussed in Section 2. The choice of SR and Mach as the target language and kernel for this work is based on several factors, which are discussed below.

In the context of this research, SR allows several mechanisms to be analyzed in relation to their implementation cost. The alternative would be to implement several different languages, each based on a different communication mechanism. Therefore, not only does SR possess many of the properties that make it a desirable language for writing operating system services, but its expressive power allows several communication methods to be evaluated in concert. SR's concurrent mechanisms are both expressive and not too high-level to prohibit efficient implementations. In addition, it appears that the fundamental objects and mechanisms found in SR correspond well to similar entities in Mach. However, the apparent relationship between language objects and kernel objects could be deceptive. It is hoped that the minimal nature of the Mach microkernel will obviate this problem.

The Mach microkernel is well established in the research community and has also made its way into industry [8]. For example, Mach is the basis of the NeXTStep operating system, OSF/1, and the GNU Hurd operating system. Mach has been well studied and also used a platform form for several microkernel research projects, such as [11], [12], [16], and [6], just to name a few.

Another useful property of both SR and Mach is that they are both freely available. Thus, the source for the SR compiler, linker, and RTS can be modified as needed. The same applies to the Mach microkernel.

The Mach microkernel is extremely flexible, giving the programmer several tools for implementing a server or task. It follows that there is no single method for implementing a language such as SR. The goal is to take advantage of the Mach primitives while preserving the semantics of SR. To expedite the development process, SRMach will preserve as much of the current SR implementation as possible. Below are four possible RTS designs for SRMach: the SSV RTS, the SMR RTS, the SMV RTS, and the MMR RTS. The first letter in each acronym specifies whether or not the RTS uses a single Mach task or multiple tasks. The second letter specifies the use of either one Mach thread or multiple threads. The last letter indicates whether or not the RTS maps SR operations onto "real" Mach port, or if the RTS supports operations internally, using "virtual" ports (which are really just queues). The four approaches presented below are not exhaustive, but other possible implementations will most likely be variations of the approaches given here.

3.1 The SSV RTS

The first, and most straightforward approach, is to implement an SR program as a single Mach task running a single Mach thread using virtual ports. In the current implementation of SR, a virtual machine is associated with a single UNIX process. In a similar manner, this approach associates a virtual machine with a single Mach task (recall that a Mach task encapsulates a single address space). Because of the similarities between a UNIX process and a Mach task, this method minimizes the work necessary to port the existing SR source code to Mach. Note that this is not the same as porting SR to the BSD emulation server that runs on Mach (which would be a trivial task in comparison). Although an SR program would execute as a Mach task, it would not use Mach's kernel threads. Similarly, all message passing (operations) within a single virtual machine would be handled by the current RTS using virtual ports rather than real Mach ports. Because a Mach task represents a single address space, shared variables between resources will work as expected. Using this approach the compiler and linker will remain virtually unchanged. The RTS would only need to be modified to use Mach system calls and the Mach port system to communicate with other virtual machines.

Figure 2 illustrates the conceptual organization of the SSV RTS. The large solid thread represents a Mach thread, while the smaller dashed threads represent SR processes implemented by the RTS lightweight thread system. An SR program and RTS are implemented using single thread within a Mach task. The solid circles denote Mach ports, which are used by tasks to communicate with the kernel as well as other tasks. In this design, ports will only be used for system calls in the RTS and as a mechanism

Task (VM)

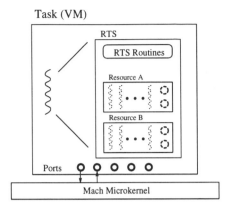

Figure 2   SSV RTS

for virtual machines to communicate. The solid boxes that enclose the resources only represent a logical separation; of course, the SR semantics still hold: resources can only communicate with other resources through imported operations or operations that are passed as arguments. Because all resources and the RTS share the same address space, the GC (generated code) can directly access all the RTS primitives.

A full implementation of SR on Mach requires two other considerations. First, a new mechanism for creating virtual machines will be needed. The current implementation uses rsh (or remsh) to start remote virtual machines. Communication between virtual machines is accomplished with UNIX sockets. Because an SR program will be implemented as a Mach task, rsh and sockets will not be available. For communication, Mach ports will be used, and because Mach is designed to insulate a program from the distributed system, Mach system calls will be used to replace rsh. Second, Mach does not directly support a file system. Mach system calls will be needed to interface with a file system server.

3.2   The SMR RTS

Another approach is to implement the SRMach RTS using both Mach threads and ports (i.e., real ports), whereby an SR virtual machine is associated with a Mach task. Using this model, SR threads are mapped to Mach threads. This approach obviates the need for many RTS routines used to simulate threads, including routines for stack allocation and management, thread scheduling, and context switching. Using Mach threads also introduces preemptive scheduling, which requires the RTS to be reentrant. MultiSR addresses this problem by protecting internal data structures with locks. Therefore, the Single Task RTS can use many of the locks employed in MultiSR. Another benefit from using Mach threads is the possibility of executing SR processes in parallel on a multiprocessor.

For message passing, SR operations can be implemented as Mach ports. In this case, rather than generating calls to the RTS to handle message passing, the compiler will translate **send** and **receive** statements into stub procedures that will ultimately use the Mach primitives to send and receive messages on ports. SR **calls** to **procs** can be implemented in the same way with the help of MIG, which implements RPC with message passing on ports (a send and reply port are used). Using Mach ports eliminates the need to implement invocation queues in the RTS. All invocations will be sent from one process to another through a Mach port.

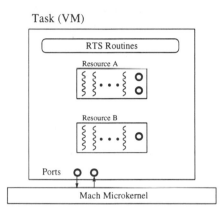

Figure 3 SMR RTS

Figure 3 illustrates the SMR RTS. An SR program is a collection of Mach threads, represented as solid lines. The solid circles located inside the resources denote Mach ports. This organization implies that SR operations will be implemented with Mach message passing. The RTS and resources all reside in the same address space, which facilitates easy access to shared variables. Mach ports will also be used to communicate with other virtual machines, rather than using a separate protocol as in the current UNIX version of SR.

Although Mach ports seem to provide a relatively easy way implement SR operations, this approach has some fundamental problems. Consider the case where a **send** or **call** is serviced by a proc. After a **send** or **call** is executed, a new process is created to service the operation. Executing a send on a Mach port will not dynamically create a new thread, therefore the proc that is servicing the operation must already have a thread associated with it that is blocked (by issuing a system call to receive a message) on the operation port. This problem can be resolved by having the RTS start up a thread for each proc in a resource when the **create** statement is executed. Each proc thread will block on a unique operation port by issuing a Mach receive message system call. When a message is sent to a operation port, the appropriate proc will be unblocked and begin execution. But now, if the same operation port is accessed again, a new proc instance will not be available to service the operation. This problem can be solved by having the original proc thread create a new thread that blocks on the same operation.

This technique will allow multiple invocations of the same proc. When the original proc has finished executing, it will simply die.

Another difficulty with using Mach ports is the inability of threads to examine the contents of a message queue. This restriction is especially important to the general input statement (**in**). An arm of the **in** statement can include a synchronization expression and scheduling expression. Both expressions require the process servicing the operation to examine the current invocations on the queue of pending invocations to determine the next invocation to service. Without being able to examine message queues, additional RTS support is required to implement the semantics of a general **in** statement. It is feasible to have an intermediate thread that buffers invocations. Through a well defined protocol, proc instances can interact with the intermediate thread to effectively "view" the message queue. Unfortunately, this complicated mechanism may introduce a bottleneck that could inhibit parallelism.

3.3   The SMV RTS

The SMR RTS attempts to take full advantage of the the Mach primitives. However, the implementation of the generalized **in** statement presents a problem because it is not possible to examine the contents of Mach port queues. An alternative approach is to take advantage of Mach threads, but continue to use the RTS to handle operations using virtual ports. This method is called the SMR RTS. This hybrid approach reduces the RTS overhead by eliminating thread simulation, but keeps the mechanism for queuing invocation blocks. This method preserves existing code that implements the **in** statement. In some respects, this implementation is similar to the MultiSR configuration. Because Mach threads are preemptive, the SR RTS will view threads as executing concurrently just as MultiSR executes processes concurrently. In fact, this approach can take advantage of a large portion of the code written for MultiSR to deal with reentrancy. MultiSR implements a set of locks used to protect internal RTS data (i.e., resource instances, invocation block queues, etc.). However, unlike MultiSR, this approach does not require the concept of a job server. In MultiSR a job server is used on each processor to fetch processes that are on the ready queue.

Figure 4 illustrates the SMV RTS. Figure 4 is similar to Figure 3, except the ports (operations) inside the resources are no longer Mach ports, but rather operations managed by the RTS using virtual ports. The ports are dashed to indicate they are not Mach ports. Similar to the SSV and SMR RTSs, all the RTS routines reside in the same address space as the processes, making them fully accessible. All program variables are also allocated in the same address space, thus pointers will operate according the language semantics.

3.4   The MMR

The Single Task RTS restricts the virtual machine to a single Mach task. Another logical organization is to associate each resource instance with a single Mach task. As in the Single Task RTS, operations can be implemented as Mach ports and procs

Task (VM)

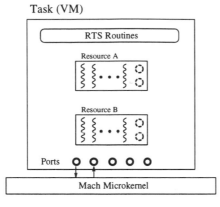

Figure 4 SMV RTS

can be handled by starting a thread for each proc in a resource instance. The RTS proper is now implemented as a separate task. Resource processes can interact with the RTS through RTS ports. Each resource task can have multiple threads representing processes. The RTS task can also have multiple threads to service requests from the resource processes.

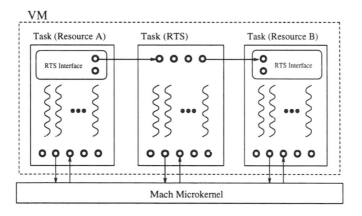

Figure 5 MMR RTS

Figure 5 illustrates the MMR RTS. Processes in different resources can communicate with other processes using operations. Depending on the type of operation, an invocation might first pass through the RTS task. This action would occur for the generalized **in** statement. For simple **in** statements, processes in different resources may communicate directly with each other through operation ports. Also notice that a virtual machine now consists of a set of tasks.

An advantage to the MMR RTS is that local resources variables can now be accessed directly, rather than having to dereference a resource pointer. However, allowing resources to be allocated as separate tasks violates the notion of a single shared address space. Recall that a Mach task and an SR virtual machine represent a single address space. However, this fact does not restrict us from using this approach because Mach allows tasks to share portions of virtual memory. Sharing can occur when a new task is created or it can occur explicitly by giving a task a port right to a range of memory. With shared virtual memory, a scheme can be developed to ensure that tasks share the appropriate data and the pointers work as expected.

4   PERFORMANCE EVALUATION

Benchmarks are required for evaluating the performance of RTS designs. Two types of benchmarks will be used: micro-benchmarks and macro-benchmarks. Micro-benchmarks only test individual mechanisms, thus they are easier to define. Unfortunately, macro-benchmarks are more difficult to develop.

The micro-benchmarks used for SRMach can be derived from previous work in performance analysis of SR's communication and synchronization mechanisms [5]. Efforts to benchmark Mach-based programs and the Mach microkernel will also be used to devise micro-benchmarks [9]. In addition, micro-benchmarks originally written in C and intended for UNIX [13] can be reformulated as SR programs.

Macro-benchmarks should represent the types of programs used by the language and microkernel (i.e., SRMach). As described in Section 2, this research primarily targets system-level programming, and secondarily, user-level programming. A logical approach is to reimplement established Mach servers in SR. This method will allow SR to be compared to C, as well as provide macro-benchmarks that can be used to evaluate different RTS designs. Possible candidates include files systems, distributed shared memory, a TCP/IP server, and portions of the UNIX single server.

5   RESEARCH PLATFORM

The SMR RTS for SRMach is currently being implemented on an i486 machine running Mach4 from the University of Utah and the Lites 4.4 BSD server from Helsinki University of Technology. Eventually, we hope to be able to run stand-alone SR programs on Mach without the aid of a UNIX server. However, in order to bootstrap SRMach we will utilize the Lites 4.4 BSD server.

6   CONCLUSIONS

This paper focuses on our efforts to design and implement a particular concurrent programming language (SR) on a particular microkernel (Mach). We presented only the key points for two of our designs, omitting several important considerations such as I/O, both file and user integration. We are also addressing the issue of interoperability between separate programs. Our effort is part of our more general work investigating issues surrounding the interfaces between languages, run-time support, and operating systems, including a workbench to help us rapidly develop and evaluate new run-time support systems.

Acknowledgements

Phil Nico and Rob Shaw helped develop some of the initial ideas behind our work. Jeff Turner, Karl Levitt, Carole McNamee, and Greg Andrews provided useful criticism and advise that helped shape this research. The anonymous referees provided valuable feedback that helped us clarify our ideas and presentation.

REFERENCES

[1] M. Accetta et al. A new kernel foundation for UNIX development. In *Proceedings of the Summer 1986 USENIX Conference*, pages 93–112, June 1986.

[2] G. R. Andrews. *Concurrent Programming: Principles and Practice.* Benjamin/Cummings, 1991.

[3] G. R. Andrews and R. A. Olsson. *The SR Programming Language: Concurrency in Practice.* The Benjamin/Cummings Publishing Co., Redwood City, California, 1993.

[4] G. R. Andrews, R. A. Olsson, M. Coffin, I. Elshoff, K. Nilsen, T. Purdin, and G. Townsend. An overview of the SR language and implementation. *ACM Transactions on Programming Languages and Systems*, 10(1):51–86, January 1988.

[5] M. S. Atkins and R. A. Olsson. Performance of multi-tasking and synchronization mechanisms in the programming language SR. *Software – Practice and Experience*, 18(9):879–895, September 1988.

[6] K. Bala, M. F. Kaashoek, and W. E. Weihl. Software prefetching and caching for translation lookaside buffers. In *Operating Systems Design and Implementation*, pages 243–253, Monterey, California, November 1994. USENIX.

[7] G. D. Benson. Microkernel support for distributed programming languages: Issues in design and implementation. Technical Report CSE-95-3, University of California, Davis, Department of Computer Science, February 1995.

[8] J. Boykin, D. Kirschen, A. Langerman, and S. LoVerso. *Programming under Mach.* Addison-Wesley, Reading, Massachusetts, 1993.

[9] D. Golub, R. Dean, A. Forin, and R. Rashid. UNIX as an application program. In *Proceedings of the Summer 1990 USENIX Conference*, pages 87–95, June 1990.

[10] E. Lazowska, H. Levy, G. Almes, M. Fischer, R. Fowler, and S. Vsetal. The architecture of the Eden system. In *Proceedings of the 8th ACM Symposium on Operating System Principles*, pages 148–159, December 1981.

[11] NSA INFOSEC Research and Technology. *Synergy: A Distributed, Microkernel-based Security Architecture*, November 1993.

[12] H. Orman, E. Menze III, S. O'Malley, and L. Peterson. A fast and general implementation of Mach IPC in a network. In *Mach III Symposium*, pages 75–88, Santa Fe, New Mexico, April 1993. USENIX.

[13] J. K. Ousterhout. Why aren't operating systems getting faster as fast as hardware? In *Proceedings of the Summer USENIX Conference*, pages 247–256, Anaheim, California, June 1990.

[14] M. L. Scott. The interface between distributed operating system and high-level programming language. In *Proceedings of the 1986 International Conference on Parallel Processing*, August 1986.

[15] D. C. Swinehart, P. T. Zellweger, R. J. Beach, and R. B. Hagmann. A structural view of the Cedar programming environment. *ACM Transactions on Programming Languages and Systems*, 8(4):419–490, October 1986.

[16] C. A. Waldspurger and W. E. Weihl. Lottery scheduling: Flexible proportion-share resource management. In *Operating Systems Design and Implementation*, pages 1–11, Monterey, California, November 1994. USENIX.

18

RUNTIME SUPPORT FOR PROGRAMMING IN ADAPTIVE PARALLEL ENVIRONMENTS

Gagan Agrawal, Guy Edjlali,

Alan Sussman, Jim Humphries

and Joel Saltz

UMIACS and Dept. of Computer Science,
University of Maryland, College Park, MD 20742, USA

ABSTRACT

There has been an increasing trend towards using a network of non-dedicated workstations for parallel programming. In such an environment, the number of processors available for parallel programming may change during the execution of a program. We are developing compiler and runtime support for data parallel programming in such an adaptive environment. Executing data parallel programs in an adaptive environment requires redistributing data when the number of processors changes, and also requires determining new loop bounds and communication patterns for the new set of processors. We have developed a runtime library to provide this support. We also briefly discuss how this runtime support can be used by compilers of HPF-like languages. We present performance results for a Navier-Stokes solver and a multigrid template run on a network of workstations and an IBM SP-2.

1 INTRODUCTION

Recently, there has been an increasing trend toward using a network of workstations for parallel execution of programs. A workstation usually has an individual owner or small set of users who would like to have sole use of the machine at certain times. However, when the individual users of workstations are not logged in these workstations can be used for executing a parallel application. When the individual user of a workstation returns, the application must be adjusted either not to use the workstation at all or to use very few cycles on the workstation. The idea is that the individual user of the workstation would not like the execution of a large parallel application to slow down the processes he/she wants to execute.

For executing a long running application in such an environment, the application must be developed in such a way that the number of processors on which it is executing can

241

be changed while the program is running. Most of the existing work in developing parallel programming support assumes that the number of processors available for programming does not change during the execution of the program.

We refer to a parallel programming environment in which the number of processors available for a given application varies with time an *adaptive* parallel programming environment. We are developing runtime support for programming applications in adaptive environments. We have extended our existing runtime library for structured and block-structured applications (Multiblock PARTI) [2, 12] to include support for adaptive environments. In this paper, we describe the functionality provided by our runtime library and how it can be used for developing applications. We also describe how our runtime support can be used by compilers for data parallel languages like High Performance Fortran (HPF).

Several other efforts have also been made for programming in an adaptive environment [4, 6, 8, 10]. However, they largely consider a task parallel model or a master-slave model. Our model for adaptive parallel programming is closest to the one presented by Proutty *et al.* [11]. We extend their work by providing routines for data remapping, whereas, in their work, this responsibility is left to the application programmer.

The rest of this paper is organized as follows: In Section 2, we discuss the runtime support required for programming in an adaptive environment. In Section 3, we discuss the runtime library we have developed. In Section 4, we briefly discuss how our runtime support can be used by compilers for HPF-like languages. Experimental results are presented in Section 5. We conclude in Section 6.

2 PROGRAMMING IN AN ADAPTIVE ENVIRONMENT

We focus our attention on data parallel programs. In compiling data parallel programs for execution on distributed memory machines, two major tasks are dividing work or loop iterations across processors, and detecting, inserting and optimizing communication between processors. To the best of our knowledge, all existing work on compiling data parallel applications assumes that the number of processors available for execution does not vary at runtime [3, 5, 14]. If the number of processors varies at runtime, runtime routines need to be inserted for determining work partitioning and communication during the execution of the program.

There are two major issues in executing applications in an adaptive environment:

- Redistributing data when the number of available processors changes during the execution of the program and,

- Handling work distribution and communication detection, insertion and optimization when the number of processors on which a given parallel loop will be executed is not known at compile-time.

Our runtime library, called Adaptive Multiblock PARTI (AMP), includes routines for handling the two tasks we have described. This runtime library can be used by compilers for data parallel languages or it can be used by a programmer parallelizing an application by hand.

In our current implementation, we have assumed a simple model for execution of adaptive programs. In this model, it is acceptable if the adaptive program does not remap immediately when the system load changes and, when the program changes from a larger number of processors to a smaller number of processors, it may continue to use a small number of cycles on the processors it no longer uses for computation. This kind of flexibility significantly eases remapping of data parallel applications, with minimal operating system support.

If an adaptive program has to remapped from a larger number of processors to a smaller number of processors, this can be done by redistributing the distributed data so that processors which should no longer be executing the program do not own any part of the distributed data. The SPMD program will continue to execute on all processors. We refer to a process that owns distributed data as an *active process* and a process from which all data has been removed as a *skeleton process*. A processor owning an active process is referred to as an *active processor* and similarly, a processor owning a skeleton process is referred to as a *skeleton processor*. A skeleton processor will still execute each parallel loop in the program. However, after evaluating the local loop bounds to restrict execution to local data, a skeleton processor will determine that it does not need to execute any iterations of the parallel loop. All computations involving writing into scalar variables will continue to be executed on all processors. The parallel program will use some cycles in the skeleton processors, because of evaluation of loop bounds for parallel loops and because of computations involving writing into scalar variables. However, for data parallel applications involving large arrays this is not likely to cause any noticeable slowdown for other processes executing on the skeleton processors.

Remapping can only be done at certain points in the program, which we refer to as *remap points*. The remap points can be chosen by the programmer and/or compiler and should be selected such that the program is not inside a data parallel loop at those points. At each remap point, the program must determine if there is a reason to remap. We assume a *detection* mechanism that determines if load needs to be shifted away from any of the processors which are currently active. This detection mechanism is the only operating system support our model assumes. All the processors synchronize at the remap point and, if the detection mechanism determines that remapping is required, data redistribution is done.

3 RUNTIME SUPPORT

In this section we discuss the runtime library we have developed for adaptive programs. The runtime library has been developed on top of an existing runtime library for structured and block structured applications. This library is called Multiblock

PARTI [2, 12], since it was initially used to parallelize multiblock applications. We have developed our runtime support for adaptive parallelism on top of Multiblock PARTI because this runtime library provides much of the runtime support required for forall loops and array expressions in data parallel languages. We refer to the new library, with extensions for adaptive parallelism, as Adaptive Multiblock PARTI (AMP).

3.1   Multiblock PARTI

This runtime library can be used in optimizing communication and partitioning work for data parallel codes in which data distribution, loop bounds and/or strides are unknown at compile-time and indirection arrays are not used. Consider the problem of compiling a data parallel loop, such as a forall loop, for a distributed memory parallel machine or network of workstations. If all loop bounds and strides are known at compile-time and if all information about the data distribution is also known, then the compiler can perform work partitioning and can also determine the sets of data elements to be communicated between processors. However, if all this information is not known, then these tasks may not be possible to perform at compile-time. In such cases, runtime analysis can be used to determine work partitioning and generate communication. The Multiblock PARTI library has been developed for providing the required runtime analysis routines.

In summary, the runtime library has routines for three sets of tasks:

- Defining data distribution at runtime; this includes maintaining a distributed array descriptor (DAD) which can be used by communication generation and work partitioning routines.

- Performing communication when the data distribution, loop bounds and/or strides are unknown at compile-time and,

- Partitioning work (loop iterations) when data distribution, loop bounds and/or strides are unknown at compile-time.

A key consideration in using runtime routines for work partitioning and communication is to keep the overheads for runtime analysis low. To this purpose, the runtime analysis routines must be efficient and it should be possible to reuse the results of runtime analysis whenever possible. In this runtime system, communication is performed in two phases. First, a subroutine is called to build a communication *schedule* that describes the required data motion, and then another subroutine is called to perform the data motion (sends and receives on a distributed memory parallel machine) using a previously built schedule. Such an arrangement allows a schedule to be used multiple times in an iterative code.

3.2 Adaptive Multiblock PARTI

The existing functionality of the Multiblock PARTI library was useful for developing adaptive programs in several ways. If the number of processors on which a data parallel loop is to be executed is not known at compile-time, it is not possible for the compiler to analyze the communication, and in some cases, even the work partitioning. This holds true even if all other information, such as loop bounds and strides, is known at compile-time. Thus runtime routines are required for analyzing communication (and work partitioning) in a program written for adaptive execution, even if the same program written for static execution on a fixed number of processors did not require any runtime analysis.

Several extensions were required to the existing library to provide the required functionality for adaptive programs. When the set of processors on which the program executes changes at runtime, all active processors must obtain information about which processors are active and how the data is distributed across the set of active processors. To deal with only some of the processors being active at any time during execution of the adaptive program, the implementation of Adaptive Multiblock PARTI uses the notion of *physical numbering* and *logical numbering* of processors. If p is the number of processors that can possibly be active during the execution of the program, each such processor is assigned a unique physical processor number between 0 and $p - 1$ before starting program execution. If we let c be the number of processors that are active at a given point during execution of a program, then each of these active processors is assigned a unique logical processor number between 0 and $c - 1$. The mapping between physical and processor numbers and logical processor numbers for active processors is updated at remap points.

In summary, the additional functionality implemented in AMP over that available in Multiblock PARTI is as follows:

- Primitives for consistently updating the logical processor numbering when it has been detected that redistribution is required.

- Primitives for redistributing data at remap points and,

- Modified communication analysis and data-move routines to incorporate information about the logical processor numbering.

4 COMPILATION ISSUES

The examples shown previously illustrate how AMP can be used by application programmers to develop adaptive programs by hand. We now briefly describe the major issues in compiling programs written in an HPF-like data parallel programming language for an adaptive environment. Our work is restricted to data parallel languages in which parallelism is specified explicitly. Incorporating adaptive parallelism in compilation systems in which parallelism is detected automatically [5] is beyond the scope of this paper.

In previous work, we successfully integrated the Multiblock PARTI library with a prototype Fortran90D/HPF compiler developed at Syracuse University [1, 2, 3]. Routines provided by the library were inserted for analyzing work partitioning and communication at runtime, whenever compile-time analysis was inadequate. This implementation can be extended to use Adaptive Multiblock PARTI and compile HPF programs for adaptive execution. The major issues in compiling a program for adaptive execution are determining remap points, inserting appropriate actions at remap points and ensuring reuse of the results of runtime analysis to minimize the cost of such analysis.

4.1   Remap Points

In our model of execution of adaptive programs, remapping is considered only at certain points in the program text. If our runtime library is to be used, a program cannot be remapped inside a data parallel loop. The reason is that the local loop bounds of a data parallel loop are determined based upon the current data distribution, and in general it is very difficult to ensure that each iteration of the parallel loop is executed by exactly one processor, either before or after remapping.

There are (at least) two possibilities for determining remap points. They may be specified by the programmer in the form of a directive, or they may be determined automatically by the compiler. For the data parallel language HPF, parallelism can only be explicitly specified through certain constructs (e.g.. forall statement, forall construct, independent statement [7]). Inside any of these constructs, the only functions that can be called are the those explicitly marked as *pure* functions. Thus it is simple to determine, solely from the syntax, what points in the program are not inside any data parallel loop and therefore can be remap points. Making all such points remap points may, however, lead to a large number of remap points which may occur very frequently during program execution, and may lead to significant overhead from employing the detection mechanism (and synchronization of all processors at each remap point).

Alternatively, a programmer may specify certain points in the program to be remap points, through an explicit directive. This, however, makes adaptive execution less transparent to the programmer.

Once remap points are known to the compiler, it can insert calls to the detection mechanism at those points. The compiler also needs to insert a conditional based on the result of the detection mechanism, so that, if the detection mechanism determines that remapping needs to be done, then calls are made both for building new Distributed Array Descriptors(DAD) and for redistributing the data as specified by the new DAD.

4.2   Schedule Reuse in the Presence of Remapping

As we discussed in Section 3, a very important consideration in using runtime analysis is the ability to reuse the results of runtime analysis whenever possible. This is relatively straightforward if a program is parallelized by inserting the runtime routines by hand. When the runtime routines are automatically inserted by a compiler, an approach based upon additional runtime bookkeeping can be used. In this approach, all schedules generated are stored in hash tables by the runtime library, along with their input parameters. Whenever a call is made to generate a schedule, the input parameters specified for this call are matched against those for all existing schedules. If a match is found, the stored schedule is returned by the library. This approach was successfully used in the prototype HPF/Fortran90D compiler that used the Multiblock PARTI runtime library. Our previous experiments have shown that saving schedules in hash tables and searching for existing schedules results in less than 10% overhead, as compared to a hand implementation that reuses schedules optimally.

This approach easily extends to programs which include remapping. One of the parameters to the schedule call is the Distributed Array Descriptor(DAD). After remapping, a call for building a new DAD for each distributed array is inserted by the compiler. For the first execution of any parallel loop after remapping, no schedule having the new DADs as parameters will be available in the hash table. New schedules for communication will therefore be generated. The hash tables for storing schedules can also be cleared after remapping to reduce the amount of memory used by the library.

5 EXPERIMENTAL RESULTS

To study the performance of the runtime routines and to determine the feasibility of using an adaptive environment for data parallel programming, we have experimented with a multiblock Navier-Stokes solver template [13] and a multigrid template [9]. The multiblock template was extracted from a computational fluid dynamics application that solves the thin-layer Navier-Stokes equations over a 3D surface (multiblock TLNS3D). The sequential Fortran77 code was developed by Vatsa *et al.* [13] at NASA Langley Research Center, and consists of nearly 18,000 lines of code. The template, which was designed to include portions of the entire code that are representative of the major computation and communication patterns of the original code, consists of nearly 2,000 lines of F77 code. The multigrid code we experimented with was developed by Overman *et al.* at NASA Langley. In earlier work, we hand parallelized these codes using Multiblock PARTI and also parallelized Fortran90D versions of these codes using the prototype HPF/Fortran 90D compiler. In both these codes, the major computation is performed inside a (sequential) time-step loop. For each of the parallel loops in the major computational part of the code, the loop bounds and communication patterns do not change across iterations of the time-step loop when the code is run in a static environment. Thus communication schedules can be generated before the first iteration of the time-step loop and can be used for all time steps in a static environment.

We modified the hand parallelized versions of these codes to use the Adaptive Multiblock PARTI routines. For both these codes, we chose the beginning of an iteration of the time-step loop as the remapping point. If remapping is done, the data distribution changes and the schedules used for previous time steps can no longer be used. For our experiments, we used two adaptive parallel programming environments. The first was a network of workstations using PVM for message passing. We had up to 12 work-

No. of Procs.	Time per Iteration	Cost of Remapping to			
		12 procs.	8 procs.	4 procs.	1 proc.
12	2213	-	3024	3740	6757
8	2480	3325	-	3715	9400
4	3242	2368	2755	-	6420
1	8244	2548	5698	5134	-

Figure 1   Cost of Remapping (in ms.): Multiblock code on Network of Workstations

No. of Procs.	Time per Iteration	Cost of Remapping to				
		16 procs.	8 procs.	4 procs.	2 procs.	1 proc.
16	59.2	-	33	49	86	159
8	91.5	34	-	54	88	156
4	139.5	47	53	-	96	160
2	215.8	78	85	95	-	171
1	526.8	143	152	156	173	-

Figure 2   Cost of Remapping (in ms.): Multiblock code on IBM SP-2

stations available for our experiments. The second environment was a 16 processors IBM SP-2.

In demonstrating the feasibility of using an adaptive environment for parallel program execution, we considered the following factors:

■   the time required for remapping and computing a new set of schedules, as compared to the time required for each iteration of the time-step loop,

■   the number of time steps that the code must execute after remapping to a greater number of processors to effectively amortize the cost of remapping, and

No. of	Time per	Cost of Remapping to			
Procs.	Iteration	8 procs.	4 procs.	2 procs.	1 proc.
8	93.2	-	14	20	36
4	135.2	18	-	22	29
2	207.5	19	23	-	29
1	950.3	33	33	36	-

Figure 3   Cost of Remapping (in ms.): Multigrid code on IBM SP-2

- the effect of skeleton processes on the performance of their host processors.

On the network of Sun workstations, we considered executing the program on 12, 8, 4 or 1 workstations at any time. Remapping was possible from any of these configurations to any other configuration. We measured the time required for one iteration of the time-step loop and the cost of remapping from one configuration to another. The experiments were conducted at a time when none of the workstations had any other jobs executing. The time required per iteration for each configuration and the time required for remapping from one configuration to another are presented in the Figure 1. In both these tables, the second column shows the time per iteration, and columns 3 to 6 show the time for remapping to 12, 8, 4 and 1 processor configuration, respectively. The remapping cost includes the time required for redistributing the data and the time required for building a new set of communication schedules. The speed-up of the template is not very high because it has a high communication to computation ratio and communication using PVM is relatively slow. These results show that the time required for remapping for this application is at most the time required for 3.5 time steps.

We performed the same experiment on a 16 processor IBM SP-2. The results are shown are in Figure 2. The program could execute on either 16, 8, 4, 2 or 1 processors and we considered remapping from any of these configurations to any other configuration. The templates obtains significantly better speed-up and the time required for remapping is much smaller. In Figure 3, we show the results from the multigrid template. Again, the remapping time for this routine is reasonably small.

Another interesting tradeoff occurs when additional processors become available for running the program. Running the program on a greater number of processors can reduce the time required for completing the execution of the program, but, at the same time, remapping the program onto a new set of processors causes additional overheads

No. of Proc.	No. of Time-steps for Amortizing when remapped to			
	12 proc.	8 proc.	4 proc.	1 proc.
12	-	-	-	-
8	12.4	-	-	-
4	2.3	3.6	-	-
1	0.4	1.1	1.0	-

Figure 4   No. of Time-steps for Amortizing Cost of Remapping: Multiblock code on Network of Sun Workstations

for moving data. A useful factor to determine is the number of iterations of the time-step loop that must still be executed so that it will be profitable to remap from fewer to a greater number of processors. Using the timings from the Figure 1, we show the results in Figure 4. These figures show that if the program will continue run for a several more time-steps, remapping from almost any configuration to any other larger configuration is likely to be profitable. Since the remapping times are even smaller on SP-2, the number of iterations required for amortizing the cost of remapping will be even smaller.

In our model of adaptive parallel programming, a program is never completely removed from any processor. A skeleton process steals some cycles on the host processor, which can potentially slow down other processes that want to use the processor (e.g. a workstation user who has just logged in). The skeleton processes do not perform any communication and do not synchronize, except at the remap points. In our examples, the remap point is the beginning of an iteration of the time-step loop. We measured the time required per iteration on the skeleton processors. Our experiments show that the execution time on skeleton processes is always less than 2% of the execution time on active processes. For the multiblock code, the time required per iteration for the skeleton processors was 4.7 ms. and 30 ms. on the IBM SP-2 and Sun-4 workstations respectively. The multi grid code took 11 ms. per iteration on the IBM SP-2. We expect, therefore, that a skeleton process will not slow down any other job run on that processor significantly (assuming that the skeleton process gets swapped out by the operating system when it reaches a remap point).

6   CONCLUSIONS

In this paper we have addressed the problem of developing applications for execution in an adaptive parallel programming environment, meaning an environment in which the number of processors available varies at runtime. We have defined a simple model for programming and program execution in such an environment. We have considered only Single Program Multiple Data (SPMD) parallel programs. Since the same program text is run on all the processors, remapping a program to include or exclude processors only involves remapping the (parallel) data used in the program.

We have presented the features of Adaptive Multiblock PARTI, which provides runtime support that can be used for developing adaptive parallel programs. We described how the runtime library can be used by a compiler to compile programs written in HPF-like data parallel languages for adaptive execution. We have presented experimental results on a hand parallelized Navier-Stokes solver template and a multigrid template run on a network of workstations using PVM and on an IBM SP-2. Our experimental results show that adaptive execution of a parallel program can be provided at relatively low cost, if the number of available processors does not vary frequently.

REFERENCES

[1] Gagan Agrawal, Alan Sussman, and Joel Saltz. Compiler and runtime support for structured and block structured applications. In *Proceedings Supercomputing '93*, pages 578–587. IEEE Computer Society Press, November 1993.

[2] Gagan Agrawal, Alan Sussman, and Joel Saltz. An integrated runtime and compile-time approach for parallelizing structured and block structured applications. *IEEE Transactions on Parallel and Distributed Systems*, 1995. To appear. Also available as University of Maryland Technical Report CS-TR-3143 and UMIACS-TR-93-94.

[3] Z. Bozkus, A. Choudhary, G. Fox, T. Haupt, S. Ranka, and M.-Y. Wu. Compiling Fortran 90D/HPF for distributed memory MIMD computers. *Journal of Parallel and Distributed Computing*, 21(1):15–26, April 1994.

[4] David Gelernter and David Kaminsky. Supercomputing out of recycled garbage: Preliminary experience with Piranha. In *Proceedings of the Sixth International Conference on Supercomputing*, pages 417–427. ACM Press, July 1992.

[5] Seema Hiranandani, Ken Kennedy, and Chau-Wen Tseng. Compiling Fortran D for MIMD distributed-memory machines. *Communications of the ACM*, 35(8):66–80, August 1992.

[6] J.Casas, R.Konuru, S.Otto, R.Prouty, and J.Walpole. Adaptative load migration systems for PVM. Technical report, Dept. of Computer Science and Engineering,Oregon Graduate Institute of Science and Technology, 1994.

[7] C. Koelbel, D. Loveman, R. Schreiber, G. Steele, Jr., and M. Zosel. *The High Performance Fortran Handbook*. MIT Press, 1994.

[8] N.Nedeljkovic and M.J.Quinn. Data-parallel programming on a network of heterogeneous workstations. *Concurrency: Practice and Experience*, 5(4), 1993.

[9] Andrea Overman and John Van Rosendale. Mapping robust parallel multigrid algorithms to scalable memory architectures. In *Proceedings of 1993 Copper Mountain Conference on Multigrid Methods*, April 1993.

[10] R.Konuru, J.Casa, R.Prouty, and J.Walpole. A user-level process package for PVM. In *Proceedings of the Scalable High Performance Computing Conference (SHPCC-94)*, pages 48–55. IEEE Computer Society Press, May 1994.

[11] R.Prouty, S.Otto, and J.Walpole. Adaptive execution of data parallel computations on networks of heterogeneous workstations. Technical Report CSE-94-012, Oregon Graduate Institute of Science and Technology, 1994.

[12] Alan Sussman, Gagan Agrawal, and Joel Saltz. A manual for the multiblock PARTI runtime primitives, revision 4.1. Technical Report CS-TR-3070.1 and UMIACS-TR-93-36.1, University of Maryland, Department of Computer Science and UMIACS, December 1993.

[13] V.N. Vatsa, M.D. Sanetrik, and E.B. Parlette. Development of a flexible and efficient multigrid-based multiblock flow solver; AIAA-93-0677. In *Proceedings of the 31st Aerospace Sciences Meeting and Exhibit*, January 1993.

[14] Hans P. Zima and Barbara Mary Chapman. Compiling for distributed-memory systems. *Proceedings of the IEEE*, 81(2):264–287, February 1993. In Special Section on Languages and Compilers for Parallel Machines.

19

DATA-PARALLEL LANGUAGE FEATURES FOR SPARSE CODES†

M. Ujaldon, E. L. Zapata, B. M. Chapman* and H. P. Zima*

Computer Architecture Department, University of Malaga,
Plaza El Ejido, s/n. 29013 Malaga, Spain

*Institute for Software Technology and Parallel Systems, University of Vienna,
Liechtensteinstr, 22, A-1090 Vienna, Austria

ABSTRACT

This paper proposes a new approach to improve data-parallel languages in the context of sparse and irregular computation. We analyze the capabilities of High Performance Fortran (HPF) and Vienna Fortran, and identify a set of problems leading to sub-optimal parallel code generation for such computations on distributed-memory machines. Finally, we propose extensions to the data distribution facilities in Vienna Fortran which address these issues and provide a powerful mechanism for efficiently expressing sparse algorithms.

1 INTRODUCTION

Many real application codes are sparse. However, it is widely recognized in the scientific community that data-parallel languages such as Vienna Fortran and High Performance Fortran(HPF) will not be particularly efficient in terms of both execution time and memory for such problems.

In this paper, we introduce new mechanisms for data distribution which support the efficient data-parallel implementation of many sparse and irregular problems on distributed-memory machines. Our ideas are based on standard sparse matrix representations [2] that only take the relevant information of the matrix of the problem without restricting its range of application.

We have carried out an analysis of a range of data distributions in terms of load-balancing and data locality [14]. We have studied their properties by using them to manually implement typical sparse algorithms [1] on parallel systems, and evaluated the performance that can be achieved by using them. However, these experiments also

† This work was supported by the Ministry of Education and Science (CICYT) of Spain under project TIC92-0942 and by the Austrian Science Foundation (FWF).

pointed out the excessive time that the implementation and debugging stages of these algorithms require if coded manually. We then developed the methods required in order to integrate these distributions in a data-parallel compiler, and initiated an implementation of the compile time and runtime strategies required for the parallelization of sparse codes [18] in the framework of the *Vienna Fortran Compilation System*. Execution times already obtained demonstrate that our compiler is able to generate target code without sacrificing performance of the parallel program[18].

This paper focusses on the language issues of such distributions and storage formats, and presents the language extensions we have designed and included into the Vienna-Fortran language to specify them. The language elements that data parallel languages have made available for this kind of application will be analyzed to demonstrate that they are not sufficient to specify our distributions.

2 REPRESENTATION OF SPARSE MATRICES ON DISTRIBUTED-MEMORY MACHINES

When a sparse matrix is mapped to a distributed-memory machine, our approach will require two kinds of information to be specified by the user. These are:

1. The representation of the sparse matrix on a *single processor*. This is called a **sparse format**.

2. The distribution of the matrix across the processors of the machine.

   In this context, the concept of a *distribution* is used as if the matrix was dense.

The combination of a sparse format with a distribution will be called a **distributed sparse representation** of the matrix.

2.1 Sparse Formats

In practice, a large variety of sparse formats are used ([10, 2]). Most approaches allocate contiguous storage in memory for the non-zero elements of the matrix. This requires a scheme for knowing where the elements fit into the full matrix, but achieves significant memory savings. To do this, auxiliary data structures are introduced. We describe this fully for one type of representation; others are constructed analogously.

For the following, assume that $A(1:n, 1:m)$ denotes a sparse matrix with α nonzero elements, which are enumerated based on a row-wise traversal.

Definition 1 *The* **Compressed Row Storage (CRS) sparse format** *is determined by a triple of functions, (DA,CO,RO):*

1. $DA : [1 : \alpha] \rightarrow \Re$, *total, the* **data function***, is defined such that* $DA(t)$ *is the t-th nonzero element, for all* $t \in [1 : \alpha]$. *

2. $CO : [1 : \alpha] \rightarrow [1 : m]$, *total, the* **column function***, is defined as follows. Assume that the t-th nonzero element is* $A(x, y)$. *Then* $CO(t) := y$.

3. $RO : [1 : n + 1] \rightarrow [1 : \alpha]$, *total, is the* **row function***. For each* $i, 1 \leq i \leq n$, $RO(i)$ *is the number of the first nonzero element in row i, if such an element exists; otherwise* $RO(i) := RO(i + 1)$. *Finally,* $RO(n + 1) := \alpha + 1$.

□

These three functions can be represented in an obvious way as vectors of α real numbers (the **data vector**), α column numbers (the **column vector**), and $n + 1$ integer numbers in the range $[1 : \alpha]$ (the **row vector**) respectively.

The storage savings achieved by this approach is usually significant. Instead of storing $n * m$ elements, we need only $2\alpha + n + 1$ storage locations.

$$\begin{pmatrix} 0 & 53 & 0 & 0 & 0 & 0 & 0 & 0 \\ 0 & 0 & 0 & 0 & 0 & 0 & 21 & 0 \\ 19 & 0 & 0 & 0 & 0 & 0 & 0 & 16 \\ 0 & 0 & 0 & 0 & 0 & 72 & 0 & 0 \\ 0 & 0 & 0 & 17 & 0 & 0 & 0 & 0 \\ 0 & 0 & 0 & 0 & 93 & 0 & 0 & 0 \\ 0 & 0 & 0 & 0 & 0 & 0 & 13 & 0 \\ 0 & 0 & 0 & 0 & 44 & 0 & 0 & 19 \\ 0 & 23 & 69 & 0 & 37 & 0 & 0 & 0 \\ 27 & 0 & 0 & 11 & 0 & 0 & 64 & 0 \end{pmatrix}$$

Figure 1 Sample sparse matrix $A_0(10,8)$ with $\alpha = 16$

Example 1 *Consider the sparse matrix* A_0 *as shown in Figure 1. Data, column and row vectors for* A_0 *are given in Figure 2.*

The **Compressed Column Storage (CCS)** sparse format is similar to CRS, but is based on an enumeration which traverses the columns of A rather than the rows.

There are a variety of additional sparse formats which exploit the structure present in certain kinds of sparse matrices frequently encountered in practice: these include *Block Compressed Row Storage* which tries to exploit dense block patterns appearing in the sparse matrix, *Compressed Diagonal Storage* and *Jagged Diagonal Storage* which can be used when the matrix A is banded, *Skyline Storage* which is used for

---

* $\Re$ denotes the set of real numbers.

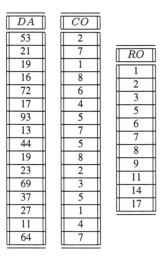

Figure 2   CRS representation for sparse matrix A_0

skyline matrices [9], and finally, the *ITPACK* format which shifts all non-zero elements to the left, after which the columns are stored consecutively and the rows are padded with zeros on the right to give them equal length.

For the purposes of our work, we assume that the CRS or CCS sparse formats are used in the source code. This is generally applicable, since it makes no assumptions about the sparsity structure of the matrix, nor does it store any unnecessary elements. The choice for a row-based or column-based format will depend largely on how array elements are accessed in the computation.

The use of these representations necessitates indirect accesses in the source code; the auxiliary arrays typically also appear in expressions for the loop bounds.

2.2   Distributed Sparse Representations

Let A denote a sparse matrix as discussed above, and δ an associated distribution.

A **distributed sparse representation** for A results from combining δ with a sparse format. This is to be understood as follows: δ is interpreted in the conventional sense, i.e., as if A were a dense Fortran array, i.e., δ determines, for each processor p, the set of array elements *local* to p. This set is again a sparse matrix. The distributed sparse representation of A is then obtained by constructing a representation of the local elements, based on the given sparse format. That is, *DA*, *CO*, and *RO* are automatically converted to the sets of vectors DA^p, CO^p, and RO^p. additional auxiliary structures may have to be set up to optimize accesses to A.

Hence the parallel code will save computation and storage using the very same mechanisms that were applied in the original program. In practice we need some additional global information to support exchanges of sparse data with other processors.

The selection of a distributed sparse representation for a given problem must find a compromise between the conflicting goals of balancing the workload, minimizing communication, saving memory, and and reducing the data access overhead. Below we discuss two approaches towards this objective based on different distributions of the sparse matrix. These strategies are applicable in different circumstances.

The first method attempts to retain data locality by mapping a single rectangle of the sparse matrix A to each target processor. Since the distribution of non-zero values in A may be highly irregular, we must have a more flexible method than BLOCK for specifying the distribution segment in order to achieve a reasonable load balance.

The second representation is based on a cyclic distribution. This does not retain locality of access; as in the regular case, it is suitable in all situations where the work load is not spread evenly across the matrix (here, across the non-zero elements). It also allows the efficient handling of a situation in which the density of the matrix varies over time.

2.3 Multiple Recursive Decomposition (MRD)

Binary Recursive Decomposition (BRD), as proposed by Berger and Bokhari [3], specifies a distribution algorithm where the sparse matrix A is recursively bisected, alternating vertical and horizontal partitioning steps until there are as many submatrices as processors. Each submatrix is mapped to a unique processor. A more flexible variant of this algorithm produces partitions in which the shapes of the individual rectangles are optimized with respect to a user-determined function [5].

In this section, we define *Multiple Recursive Decomposition (MRD)*, a generalization of the BRD method, which attempts to improve the communication structure of the code.

Definition 2 MRD Distribution

We assume the processor array to be declared as $P(0 : X - 1, 0 : Y - 1)$. Let $X * Y = P_1 * P_2 * ... * P_k$ be the prime factor decomposition for $X * Y$, ordered in such a way that the prime factors of X, sorted in descending order, come first and are followed by the factors of Y, sorted in the same fashion.

The MRD distribution method produces an $X * Y$ partition of matrix A in k steps, recursively performing horizontal divisions of the matrix for the prime factors of X, and vertical ones for the prime factors of Y:

- *Step 1: Matrix A is partitioned into P_1 submatrices in such a way that the non-zero elements are spread across the submatrices as evenly as possible. When a* *submatrix is partitioned horizontally, any rows with no non-zero entries which are not uniquely assigned to either partition are included in the lower one; in a vertical step, such columns are assigned to the right partition.*

■   *Step i ($1 < i \leq k$): Each submatrix resulting from step i-1 is partitioned into P_i submatrices using the same criteria as before.*

□

This distribution defines the local segment of each processor as a rectangular matrix which preserves neighborhood properties and achieves a good load balance.

The fact that we perform all horizontal partitioning steps before the vertical ones reduces the number of possible neighbors that a submatrix may have, and hence the number of processors with which communication will be necessary.

Many applications involving sparse matrices may be characterized by the fact that interaction between elements is local. That is, access to elements is structured in the same way as for regular problems. For such codes, the MRD distribution is an appropriate choice for the sparse array. If row traversals of the matrix dominate in the code, a suitable distributed sparse representation is obtained by combining MRD with the CRS sparse format; if column traversals dominate, the CCS format is used instead.

2.4   The BRS and BCS Distributed Sparse Representations

Cyclic distributions are used to impose some kind of load balance in situations where the amount of work may be highly uneven across the domain, and is not known in advance. In this section, we assume both dimensions of A to be distributed cyclically with block length 1, as specified by the annotation in the Vienna Fortran declaration below:

REAL $A(N, M)$ **DIST** $(CYCLIC, CYCLIC)$ **TO** P

We consider two distributed sparse representations based on this distribution:

■   **Block Row Scatter (BRS)** which uses CRS as the sparse format, and

■   **Block Column Scatter (BCS)** which uses CCS.

The choice among these two representations will depend on the way in which the sparse matrix is accessed in the code. If column traversals predominate, a column storage is preferred. A typical case for this is the sparse LU decomposition.

The BRS and BCS representations are good choices for irregular algorithms with a gradual decrease or increase in the workload, and for those where the workload is not identical for each non-zero element of the sparse matrix. Many common algorithms

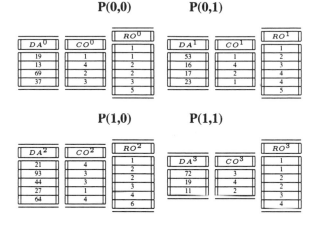

Figure 3 BRS representation for A_0 and processor array $P(0:1,0:1)$

are of this nature, including sparse matrix decomposition (LU, Cholesky, QR, WZ), image reconstruction, least square minimum, iterative methods for the solution of linear systems, and Lanczos' algorithm for determining eigensystems.

The mapping which is established by the choice of a CYCLIC distribution and a BRS or BCS representation requires complex auxiliary structures and translation schemes within the compiler. However, if such data are used together with cyclically distributed dense arrays, then the structures are properly aligned, leading to savings in communication.

Example 2 *Assume A_0 with a BRS distributed sparse representation. The data, column and row vectors for A_0 on each processor are shown in Figure 3.*

3   VIENNA FORTRAN/HPF EXTENSIONS FOR THE SUPPORT OF SPARSE MATRIX COMPUTATIONS

3.1   Language Considerations

In this section, we propose new language features specifically suited to the requirements of sparse matrix computations. An analysis of the support provided by existing data-parallel languages has to consider these two issues separately:

- **Sparse Formats**
  Since Fortran 77 offers no features for structured types or type abstractions, the arrays needed for the different variants of sparse formats must be explicitly declared and manipulated by the user when using this language.

In contrast, Fortran 90 provides *derived types*, a data structuring facility. This feature is, however, too weak for our purposes, since derived types cannot be properly parameterized.

■ **Distributions**
Regular distributions, in particular the cyclic distributions used in the BRS and BCS representations, are offered by most data-parallel languages. While HPF is restricted to regular distributions, Vienna Fortran provides two more general mechanisms: **INDIRECT** distributions permit the specification of a distribution via a *mapping array*, which defines a point-to-point relationship between array and processor indices. Furthermore, *user-defined distribution functions (UDDFs)* provide a structured mechanism for extending the intrinsic set of distributions, using a variant of the Fortran subroutine syntax.

Both methods are powerful and can, in principle, be used to handle sparse matrix codes, but not necessarily in the manner we aim for: in particular, indirect distributions incur significant memory overhead, and, in addition, do not reflect the structure of the problem. Runtime handling is expensive. On the other hand, UDDFs do not allow explicit control of a distribution's representation.

In the following we discuss new language features for data parallel languages. They provide sufficient information to the compiler to enable it to generate efficient parallel code as discussed later on.

It is generally not possible to construct the distributed sparse representation at compile time, since this requires both the specific sparse matrix structure and the number of processors. Hence the original matrix (or, rather, the representation of its structure) must be read from a file and distributed at runtime. The processor-local data structures can then be constructed.

If the data is not available at the time the declaration is processed, then an explicit **DISTRIBUTE** statement must be used to mark the position in the program where they become available; this is where the distributed sparse representation will be constructed.

The data is accessed in the source code according to the underlying sparse format. We thus require the associated auxiliary structures to be declared and used according to one of the representations known to the compiler. The compiler utilizes this information to construct the local data sets as described in the previous section.

In all, the following information is communicated to the compiler:

■ The *name*, *index domain*, and *element type* of the sparse matrix are declared.

■ An annotation is specified which declares the array as being **SPARSE** and provides information on the representation of the array.

■ The keyword **DYNAMIC** is used in a manner analogous to its meaning in Vienna Fortran: if it is specified, then the distributed sparse representation will be determined dynamically, as a result of executing a **DISTRIBUTE** statement. Otherwise, all components of the distributed sparse representation (possibly excepting the actual non-zero values of the matrix) can be constructed at the time the declaration is processed. Often, this information will be contained in a file whose name will be indicated in this annotation.

As an example, consider the following code fragment which illustrates some details of the syntax, based upon Vienna Fortran notation:

```
REAL C(NA,NC)  DIST (CYCLIC,CYCLIC)
INTEGER I, J, K

C A and B use CRS format:
    REAL A(NA, NB), SPARSE(CRS(AD,AC,AR)), DYNAMIC
    REAL B(NB, NC), SPARSE(CCS(BD,BC,BR)), DYNAMIC

    . . .
C — Read A and B —
    . . .
    DISTRIBUTE A,B :: (CYCLIC, CYCLIC)

    . . .

C Now A and B can be accessed via AD,...BR as in the sequential code.
```

4 DATA STRUCTURES AND TRANSLATION STRATEGIES

4.1 Runtime Handling

Our run time implementation for sparse data structures is based on the familiar *inspector-executor* paradigm [20] which can be used to deal with indirect array references inside loops.

As usual, the inspector phase comprises all the work needed to determine which data references are made by a processor, calculate which non-local data need to be fetched and where these data will be stored once they are received. Before the loop in which the sparse references appear is executed, it is traversed and the expressions inside each sparse reference are analyzed to determine whether the datum accessed is local or not. At the end of this inspection phase, the set of sparse accesses has been determined on each processor, and grouped into two different lists: One for the local accesses and other for the non-local ones.

The executor phase then accomplishes the work necessary to perform the communications required for the non-local accesses. When all the computations inside the original loop can be performed locally, this loop is executed.

4.2   MRD Compilation

An efficient implementation of MRD-based distributed sparse representations is relatively simple, due to the simple geometry – a rectangular region – associated with each distribution segment.

We propose the following data structures for the representation of MRD distributions:

■   a vector $H(1 : X - 1)$ specifies the *horizontal* boundaries, and

■   an array $V(0 : X - 1, 1 : Y - 1)$ specifies the *vertical* boundaries in each row.

H and V together provide a complete specification of an MRD distribution. These data structures – whose size depends only on the number of processors and not on the problem size – are stored on each processor, together with the three local auxiliary vectors DA, CO and RO. Since now each processor has locally complete knowledge of the data distribution, no communication is required for local data accesses, and exactly one communication must be performed for non-local accesses.

4.3   BRS Compilation

The implementation of the BRS distributed sparse representation is far more complex than that of MRD. We have worked out a scheme that, based on additional auxiliary structures, improves performance considerably relative to a pure PARTI-based implementation. These improvements are obtained by exploiting the knowledge about the representation in such a way that some communications otherwise required for data accesse can be suppressed. Details are described in [18].

5   CONCLUSION

In this paper, sparse data distributions and a specific language extension have been proposed which may be added to a data-parallel language such as Vienna Fortran or HPF to improve their handling of sparse irregular computation. These features enable the translation of codes which use typical sparse coding techniques, without any necessity for rewriting. Such codes may be translated so that the resulting code retains significant features of sequential sparse applications. In particular, the savings in memory and computation which are typical for these techniques are retained and can lead to high efficiency at run time. The data distributions have been designed to retain data locality when appropriate, support a good load balance, and avoid memory wastage.

The compile time and run time support translates these into structures which permit a sparse representation of data on the processors of a parallel system.

The language extensions required are minimal, yet sufficient to provide the compiler with the additional information needed for translation and optimization.

Although there are a variety of languages and compilers targeted at distributed memory multiprocessors ([21, 6, 11, 12, 20, 13]), only relatively few [11, 21, 20] provide facilities to deal with irregular codes at all. The method proposed by Saltz et al. uses runtime libraries [15, 16] to handle such features. Our approach differs from these other proposals in that it extends the language and develops specialized compilation and runtime routines tailored to sparse matrices. Experimental results have been given in [18].

An alternative strategy is used by Bik and Wijshoff [4], who implemented a restructuring compiler that automatically converts programs operating on dense matrices into sparse code.

REFERENCES

[1] R. Asenjo, L.F. Romero, M. Ujaldon and E.L. Zapata, *"Sparse Block and Cyclic Data Distributions for Matrix Computation"*. High Performance Computing, Technology and Applications. Eds. L. Grandinetti, G.R. Joubert, J.J. Dongarra and J. Kowalik. Elsevier Science, Amsterdam, 1995.

[2] R. Barrett, M. Berry, T. Chan, J. Demmel, J. Donato, J. Dongarra, V. Eijkhout, R. Pozo, C. Romine and Henk van der Vorst, *Templates for the solution of linear systems: Building blocks for iterative methods*, SIAM 1994.

[3] M. J. Berger and S.H. Bokhari, *A Partitioning Strategy for Nonuniform Problems on Multiprocessors*, IEEE Trans. Comput., vol. 36, no. 5, pp. 570-580, 1987.

[4] A.J.C. Bik and H.A.G. Wijshoff, *Compilation Techniques for Sparse Matrix Computations*, ACM Int'l Conf. on Supercomputing (Tokyo), pp. 416-424, July 1993.

[5] S.H. Bokhari, T.W. Crockett and D.M. Nicol *Parametric Binary Dissection* ICASE Report No. 93-39, NASA Langley Research Center, 1993.

[6] B. Chapman, S. Benkner, R. Blasko, P. Brezany, M. Egg, T. Fahringer, H.M. Gerndt, J. Hulman, B. Knaus, P. Kutschera, H. Moritsch, A. Schwald, V. Sipkova, H. Zima: *Vienna Fortran Compilation System*, User's Guide, 1993.

[7] B. Chapman, P. Mehrotra, and H. Zima. Programming in Vienna Fortran. *Scientific Programming* 1(1):31-50, Fall 1992.

[8] R. Das, J. Saltz, K. Kennedy, P. Havlak *Index Array Flattening Through Program Transformations*. Submitted to: PLDI'95.

[9] I.S. Duff, A.M. Erisman and J.K. Reid, *Direct Methods for Sparse Matrices*, Clarendon Press, Oxford, 1986.

[10] M. Eijkhout, *LAPACK working note 50: Distributed sparse data structures for linear algebra operations*, Tech. Report CS 92-169, Computer Science Department, University of Tennessee, Knoxville, TN, 1992.

[11] G. Fox, S. Hiranandani, K. Kennedy, C. Koelbel, U. Kremer, C. Tseng, and M. Wu, *Fortran D language specification*, Dept of Computer Science Rice COMP TR90079, Rice University, 1991.

[12] *High Performance Language Specification*. Version 1.0, Technical Report TR92-225, Rice University, May 3, 1993. Also available as Scientific Programming 2(1-2):1-170, Spring and Summer 1993.

[13] P. Mehrotra and J. Van Rosendale. *Programming distributed memory architectures using Kali*. In A. Nicolau, D. Gelernter, T. Gross and D. Padua, editors, Advances in Languages and Compilers for Parallel Processing, pp. 364-384. Pitman/MIT-Press, 1991.

[14] L.F. Romero and E.L. Zapata, *Data distributions for sparse matrix vector multiplication solvers*, J. Parallel Computing (to appear).

[15] J. Saltz, K. Crowley, R. Mirchandaney, and H. Berryman. Run-time scheduling and execution of loops on message passing machines. *Journal of Parallel and Distributed Computing*, 8(2):303–312, 1990.

[16] J. Saltz, R. Das, B. Moon, S. Sharma, Y. Hwang, R. Ponnusamy, M. Uysal *A Manual for the CHAOS Runtime Library*, Computer Science Department, University of Maryland, December 22, 1993.

[17] M. Ujaldon, E. L. Zapata, B. Chapman and H. Zima. New Data-Parallel Language Features for Sparse Matrix Computations. Proceedings of 9th International Parallel Processing Symposium. Santa Barbara, California. April, 1995 (to appear).

[18] M. Ujaldon, E. L. Zapata, B. Chapman and H. Zima. *Vienna Fortran/HPF Extensions for Sparse and Irregular Problems and its Compilation*. Technical Report TR 95-4, Institute for Software Technology and Parallel Systems, University of Vienna, Austria.

[19] M. Ujaldon and E.L. Zapata, *Efficient Resolution of Sparse Indirections in Data-Parallel Compilers*. Proc. 9th ACM International Conference on Supercomputing. Barcelona (Spain), July 1995.

[20] J. Wu, R. Das, J. Saltz, H. Berryman, S. Hiranandani *Distributed Memory Compiler Design for Sparse Problems*. To appear in: "IEEE Transactions on Computers".

[21] H. Zima, P. Brezany, B. Chapman, P. Mehrotra, A. Schwald : *Vienna Fortran - A language Specification Version 1.1*, University of Vienna, ACPC-TR 92-4, March 1992.

[22] H. Zima and B. Chapman, *Compiling for Distributed Memory Systems*, Proceedings of the IEEE, Special Section on Languages and Compilers for Parallel Machines, pp. 264-287, February 1993. Also: Technical Report ACPC/TR 92-16, Austrian Center for Parallel Computation, November 1992.

20

THE QUALITY OF PARTITIONS PRODUCED BY AN ITERATIVE LOAD BALANCER

Carlo L. Bottasso, Joseph E. Flaherty*, Can Özturan*,
Mark S. Shephard, Boleslaw K. Szymanski*,
James D. Teresco*, Louis H. Ziantz*

Scientific Computation Research Center (SCOREC)
* and Department of Computer Science,
Rensselaer Polytechnic Institute,
Troy, NY 12180 USA

ABSTRACT

We examine the quality of partitions produced by an iterative load balancer in parallel adaptive finite element calculations. We present several metrics which we use to evaluate the quality of a mesh partitioning, and report statistics generated from our analysis of adaptively refined meshes produced during the solution of computational fluid dynamics problems. Timings from the finite element solution phase for runs involving these meshes on 16 and 32 processors of an IBM SP2 are also presented.

1 INTRODUCTION

Adaptive finite element methods (FEMs) have gained importance based on their ability to offer reliable solutions to partial differential equations. In such an analysis, the computational domain is first discretized to create a mesh. During the solution process, portions of this mesh are recursively refined or coarsened (h-refinement) and/or the finite element approximation is varied in order (p-refinement) to improve the convergence rate and concentrate the computational effort in parts of the domain where the solution resolution is inadequate [3].

In order to solve large problems within a reasonable period of time, these methods have been implemented on parallel computers. The current methodology for optimizing parallel FEM programs relies on the initial partitioning of the meshes involved in the computation. However, in parallel adaptive codes, a good initial partitioning is not sufficient to assure high performance throughout the computation. Load imbalance caused by adaptive enrichment necessitates a dynamic redistribution of data. Since

265

performing a global repartitioning of the entire mesh can be costly relative to the time spent in actual computation, a number of iterative dynamic load balancing techniques that incrementally migrate elements from heavily to lightly loaded processors have been proposed [2, 3, 5, 15]. While these methods have proven to be inexpensive and effective ways to achieve a balanced load, they can lead to degradation in the partition quality of the resulting subdomains. On a distributed-memory parallel computer, this generally results in a larger communication penalty during the finite element solution phase. The two pieces of information readily available to aid in the element-migration process are coordinates and local topological entity connectivity. Vidwans, *et al.* [15] experiment with using both types of information. Others [3, 5] use prioritized connectivity information, whereas our system [2] utilizes local connectivity information among various entities.

The primary goal of most mesh-partitioning algorithms is the minimization of the number of "cuts" that the subdomains create when the partitioning is viewed as a communication graph [7, 8, 14]. With many finite volume and finite element schemes this would closely correspond to the task of minimizing the number of element faces on interprocessor boundaries. Thus, the number of faces on the boundary or "surface" of each partition is related to the amount of non-local data that must be communicated to perform the computation. But, both iterative load-balancing and partitioning methods require other important measures of partition quality. In particular, we focus on three complementary measures: (*i*) different estimates of the number of faces on the boundary (normalized by the total number of faces), (*ii*) the spatial connectivity within partitions, and (*iii*) the degree of interconnection between partitions.

Our parallel adaptive FEM system is described in Section 2. In Section 3, we briefly discuss the characteristics of a "good" partition. Sections 4–6 provide a more detailed description of the various measures of partition quality. We present statistics and timings for meshes generated during an analysis of a compressible, inviscid flow about an Onera M6 wing in Section 7. In Section 8, we discuss future modifications to the load-balancing scheme that may improve partition quality.

2   EXISTING SYSTEM

The system we are using is built upon the *SCOREC Mesh Database* [1], which provides a hierarchical representation of a finite element mesh. It also includes a set of operators to query and update the mesh data structure. The basic hierarchy consists of three-dimensional *regions*, and their bounding *faces*, *edges*, and *vertices*. In our case, each region is a tetrahedral finite element.

A *Parallel Mesh Database* [2, 10] (PMDB) which provides operators to create and manipulate distributed meshes is built on top of the SCOREC Mesh Database. The package includes routines for partitioning using the Orthogonal Recursive Bisection (ORB) and the Inertial Recursive Bisection (IRB) algorithms [9] and for load balancing through iterative element migration. Once an adaptive FEM calculation begins, it consists of alternating phases of computation, mesh-refinement, and load balancing.

PMDB data structures and operators are used to perform an incremental load balancing. Balance is achieved through mesh migration, which occurs between processors that control neighboring spatial regions. Each processor requests load from its most heavily loaded neighboring processor. These requests are viewed as a tree, and a logarithmic time scan operation is used to compute load flows on this tree. The amount of data to be migrated is determined by these flows. Single layers of regions on interprocessor boundaries are moved from heavily loaded to lightly loaded processors based on the load to be migrated. This process is repeated until the load becomes balanced to within a tolerance, or until the maximum number of iterations has been performed [2, 10]. The iterative migration can also be run periodically with only a few iterations to help maintain balance between substages of an operation like refinement (cf. [2]) without a large run-time penalty.

The results that we present were generated using a parallel adaptive FEM program called *Fluid Analysis in Space-Time* (FAST) [2] which uses a Time Discontinuous Galerkin/Least-Squares method [12] and the Generalized Minimum Residual (GM-Res) [11] algorithm for linear systems to analyze compressible, inviscid fluid flows. It utilizes PMDB to perform parallel mesh operations. The code can do any number of solution steps on a mesh and can apply refinement and load balancing based on user-supplied parameters.

3 PARTITION QUALITY

We are interested in quantifying the notion of a "high quality" partition. The basic requirement of a good partition is that the computational load be balanced. If some processors have more work than others, then the lightly loaded processors will sit idle while the heavily loaded processors finish their computation. Another important measure is the interprocessor communication volume. We use metrics based on ratios of faces on interprocessor boundaries to total faces to indicate of the amount of interprocessor communication relative to on-processor data access. We also examine the number of geometrically disjoint components within each processor. Our final measure of partition quality is the number of processors that need to communicate with each other. This is a lower bound on number of message startups that will be required during the finite element computation, which can be significant when message startups are expensive relative to sustained communication. Each is detailed in the following three sections. Note that we consider only fixed-order elements and assume a homogeneous processing environment in our descriptions.

Our goal is to evaluate the influence of these measures on the performance of our parallel adaptive calculations and to use them to estimate the quality of partitions generated by our current load-balancing scheme, as well as to help design and appraise new selection and load-balancing techniques.

4 METRICS

On most distributed-memory parallel computers, interprocessor communication is expensive relative to computation and on-processor data access. We estimate the cost of interprocessor communication by computing two *surface index* metrics of partitions. We use the number of boundary faces as an indication of the partition "surface area," since a face on the boundary will also have its edges and vertices on the interprocessor boundary. A face is called a *boundary face* if it is shared by two regions that are assigned to different processors. Intuitively, the surface index metrics can be thought of as surface-to-volume ratios, although the concepts of surface and volume do not fit conventional notions.

Given a set of n partitions $\mathcal{P} = \{P_1, P_2, \ldots, P_n\}$, let b_i denote the number of faces on the boundary of P_i, f_i the number of faces in the partition P_i, b_t the total number of faces on all partition boundaries, and f_t, the total number of faces in all partitions, then the *maximum local ratio* r_M and the *global ratio* r_G are defined as

$$r_M = \max_{i=1,\ldots,n} \left(\frac{b_i}{f_i} \right) \text{ and } r_G = \frac{b_t}{f_t} \ .$$

The surface index metrics are inexpensive to compute. The PMDB maintains structures representing interpartition boundaries, so computing r_M involves traversing the boundary structure on each processor in parallel, followed by a global reduction operation and a local division. The total number of faces on a boundary can be computed by first moving through the boundary structure of a processor and counting a face only if the current processor's number is less than that of the processor which shares the face. This is done in parallel on all processors, and a global summation is then carried out to produce b_t. Alternately, all of the boundary faces can be counted on each processor in parallel, and the result of a subsequent global summation is divided by two. In either instance, the computation assures that a particular face on the boundary between two partitions will be counted only once. After b_t has been determined,

$$f_t = \left(\sum_{i=1}^{n} f_i \right) - b_t \ .$$

An estimate of the worst case communication relative to the amount of on-processor data is provided by r_M. On some systems, the number of the processor that produced r_M may identify the processor that will be the last to complete its communication. The global metric r_G represents the total volume of communication normalized by computation and is the number of cuts [7, 8, 14] divided by the total number of faces in the mesh.

5 CONNECTIVITY OF PARTITIONS

A second quality metric involves statistics that quantify the geometric connectivity of the mesh assigned to each processor. Having multiple disjoint connected components within a processor's mesh, called *subdomain splitting* [9], is undesirable. The inter-processor boundary may be larger than necessary if a processor's mesh is not a single geometrically connected entity, and domain-decomposition methods for solving linear systems may converge slowly in this case [4]. If a relatively small disjoint part of one subdomain can be merged into a neighboring partition, the surface area on the interprocessor boundary will decrease to improve the surface index metrics.

In a three-dimensional mesh, the definition of a "connected partition" depends on the degree of the geometric entity that must be shared by two regions for them to be considered "connected." We consider *face connectivity*, *edge connectivity*, and *vertex connectivity*. As the names suggest, two regions are face-connected if they share a common face, edge-connected if they share a common edge, and vertex-connected if they share a common vertex. Face-connected partitions are the most desirable, since two regions that share a face will also share the edges of that face, and the vertices of those edges. A higher degree of face connectivity means less interprocessor communication during the computation phase, as a face on the boundary will also have its edges and vertices on the boundary as well.

The algorithm for computing connectivity starts with a region that has not been visited, and successively marks all adjacent elements as visited until all the regions that make up a connected component have been marked. This process continues until all regions in the partition have been visited. The cost of this computation increases significantly as the type of connectivity being considered moves from face to edge to vertex. There are at most four face-adjacent regions to consider at each step, but there can be many more when edge and vertex adjacency are considered.

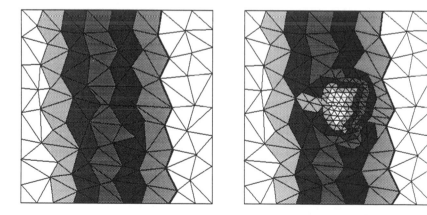

Figure 1 Slice migration of elements from right to left with all elements nearly the same size (left). Disconnected partition resulting when the same load-balancing selection is applied following refinement (right).

None of the partitioning algorithms in our system guarantee that each resulting partition consists of a single connected component. Others do ensure this [4], but they may not produce a balanced computational load. Also, a connected initial partition is no guarantee that meshes on the processors will not become disjoint after repeated applications of adaptivity and load balancing. In Figure 1, we illustrate how a connected initial partition may be split into more than one connected component in a two-dimensional mesh after refinement and load balancing are applied. Elements to the left of the heavy black line belong to Processor 0, while those to the right belong to Processor 1. The different shadings represent the "slices" that are migrated along the interprocessor boundary from Processor 0 to 1. On the left of Figure 1, we show that when the element sizes are close to uniform, this algorithm preserves the shape of the interprocessor boundary. However, on the right of Figure 1, we demonstrate that the domain becomes disconnected if refinement is applied to elements on Processor 0 that are near the boundary of Processor 1 before migration is done. The interprocessor boundary moves across areas with coarser elements more quickly than it does through the refined area. After several iterations of migration have been applied, a cluster of elements still assigned to Processor 0 has been completely surrounded by elements of Processor 1. Similar situations can occur in three dimensions.

6 INTERPROCESSOR CONNECTION DENSITY

A final measure of partition quality is the degree of interconnection between partitions. During the solution phase, a processor needs to exchange information with all of its vertex-adjacent neighbors. On a computer with a specific communication topology, this could impact performance significantly since direct neighbor communications can be significantly cheaper than more general communication. Having a large number of adjacent processors can also degrade performance on a computer like the IBM SP2 which has a high software latency for interprocessor communication compared to the speed of its processors.

We compute both the average and maximum number of processors that each processor must communicate with. These are expressed as a percentage of the largest possible number of adjacent processors (*i.e.*, $n - 1$, when using n processors).

7 EXAMPLES

The test problem that we are using involves transonic flow about an Onera M6 wing. On the left of Figure 2, we show the initial partitioning of the mesh onto 16 processors using IRB. This picture shows the mesh elements at the surface of the wing along with some of the regions that are part of the surrounding flow. The different shadings indicate elements that are assigned to different processors. This is only a small portion of the entire mesh, but it contains the interesting part at the wing's surface.

On the right of Figure 2, we show the part of the mesh that is assigned to processor number 12 of the initial partition. Notice that there is a large cluster of small elements with several larger elements outside of the main cluster. Some elements are disjoint from the main component of this partition. This looks like a poor partition, but quantitative measures are needed for an objective determination.

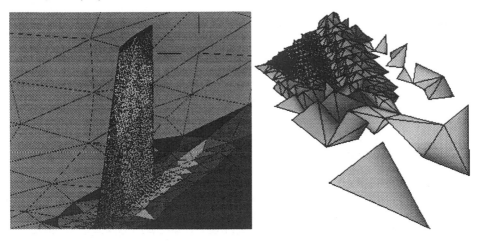

Figure 2 Initial partitioning of a portion of the mesh about an Onera M6 wing on 16 processors (left). The mesh associated with Processor 12 of this initial partition (right).

Refinements Performed on 16 Processors				
Test Case	Number of Tetrahedra	Maximum Load		
		Unbalanced	Migration	Partitioned
1. **onera0**	85567	—	—	5348
2. **onera1**	130454	12701	8156	8154
3. **onera2**	258045	30698	16303	16128
4. **onera3**	317756	26399	19865	19860

Refinements Performed on 32 Processors				
Test Case	Number of Tetrahedra	Maximum Load		
		Unbalanced	Migration	Partitioned
1. **onera0**	85567	—	—	2674
2. **onera1**	131006	7588	4095	4095
3. **onera2**	223501	12222	6992	6985
4. **onera3**	388837	19639	12162	12152

Table 1 Data for three h-refinements of an Onera M6 wing mesh performed on 16 (top) and 32 (bottom) processors.

Table 1 shows the mesh sizes for a series of three refinements of this initial Onera wing mesh. The initial mesh consisted of 85,567 tetrahedra which were distributed by IRB onto 16 or 32 processors. The 16- and 32-processor runs were done on IBM SP2s at Rensselaer and the NASA Ames Research Center, respectively. The other meshes were generated by performing an adaptive *h*-refinement of the prior mesh. The "Maximum Load" columns contain the maximum number of elements on any processor. The first column shows the maximum processor load before load-balancing was applied and the second shows the maximum processor load after our migration-based iterative load balancing algorithm was applied (for at most ten iterations) [2, 10]. The third column shows the maximum number of elements on any processor after a parallel global IRB was performed [6, 13].

7.1 Surface Index Statistics

In Figure 3, we show r_G as a function of mesh size for the four Onera meshes from 16- and 32-processor runs. The scale for mesh size is normalized by the number of elements of the initial mesh (**onera0**). The surface index metrics are expressed as percentages by multiplication by 100. In both cases, the global IRB repartitioning does better than the migration-based load balancing for all mesh sizes. With 32 processors, the percentages of faces on the interprocessor boundaries increases as expected for problems having the same mesh sizes.

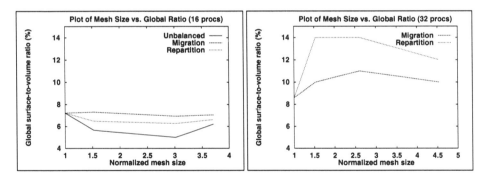

Figure 3 Global surface index r_G vs. mesh size for the meshes of Table 1 on 16 (left) and 32 (right) processors.

In Figure 4, we show data similar to Figure 3 for the maximum local ratio r_M on 16 and 32 processors. The vertical line in the left graph will be discussed in Section 7.4. In general, both the partitions produced by repartitioning and migration show an increase in this ratio relative to the unbalanced mesh. While the partitions generated by migration are slightly superior to those produced by repartitioning for the smaller meshes, this trend disappears as the mesh size increases.

In particular, there are two instances in which the ratio computed on the subdomains balanced by migration is significantly higher than for the repartitioned ones (*i.e.*, from **onera1** to **onera2** for 16 processors and from **onera2** to **onera3** for 32 processors). In both cases, the meshes nearly double from one refinement to the next and the resulting meshes showed a large increase in the maximum load on a processor relative to the previous mesh. Global repartitioning has a better chance of reducing the worst surface index after such a massive change in the mesh than local migration. Indeed, with 16

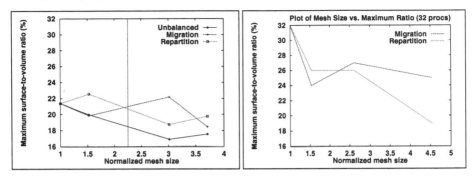

Figure 4 Maximum local surface index r_M vs. mesh size for the meshes of Table 1 on 16 (left) and 32 (right) processors.

processors, it is clear that migration would need more than the ten iterations it was allowed in order to fully balance the load (cf. Table 1). Thus, for large mesh changes, full repartitioning should be a better choice than iterative migration.

7.2   Intraprocessor Connectivity

In Figure 5, we examine the intrapartition connectivity of the meshes in Table 1 that have been balanced using iterative migration. The figure shows plots of the average and maximum number of disjoint connected components *vs.* mesh size.

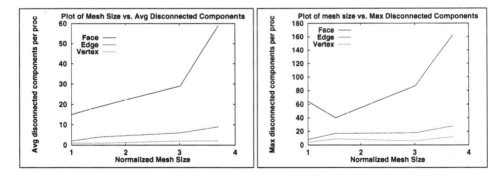

Figure 5 Average (left) and maximum (right) number of connected components per processor vs. mesh size for the meshes of Table 1 on 16 processors.

Notice that even the starting mesh (**onera0**), partitioned with IRB, has an average of 15 face-connected components (cf. Section 5) in each processor. In fact, the submesh assigned to a single processor shown on the right of Figure 2 from the IRB partitioning of the **onera0** mesh has 64 disjoint face-connected components. Further, as refinement and the migration-based load balancing are applied to obtain the later meshes, both the average and maximum number of disjoint connected components consistently increase.

This indicates that the situation illustrated in on the right of Figure 1 is occurring. Our current selection scheme for migration does not take the sizes of the elements into consideration, so the interprocessor boundaries move quickly across coarse areas as compared to highly-refined ones.

7.3 Interprocessor Adjacency

Finally, we consider the interprocessor adjacency values for the Onera meshes. In Figure 6, we show the interprocessor adjacency for the 16-processor Onera meshes. Again, the vertical line in the right plot will be discussed in Section 7.4. Maximum adjacency values are close to or at 100 percent. Even the average adjacency remains in the 75 to 85 percent range, demonstrating a very dense interconnection among the processors. A 16-processor run is too small to see any consistent difference between results for meshes after load balancing through migration and after global repartitioning.

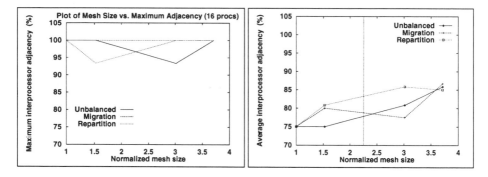

Figure 6 Maximum (left) and average (right) interprocessor adjacency vs. mesh size for the meshes of Table 1 on 16 processors.

With 32 processors, we have more meaningful results as presented in Figure 7. Both maximum and average adjacencies for partitions generated by the migratory load balancing are higher than those produced by repartitioning. This indicates that it may be worthwhile to concentrate more on avoiding increases in interprocessor connectivity when applying load balancing techniques. However, even 32 processors may still be too few to draw definite conclusions. Moving to 64 or 128 processors in future tests will help resolve this issue.

7.4 Timings

The most meaningful statistic is solution speed. Table 2 contains the average times, in seconds, to complete a single solution step of the FAST solver on 16 and 32 processors using some of the meshes we have been discussing. Only data for the last test mesh was available for the 32-processor case (and only for the load-balanced computations). The "Gain" column in the upper portion of the table indicates the percent improvement

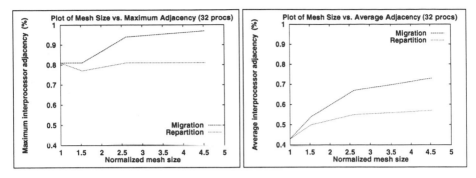

Figure 7 Maximum (left) and average (right) interprocessor adjacency vs. mesh size for the meshes of Table 1 on 32 processors.

in time for partitions produced by each algorithm relative to an unbalanced mesh. The "Difference" column for the 32-processor solution gives the percent decrease in time for the repartitioned mesh *versus* the mesh produced by migration.

Refinements Performed on 16 Processors						
Test Case	Number of Tetrahedra	Time Per Step (s)			Gain (%)	
		Unbal.	Mig.	Repart.	Mig.	Repart.
2. **onera1**	130454	434.1	229.6	218.4	47.1	49.7
3. **onera2**	258045	1821.0	692.9	722.4	61.9	60.3
4. **onera3**	317756	1356.6	919.1	1076.8	32.2	20.6

Refinements Performed on 32 Processors				
Test Case	Number of Tetrahedra	Time Per Step (s)		Difference (%)
		Mig.	Repart.	
4. **onera3**	388837	294.2	243.4	17.26

Table 2 Sizes, timings, and relative improvements in run times for example meshes from Table 1 for 16 (top) and 32 (bottom) processors.

Initial results from production runs with 32 processors of an SP2 at the NASA Amcs Research Center suggested that a global repartitioning produced a significant reduction in solution time relative to the migration-based load balancing (see the 32-processor portion of Table 2). These runs indicated that interprocessor adjacency is a major factor, since repartitioning clearly beat migration in this area.

However, when similar runs were performed on 16 processors of the SP2 at Rensselaer, we found that migration produced faster solution times than the global repartitioning for the **onera3** mesh. For refinements that had similar numbers of finite elements per processor to the 32-processor **onera3** mesh, the times were comparable for both redistribution methods. Migration-generated partitions yielded slightly better results for the **onera2** mesh whereas the partitions produced by repartitioning were slightly better than those created by migration in the case of the **onera1** mesh. Recall that the plots of interprocessor adjacency for the 16-processor meshes (see Figure 6) failed to show a clear pattern and any differences were reasonably small. In addition, none of the other statistics showed any meaningful trends when compared to the timing results. There are clearly other factors influencing the 16 processor runs, which we are investigating. In particular, cache size and the amount of physical memory may have played a role in the results for the larger Onera meshes on Rensselaer's SP2 because its processors have less memory bandwidth than those of the SP2 at the NASA Ames Research Center.

The 32-processor mesh consisted of approximately 12,000 regions per processor, whereas the 16-processor meshes had about 8,000, 16,000 and 20,000 elements per processor. If we compare the values intersecting the vertical line on the left of Figure 4 to the rightmost values on the right graph of Figure 4 and the values intersecting the vertical line in the right portion of Figure 6 to the rightmost values in the right graph of Figure 7, we see that 16- and 32-processor partitions with a similar number of elements on each processor would still have different characteristics. Based on this observation, even if the refinement were adjusted to get a mesh with about 12,000 regions per processor, it is likely that there would still be a difference between the 16- and 32-processor run times on the same machine.

8   SUMMARY AND FUTURE GOALS

In summary, we have taken measures of partition quality and computed values for them on the meshes used to solve a problem involving a transonic flow about an Onera M6 wing. Our statistics have yet to establish any firm relationship to performance. Interprocessor adjacency, at least in the 32-processor case, appears to be a significant factor, but more test cases on a wider range of processor sets on a single machine are needed to quantify its importance and draw firm conclusions.

Using smaller test meshes and academic problems, we might have found some correlations between the mesh statistics and running times. However, smaller meshes, with artificially induced refinement and load imbalance, may not exhibit important characteristics, such as those which lead to the situation described in Figure 1, and therefore might not point out potential problems with a load-balancing scheme. By concentrating on meshes that arise in computational fluid dynamics problems, we can isolate the properties of a mesh partitioning strategy that lead to a performance improvement of our adaptive software in practical situations.

We would like to measure the effect that the initial partitioning has on subsequent repartitionings necessitated by h-refinement. At present, we have ORB, IRB, and Spectral Recursive Bisection (SRB) available to us. Only ORB and IRB are implemented directly as part of our system. *Chaco* [7], the SRB package made available to us by Sandia National Laboratories, runs serially and does not operate directly on meshes in our framework.

Since initial partitions are often used only briefly before adaptivity and rebalancing will be necessary, a good starting partitioning is not as important for parallel adaptive techniques as for other methods. This is especially true when using a repartitioning algorithm because it generates an entirely new partitioning. However, iterative migratory load balancing simply modifies existing partitions to rebalance load, and so undesirable features of a poor initial partitioning may propagate to subsequent partitionings. Thus, it might be worthwhile to investigate partitioning methods that guarantee geometrically connected initial partitions [4], as well as developing others that focus on minimizing the number of interprocessor connections, though the importance of these characteristics is still under study.

A major area of current and future work is to use these measures of partition quality to develop, implement, and analyze the performance of alternate schemes to choose elements for migration during load balancing. We are now experimenting with geometric methods which take advantage of the geometric location of elements that are candidates for migration and their positions in space relative to the centroids of the processors which are sending and receiving load. Vidwans *et al.* [15] have presented divide-and-conquer load balancing methods that take advantage of the geometric information in a similar framework. We have yet to work with inertial heuristics, but such algorithms should give results similar to geometric methods while being potentially less expensive. Methods that select elements to maintain "compactness" of partitions, and those that move elements to improve interprocessor adjacency are also being considered. However, when any type of information is used to improve the partitions, we must also be sure that the cost of doing so does not exceed the savings we wish to realize during the computation phase.

Acknowledgements

We would like to thank Mark Beall for access to the SCOREC Mesh Database, Hugues de Cougny for the use of the parallel mesh refinement and parallel inertial repartitioning packages that he developed, and the NASA Ames Research Center for access to their SP2. The first and fourth authors were supported by ARO grant DAAH04-93-G0003, and the second, fourth, and sixth authors were funded under ARO grant DAAH04-95-1-0091. Support was provided to the second, third, fourth, fifth, and seventh authors via NSF Grant ASC-93-18184. In addition, the second, fifth, and seventh authors were supported under NSF Grant CCR-92-16053, and the fifth and seventh authors were funded by ONR Grant N00014-93-1-0076.

REFERENCES

[1] M. W. Beall. SCOREC mesh database version 2.3 user's guide. Scientific Computation Research Center, Rensselaer Polytechnic Institute, Troy, 1994.

[2] C. L. Bottasso, H. L. de Cougny, M. Dindar, J. E. Flaherty, C. Özturan, Z. Rusak, and M. S. Shephard. Compressible aerodynamics using a parallel adaptive time-discontinuous galerkin least-squares finite element method. In *Proceedings of the Twelveth AIAA Applied Aerodynamics Conference*, pp. 1–11, Colorado Springs, 1994.

[3] K. Clark, J. E. Flaherty, and M. S. Shephard, Eds. *Applied Numerical Mathematics*, 14, special ed. on Adaptive Methods for Partial Differential Equations, 1994.

[4] L. Dagum. Automatic partitioning of unstructured grids into connected components. In *Proceedings of the Supercomputing Conference 1993*, pp. 94–101, Los Alamitos, 1993.

[5] H. L. de Cougny, K. D. Devine, J. E. Flaherty, R. M. Loy, C. Özturan, and M. S. Shephard. Load balancing for the parallel adaptive solution of partial differential equations. *Applied Numerical Mathematics*, 16:157–182, 1994.

[6] H. L. de Cougny, M. S. Shephard, and C. Özturan. Parallel three-dimensional mesh generation on distributed memory MIMD computers. Submitted to *Engineering with Computers*.

[7] B. Hendrickson and R. Leland. The Chaco user's guide, version 1.0. Technical Report SAND93-2339, Sandia National Laboratories, Albuquerque, 1993.

[8] B. Hendrickson and R. Leland. Multidimensional spectral load balancing. Technical Report SAND93-0074, Sandia National Laboratories, Albuquerque, 1993.

[9] S.-H. Hsieh, G. H. Paulino, and J. F. Abel. Evaluation of automatic domain partitioning algorithms for parallel finite element analysis. Structural Engineering Report 94-2, School of Civil and Environmental Engineering, Cornell University, Ithaca, 1994.

[10] C. Özturan. Distributed environment and load balancing for adaptive unstructured meshes. PhD dissertation, Computer Science Dept., Rensselaer Polytechnic Institute, Troy, 1995.

[11] Y. Saad and M. Schultz. A generalized minimum residual algorithm for solving nonsymmetric linear systems. *SIAM Journal on Scientific and Statistical Computing*, 7:856–869, 1986.

[12] F. Shakib, T. J. R. Hugues, and Z. Johan. New finite element formulation for computational fluid dynamics: X. The compressible Euler and Navier-Stokes equations. *Computer Methods in Applied Mechanics and Engineering*, 89:141-219, 1991.

[13] M. S. Shephard, J. E. Flaherty, H. L. de Cougny, C. Özturan, C. L. Bottasso, and M. W. Beall. Parallel automated adaptive procedures for unstructured meshes. To appear in *Parallel Computing in CFD*, AGARD, Neuilly-Sur-Seine, 1995.

[14] H. D. Simon. Partitioning of unstructured problems for parallel processing. *Computer Systems in Engineering*, 2:135-148, 1991.

[15] V. Vidwans, Y. Kallinderis, and V. Venkatakrishnan. Parallel dynamic load-balancing algorithm for three-dimensional adaptive unstructured grids. *AIAA Journal*, 32:497–505, 1994.

21

A NEW COMPILER TECHNOLOGY FOR HANDLING HPF DATA PARALLEL CONSTRUCTS

Françoise André, Peter Brezany*, Olivier Chéron,
Will Denissen**, Jean-Louis Pazat, Kamran Sanjari*

IRISA, Campus de Beaulieu, 35042 Rennes, France
({fandre,ocheron,pazat}@irisa.fr)
* Institute for Software Technology and Parallel Systems,
A-1092 Vienna, Austria ({brezany,sanjari}@par.univie.ac.at)
** TNO, POB 155, 2600 AD Delft, The Netherlands (den-wja@tpd.tno.nl)

1   INTRODUCTION

The HPF language provides the user with means to specify complex data parallel Fortran 90 (F90) applications to be executed on distributed memory parallel computers. HPF offers several data distribution modes including **BLOCK**, **BLOCK(M)**, **CYCLIC** and **CYCLIC(M)** combined with alignment features and provides a wide range of data parallel constructs: HPF **FORALL** and **DO INDEPENDENT** loops, F90 array assignments and **WHERE** statements, and F77 **DO** loop-nests that are proved to show no loop-carried data dependencies. Since the HPF language is gaining acceptance, handling all these features efficiently by HPF compilers is a challenging problem of growing importance.

An advanced HPF compilation environment is currently being developed within the PREPARE project [6]. This compilation system relies on the CoSy technology [1] developed in the associated COMPARE project. The CoSy model is an innovative compilation framework that makes it possible to configure highly optimizing compilers from a large set of building blocks called *engines*. These engines work concurrently (when they run on a set of processors the compilation process is speeded up); they share a generic Internal Representation (IR) in which all HPF data-parallel constructs are mapped to one canonical form (the ARRAYASSIGN). A dedicated engine performs automatic DO loop vectorization which maps parallel loops to ARRAYASSIGN's. The PREPARE HPF compiler includes about thirty engines and is able to generate: (1) binary code for several target distributed-memory systems (Parsytec GC, cluster of Sun Sparc stations and other systems built upon Sparc or PowerPC processors), (2) message passing C code with MPI communications.

The binary code generation focuses on gaining high performance (integration of intra- and interprocessor parallelism) and the C code generation guarantees a high portability of the parallel code.

This paper concentrates on the description of the Parallelization Engine (PE) that is responsible for the restructuring of HPF programs and for the SPMD code generation. The methods used by the PE for processing HPF codes are presented: the implementation of HPF distributed arrays and the compilation techniques are discussed. According to the access functions used in distributed array references (regular or irregular case), the compiler applies two different techniques detailed in the subsequent sections. The work described in this paper was carried out as part of the European ESPRIT project EP 6516 PREPARE.

2   ALLOCATING AND REFERENCING HPF DISTRIBUTED ARRAYS

We have developed a general method [5] which unifies the handling of all HPF distribution mappings. Both collapse and replication mappings are implemented. As mappings may not be known at compile time, runtime descriptors are used. Nevertheless, thanks to constant propagation, distribution information is made available to the PE where possible allowing compile-time optimizations. The main aspects of the implementation of distributed arrays include:

- The allocation of local arrays: the elements of a distributed array which are owned by a processor are allocated and some extra space is reserved in order to keep the global to local index conversion simple (e.g. *overlap*),

- The global to local index conversion: the conversion functions are inlined on a per dimension basis. The general global to local index conversions can handle inherited distributions. For prescriptive and descriptive mappings, specific efficient conversion functions are implemented,

- The global to processor index conversion: for prescriptive and descriptive mappings this index conversion is also inlined per dimension. For inherited mappings the ownership computation must be performed for all dimensions together.

3   HANDLING REGULAR CONSTRUCTS

An ARRAYASSIGN is said to be *regular* if inside it all distributed arrays are referenced through linear access functions, else it is referred to as *irregular*. Regular ARRAYAS-SIGN's are transformed in different phases and end up as separate send, receive and computation loop nests:

- The original ARRAYASSIGN is decomposed into COMMUNICATION ARRAYAS-SIGN's and one LOCAL ARRAYASSIGN by analyzing the rhs distributed array references with respect to that of lhs. Aligned rhs and lhs array references are detected by symbolic evaluation and, in such cases, no COMMUNICATION AR-RAYASSIGN is generated.

- A COMMUNICATION ARRAYASSIGN is translated into a separate send and receive loop nest. Collapse and replication of dimensions are taken into account. All elements which must be communicated between two processors are collected into one message. For HPF codes implementing stencil operations, *overlap communications* are generated.

- In the LOCAL ARRAYASSIGN resulting from the decomposition, it is guaranteed that all rhs distributed elements are locally available to the processor which owns the lhs distributed elements. Our loop bound reduction technique based on diophantine equation resolution generates an efficient computation loop nest from the LOCAL ARRAYASSIGN.

4 HANDLING IRREGULAR CONSTRUCTS

For irregular ARRAYASSIGN the PREPARE compiler generates three phases*: the Work Distributor (WD), the Inspector and the Executor [2, 4]. The WD characterizes the iterations that are local and may apply various distribution strategies; the decision is based on the results of program analysis and some heuristics. The Inspector phase generates the communication pattern descriptors (*schedules*) that describe the non-local accesses performed by the process on a given distributed array. In the case of arrays with multi-dimensional distributions, organization of communication and addressing is based on viewing every rhs distributed array as a one-dimensional array whose distribution is determined by the dimensional distributions of the original array. Finally, the Executor phase gathers/scatters the non-local data and performs the local iterations. For indices with multi-level indirections, the *multi-phase inspectors and executors* are generated using the techniques proposed in [3].

As the runtime analysis is rather costly, the PREPARE compiler tries to optimize the two first analysis phases where possible. On the IR level, specific abstractions have been introduced for each phase in order to ease the optimization task. A dedicated engine checks the reusability of results of the WD and Inspector phases: the first version implements loop invariant code motion and the full-fledged version will employ general partial redundancy elimination techniques.

The generated code relies on a special runtime support provided by the PARTI+ library which deals with address and *schedule* computation as well as with communication by implementing efficient global exchange algorithms. PARTI+ is an extension of the PARTI library [2] whose kernel was revised and new techniques for hash table manipulations were applied. Moreover, the PARTI+ routines can handle any HPF multi-dimensional distributions and provide support for operations on all F90 intrinsic

---

*The WD and the Inspector actually perform dynamic analysis of the construct attributes.

data types. Preliminary performance results [4] show that in some cases, due to improved hashing, PARTI+ dramatically speeds up the inspector phase when comparing with PARTI and CHAOS.

5 CONCLUSION

The PREPARE compiler handles any HPF data parallel constructs with almost no restriction; especially, the following cases are supported by the compiler: (1) BLOCK(M) and CYCLIC(M) data distributions combined with alignment, (2) linear as well as non-linear access functions to distributed arrays (aggregate communication are generated in both cases), (3) irregular access functions combined with multidimensional data distributions and distributed indirections.

Moreover, the PREPARE compiler combines the classical compiler optimizations (common subexpression elimination, constant folding) provided by COMPARE engines with automatic vectorization and the specific SPMD code generation techniques described above in order to produce efficient parallel code.

The results of our first product give us confidence in the efficiency of our implementation. We expect to have a complete compilation environment for the official HPF subset and full F90 by the end of 1995.

REFERENCES

[1] M. Alt, U. Aßmann, and H. van Someren, *"Cosy Compiler Phase embedding with the CoSy Compiler Model,"* 5th Int. Conf. CC'94, Edinburgh, LNCS, Vol. 786, April 1994, 278–293.

[2] H. Berryman, J. Saltz and J. Scroggs, *"Execution time support for adaptive scientific algorithms on distributed memory machines,"* Concurrency: Practise and Experience, June 1991, 3(3):159–178.

[3] P. Brezany, B. Chapman, R. Ponnusamy, V. Sipkova, and H Zima, *"Study of Application Algorithms with Irregular Distributions,"* tech. report D1Z-3 of the CEI-PACT Project, University of Vienna, April 1994.

[4] P. Brezany, O. Chéron, K. Sanjari, and E. van Konijnenburg, *"Processing Irregular Codes Containing Arrays with Multi-Dimensional Distributions by the PREPARE HPF Compiler,"* HPCN Europe'95, Milan, Springer-Verlag, 526–531.

[5] C. van Reeuwijk, W. Denissen, H.J. Sips, and E.M. Paalvast, *"Implementing HPF distributed arrays on a message-passing parallel computer system,"* submitted for publication.

[6] A. Veen, and M. de Lange, *"Overview of the PREPARE Project,"* 4th Int. Workshop on Compilers for Parallel Computers, Delft, The Netherlands, Dec. 1993.

22

AN IMPROVED TYPE-INFERENCE ALGORITHM TO EXPOSE PARALLELISM IN OBJECT-ORIENTED PROGRAMS

Sandeep Kumar[†], Dharma P. Agrawal[†]
and S. Purushothaman Iyer[‡]

North Carolina State University, Raleigh, North Carolina 27695, USA.

1 INTRODUCTION

The popularity of object-oriented (OO) programming has been on the rise. Unlike the procedural programming approach, OO programming provides a natural facility for modeling and decomposing a problem into self-contained entities called *objects*. The objects interact with each other through a message passing mechanism. At different program-points, the objects assume different *implementation* (or *concrete*) types, which are sets of *classes* or built-in types.

A recent study [2] reveals that OO programs tend to have (i) a large number of method calls, (ii) basic blocks which are larger in methods than in non-methods, and (iii) many indirect jumps, primarily due to virtual-function calls. Note that the occurrence of dynamically bound calls in OO programs is a very common phenomenon [2]; this is in part due to either (a) late binding of objects to one concrete type, (b) use of function pointers, or (c) an assignment to such variables (as in C++). Furthermore, the primary cause for OO programs to be inefficient is due to the late binding of objects to one particular concrete type. Based on these facts we observe that there are ample opportunities for exploiting hidden parallelism in OO programs. A supercompiler can therefore, detect, expose and translate a sequential OO program for execution on parallel machines.

For imperative programs, a number of code optimization and parallelization techniques have been developed. Often, most of these optimizations use program's *call graph*. Unfortunately, a precise enough construction of call graph for an OO program is difficult due to the lack of information about the exact program-point-specific concrete

[†] Sandeep Kumar and Dharma P. Agrawal are with Department of Electrical & Computer Engineering and supported by ARO under contract DAAH04-94-G-0306.
[‡] S. Purushothaman Iyer is with Department of Computer Science and supported in part by NSF under contract CCR-9404619.

type information about the objects. Consequently, many known program analysis techniques are rendered useless or imprecise.

Recently, we have been attempting to restructure programs written in a simple OO language called BOPL (Basic Object-Programming Language), as described in [6]. Note that, in principle, programs in most of the existing OO languages such as, C++, Smalltalk, Self, BETA, Eiffel, etc. can be expressed in BOPL [6]. We discovered that the opportunities for exposing and exploiting hidden parallelism in an OO program increase with the availability of program-point specific type information about the objects.

Earlier, Pande et al [7] have used the *conditional analysis* approach for determining program-point specific type information for C++ programs . However, their algorithm is unable to provide type information for untyped OO languages such as, Self and Smalltalk . The basic constraint-based type-inference algorithm, as described in [6], is more generic and has been used by several researchers [1, 4, 5, 8]. For Concurrent Aggregates programs, Plevyak et al [8] iteratively execute the algorithm in [6], but split the *entry-sets* and *creation-sets* in a demand-driven fashion to improve the precision. However, the derived precision is dependent upon the number of iterations. Similarly, a few other variants of the basic constraint-based algorithm such as, 1-level [5] and p-level expansion [4] algorithms, fail to provide program-point-specific (and precise) type information.

This paper is based on the thesis that a precise enough program-point specific type analysis can assist in obtaining a more precise call-graph, and, consequently, improve the overall program analysis necessary for program parallelization. The following section gives an outline of our type-inference approach followed by an illustration with an example BOPL program. Later, we present our conclusions.

2   AN IMPROVED TYPE INFERENCE APPROACH

The basic constraint-based type-inference algorithm derives the "union" of types for program variables and objects from all program points. Thus, multiple assignments to a variable from expressions of different types account for imprecision in type inference for that variable. To remedy this type-imprecision and to compute program-point-specific type information for an OO program, we first cast the input program into its *Static Single Assignment* (SSA) form [3], before applying the basic constraint-based type inference algorithm of [6]. Thus, we avoid the unioning of types due to multiple and polymorphic assignments to a data member by exploiting the SSA property of the program. Furthermore, a program in its SSA form is known to be useful for other code optimizations as well [3].

Consider the BOPL program shown in upper part of Figure 1. In class, `main`, for all program-points, the basic-constraint based algorithm imprecisely computes `Base` and `Derived` as the types for the object, `pb`. In contrast, as shown in lower part of Figure 1, our approach precisely computes the types for different SSA-incarnations of

```
class Base
  var a: Int
  method foo() returns Int
    a:=5
  end
end
class Derived                    class Main
  var a: Int                       var pb: {Derived, Base}
  var b: Int                       var pd: Derived
  method foo$Base() re-            method main() returns Int
turns Int                            pb:=Base new;
    a:=5                             pd:=Derived new;
  end                                pb.foo();
  method foo() returns Int           pb:=pd;
    b:=5                             pb.foo()
  end                              end
end                              end
```

```
Main new.main()
```

```
class Base
  var a$0,a$1,a$2: Int
  method foo() returns Int
    a$1::=(a$0);
    a$2:=5;
    a$0::=(a$1, a$2)
  end
end
class Derived                    class Main
  var a$0,a$3: Int                 var pb$0,pb$3: Derived
  var a$2: {}                      var pb$1: {}
  var b$1,b$2,b$3: Int             var pb$2: Base
  method foo$Base() re-            var pb$0,pd$2: Derived
turns Int                          var pd$1: {}
    a$2::=(nil);                   method main() returns Int
    a$3:=5;                          pd$1::=(nil);
    a$0::=(a$2, a$3)                 pb$1::=(nil);
  end                               pb$2:=Base new;
  method foo() returns Int          pd$2:=Derived new;
    b$2::=(b$1);                     pb$2.foo();
    b$3:=5;                          pb$3:=pd$2;
    b$1::=(b$2, b$3)                 pb$3.foo();
  end                               pd$0::=(pd$1, pd$2);
end                                 pb$0::=(pb$1, pb$3)
                                   end
                                 end
```

```
SSA-form of Main new.main()
```

Figure 1   Derived types for the original BOPL program and its SSA-form.

pb. Clearly, with the availability of precise program-point-specific type information, as shown in Figure 1, a parallelizer can generate code such that the two method calls – pb\$2 . foo () and pb\$3 . foo () – execute in parallel.

3   CONCLUSIONS

Type-inference for OO programs is a major challenge due to the presence of inheritance, assignment, and late binding. We have shown that an OO program in its SSA form can be used to compute program-point-specific type information. We also show that with the availability of program-point-specific type information, the opportunities for exposing and exploiting hidden parallelism in an OO program increase. Our SSA-based approach is language independent and can be used with constraint-based type inferencing algorithms for other OO languages.

REFERENCES

[1] Agesen, O., Palsberg, J., and Schwartzbach, M. I., "Type Inference For SELF: Analysis of Objects With Dynamic and Multiple Inheritance," *Proc. of ECOOP'93*, Kaiserslautern, Germany, July 1993, pp. 247-267.

[2] Calder, B., Grunwald, D., and Zorn, B. "Quantifying Behavioral Differences Between C and C++ Programs," *Tech. Rep. CU-CS-698-94*, Dept. of Computer Sci., Univ. of Colorado, Boulder, Jan 1994, pp. 1-28.

[3] Cytron, R., et al., "Efficiently Computing Static Single Assignment Form and the Control Dependence Graph," *ACM TOPLAS*, Vol. 13, No. 4, Oct 1991, pp. 451-490.

[4] Gautron, P. and Shepard, T., "Static Typing Without Explicit Types," *Technical Report*, Dept. of Electrical and Computer Engg., Royal Military College of Canada, Ontario, Canada, 1994.

[5] Oxhøj, N., Palsberg, J., and Schwartzbach, M. I., "Making Type Inference Practical," *Proc. of ECOOP*, Springer-Verlag, LNCS 615, Utrecht, The Netherlands, July 1992.

[6] Palsberg, J. and Schwartzbach, M. I., *Object-Oriented Type Systems*, John-Wiley & Sons Ltd., 1994.

[7] Pande, H. and Ryder, B., "Static Type Determination for C++," *USENIX Sixth C++ Tech. Conf.*, Cambridge, MA, April 11-14, 1994, pp. 85-98.

[8] Plevyak, J. and Chien, A. A., "Precise Concrete Type Inference of Object-Oriented Programs," *Proc. of OOPSLA*, Portland, OR, Oct. 1994.

23

AUTOMATIC DISTRIBUTION OF SHARED DATA OBJECTS[†]

**Koen Langendoen, Raoul Bhoedjang
and Henri E. Bal**

*Dept. of Mathematics and Computer Science,
Vrije Universiteit, Amsterdam, The Netherlands*

1 INTRODUCTION

Object-based distributed shared memory is a form of shared virtual memory in which shared data are encapsulated in objects. One of the main research issues related to shared objects is how to implement them efficiently on a distributed-memory system. Our Orca system [1, 3] uses two distribution strategies. In the simplest case, an object is stored on one processor (single-copy mode), and other processors access it through remote invocations. To reduce communication overhead, each object is migrated to the processor that accesses it most frequently. The other strategy we use is to *replicate* shared objects that have a high read/write ratio. With a replicated object, read-only operations can be executed locally. Operations that change the object update all copies in a consistent way, using totally-ordered group communication [2]. For reasons of transparency and portability we want to decide *automatically* which of these strategies to use for a given object.

2 AUTOMATIC OBJECT DISTRIBUTION

We first consider the approach currently used by Orca, which is based on compile-time information [1]. The compiler analyses the access behavior per process type using simple heuristics; for example, operations inside a loop will be executed more often than operations outside a loop. The compiler passes a summary of its access analysis to the runtime system (RTS). Whenever the RTS creates a new process, it will have some hints about how the process is going to access shared objects. The RTS sums this information across all processes and uses the result to determine the distribution strategy for each object.

[†]This research is supported by a PIONIER grant from the Netherlands Organization for Scientific Research (N.W.O.).

With this approach, the RTS usually is able to make the right decision regarding object distribution. The approach, however, has several disadvantages. First, the strategy for an object will only be changed as the result of a process fork, since this is the only time the RTS receives new information. Second, the use of heuristics makes the compiler-generated information inaccurate. Third, the effectiveness of the approach depends on how much analysis is done by the Orca compiler. Currently, the compiler does not perform access analysis on array elements. Therefore, programs using an array of shared objects are not properly handled by the RTS since it treats all objects equally. For example, the implementation of a distributed job queue using an array of objects performs best when each queue object is placed at its "logically" associated processor, but the compiler does not generate this locality information.

To avoid choosing an inefficient object distribution strategy when the compiler analysis is incorrect, we have modified the RTS to use *runtime statistics* of object invocations. For each shared object the RTS dynamically keeps track of the number of read and write operations issued by each processor, so it can base its decisions on the "true" access patterns. Only using runtime statistics, however, does not take advantage of the compiler's capabilities to estimate future behavior, so the RTS necessarily lags behind. Therefore, it is best to combine both approaches: runtime statistics are used to detect when the compiler-generated information is incorrect, so that the RTS can reconsider its earlier decision and switch to the most efficient object distribution strategy. The RTS uses the heuristic that whenever the runtime statistics and compiler information contradict, the one with the largest ratio between the costs for replicating and single-copy mode determines the object implementation strategy.

The bookkeeping of the runtime statistics for nonreplicated objects is straightforward: whenever an operation is executed on a nonreplicated object, a corresponding read or write counter is incremented. Next, the RTS reconsiders its choice of distribution strategy. If the strategy has to be changed, the RTS broadcasts a message to inform all processors of the new strategy.

The bookkeeping for replicated objects is more difficult. To reduce storage consumption, the runtime statistics are stored at a single processor named the *manager*. The statistics are updated at each object invocation at the manager processor: all write operations and *local* read operations. The read operations invoked on other processors are invisible to the manager because they are handled locally to avoid communication. Therefore the RTS piggybacks on each *write* operation the number of hidden reads on the source processor, so the manager can catch up with the runtime statistics.

3   EXPERIMENTAL RESULTS

Here we present our initial experiences with the new Orca runtime system. The RTS can be used in three modes. *RTS-static* only makes decisions when new processes are forked; these decisions are based solely on the compiler-generated information. *RTS-dynamic* ignores all compiler information and uses only dynamic operation counts. *RTS-combined* is a hybrid version that uses both static and dynamic information. We

Orca	Object Distribution			
Application	static	dynamic	combined	manually
ASP	43	42	43	43
PSRS	29	29	29	5
IDA*	232	129	104	85

Table 1   Execution times [sec] on 64 CPUs.

used several Orca programs to measure the effects of incorrect compiler estimates on the object distribution strategies chosen by each RTS mode, and compared the performance to the optimal case of placing objects manually. The programs were run on an Amoeba processor pool consisting of 64 SPARC Classic clones (50Mhz, 32Mb memory, 4+2 Kb I+D cache) connected by Ethernet. All measurements reported in Table 1 are averaged values of 10 runs with standard deviations less than 11%.

The All-Pairs Shortest Paths (ASP) application uses an iterative matrix algorithm to compute all shortest paths between the nodes of a graph. At the start of each iteration, one processor adds a row to the shared matrix object, which is subsequently read by *all* other processors. Hence, the shared matrix should be replicated to obtain good performance. The Orca compiler (overly conservative) estimates that the read/write ratio equals 1, so RTS-static and RTS-combined immediately decide to replicate the object. RTS-dynamic, on the other hand, starts by migrating the object to the processor that performs the first series of updates, before it records the large number of read operations and decides to replicate the object. Because of the many iterations, however, the incorrect first decision has no impact on performance, see Table 1.

The Parallel Sorting by Regular Sampling (PSRS) application contains one phase where each processor sends its locally sorted numbers to their destination processor. This is accomplished by issuing a Put operation on a buffer object associated with the specific processor. Since each processor has to communicate with all other processors, the program uses an array of shared buffer objects. For optimal performance, each buffer object should be placed at "its" processor. The Orca compiler, however, does not analyze array elements individually, so the RTS treats all objects equally and, as a consequence, places them on the same processor. This clearly is a bad allocation scheme, which results in a factor six slowdown, because the RTSs decide for each object independently what the best strategy is without regard of the "load" of the processors involved.

The Iterative Deepening A* (IDA*) program implements a branch-and-bound search strategy and uses a distributed job queue for load balancing. The job queue is implemented as an array of shared queue objects. Each processor is associated with a specific queue object. If a processor runs out of work and its local queue is empty then it will check the other queues to steal work. RTS-static allocates all objects at a single processor because the Orca compiler estimates that all objects are accessed equally. RTS-dynamic and RTS-combined, however, base their decisions on the runtime statistics that show that a processor frequently accesses its local queue and rarely accesses other queues. Hence, a shared queue object is quickly migrated to its owning processor. The results in Table 1 show that the usage of runtime statistics roughly halves the execution time, but still better performance is achieved by manually placing objects. The reason is that at the beginning many processors are out of work and poll other queues, which are empty too. The failing Get operations just read the state of the object, so the runtime statistics show that replication is the best policy. As soon as work is distributed equally, the access behavior changes into each processor using its local queue only, so objects have to be made single-copy. The iterative nature of IDA* causes several transitions between replicated and single-copy state, which explains the loss in performance. RTS-dynamic differs more from this thrashing behavior than RTS-combined because the latter has to overrule the static decisions based on the compiler estimates.

4   CONCLUSIONS

The Orca system frees the programmer from the burden of distributing the shared objects used for inter-process communication. The RTS uses a combination of compiler estimates and runtime statistics to automatically decide on an distribution strategy for each object. Both sources of information are required to efficiently handle as many applications as possible. The analysis of Orca programs has shown that the compiler fails to correctly predict access behavior when arrays of shared objects are involved. In these cases the runtime statistics allow the RTS to select a better object distribution strategy.

REFERENCES

[1] H.E. Bal and M.F. Kaashoek. Object distribution in Orca using compile-time and run-time techniques. Proc. *OOPSLA*, pp 162–177, Washington D.C., 1993.

[2] M. Kaashoek. *Group Communication in Distributed Computer Systems*. PhD thesis, Vrije Universiteit, Amsterdam, 1992.

[3] A.S. Tanenbaum, M.F. Kaashoek, and H.E. Bal. Parallel programming using shared objects and broadcasting. *IEEE Computer*, 25(8):10–19, August 1992.

24

BOTTOM-UP SCHEDULING WITH WORMHOLE AND CIRCUIT SWITCHED ROUTING

Kanad Ghose and Neelima Mehdiratta

Department of Computer Science

State University of New York, Binghamton, NY 13902-6000

{ghose, neelima}@cs.binghamton.edu

1 INTRODUCTION

We present a static list scheduling technique for assigning tasks of a parallel program described as a task graph onto a distributed memory multiprocessor (DMM). Our technique factors in the impact of inter-task communication delays in heuristics for processor selection and channel assignment. Unlike conventional list schedulers that schedule task graph nodes top-down, we schedule task graph nodes bottom-up to get a better estimate of the scheduling weight of a task in the face of finite communication delays [2]. In [3] and [4], we applied and evaluated our scheduler for message switched architectures for a variety of interconnection topologies. This paper describes our scheduling technique as applied to hypercube connected systems using wormhole and circuit-switched routing.

List schedulers take as input a task graph (nodes: tasks, edges: inter-task communication) and output a schedule for a target machine by associating two priority levels with each task: (i) *precedence level* (plevel), which is given by the maximum number of edges along any path to the node from the start node(s); plevel implies how soon a task becomes eligible for scheduling, (ii) *scheduling level* (slevel), which indicates the order in which tasks eligible for scheduling are actually assigned to processors. The computation of slevel is specific to the scheduling technique. A number of scheduling schemes, such as the one in [1] and ours, use the length of the longest path from the task to a terminal node (including the computation cost for nodes and the communication costs for edges on the path) as the value of slevel.

Top down scheduling schemes do not use an accurate estimate for the slevel, since the slevel for a task node is a function of the communication costs associated with the successor nodes along the longest path. These costs are not known accurately, since successors are scheduled later in the top down approach.

2   THE BOTTOM UP SCHEDULER

We schedule nodes (tasks) of the task graph *bottom up*, assigning terminal nodes first and start nodes last:

1. Compute the plevel (precedence level) of all nodes in the DAG.

2. Compute the slevel (scheduling level) of all tasks in the DAG. This is computed bottom up plevel by plevel. Form a list of all the nodes on the critical path as the slevels are computed.

3. Find the critical path of the task DAG from the start node(s).

4. Assign tasks on the critical path to the same processor node. Mark these tasks as assigned, and update processor load after each assignment. Mark as zero the (communication) edges among all nodes on the critical path since they are assigned to the same processor.

5. Assign the rest of the nodes in order of their plevels starting with the highest plevel (i.e., task nodes are assigned bottom up) using the following steps:

   - Re-compute the scheduling level (slevel) of all nodes at that plevel.

   - Sort these nodes at the same plevel in decreasing order of their slevels creating list L.

   - For each task in L, assign a processor using the processor selection heuristic, as described later.

   - Re-compute slevels of all tasks at this plevel, (except terminal nodes) to reflect the processor assignments.

6. Assign communication channels in a top-down fashion. A variety of channel allocation heuristics [3], [4] can be used for channel allocations. Alternatively, the default routing strategy can be used, since most systems do not allow users to set up routing information.

Since the start node(s) is(are) scheduled last, it is not possible to determine the time at which a task can start executing (i.e., the startup time of the task). Consequently, link contention cannot be accurately determined till all the tasks are scheduled on the processors. We therefore make a second pass through the scheduled task graph (top down) to assign channels. Terminal nodes are assigned to any processor with the minimum load.

3   PROCESSOR ALLOCATION & CHANNEL ALLOCATION

Our processor selection heuristic (PSH) attempts to make a compromise between minimizing the communication delays and maximizing parallelism, keeping a balanced load across the CPUs.

We define the *dominant successor*, Dom(T), of a task node T to be that successor Q of T, such that the edge from T to Q has the maximum weight among all edges from T to any of its successors. The weight of this edge determines the slevel for T. In other words, Q is the successor with which T communicates most heavily. The basic processor selection heuristic attempts to assign a task node T on the same processor as Dom(t) if the ratio of the communication delay to the successor and the computation time of T exceeds a predefined threshold. The result of this allocation is to reduce the adverse impact of the relatively large communication time between T and Dom(T). In all other cases, the heuristic attempts to assign T to a processing node that is lightly loaded and as close as possible to the processing node on which the dominant successor is assigned. The reader is referred to [3] for details, including two variations of the basic heuristic dubbed PSH2 and PSH3.

In wormhole routing, the communication cost C(T,Q) between two tasks T and Q assigned to two different processors assuming that there is no delay due to channel contention is given by:

$$C(T, Q) = FT * H(T,Q) + (MS-1) * FT$$

where FT is the network cycle time and MS is the message size in number of flits. H(T, Q) is the hop distance between the two processors on which T and Q are assigned. The communication cost given by the above equation are used in the PSHs. A similar delay equation was used for circuit switching. Two routing strategies were used for the circuit-switched and wormhole routed hypercube DMMs assumed as target machines. The first is the default e-cube routing of the hypercube. The second routing strategy used was the adaptive and deadlock-free p-cube routing strategy of Glass and Ni.

4 AN ASSESSMENT

We evaluated the performance of our scheduler by letting it schedule randomly generated graphs. Figure 1 shows the execution times for the schedules produced for randomly generated task graphs on a 32-node wormhole routed hypercube. Figure 2 shows how the schedules produced for two 800-node task graphs, one communication intensive and the other computation intensive, scale with the number of CPUs for wormhole routed hypercubes. Although not depicted here, the results for circuit-switched systems were quite similar. Our results also show that the load imbalance among CPUs is less than 10% in most of the cases. Our earlier results presented in [3] and [4] for a variety of message switched architectures are also quite similar. The applicability of our scheduler is thus quite general, encompassing a variety of routing techniques and arbitrary interconnection topologies.

REFERENCES

[1] H. El-Rewini and T. G. Lewis, "Scheduling Parallel Program Tasks onto Arbitrary Target Machines," Journal of Parallel and Distributed Computing, 9, pp. 138-153, 1990.

[2] K. Ghose and N. Mehdiratta, "A Universal Approach for Task Scheduling for Distributed Memory Multiprocessors", in Proc. Scalable High Perf. Computing Conf. 1994 (SHPCC 94), pp. 577-584.

[3] N. Mehdiratta and K. Ghose, "Scheduling Task Graphs onto Distributed Memory Multiprocessors Under Realistic Constraints", in Proc. Parallel Architectures and Languages Europe, pp. 589-600, 1994 (PARLE 94).

[4] N. Mehdiratta and K. Ghose, "A Bottom-Up Approach To Task Scheduling on Distributed Memory Multiprocessors", in Proc. Int. Conf. Parallel Processing, vol. 2 pp. 151-154, 1994.

25

COMMUNICATION-BUFFERS FOR DATA-PARALLEL, IRREGULAR COMPUTATIONS

Andreas Müller and Roland Rühl

Centro Svizzero di Calcolo Scientifico (CSCS-ETHZ),
La Galleria, Via Cantonale, CH-6928 Manno, Switzerland

1 INTRODUCTION

In a team of six software engineers, we are currently developing the portable integrated tool environment *Annai* [1] for distributed-memory parallel processors. *Annai* consists of a High Performance Fortran (HPF) compiler, extended for the support of unstructured computations, a performance monitor and analyzer [2], and a source-level debugger [3] for distributed programs, all sharing a common user-interface. The recently-defined Message Passing Interface (MPI) serves as our low-level machine interface. Our HPF extensions are implemented by a compiler generically called Parallelization Support Tool (PST). All PST HPF extensions are fully supported by both the performance analyzer and debugger.

Much like Arf, Fortran D, Kali, and Oxygen, PST supports unstructured computations through the run-time preprocessing of critical code segments. In a previous report [4] we have described PST's language extensions, compilation mechanisms and run-time support in detail. Performance of compiler-generated parallel programs was discussed and execution-time overhead was measured. In this summary we focus on one of PST's advanced features, namely the availability of different buffer organizations for distributed data.

Note that the main concept presented in this paper, namely the compiler-supported communication buffering for unstructured computations is not new and related performance measurements with simpler buffer organizations and a simple test algorithm were already collected in 1991 by J. Saltz and his colleagues [7]. The results presented in this report however, stem from our experience with a full application, parallelized by an HPF compiler which also accepts extensions for the support of unstructured computations.

295

2 EXTENDING HPF WITH PST

Using Oxygen [5], we previously parallelized PILS, a *Package of Iterative Linear Solvers*, on the Intel Paragon and the Fujitsu AP1000 [6]. Our experience with Oxygen and PILS as well as the requirements of a group of application developers who is working with us led us to include the following major features in PST: (1) replicated variables and shared-memory semantics, (2) user-defined data distributions, (3) user-defined loop distributions, (4) re-distribution and re-mapping, and (5) saving of communication patterns.

PST supplements an HPF compiler developed by NEC Tokyo by providing an extended input language, and a different underlying programming paradigm and compilation technique. To achieve a clear separation, routines that use PST extensions and rely on PST's programming model have to be declared EXTRINSIC (PST_LOCAL). PST supports all regular HPF data distribution directives plus three dynamic (user-defined) data distributions. By default, data are replicated and private, i.e., the compiler does not enforce consistency of non-distributed data across processors. Distributed data are part of the global name space which is implemented by run-time analysis.

By default, all code runs *locally* and a global name space is not enforced. The user can specify certain code segments *public*, and for such segments, PST generates a run-time preprocessing phase, called *symbol handler*, and an executions phase, called *executor*. The symbol handler prepares the data transfers necessary to execute statements with references to distributed arrays in the executor. Executors consist of computational chunks and communication checkpoints in between. Remote data are fetched or updated in the checkpoints and the computational chunks operate on buffers to access remote data. These buffers are loaded by receives in a previous checkpoint for fetches and they are used in a send in the next checkpoint for data updates.

We call the buffers mentioned above *communication caches* because of their faint structural resemblance to hardware caches. Also the problematic nature is similar: a compromise has to be made between memory consumption and run-time overhead. Fig. 1 depicts the four alternatives: In the simplest organization (0), we completely replicate the allocation of distributed data on all processors. With organization (1), the global index of a distributed array element is hashed by first computing the element's owner (i.e., the processor which maintains a consistent copy of the element), and then by allocating a complete copy of that processor's part of the distributed array. Organization (2) differs from organization (1) in the fact that a processor's local array segment is allocated in blocks of fixed size (b) rather than as a whole. The index of an array element in such a block is equal to the element's local index, modulo b. When remote data are accessed, organization (3) inserts remote values of a distributed array in a sorted buffer. The buffer includes both data values and global array indices.

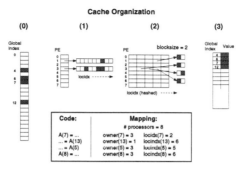

Figure 1 *Different communication cache organizations implemented in PST.*

3 EXPERIMENTAL RESULTS

We have parallelized PILS with PST and compiled it for all four organizations. For the test runs, the library was applied to the solution of four sparse linear systems of equations stemming from two 3D finite-element simulations of sub-micron DRAM cells with trench capacitors (DR15E and DR15C) and from two bipolar transistors (BIPOL3D20KH and BP25E). As iterative solution method Bi-CGSTAB was used, preconditioned by a D-ILU preconditioner in split position.

Tab. 1 summarizes measurements on a 64 processor NEC Cenju-3. The top part of the table describes the four equation systems in more detail. The lower part shows maximum local memory requirements (in Kbytes) for storing distributed vectors and their communication cache, as well as time (in seconds) spent in the executors of the four main PILS matrix-vector operations during one iteration of the solution process' steady state. Already with cache organization (1) memory consumption due to data replication can be significantly reduced (depending on the problem by a factor of 2.4 to 4.4), while execution time increases by less than 10%. When applying cache organization (2) with different block sizes b, on the one hand, execution times increase with decreasing b, because the use of more and smaller cache blocks destroys the program's spacial locality. On the other hand, memory consumption depends on b: as b increases, the pointer array allocated for the cache becomes smaller, but more memory is consumed for irregular remote memory accesses; in the worst case, for each access one block is allocated. The most time consuming operation for cache organization (3) is the test on locality when distributed vectors are accessed.

REFERENCES

[1] C. Clémençon, A. Endo, J. Fritscher, A. Müller, R. Rühl, and B. J.N. Wylie. The "Annai" Environment for Portable Distributed Memory Parallel Programming. *Proc. 28th Hawaii International Conference on System Sciences*, IEEE, Mauii, Hawaii, January 1995

[2] B. J. N. Wylie and A. Endo. Design and realization of the Annai integrated parallel

Equation System		dr15e	bipol3D20kh	bp25e	dr15c
Problem Characteristics					
# unknowns		15564	20412	25642	46692
# nonzeros		143710	263920	234436	986042
matrix density		9.2	13.0	9.1	21.1
Cache Organization		Performance			
(0)	memory	1874	2456	3084	5610
	ex. time	0.056	0.095	0.132	0.213
(1)	memory	491	564	1267	1705
	ex. time	0.060	0.099	0.140	0.222
$(2), b = 8$	memory	232	300	587	678
	ex. time	0.093	0.160	0.189	0.463
$(2), b = 16$	memory	210	259	632	601
	ex. time	0.078	0.128	0.161	0.343
$(2), b = 32$	memory	219	262	749	628
	ex. time	0.069	0.114	0.146	0.281
$(2), b = 64$	memory	261	299	934	755
	ex. time	0.063	0.108	0.137	0.252
(3)	memory	38	50	71	106
	ex. time	0.070	0.132	0.292	0.322

Table 1 *PILS performance when parallelized with PST and running with different communication cache organizations on a 64 processor Cenju-3.*

programming environment performance monitor and analyzer. Technical Report CSCS-TR-94-07, Aug. 1994.

[3] C. Clémençon, J. Fritscher, and R. Rühl. Execution Control, Visualization and Replay of Massively Parallel Programs within Annai's Debugging Tool. To appear in Proc. *HPCS'95*, Montréal, CA, July 1995.

[4] A. Müller and R. Rühl. Extending High Performance Fortran for the Support of Unstructured Computations. To appear in Proc. *9-th International Conf. on Supercomputing*, ACM, Barcelona, Spain, July 1995.

[5] R. Rühl. *A Parallelizing Compiler for Distributed-Memory Parallel Processors.* PhD thesis, ETH-Zürich, 1992. Published by Hartung-Gorre Verlag, Konstanz, Germany.

[6] C. Pommerell and R. Rühl. Migration of Vectorized Iterative Solvers to Distributed Memory Architectures. To appear in SIAM J. Sci. Comput., January 1996.

[7] S. Hiranandani, J. Saltz, P. Mehrotra and H. Berryman, Performance of Hashed Cache Data Migration Schemes on Multicomputers. Journal of Parallel and Distributed Computing, 12, 415–422, 1991

26

COMPILING ASSEMBLY PATTERN ON A SHARED VIRTUAL MEMORY

Mounir Hahad, Thierry Priol and Jocelyne Erhel

IRISA/INRIA, Campus de Beaulieu, 35042 Rennes-France

1 INTRODUCTION

Among the variety of tools in a programming environment (debugger, performance analyzer, data mapping assistant, user interface, compiler, runtime support), we focus here on the compiler item. The definition of machine-independent parallel programming languages is a relevant example of the need for portability. However, we believe that rather than focusing exclusively on data distribution approaches, we may merge both data distribution and control distribution to target a wider range of applications. To rely on control distribution, we need a global address space, which, on scalable multiprocessors, may be afforded by a Shared Virtual Memory (SVM). Thanks to the SVM, the code generation process is much simpler : there is no need to an explicit data distribution, nor localization of array subscripts, nor management of non-local data buffers, nor communication schedules generation (with message vectorization, coalescing, aggregation). All this is handled automatically by the runtime support. Furthermore, the compilation of procedure and function calls within a parallel loop becomes easily feasible. Incremental (step by step) parallelization of codes thanks to the global address space is an interesting advantage. The drawback is the coherence grain which is not always well suited to the application.

Our prototype code generator Fortran-S [1] is based on the Fortran77 specifications, to which it adds some directives to tag the data to be shared and the parallel loops. Several optimizations are also implemented, like coherence protocol switching, memory page shuffles and broadcast, and some efficient message-based functions (synchronization mechanisms). The use of directives rather than language extensions enables straightforward compilation on sequential computers for debugging purposes. Fortran-S generates a SPMD fortran77 code targeted to the PARAGON XP/S (augmented with the MYOAN SVM [3]), the KSR1 or the iPSC/2 (augmented with the KOAN SVM [5]). In this paper, we introduce new functionalities of Fortran-S allowing it to generate a more efficient code for irregular access patterns loops. Our sample loop is shown in figure 1.

where tmp stands for the result of independent computations (even function calls with non local data arguments), S is a shared array of size n, La and Lb are indirection

```
Do t=1,ntimes
  Do i=1,m
    tmp = ...
    S(La(i)) = S(La(i))  op  F¹(tmp)
    S(Lb(i)) = S(Lb(i))  op  F²(tmp)
  EndDo
EndDo
```

```
Do t=1,ntimes
  Do i=1,m
    S(L(i)) = S(L(i))  op ...
  EndDo
EndDo
```

Figure 1   Loop ℓ **Figure 2**   Loop ℓ_1

arrays of size m with $m > n$ and *op* is a commutative and associative operation. This loop arises from an assemblage code of an unstructured triangular mesh, discretizing different domain shapes [2]. On a SVM, data coherence is maintained at a page (or cache line) level. Uncareful distribution of the inner loop iterations can lead to a false sharing problem and a dependence violation if the read/write in S is not atomically executed. To compile this loop, our proposal relies on two major contributions : first, a *virtual* page-ownership oriented computation that we call *Conditioned Iterations Loop* (CIL), and second, a learning technique (LEARN) to enhance the efficiency of subsequent computations.

2   PRINCIPLE : CIL AND LEARN

Let us first consider a simpler loop structure, like the one in Figure 2.

Definition 1 *A Conditioned Iterations Loop (CIL) is a loop which iterations are wholly contained into a conditional statement (Figure 3) so that if an iteration is executed by several processors, the condition* Cond *is true on one and exactly one processor (and False on the others)*   □

The owner-computes rule is a particular case of the CIL, where the condition Cond is evaluated on the basis of the actual mapping of the left hand side data S on the local memories of a DMPC. On a SVM, the ownership of data is not static, memory pages are free to move between local memories. Thanks to this property, CIL may rely on a *virtual* (default or user defined) page ownership rather than the actual page distribution. Thus, load imbalance which could occur because of an inadequate initial data distribution, is quite easily avoided. In other words, virtual page ownership acts as a page remapping, but without any compiler support overhead. To execute the ℓ_1 loop in parallel, we compile it into a CIL form, that respects the following execution conditions :

- all the processors execute all the iterations,

- Cond = I (virtually) own the page containing S(L(i)).

Do i=1,m
  if (Cond) then
    S(L(i)) = S(L(i)) *op* ...
  Endif
EndDo
	Do i=1,m
	  if (Cond) then
	    i1 = i1 + 1
	    Iter(i1) = i
	    S(L(i)) = S(L(i)) *op* ...
	  Endif
	EndDo
	Do t=2,ntimes
	  Do i=1,i1
	  i = Iter(i1)
	  S(L(i)) = S(L(i)) *op* ...
	  EndDo
	EndDo

Figure 3 CIL   **Figure 4** LEARN

This is a program distribution based on the virtual distribution of the data. Consequently, each processor is responsible of the iterations modifying a subset of the pages of S. In our present implementations, this subset is equal either to the actual page ownership, or to a subset derived from a regular distribution of the pages of S over the processors (block and cyclic). Thanks to the CIL, all updates to S are atomic, and the page write misses are limited to cold-start ones. Notice also that the CIL performs the updates to a single element of S in the same order as the sequential execution of the loop. An analytical model of the CIL and a comparison with different compilation schemes are discussed in [4]. The next step is to avoid the execution of *all* the inner loop iterations by *all* the processors. We adopt a modified Inspector/Executor scheme [6] : the inspection process is performed *while* executing, rather than *before* executing. So we take advantage of the first iteration of the outermost loop, to collect information about the CIL loop. This information, stored in private arrays Iter, will reduce the CIL loop bounds of the next iterations of the outermost loop and discard the test of page ownership. The corresponding generated code for each processor is shown in Figure 4.

3 HIGH LEVEL LANGUAGE SUPPORT

Presently, the code showed above is automatically generated by Fortran-S. Directives indicate that the inner loop should be compiled into CIL and that the outer loop should be compiled as a LEARN loop. The source code provided by the user includes some directives presented here in Fortran-S syntax :

```
C$ann[LEARN(1)]
  Do t=1, ntimes
C$ann[CIL(STATIC,BLOCK)]
    Do i=1,m
      S(La(i)) = S(La(i)) op ...
    EndDo
  EndDo
```

The parameter of the CIL annotation can be either DYNAMIC to use the actual page ownership as Cond, or STATIC coupled to BLOC/CYCLIC to use a simple virtual page ownership. The parameter appended to the LEARN annotation indicates which inner loop, if there were several, is to be used to learn about the data access pattern.

4 EXTENDING CIL

In the initial loop structure ℓ, there are two write accesses to the shared variable S in the inner loop body. The shortcomings of CIL is its ability to deal with only one write access to a shared variable per iteration. Thus it may have some difficulty in assigning the iterations of the ℓ loop to processors while reducing false sharing. Our solution is to split the loop in as many loops as there are write accesses to shared arrays, then expanding the local scalar variables in vectors. Each loop with a shared variable is then compiled into CIL, and LEARN can be used with individual loops.

5 CONCLUSION

We have developed and implemented a set of runtime techniques to handle efficiently assemblage-like irregular loops. They are derived from a custom inspect/execute paradigm suited to Shared Virtual Memory machines. Our results on an Intel iPSC/2 and a KSR1 [4] show a large improvement in performance in comparison with other runtime techniques.

REFERENCES

[1] François Bodin, Lionnel Kervella, and Thierry Priol. Fortran-S : a fortran interface for shared virtual memory architectures. In *Supercomputing'93*, pages 274–283, November 1993.

[2] Marie Odile Bristeau, Jocelyne Erhel, Philippe Feat, Roland Glowinski, and Jaques Périaux. Solving the helmholtz equation at high wave numbers on a parallel computer with a shared virtual memory. *International journal of supercomputer applications and high performance computing*, (9.1), 1995.

[3] Gilbert Cabillic, Thierry Priol, and Isabelle Puaut. *MYOAN: an Implementation of the KOAN Shared Virtual Memory on the Intel Paragon*. Technical Report 2258, INRIA, April 1994.

[4] Mounir Hahad, Thierry Priol, and Jocelyne Erhel. *Irregular Loop Patterns Compilation on Distributed Shared Memory Multiprocessors*. Technical Report 2361, INRIA, Campus de Beaulieu - 35042 Rennes Cedex - France, September 1994.

[5] Zakaria Lahjomri and Thierry Priol. Koan : a shared virtual memory for an ipsc/2 hypercube. In *Proceedings of CONPAR/VAPP*, pages 441–452, Springer-Verlag, France, September 1992.

[6] J. Saltz, K. Crowley, R. Mirchandaney, and H. Berryman. Run-time scheduling and execution of loops on message passing machines. *Journal of Parallel and Distributed Computing*, 8:303–312, 1990.

27

DISTRIBUTED MEMORY IMPLEMENTATION OF A SHARED-ADDRESS PARALLEL OBJECT-ORIENTED LANGUAGE

Chu-Cheow Lim, Jerome A. Feldman*

International Computer Science Institute (ICSI)
Berkeley, California 94704

* and Computer Science Division, U.C. Berkeley
Berkeley, California 94720
USA

1 INTRODUCTION

Parallel Sather* (pSather [1]) is a parallel object-oriented language with a shared address space programming model, independent of the underlying multiprocessor architecture. To account for distributed-memory machines, pSather provides a cluster model in which processors are grouped in clusters. Associated with a cluster is a part of the address space with fast access; access to other parts of the address space is ≤ 2 orders of magnitude slower.

We have an implementation of pSather on the CM-5. The prototype shows that even on distributed-memory machines without hardware/operating system support for a shared address space, it is still practical and reasonably efficient for the shared address abstraction to be implemented in the compiler/runtime. This paper describes some optimizations that we use for efficient compiler/runtime implementation.

Section 1.1 briefly describes pSather's machine and and execution model. Section 2 briefly describes the runtime implementation of pSather on the CM-5, and (as an example of the optimization strategies) how the compiler and runtime optimize the accesses of remote object attributes. ([1] describes other optimizations, e.g. strategies to improve the timings of remote calls/threads and synchronization objects.) Section 3 summarizes our experience for the pSather CM-5 prototype.

---

*This abstract describes pSather 0.2 based on an earlier version of Sather (version 0.2). A new version of pSather 1.0 (based on Sather 1.0) is currently being implemented at ICSI.

1.1   Machine and Execution Model

PSather adopts an MIMD programming model. Its abstract machine model has P asynchronous processors grouped in C clusters. The model presents a shared logical address-space to the programmers, but divides the address space such that each cluster has its own physical address-space. Clusters may have one or more processors and each cluster may have a different number of processors. A processor belongs to exactly one cluster. Processors and memory locations belonging to the same cluster are *near* to each other. Processors and memory locations belonging to different clusters are *far* (or remote) from each other. Far accesses are consistently less efficient than near accesses.

This model unifies many multiprocessor configurations, ranging from shared-memory machines (e.g. SGI Power Challenge) to distributed-memory machines (e.g. CM-5), each cluster consists of only one processor. An example of multiple processors per cluster is a network of shared-memory multiprocessors.

In the cluster model, an object has a *cluster location* which is the cluster from which access to the object is most efficient. The location of a dynamically allocated object x is given by x.where, and does not change during its lifetime. Such an object can be allocated on a cluster specified explicitly by a programmer, using an @-operator.

In pSather's multithreading model, an activation frame has a fixed *cluster location*. We treat this activation frame + cluster location as a *subthread*. So as a thread's execution unfolds, it consists of a stack of subthreads and a subthread may be on a different cluster from previous subthreads. There is no limit to the number of subthreads executing in an object at the same time. The location of subthread is specified by using the @-operator in the language.

A language fork construct allows user to start asynchronous execution threads on local cluster (default) or remote clusters (using the @-operator.)

2   CM-5 IMPLEMENTATION OF PSATHER

On the CM-5, all pSather remote operations are implemented by using the CM-5 Active Message (CMAM) library [2]. Because the CMAM library uses polling to receive requests from the network, in order to ensure that all active messages are received, the compiler introduces additional polling statements into the generated code.

2.1   Accessing Object Attributes

We support shared address in the compiler and runtime, and represent pointers as 64-bit entities. The first word denotes a cluster id and the second word is an address

	Time/write (μs)
Sather on Sparc workstation	0.48 – 0.5
PSather on Sparc workstation	0.48 – 0.5
Remote Object	
PSather on CM-5 (no optimization)	63.1
PSather on CM-5 (optimzed remote dispatch/access)	30.1
Local Object	
PSather on CM-5 (no optimization)	3.9
PSather on CM-5 with `with-near` statement	1.6
PSather on CM-5 with `with-near` statement and eliminating polling statements	0.67

Table 1   Times to read local/remote object attributes.

within the specified cluster. The implementation is a straight-forward one in which each access to a object is tested for remote access.[†]

Dispatching for Remote Objects

A dynamic dispatch might involve two remote accesses – first to get an object's actual type, then the actual (potentially remote) operation on an object. We reduce the number of messages by having compiler-generated routines which act as remote handlers to perform dispatch and read/write specific object attributes.

If the object is local, then we invoke the dispatching mechanism locally (using a local cache). Otherwise, we invoke a runtime routine to invoke the remote handler which has its own dispatch cache.

Eliminating Overheads in Pointer Dereference

In the pSather CM-5 prototype, whenever an object attribute is read/written, the cluster id of the address is checked for local vs. remote access. To reduce this source of overhead, we make use of a language construct (`with-near` statement) which asserts that pointers are local relative to the executing thread.

The compiler uses the `with-near` statement to mark near variables and to record expressions which use near variables. This information is further propagated via inlining to other variables (including object attributes). [1] describes the implementation details.

Performance

[†] Value objects (not dynamically allocated) such as `INT` retain their shared memory representation and do not impose any overhead.

Table 1 shows a summary timings for dispatched attribute reads. There are two major sources of overheads for local access. The first is the extra check for remote object. This can be eliminated when the programmer uses the `with-near` statement and the compiler uses this statement as a hint to optimize pointer dereferences. The second source is from the (compiler-generated) polling statements. By removing them, the read time is reduced from 1.6 to 0.67 μs. Unfortunately, we must keep the polling statements in order to make sure messages are always received.

3 CONCLUSIONS

Although active messages were developed as support for dataflow languages, we find that they are also useful as part of the runtime support for pSather, a high-level object-oriented language with a completely different paradigm. The performance figures also suggest that when selecting a low-level message library for language runtime, it would be more efficient to use an interrupt-driven library (as opposed to one based on polling).

[1] describes the implementation of a few abstractions which are reusable by applications with very different characteristics (including a fast-multipole N-body program and a Gröbner basis computation). They are examples of how software can be reused in both small and medium-sized parallel applications. The performance of our applications shows reasonable speedups even when compared to similar C programs executing on a CM-5 node. The pSather programs on CM-5 have been able to make absolute performance gains over comparable sequential processors. We think that pSather will serve as a practical and efficient platform for experimenting with new parallel algorithms and data structures.

Work on pSather is continuing, to get a design and implementation which is compatible to a new version of Sather (Sather 1.0).

REFERENCES

[1] Chu-Cheow Lim. *A Parallel Object-Oriented System for Realizing Reusable and Efficient Data Abstractions.* PhD thesis, University of California at Berkeley, October 1993. Also available as: TR-93-063, International Computer Science Institute, 1947 Center Street, Suite 600, Berkeley, CA 94704-1105, October 1993.

[2] Thorsten von Eicken, David E. Culler, Seth Copen Goldstein, and Klaus Erik Schauser. Active Messages: A Mechanism for Integrated Communication and Computation. In *Proceedings of the 19th International Symposium on Computer Architecture.* ACM Press, May 1992. Also available as technical report from University of California at Berkeley, CS Division, UCB/CSD 92/675, March 1992.

DISTRIBUTED TREE STRUCTURES FOR N-BODY SIMULATION[†]

A. Satish Pai, Young-il Choo*, Marina Chen**

Computer Science Dept., Yale University, New Haven, CT 06520, USA

* IBM, Kingston, NY 12401, USA

** Computer Science Dept., Boston University, Boston, MA 02215, USA

1 IRREGULAR DYNAMIC DATA STRUCTURES

Several particle simulation algorithms, such as the Barnes-Hut [1] and the Fast Multipole method [2], proceed by hierarchically decomposing the simulation space and representing the distribution of the simulated particles in an adaptive tree data structure which varies as the simulation proceeds. Such tree structures are also used in radiosity calculation, computational fluid mechanics, and other applications. Managing such a structure on a distributed-memory machine poses significant difficulties in terms of communication costs and partitioning strategies. The irregular nature of the structures rules out the usual optimization techniques used with arrays. Hand-coding these irregular and dynamic data structures is error-prone and not easily portable.

We present the design and an object-oriented implementation of a Virtual Distributed Tree (VDT) structure that provides a high-level view of a dynamic and irregular tree data structure to the application developer while hiding the low-level communication and tree management functions that are implemented using a message-passing system below the class interface. The application interface provides various methods to manipulate the tree in a global fashion while the run-time system handles most of the other details of parallel execution, including the partition of the data structure across several processors, communication, and load-balancing. Our emphasis is on programmability and ease of use: we want an easily comprehensible framework using which various applications that require adaptive trees can be coded up quickly.

The VDT class has been designed to provide a clear separation between the application code for the tree-based algorithm, and the implementation of the methods of the VDT class itself. There is also a clear separation between the algorithmic details of the VDT

[†]This research was supported in part by grant N00014-93-1-0114 from ONR and CCR8908285 from NSF.

class methods and the low-level message-passing and machine-dependent code, so that the class may be ported to different machines with ease. Lastly, we have provided for a certain degree of flexibility in the class by allowing different strategies to be used for partitioning the data structure.

We have used the VDT class in implementing the Barnes-Hut algorithm for particle simulation on a network of workstations and a distributed memory machine.

2   THE BARNES-HUT ALGORITHM

The hierarchical decomposition of the simulation space according to the density of the particles in each sub-region naturally yields a tree structure that is deeper in the regions where the particles are denser. In order to avoid the $O(N^2)$ force computations, several algorithms use approximations by considering various mass moments of groups of particles. Several implementations of these algorithms exist [3, 4, 5, 6] The data sets involved are normally very large and there is significant parallelism to be availed of, hence running these algorithms on parallel machines is attractive.

On distributed-memory parallel machines (or workstation clusters) with message passing, the main challenge is how to distribute the large tree that is created and manage the irregular patterns of communication as the computation progresses. For extended simulation, the tree also needs to be repartitioned periodically to balance the load on each processor.

3   THE VIRTUAL DISTRIBUTED TREE

In the VDT class, we provide the application programmer with several operations that correspond to certain simple and natural operations such as sweeps and traversals over the trees. Many algorithms such as Barnes-Hut can be expressed easily using a small set of such generic operations. Each global operation induces some local computation on each processor's piece of the distributed tree, and the results of all the local computations are then put together.

The VDT abstraction has been implemented as a class in the C++ language. The application programmer declares an object of this class in the main program, and then performs all computations by invoking the methods of the object. The object can be treated as a single monolithic global data structure in the program even though in reality it exists as a number of collections of subtrees across all the processors. The runtime system ensures that the subtrees remain coherent and synchronized at all times. There is a subsidiary class that describes the nodes of the adaptive tree; this can be customized for the particular geometry needed by the application.

After initialization the component of the tree containing the tree root behaves as a master unit to coordinate the actions of all the components. Message-passing initiated by this master unit results in appropriate local computations at all the components. Though this appears asymmetric in terms of the control flow, in practice the numerical computations that occur in the distributed components dominate the run time and the load can be kept fairly balanced across all processors. The model of computation is similar to the "bulk synchronous" model in that we alternate between phases of computation with local data and phases of communication to exchange partial results and control information. The system is loosely coupled—some processors may block waiting for data at times, but otherwise each processor proceeds computing with local data to the extent possible.

The methods of the tree class include methods to insert nodes in a tree, to build the tree in a specified manner, to perform various kinds of computations on the nodes of the tree, and to traverse the tree in various ways. These methods are all generic in that they are not specific to any particular application; rather, the application programmer needs to define specific functions to perform the computations needed, and these have to be provided as parameters to the generic methods of the tree.

For different applications, and for execution on different platforms, it is desirable to have different methods of partitioning the tree and balancing the load across the processors of the machine. The VDT class provides generic function hooks that can be customized for various partitioning strategies. We have used the Orthogonal Recursive Bisection (ORB) and the static allocation schemes as demonstrations.

4 BARNES-HUT WITH THE VDT CLASS

The following shows what the Barnes-Hut algorithm using the ORB method of partitioning looks like when programmed using the VDT class. A pointer dt is used to create and manipulate a global distributed tree.

```
DistTree *dt;
dt=new DistTree(init_node,8,0);
      // init, degree 8 for 3-D
dt->setup_balance_hooks(ORB_prebalance,...);
      // set up ORB
dt->free_action(read_input_file);// read input data
dt->iterated_grow_at_leaves; // build tree from input
// the following are in a loop for the simulation
   dt->act_on_leaves(init_leaf_com);
      // leaves' centers of mass
   dt->up_sweep(compute_all_com);
      // internal centers of mass
   dt->down_sweep(send_edata);// exchange data
   dt->tree_action(select_leaf, select_node,
      compute_forces, update_particle_forces);
      // compute forces
   dt->act_on_leaves(update_particles);
      // move particles
   dt->balance_tree(1);                     // invoke ORB
```

```
dt->free_action(print_particles);          // output
```

5 THE CURRENT IMPLEMENTATION

We have implemented the VDT abstraction on two different message-passing plat-forms. One uses the p4 message-passing package running on a networked cluster of Sparc workstations. The other uses the CMMD message-passing library on a CM5-E Connection Machine equipped with vector units. The tree abstractions have been used to implement the Barnes-Hut algorithm for N-body simulation involving gravitational fields, and we are working on implementing the Fast Multipole Method. The partition-ing strategies used for both include the Orthogonal Recursive Bisection and a form of static allocation.

On a 32-node CM-5E experiments have been run with up to 4 million particles in a simulation. On Sparc workstations memory and other constraints restrict us to smaller numbers of particles per node. For a typical run with 2 million particles on a 32-node CM-5E the breakup of the run time is approximately as follows: 65% for force computation and essential data exchange; 20% for center of mass computation; 15% for synchronization, control data exchange, etc. Tree-building takes about 25% of the time for one time step, but this is amortized over the number of time steps between load balances. The raw run time for one time step is about 450 sec (force computation 302 sec, centers of mass 94 sec) tree-building takes around 110 sec.

REFERENCES

[1] J. Barnes and P. Hut. A hierarchical O(N log N) force-calculation algorithm. *Nature*, page 324, 1986.

[2] L. Greengard and V. Rokhlin. A fast algorithm for particle simulations. *Journal of Computational Physics*, page 73, 1987.

[3] M. Warren and J. Salmon. Astrophysical N-body simulations using hierarchical tree data structures. In *Proceedings of Supercomputing*, 1992.

[4] J. Singh. *Parallel Hierarchical N-body Methods and their Implications for Multiproces-sors*. PhD thesis, Stanford University, 1993.

[5] S. Bhatt, M. Chen, J. Cowie, C. Lin, and P. Liu. Object-oriented support for adaptive methods on parallel machines. In *Object Oriented Numerics Conference*, 1993.

[6] S. Bhatt, M. Chen, C.-Y. Lin, and P. Liu. Abstractions for parallel N-body simulations. In *Scalable High-Performance Computing Conference*, 1992.

29

COMMUNICATION GENERATION AND OPTIMIZATION FOR HPF

A. Thirumalai, J. Ramanujam and A. Venkatachar

Department of Electrical and Computer Engineering,
Louisiana State University, Baton Rouge, LA 70803, USA.

1 INTRODUCTION

Programming massively parallel distributed memory machines involves partitioning data and computation across processors. In order to ease this difficult task, languages such as Fortran D [3] and High Performance Fortran [2] include directives that allow programmers to specify data mappings. In these languages, arrays are aligned to an abstract Cartesian grid called a *template* ; the template is then distributed across the various processors. A compiler for HPF that generates code for each processor has to compute the sequence of local memory addresses accessed by each processor and the sequence of sends and receives for a given processor to access non-local data. The distribution of computation in most compilers follows the *owner-computes* rule. That is, a processor performs only those computations (or assignments) for which it owns the left hand side variable. Access to non-local right hand side variables is achieved by inserting sends and receives. In this paper, we present a novel approach to communication generation for general block-cyclic distributions based on the fact that the set of elements referenced form a lettice, i.e., they can be generated by integer linear combinations of basis vectors and that this set has a repeating pattern. Experiments on an IBM SP-2 show that the communication table generation times are small.

2 ADDRESS GENERATION

We consider an array A identically aligned to a template T, i.e., $A(i)$ is aligned with $T(ai + b)$, where the alignment stride $a = 1$ and the alignment offset $b = 0$. We assume that this template is distributed in a block-cyclic fashion onto p processors with a block size of k. This is also known as a $\text{CYCLIC}(k)$ distribution [2]. A typical HPF assignment statement is of the form $A(l : h : s) = \cdots$ where s is the access stride. Given an array statement with HPF-style data mappings, it is our aim to generate code including the communication for each processor.

Under the mapping, we assign a set of k cells of the template to each of the p processors and then wrap around and assign the rest of the cells in a similar fashion. We refer to each set of pk elements as a course. The set of elements of A that are accessed form a *lattice* [10]; every lattice can be described by its *basis,* which is a collection of vectors, integer linear combinations of which can generate every point that belongs to the lattice. Since we want to enumerate the points of the lattice in lexicographic order, we use a set of *extremal basis* vectors non-negative integer linear combinations of which generate all the accessed points; this is useful in code generation, since nested loops can be used for lattice enumeration. The vectors $(1, - pk \bmod s)$ and $(0, s)$ form an extremal basis; details can be found in [9, 10].

Let $B = \begin{bmatrix} 1 & 0 \\ -(pk \bmod s) & s \end{bmatrix}$ be the basis matrix of the array section lattice; The determinant of B is the access stride s itself. Using a transformation $T = B^{-1}$ and Fourier-Motzkin elimination, we derive the code for processor $m (0 \le m < p)$ as shown to the right. For details, the reader is referred to [8, 9, 10]. The access pattern for the LHS array A repeats after every $\frac{s}{\gcd(s,pk)}$ courses of elements. Hence, it is sufficient to store the access pattern of the elements in the first $\frac{s}{\gcd(s,pk)}$ courses and use this information to determine the remaining elements accessed. In the code shown to the right, the array U stores the access pattern. Details of code generation for an arbitrary array section $A(\ell : h : s)$ can be found in [8, 9, 10].

$\alpha = pk \bmod s;\ \beta = mk;\ w = 0;$
$s' = \frac{s}{\gcd(s,pk)};\ N' = \lceil \frac{N}{s'} \rceil;$
DO $u = 0, s' - 1$
$\quad t = \alpha u + \beta$
$\quad$ **DO** $v = \lceil \frac{t}{s} \rceil, \lfloor \frac{k'+t}{s} \rfloor$
$\quad\quad U[w] = uk + vs - t;$
$\quad\quad$ Increment w;
$\quad$ **ENDDO**
ENDDO
$length = w;\ offset = 0;$
DO $i = 0, N'$
$\quad$ **DO** $j = 0, length - 1$
$\quad\quad A[offset + U(j)] = \cdots$
$\quad$ **ENDDO**
$\quad offset = offset + ks'$
ENDDO

3 COMMUNICATION GENERATION

Receive pattern generation

We consider a typical HPF-style assignment statement: $A(l_1 : h_1 : s_1) = B(l_2 : h_2 : s_2)$. Given a LHS element, we can easily determine the processor that owns the RHS element and the local address of the RHS element on that processor using the following expressions: $m = (i \text{ div } k)$ and $L = k * (i \text{ div } pk) + i \bmod k$, where i is a global address, m is the processor to which i belongs to and L is the local address of i on processor m. The access pattern in the global address space repeats itself after pk elements are accessed, i.e. after every s_1 courses, where s_1 is the access stride of the LHS array. To generate the receive pattern, it is sufficient to run the code generated in the previous sections to obtain the global address of the first pk elements accessed on the LHS. For each of these elements we calculate the processor that owns the corresponding RHS element and local address of that element on it. This code is shown in Figure 1(a).

$\alpha = pk \bmod (s_1) \; ; \; k' = k - 1$
$\beta = m * k - l_1 \; ; \; q = 0$
DO $u = \frac{l_1}{pk}, s_1 - 1 + \frac{l_1}{pk}$
  $t = \alpha u + \beta$
  DO $v = \left\lceil \frac{t}{s_1} \right\rceil, \left\lfloor \frac{k'+t}{s_1} \right\rfloor$
    $i = (upk + mk + vs_1 - t - l_1)$
    $RProcpattern_m[q] = (i \text{ div } k) \bmod p$
    $RPattern_m[q] = (k(i \text{ div } pk) + i \bmod k)$
    Increment q
  ENDDO
ENDDO

(a): Code for computing the receive pattern

$\alpha = pk \bmod (s_2) \; ; \; k' = k - 1$
$\beta = m * k - l_2 \; ; \; q = 0$
DO $u = \frac{l_2}{pk}, s_2 - 1 + \frac{l_2}{pk}$
  $t = \alpha u + \beta$
  DO $v = \left\lceil \frac{t}{s_2} \right\rceil, \left\lfloor \frac{k'+t}{s_2} \right\rfloor$
    $i = \frac{(upk + mk + vs_2 - t - l_2)s_1}{s_2} + l_1$
    $SProcpattern_m[q] = (i \text{ div } k) \bmod p$
    $SPattern_m[q] = (k(i \text{ div } pk) + i \bmod k)$
    Increment q
  ENDDO
ENDDO

(b): Code for computing the send pattern

Figure 1 Computing the receive and send patterns for $A(l_1 : h_1 : s_1) = B(l_2 : h_2 : s_2)$

Send pattern generation

Our algorithm for send pattern generation is very similar to the algorithm for receive pattern generation dicussed above. We exploit the fact there is a one to one correspondence between the LHS array element and the RHS array elements. So the send pattern for a processor is the same as the receive pattern calculated assuming that the RHS element is actually the LHS element. Here again we notice that the send pattern pattern should repeat after every s_2 courses. The code that generates the send pattern is shown in Figure 1(b).

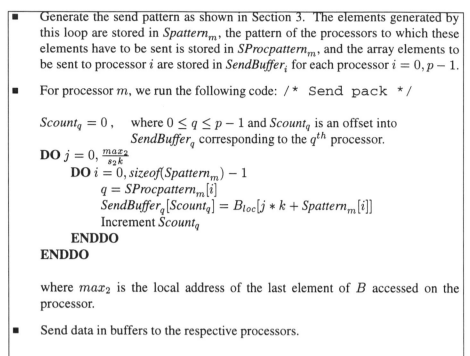

- Generate the send pattern as shown in Section 3. The elements generated by this loop are stored in $Spattern_m$, the pattern of the processors to which these elements have to be sent is stored in $SProcpattern_m$, and the array elements to be sent to processor i are stored in $SendBuffer_i$ for each processor $i = 0, p - 1$.

- For processor m, we run the following code: /* Send pack */

  $Scount_q = 0$,   where $0 \le q \le p - 1$ and $Scount_q$ is an offset into $SendBuffer_q$ corresponding to the qth processor.

  DO $j = 0, \frac{max_2}{s_2 k}$

      DO $i = 0, sizeof(Spattern_m) - 1$
          $q = SProcpattern_m[i]$
          $SendBuffer_q[Scount_q] = B_{loc}[j * k + Spattern_m[i]]$
          Increment $Scount_q$
      ENDDO
  ENDDO

  where max_2 is the local address of the last element of B accessed on the processor.

- Send data in buffers to the respective processors.

Figure 2   Send phase generation algorithm

Communication Algorithm

The communication algorithm for an array assignment statement is shown in Figures 2 and 3. We assume that each processor maintains a separate send and receive buffer for all the m processors. As we have assumed a single template model, closed form expressions for the communication set generation exist for the case where $k = 1$ (template is cyclically distributed) and $k = \left\lceil \frac{N}{p} \right\rceil$ (template is block distributed) [6]. The algorithm shown in Figures 2 and 3 simplifies for these cases as well as the case where, s_{lhs} divides s_{rhs} or vice-versa.

Experimental Results   Communication generation times for an IBM SP-2 are shown in table 1.

Acknowledgments   We gratefully acknowledge the support from NSF through an Young Investigator Award CCR–9457768, an NSF grant CCR–9210422, and from the Louisiana Board of Regents through contract LEQSF (1991-94)-RD-A-09.

REFERENCES

[1] S. Chatterjee, J. Gilbert, F. Long, R. Schreiber, and S. Teng. Generating local addresses and communication sets for data parallel programs. In *Proc. ACM Symposium on Principles and Practice of Parallel Programming*, pp. 149–158, May 1993.

- Receive data from the p processors

- Run the receive pattern generation code shown in Section 3. We assume that elements received in this loop are stored in $Rpattern_m$ and array elements received from processor i is stored in $ReceiveBuffer_i$ for each processor $i = 0, p - 1$. $Apattern_m$ holds A's access pattern.

- For processor m, we run the following code:

$Rcount_q = 0$,   where $0 \le q \le p - 1$ and $Rcount_q$ is an offset into
         $ReceiveBuffer_q$ corresponding to the qth processor.

DO $j = 0, \frac{max_1}{s_1 k}$
    DO $i = 0, sizeof(Rpattern_m) - 1$
        $q = RProcpattern_m[i]$
        if m = q
            $A_{loc}[j * k + Apattern_m[i]] = B_{loc}[Rpattern_m[i]]$
        else
            $A_{loc}[j * k + Apattern_m[i]] = ReceiveBuffer_q[Rcount_q]$
            Increment $Rcount_q$
        endif
    ENDDO
ENDDO

where max_1 is the local address of the last element of A accessed on the processor.

Figure 3   Receive phase generation algorithm

k	p	s_{lhs}	s_{rhs}	Comm. Gen. Time (microseconds)
4	3	5	3	41
4	3	3	5	40
8	4	3	5	49
8	4	5	3	49
8	32	7	99	84
16	32	7	99	128
32	32	7	99	240
8	32	99	7	84
16	32	99	7	127
32	32	99	7	228

Table 1   Communication generation times for an IBM SP-2 system.

[2] High Performance Fortran Forum. High Performance Fortran language specification version 1.0. Technical Report CRPC-TR92225, Rice University, May 1993.

[3] G. Fox, S. Hiranandani, K. Kennedy, C Koelbel, U. Kremer, C.-W. Tseng, and M. Wu. Fortran D Language Specification. TR-91-170, Rice University, Dec. 1991.

[4] S. Gupta, S. Kaushik, C. Huang, and P. Sadayappan. On compiling array expressions for efficient execution on distributed-memory machines. OSU-CISRC-94-TR19, Apr. 1994.

[5] S. Hiranandani, K. Kennedy, J. Mellor-Crummey, and A. Sethi. Advanced compilation techniques for Fortran D. Report CRPC-TR-93-338, Rice University, Oct. 1993.

[6] C. Koelbel. Compile-time generation of communication for scientific programs. In *Supercomputing '91*, pp. 101–110, Nov. 1991.

[7] J. M. Stichnoth. Efficient compilation of array statements for private memory multi-computers. Technical Report CMU-CS-93-109, School of Computer Science, Carnegie Mellon University, Feb. 1993.

[8] A. Thirumalai and J. Ramanujam. Code generation and optimization for array statements in High Performance Fortran. Technical Report TR-94-11-02, Dept. of Electrical and Computer Engineering, Louisiana State University, Nov. 1994.

[9] A. Thirumalai and J. Ramanujam. An Efficient Compile-Time Approach to Compute Address Sequences in Data Parallel Programs. In *Proc. 5th International Workshop on Compilers for Parallel Computers,* Malaga, Spain, June 1995.

[10] A. Thirumalai and J. Ramanujam. Fast Address Sequence Generation for Data-Parallel Programs Using Integer Lattices. In *Proc. 8th Annual Workshop on Languages and Compilers for Parallel Computing,* Columbus, Ohio, August 1995.

30

PREDICTION BASED TASK SCHEDULING IN DISTRIBUTED COMPUTING†

Mehrdad Samadani and Erich Kaltofen

Department of Computer Science,
Rensselaer Polytechnic Institute,
Troy, NY 12180-3590 USA

1 INTRODUCTION

The effectiveness of task scheduling in a distributed environment is critically dependent on the timely identification of the least loaded nodes. Whether the issue of interest is load-sharing or distributed parallel computation, overall system performance is determined in large part by the characteristics of the nodes participating in a particular computation. The diversity of node characteristics across the network frequently results in a spectrum of available compute powers on different nodes. Due to the high cost of task migration, effective evaluation of the relative available compute powers of the nodes in the network and the use of that information in task distribution are essential components of successful task scheduling in a distributed environment.

A few implementations of systems for distributing large scale computations over a network of computers rely on schemes based on the current as well as the prior state information on each node to make better task distribution decisions [2]. The goal of such algorithms is to uncover the hidden information that may be present in the past load data, and use that information to better evaluate the available compute power of the nodes in the network. These approaches tend to rely on extensive fine-tuning often due to the ad-hoc design of the data analysis procedures employed.

We present a systematic and statistically sound method for uncovering the information present in the past load data and using that information to predict the future processor load. Using time series statistical methods we analyze the compute intensive load on actual and simulated processors to identify stochastic models that suitably represent the load behavior on those processors. We then use these models to obtain the minimum mean square error load forecasts for various times in the future and discuss how they can be used in task scheduling in distributed systems. In particular, we use

---

†This material is based on work supported in part by the National Science Foundation under Grant No. CRR-93-19776.

these forecasts to reduce the performance degradation caused by the outdated state information resulting from delays in collecting it.

The performance of the minimum mean square error load forecasts are then compared against those obtained by using the current load levels as predictors of the future state of the nodes. We show that the relative performance of these approaches depends on factors including the statistical characteristics of the load on each processor and the number of nodes in the system.

2 TIME SERIES ANALYSIS

Conceptually, the load on a processor can be modeled by a theoretical stochastic process. In the following, we express the computation load on a processor by the length of its CPU ready queue. Let x_t denote the load on the processor X at time t. We refer to the sequence $\{x_{t-j}\}$, where $j = 1, 2, \dots$ as the load time series on node X. The special feature of this type of load time series is the fact that successive observations are usually not independent and that any analysis of such time series must take into account the time order of the observations. Since successive observations are dependent, future values may be predicted from past observations. The load time series are stochastic in that the future is only partly determined by past values, so that exact predictions are impossible and must be replaced by the idea that future values have a probability distribution which is conditioned by a knowledge of past values. The information present in the load time series can be extracted by appropriate statistical analysis methods.

2.1 Preliminaries

Suppose $\{a_t\}$ is a sequence of independent and identically distributed random variables from a distribution with mean zero and variance σ_a^2. A powerful model for describing time series is the general autoregressive integrated moving average (ARIMA) process of order (p, d, q), defined by

$$\Phi(B)w_t = \Theta(B)a_t$$

where

$$w_t = \nabla^d x_t = (1 - B)^d x_t,$$
$$\Phi(B) = 1 - \phi_1 B - \phi_2 B^2 - \dots - \phi_p B^p,$$
$$\Theta(B) = 1 - \theta_1 B - \theta_2 B^2 - \dots - \theta_q B^q,$$

and where B is defined by $Bz_t = z_{t-1}$ for any time series $\{z_t\}$. The operators B and ∇ are called the backward shift and the backward difference operator respectively. The coefficients ϕ_i and θ_i are constants.

Given a model ARIMA(p, d, q) and a time series $\{x_{t-j}\}$, where $j = 1, 2, \dots$ generated by it we would like to forecast the value of x_{t+l}, where $l \geq 1$, when we are currently at time t. Equivalently, we would like to obtain $\hat{x}_t(l)$, the minimum mean square error forecast at origin t for lead time l. It can be shown ([1]) that

$$\hat{x}_t(l) = E[x_{t+l} \mid x_t, x_{t-1}, x_{t-2}, \ldots]$$

where the right hand side denotes the conditional expectation of x_{t+l} given $\{x_{t-j}\}$, $j = 0, 1, 2, \ldots$. When $\hat{x}_t(l)$ is regarded as a function of l for fixed t, it is referred to as the forecast function for origin t.

Our approach to forecasting is first to derive a suitable stochastic model based on the available data for the particular load time series under study. Once an appropriate model for the series has been determined, it will be used in obtaining the forecast function.

2.2 Application to Task Scheduling

A daemon task is placed on each node in the system. The daemon is responsible for periodic collection of load data on its node. Once fifty or more load observations have been recorded, the daemon uses the data to test the validity of the current stochastic model by applying diagnostic checks to the model. One possible check could be carried out by computing the residuals $a_t = x_t - \hat{x}_{t-1}(1)$ from the data and testing whether or not they appear to be random. Alternatively, the daemon could simply identify and estimate a new stochastic model periodically. In either case, the new model is communicated to the central scheduler in the next status update message. The daemon sends a status update message to the central scheduler at regular intervals. These messages contain the current stochastic model as well as the most recent data required by the model for forecasting purposes.

The central scheduler maintains the stochastic model and forecasts for each node in the system. The scheduler periodically receives status update messages from the local daemons. It then uses the new information to update the stochastic model it uses for prediction purposes and computes new forecasts for the affected node. When a task arrives at the central scheduler, the forecasts are used to identify the node with the highest expected available compute power and the task is assigned to the identified node.

3 NUMERICAL STUDY

As part of our numerical study, load data were obtained and analyzed for actual as well as simulated systems. The results were used to compare the performance of the minimum mean square error load forecasts against those obtained by using the current load levels as predictors of the future state of the nodes. We refer to the latter approach as the single point prediction method.

Virtually every load time series obtained from the experiments turned out to be non-stationary, indicating the absense of a natural mean. The model fitted to one of the actual load time series after an initial transformation is the ARIMA$(2, 1, 0)$

$$(1 + 0.30B + 0.32B^2)\nabla x_t = a_t.$$

In the case of the simulated nodes, the models fitted to a few of the load time series were very close to Markov process, or ARIMA$(0, 1, 0)$

$$\nabla x_t = a_t.$$

However, in other simulated cases, we obtained models such as the ARIMA$(1, 1, 1)$

$$(1 - 0.22B)\nabla x_t = (1 - 0.79B).$$

The performance comparison study that was carried out using this ARIMA(1, 1, 1) model resulted in increasing number of instances where the two forecasting methods led to different scheduling decisions as the number of nodes was increased. When they disagreed, the minimum mean square error forecast was about twice as likely to make a better decision than the single point predictor.

REFERENCES

[1] G. E. P. Box, G. M. Jenkins, "Time Series Analysis: Forecasting and Control", Holden-Day, 1976.

[2] A. Diaz, M. Hitz, E. Kaltofen, A. Lobo, T. Valente, "Process Scheduling in DSC and the Large Sparce Linear Systems Challenge", *Proc. DISCO '93, Springer Lect. Notes Comput. Sci.*, A. Miola (ed.), Vol. 722, pp. 66–80, 1993. *J. Symbolic Computation*, to appear.

[3] A. Geist, A. Beguelin, J. Dongarra, W. Jiang, R. Manchek, V. Sunderam, "PVM Parallel Virtual Machine A Users' Guide and Tutorial for Network Parallel Computing", MIT Press, Cambridge, MA, 1994.

[4] K. K. Goswami, M. Devarakonda, R. K. Iyer, "Prediction-Based Dynamic Load-Sharing Heuristics", *IEEE Trans. Parallel and Distributed Systems*, Vol. 4, No. 6, June 1993.

[5] K. G. Shin, C.-J. Hou, "Design and Evaluation of Effective Load Sharing in Distributed Real-Time Systems", *IEEE Trans. Parallel and Distributed Systems*, Vol. 5, No. 7, July 1994.

31

REFINED SINGLE-THREADING FOR PARALLEL FUNCTIONAL PROGRAMMING[†]

George Becker, Neil V. Murray, Richard E. Stearns

Department of Computer Science, University at Albany, Albany, NY 12222

1 OVERVIEW

Fortran, C and C++ are three dominant languages used in scientific computation. As a result, derivatives of these languages prevail in parallel computation as well. However, imperative languages do not naturally support parallelism. Functional languages, such as EPL, SISAL, Haskell, etc. [11] isolate the programmer from the complexities of parallel programming. These languages expose implicit parallelism through data independence. Functional programs that run correctly on a single processor are guaranteed to run correctly on any multiprocessor regardless of architecture.

The difficulty with functional programming is in the area of implementation. In order to preserve referential transparency, the physical representation of values must be considered. We could eliminate dependency between function execution and representation of input arguments by always copying input data, but copying of data aggregates (e.g., array, list, tree, tuple) introduces unacceptable run-time and memory space costs, giving rise to the *aggregate update problem* [3].

The conventional approach to this problem, used in, for example, Haskell, utilizes *analytical methods* to detect *single-threading* (i.e. using a value only once) of aggregate data. Such analytical methods are known to have exponential time complexity. More seriously, the analytical methods may fail to find all singly-threaded uses of aggregate data. Finally, large programs must be expected to contain a number of uses of aggregate data that are not singly-threaded and thus cannot be optimized at all.

The alternative approach to the aggregate update problem, used in, for example, Linear LISP [2], makes single-threading explicit at the programmer's level. This approach *restricts* a functional programming language so that *only singly-threaded programs can be expressed.* However, rigid enforcement of single-threading is a severe constraint on

---
[†]Supported in part by NSF Grant CCR-9101280.

the expressiveness of a programming language. Thus, rigid single-threading appears to be self-defeating. Yet, a similar approach used in Concurrent Clean [8] achieved efficient pure functional input/output.

Our approach [4] relaxes single-threading to restore expressiveness while still avoiding the problems of aggregate update. The central idea is to divide *function input arguments* into *two categories* called *inert inputs* and *active inputs*. This distinction is crucial for aggregate data arguments because for the sake of efficiency such arguments are passed by reference. *Inert* inputs are used for operations like determining the length of a list or computing the sum of an array of numbers. Such operations can be performed without altering the input and hence do not need to be implemented through copying the input data. *Active* inputs are used for aggregate data subject to updating in a given operation.

Our proposed solution to the aggregate update problem has two aspects. First, our *structured function composition* defines legal uses of inert and active inputs when composing functions. Second, our *memory axioms* stipulate how predefined primitive functions must be implemented. We have shown in [4] that evaluation of any structured function composition of primitive functions is free of aliasing, i.e., single-threading is preserved. Thus, referential transparency is achieved despite in-place updating of active input data. We use parallel graph grammars to extend our model to include recursive functions and higher order functions. This is similar to parallel programming with *skeleton functions* [6]. To show the benefits of this basic theoretical result, we have designed and implemented an experimental functional language.

2   FORMAL MODEL

In [4], we introduce a discipline for composition of functions with inert and active inputs. The primary constraint is that each output of any function may be supplied to only one active input. There is no restriction on the number of uses of function outputs for inert inputs. The discipline stipulates that, for each output of any function, all functions using this output for their inert inputs must finish executing before a function using this same output for its active input starts executing.

We formalize the manipulation of memory through two *memory axioms*. First, we state the *primitive operator memory axiom* for computer implementations of predefined (primitive) functions. Second, as primitive operators may entail allocation and deallocation (disposal) of memory, we stipulate the *memory manager axiom* capturing the correct (possibly concurrent) operation of the memory manager. We then prove that the evaluation of composition of functions with inert and active inputs preserve our *memory partitioning property*. This property is closely related to *store fragmentation* [9].

Additional higher order functions, such as *apply-to-all* (i.e. FORALL), [1], or *skeleton functions* [6], are employed in order to utilize data-parallel machines.

3 EXPERIMENTAL RESULTS

We have designed and implemented a simple functional language called RETRAN (for REferential TRANsparency) which incorporates our theoretical concepts. Referential transparency is guaranteed in all aspects including external input/output. RETRAN supports recursion and higher order functions. Typing in RETRAN is fully static with four categories of data type: scalars, function references, aggregates and input/output streams. Scalar types are boolean, character, integer, and real. Aggregate data types are vectors, matrices and lists. Unlike other data types, I/O streams may not be copied.

RETRAN employs the relaxation of strict single-threading described in earlier sections. Its purpose is to overcome the lack of expressiveness of strict single-threading, while allowing in-place modification of data aggregates without loss of referential transparency. RETRAN permits those side-effects that are invisible due to single-threading. RETRAN programs are guaranteed to maintain dynamic data references with a single count only. Any heap memory segment can therefore be explicitly deallocated at the end of the memory reference life span. Consequently, no garbage collection is needed.

A prototype compiler has been implemented for RETRAN. The prototype translates RETRAN programs into C, which can then be compiled with a standard C-compiler. Several standard algorithms, such as *histogram* and various *sort* algorithms, which give rise to the aggregate update problem in contemporary pure functional languages, were programmed in RETRAN. Our results demonstrate that the asymptotic time complexity of these programs is the same as that of their hand coded versions. For example, on a SUN4/Sparc, our RETRAN quick-sort program ran only 30% to 40% slower than the C library function *qsort*.

4 CONCLUSIONS

We have presented a conceptual framework to reconcile referential transparency with in-place updating of aggregate data. This framework circumvents the aggregate update problem by a novel relaxation of strict single-threading. Our method is fully static, and is applied to each function definition separately.

We use a simple analysis of the constraints of structured function composition. This analysis is linear in the size of function definitions, and additive between functions. Unlike approaches utilized in optimizing compilers, our method naturally *scales up* to large programs, and it guarantees the asymptotic time complexity of corresponding imperative programs while obviating the need for garbage collection.

We have demonstrated the viability of this approach by designing and implementing a simple functional language. This experimental confirmation shows that our solution to the aggregate update problem indeed results in efficient pure functional programming, which is competitive with conventional imperative programming. Our framework can express SIMD as well as MIMD computations. Moreover, higher-order functions (skeletons) can be nested. Since our memory partitioning guarantees separation of data between outer and inner skeletons, the *skeleton composition problem* [10] does not arise.

REFERENCES

[1] John Backus: "Can Programming Be Liberated from the von Neumann Style? A Functional Style and Its Algebra of Programs", *Comm of ACM*, Aug 1978

[2] Henry G. Baker: "A 'Linear Logic' Quicksort", *ACM Sigplan Notices*, Feb 1994

[3] Adrienne Bloss: "Update Analysis and the Efficient Implementation of Functional Aggregates", FPCA, ACM 1989

[4] George Becker, Neil V. Murray: "Efficient execution of Programs with Static Semantics", *ACM Sigplan Notices*, April 1995

[5] David Cann: "Retire Fortran? A debate rekindled", *Comm of ACM*, Aug 1992

[6] J. Darlington *et al.*: "Parallel Programming Using Skeleton Functions", PARLE'93, LNCS 694

[7] Peter Landin: "The Next 700 Programming Languages", *Comm. of ACM*, March 1966

[8] E. Nöcker, J. Smetsers, M. v. Eekelen, M. Plasmeijer: "Concurrent Clean", PARLE'90, LNCS 505

[9] Bjarne Steensgaard: "Sparse Functional Stores for Imperative Programs", Workshop on Intermediate Representations, POPL'95

[10] Mario Südholt: "Data Distribution Algebras - A Formal Basis for Programming Using Skeletons", *Programming Concepts, Methods and Calculi*, IFIP, North-Holland, June 1994

[11] B. Szymanski: *Parallel Functional Languages and Compilers*, ACM Press, 1991

32

SYMMETRIC DISTRIBUTED COMPUTING WITH DYNAMIC LOAD BALANCING AND FAULT TOLERANCE

T. Bubeck, W. Küchlin and W. Rosenstiel

Universität Tübingen
Wilhelm-Schickard-Institut für Informatik
Sand 13, 72076 Tübingen
Germany

We present a system for *functional* parallel computing on distributed memory machines, which does dynamic load balancing and is totally symmetric. This means that every node can perform any computation and is client and server at the same time. Furthermore, the calling convention is similar to threads on shared memory machines to allow a uniform usage of parallel and distributed procedure calls. Finally the communication and computation is strictly separated for easy maintenance of the user program.

1 PROPERTIES

The *Distributed Threads System* (DTS) [Bub93, BR94, SB94] provides a framework to parallize a program on a number of heterogeneous workstations. They are connected in a way, that the programmer sees one single computer consisting of multiple processors.

DTS consists of a run-time environment and some library functions (two most important functions are `dts_fork()` and `dts_join()`). They can be used in standard programming languages, like C or FORTRAN and are currently implemented on top of a message passing system and a thread package. The former (currently PVM [DGMS93]) is used to exchange data between different machines easily, whereas the later (depending on the computer architecture e. g. Solaris threads) is used to achieve local parallelism at each node.

Following the programming pattern of thread packages, the user of DTS is able to submit a procedure call using `dts_fork()`. This procedure runs in parallel to the caller and gets normally executed on one of the hosts in a user-defined pool of worker machines. In contrast to Remote Procedure Call (RPC), the calling program does *not* block until the result is returned. Instead it is possible for the program to create further jobs. After starting all parallel tasks, the caller typically waits for the running procedures to complete and gets each result using dts_join().

A cluster of workstation can be seen as a distributed memory machine and therefore each machine holds its own memory. The change of any memory data is therefore not done on all machines. This means that only procedures without any side-effects, which do not rely on global data, can be parallelized through DTS in a straight-forward way.

Starting a procedure on a remote workstation is more expensive than running it on the local machine using threads. Therefore DTS should be used for the coarse-grained jobs and these should be divided—if necessary—onto the local processors using threads. Figure 1 shows a snapshot of a typical DTS application. It has distributed three coarse-grained jobs to three machines, and one machine has split its job further onto three local threads.

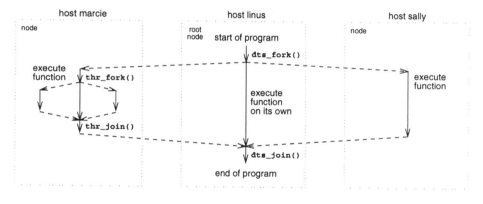

Figure 1 Three machines taking part in DTS

DTS follows the SPMD model (*single program, multiple data*), which means that all machines run an identical program and have the same functionality. Each can make arbitrary parallel procedure calls which get executed on another machine. DTS decides at a given time, which job should be executed on which machine and tries to keep all machines busy. But although DTS uses the SPMD model, it is still able to work on heterogeneous workstation clusters, because it translates all values (procedure pointers and user data) between the different representations. It is currently implemented on Sun workstations with one or more processors (under SunOS 4.1.x or Solaris 2.x), Solbourne multiprocessors, and on IBM RS/6000 and PowerPC under AIX 3.2.x. It is easy to port to other architectures, relying on UNIX, PVM, and a threads package.

Load Balancing

In order to achieve good performance, parallel systems must balance their jobs on the processors. Ideally *all* machines should have work until the end of the computation, where all should stop at the same time. The situation where nearly all machines have finished and are waiting for the last machine to complete its jobs should be avoided.

DTS tries to achieve this by *not* immediately starting all forked procedures. Instead it runs only MAXJOBS on each machine and keeps the remaining jobs in a queue. Running more than one task per machine has the advantage that most communication can be overlapped by useful computation. On the other hand, not too many jobs should be started on each machine to avoid the risk of unbalanced workload or overloading a single machine. Otherwise efficiency will go down because of paging and other unwanted activities.

If the queue gets smaller and the possible end of the computation arrives, the number of running jobs at each node is even more reduced, by not starting a new job on a therefore "overloaded" machine. Fewer jobs per machine reduce the probability of an unbalanced job distribution and is therefore very important at the end.

The maximum number of jobs on each node is limited through $l(\# \ of \ items \ in \ queue) = \min(\text{MAXJOBS}, \lceil \frac{\# \ of \ items \ in \ queue}{\# \ of \ hosts} \rceil)$, where MAXJOBS as 5 has produced good results on different test cases.

Fault tolerance

All programs taking part in DTS exchange messages over the network and are therefore in contact all the time. If DTS registers the crash of a machine, it automatically restarts all jobs executed on the crashed host on another machine, without concern or knowledge by the user program. This ensures that the application continues, even if some machines go down. If a dropped machine restarts, it is automatically integrated again.

This mechanism allows to reconfigure the system during run-time, without the need to stop the computation, which makes it possible to delete or add machines manually.

2 EXAMPLES AND TIMING RESULTS

To demonstrate the power of DTS, a few sequential or partly parallel programs where distributed. We focus on non-trivial test cases to get as general results as possible. For this reason we selected some algorithms of the computer algebra system PARSAC-2, which need not much change to fit the requirements of DTS. In addition, DTS was applied in a numerical interval package written in C++ and in FORTRAN programs for computations in physics.

There are quite a few algorithm of PARSAC-2 distributed through DTS. We will concentrate on one example—an implementation of the RSA public key encryption system. The timing results presented here (see figure 2) are computed with a 600 bit wide key on a different number of Sun ELC machines. The figure shows the run time as the sum of the encryption and decryption time taken on messages with three different sizes: 100 KByte, 50 KByte, and 10 KByte. All timing results are measured with real wall clock time and printed in seconds. The given speedup is relative to the sequential execution mentioned as execution time for a single machine.

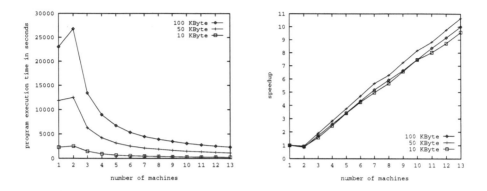

Figure 2   The program execution time and speedups of the RSA encryption system

The distributed program starts by dividing the message into small chunks and encrypting them in parallel on all remaining machines. So one machines does only fork and join, while the others do the encryption work. This is why two machines are slower than a single machine. With more than two machines, we get a significant speed improvement.

REFERENCES

[BR94]   Tilmann Bubeck and Wolfgang Rosenstiel.   Verteiltes Rechnen mit DTS (Distributed Thread System).   In Marc Aguilar, editor, *Proceedings of the '94 SIPAR-Workshop on Parallel and Distributed Computing*, pages 65–68, Fribourg, Suisse, October 1994.

[Bub93]   Tilmann Bubeck. Eine Systemumgebung zum verteilten funktionalen Rechnen. Technical Report WSI-93-8, Eberhard-Karls-Universität Tübingen, August 1993.

[DGMS93]   J. Dongarra, A. Geist, R. Manchek, and V. S. Sunderam. Integrated PVM framework supports heterogeneous network computing. *Computers in Physics*, 7(2):166–175, April 1993.

[SB94]   Mark J. Schaefer and Tilmann Bubeck.   A Parallel Complex Zero Finder.   *Interval Computations*, 1994. to appear.

33

THE RELATIONSHIP BETWEEN LANGUAGE PARADIGM AND PARALLELISM: THE EQ PROTOTYPING LANGUAGE

Thomas Derby, Robert Schnabel, and Benjamin Zorn

Department of Computer Science
University of Colorado at Boulder

1   INTRODUCTION

Both the imperative (Fortran [1], APL [4], Matlab [5], etc.) and functional (Sisal [2], Id [6], EPL [7] , etc.) language paradigms have attractive features. Imperative languages are able to easily express changing quantities, something which functional languages find more difficult. However, the side-effects of imperative languages makes parallelization more difficult than in functional languages. The EQ language is an attempt to blend these two paradigms, in order to try and achieve the advantages of both. While designed for sequential execution, it turns out that EQ makes the parallelism in a program explicit to the user, without introducing special "parallel" constructs. We feel this property makes EQ a good target for further parallel language research.

2   FEATURES OF EQ

2.1   Unordered Equations

Mathematical notations, in general, are not ordered; a set of equations is given. Typical examples have extra words between these equations; "x = sin y, where y = ..." and "let y = ... in x = sin y" are common examples. To model these kinds of notation more simply, EQ provides a simple unordered model. For example,

```
a = 4;
b = a + correction;
correction = sqrt (a);
```

would compute a = 4, `correction` = 2, and therefore b = 6. This "unordered" paradigm allows the programmer much greater flexibility and similarity to the "natural" way of expressing algorithms; statements that logically belong together can be placed in proximity, even if they cannot be executed sequentially. These properties are shared by many functional and data flow languages. It also allows easy expression of functional parallelism.

2.2 Computation over Sets

Performing computations over a set of values is a very common activity in programming. In numerical computations, typically these sets are sets of subscripts. Using loop notation (as is required in FORTRAN) obscures the intent, in addition to expanding code volume.

To address these issues, EQ provides a range variable; a variable that takes on a consecutive set of integer values. This construct is very similar to EPL's subscript variables. Statements that involve a range variable are performed for each possible value of the variable. For example:

```
i = 1..20;
a[i] = 0;
```

makes a length 20 vector of zeros. Range variables are also used in many other contexts, including reduction operations. For example:

```
s = sum [i]: a[i];
```

adds up the elements of array a. Combining different uses of range variables can yield tremendous expressive power:

```
i = 1..10;   j = 1..10;   k = 1..10;
c[i,k] = sum[j]: a[i,j] * b[j,k]
```

is a matrix multiplication program for 10x10 matrices.

Since recurrences are not permitted (EQ considers these to be circular definitions), range variables inherently represent data parallel computations. This fact (which is not true of EPL's subscripts) allows an EQ programmer to directly express data parallelism.

2.3 Explicit Notations for Change

In an unordered notation, each name can represent only a single value; thus, the FORTRAN-style assignment statement is not effective in such a context. We turn to notation used for writing down algorithms that have iteration as a major component, and often find such notation as:

$$x_+ = x_c + x_p$$

where the subscripts +, c, and p stand for the next value, current value, and previous value, respectively. EQ models this notation very closely:

```
next x = x + prev x;
```

This notation corresponds more closely to the algorithmic ideas than the FORTRAN code, which would require a temporary to be introduced to express this computation.

In order to use this notation, there must be a framework that specifies which iteration or time step one is currently in. EQ provides several mechanisms for incrementing the time step. Two of these are the do loop, which goes through a series of time steps, one for each time through the loop's body, and the followed-by operator =>, which performs a single time step:

```
a = 5 =>
a = prev a * 2;
```

computes the final value a = 10.

Note that these notations allow the user to express explicitly non-parallel loops and sequential control flow. This property means that the parallelism or non-parallelism of a given loop is explicit in its syntax. In addition to simplifying analysis, this means that the programmer is more aware of the parallel and sequential parts of the algorithm.

3   EXAMPLE PROGRAM

We present a short program for computing an LU decomposition with partial pivoting. More information about this and other example EQ programs can be found in [3].

```
k = 1..n;
p [k] = k;
over k: {
  i, j = k+1..n;
  piv = k..n;
  at max [piv]: |a [piv, k]| {
  t1 = p [k] => p' [k] = p [piv] => p' [piv] = t1;
  t2 = a [k,] => a' [k,] = a [piv,] => a' [piv,]
      = t2;
  } =>
  a' [i,k] /= a [k,k] =>
  a' [i,j] -= a [i,k] * a [k,j];
}
```

4   RESULTS

A prototype compiler for the EQ language has been implemented. It translates an EQ program into an equivalent sequential C program, which can then be compiled using a standard C compiler. Timing results indicate that execution times are 1.2 to 1.4 times as long as comparable hand-written C code, if some simple memory optimization techniques are applied. For more information, see [3].

5 SUMMARY

Our goal in this research is to investigate a new paradigm for programming a large class of scientific algorithms that expresses these algorithms in a natural manner, and is also easy to use and leads to reasonably efficient code. The examination of the possibilities for parallel implementation is an important step, even in the design of a sequential language. The likelihood of a parallel version of a language being desirable at some future date is too large to ignore these questions. The blending in EQ of both functional implicit parallelism and imperative "changeability" means that parallel programming paradigms from both language communities can be tried within the same basic language.

For additional information about the EQ project, see [3].

REFERENCES

[1] ANSI. American National Standard Programming Language Fortran ANSI X3.9-1978.

[2] A. P. W. Bohm, R. R. Oldehoeft, D. C. Cann, and J. T. Feo. Sisal Reference Manual, Version 2.0.

[3] Thomas Derby, Robert Schnabel, and Benjamin Zorn. Design Ideas for Prototyping Scientific Computations: the EQ Language. Technical Report, University of Colorado at Boulder, Dept. of Computer Science.

[4] Kenneth E. Iverson. A Programming Language. Wiley, New York, New York, 1962.

[5] Math Works Inc. MATLAB User's Guide, 1992.

[6] Rishiyur S. Nikhil. Id language reference manual, version90.1. Postscript available via FTP from Massachusetts Institute of Technology, July 1991.

[7] Boleslaw K. Szymanski. "EPL - parallel programming with recurrent equations". In Boleslaw K. Szymanski, editor, Parallel Functional Languages and Compilers, chapter 3, pages 51-104. ACM Press, New York, New York, 1991.

INDEX